MUSICAL CANADA

*To Harmon,
with lots of thanks
From
Trish (Aug '89)*

EDITED BY JOHN BECKWITH
AND FREDERICK A. HALL

Musical Canada

Words and Music Honouring Helmut Kallmann

UNIVERSITY OF TORONTO PRESS
Toronto Buffalo London

© University of Toronto Press 1988
Toronto Buffalo London
Printed in Canada

ISBN 0-8020-5759-4

Printed on acid-free paper

Canadian Cataloguing in Publication Data

Main entry under title:

Musical Canada

Includes index.
ISBN 0-8020-5759-4

1. Kallmann, Helmut, 1922– . 2. Music – Canada – History and criticism.
I. Kallmann, Helmut, 1922– . II. Beckwith, John, 1927– . III. Hall,
Frederick Albert.

ML55.K2M98 1988.   780′.971   C87-094958-6

FRONTISPIECE: Helmut Kallmann
Photograph courtesy of the National Library of Canada

Contents

Preface
xi

The Transmission of Algonkian Indian Hymns:
Between Orality and Literacy
BEVERLEY CAVANAGH
3

Catalogue des imprimés musicaux d'avant 1800
conservés à la bibliothèque de l'Université Laval
CLAUDE BEAUDRY
29

Musique spirituelle (1718):
Canada's First Music Theory Manual
ERICH SCHWANDT
50

La fortune de deux oeuvres de Jean-Jacques Rousseau
au Canada français entre 1790 et 1850
LUCIEN POIRIER
60

Music Instruction in Nova Scotia before 1914
NANCY F. VOGAN
71

John Lovell (1810–93):
Montreal Music Printer and Publisher
MARIA CALDERISI BRYCE
79

A Little Fantasy on J.P. Clarke's Ballad
'Summer and Winter'
CLIFFORD FORD
97

Orchestras and Orchestral Repertoire
in Toronto before 1914
CARL MOREY
100

Musical Activity in Canada's
New Capital City in the 1870s
ELAINE KEILLOR
115

Homage to Helmut
RICHARD JOHNSTON
134

Ships of the Fleet: The Royal Navy
and the Development of Music in British Columbia
ROBERT DALE McINTOSH
143

Maurice Ravel au Canada
GILLES POTVIN
149

Ernest MacMillan: The Ruhleben Years
KEITH MacMILLAN
164

CanOn Stride
JOHN WEINZWEIG
183

Contents vii

Notes on Violet Archer
GEORGE A. PROCTOR
188

Healey Willan's Unfinished *Requiem*
F.R.C. CLARKE
203

Thisness: Marks and Remarks
ISTVAN ANHALT
211

Sun-Father Sky-Mother
R. MURRAY SCHAFER
232

Sounds in the Wilderness:
Fifty Years of CBC Commissions
PATRICIA KELLOGG
239

The Canadian Music Council:
A Brief History
RONALD NAPIER
262

Three Masses by Maritime Composers
WALTER H. KEMP
274

Towards the 'One Justifiable End':
Six Discs
KENNETH WINTERS
286

The Glenn Gould Outtakes
GEOFFREY PAYZANT
298

Writings by Helmut Kallmann
315

Notes
325

Notes on Contributors
345

Index
349

Illustrations

L'Incantation de la Jongleuse by Ernest Gagnon
85

Souvenir de Venise by Ernest Gagnon
86

Prince Arthur Galop by H. Gowan
119

Programme du concert Ravel à Vancouver le 14 février 1928
153

Ernest MacMillan as Lady Bracknell
173

The cast and orchestra for *The Mikado*, December 1916–January 1917
178

Healey Willan's sketch for the Benedictus of his *Requiem*
209

Two sketches for the costume and set designs for *Thisness*
225

Preface

The career activities of Helmut Max Kallmann (b. 1922) have touched Canadian musical life in numerous ways. His 1960 book *A History of Music in Canada 1534-1914* remains the seminal work in the field. His writings and scholarly advice have placed the details of Canada's musical repertoire and musical history in accessible form not only at home (in the *Encyclopedia of Music in Canada*, for which he was research editor) but also abroad (in publications such as *Die Musik in Geschichte und Gegenwart* and *The New Grove Dictionary of Music and Musicians*, to both of which he contributed organizational guidance as well as many original articles). His numerous bibliographies, beginning with his 1952 revision of the CBC's *Catalogue of Canadian Composers*, are irreplaceable tools in research into Canadian music. He has held executive posts with several national music organizations including the Canadian Music Council, the Canadian Association of Music Libraries, and the Canadian Musical Heritage Society. All this is in addition to his enduring work as music librarian of the CBC for twenty years and founding chief of the Music Division, National Library of Canada, for seventeen.

The present collection – prepared by past and present colleagues to honour him on his retirement from the latter position in mid-1987 – takes its theme from the centre of Dr Kallmann's life-work, the music and musical lore of his adopted country, Canada. The title recalls a pair of once-thriving Canadian music periodicals, *Musical Canada* (English, 1906-33) and *Le Canada musical* (French, 1866-7, 1875-81, 1917-24, 1930).

Reflecting Dr Kallmann's exceptionally broad musical interests, the contributions include critical and scholarly essays, bibliographic studies, and newly composed musical pieces (Dr Kallmann has maintained a steady interest in, and range of contacts with, composers ever since his voluntary service as archivist of the Canadian League of Composers in the 1950s). Though not initially planned as such, the volume has evolved into a continuation of the series of multi-authored investigations of Canadian musical life that began with *Music in Canada* (edited by Sir Ernest MacMillan, Toronto 1955) and continued with *Aspects of Music in Canada* (edited by Arnold Walter, Toronto 1969)/*Aspects de la musique au Canada* (edited by Maryvonne Kendergi and Gilles Potvin, Montreal 1970); Dr Kallmann was a major contributor to both. The breadth of specializations represented among the contributions may be taken, we believe, as a fair sampling not only of Helmut Kallmann's own approaches and enthusiasms but of current emphases in Canadian composition and in the study of Canadian music.

Beverley Cavanagh examines hymn tunes and related sacred music forms as found both in publications in aboriginal languages and in transcriptions from recent field recordings among particular native groups. The music of New France and post-conquest Quebec is the subject of a bibliography by Claude Beaudry, an annotated transcription of an early treatise by Erich Schwandt, and an investigative essay by Lucien Poirier.

Aspects of local music history, an essential ingredient of any national view of the subject, arise in the contributions of Nancy Vogan (Nova Scotia), Maria Calderisi Bryce (Montreal), Carl Morey (Toronto), Elaine Keillor (Ottawa), and Robert Dale McIntosh (British Columbia), and these authors touch in turn on music education, publishing, orchestras, and local music-making. Gilles Potvin recounts the tour sixty years ago of the composer Maurice Ravel to three Canadian cities, and Keith MacMillan the crucial early phase of Sir Ernest MacMillan's musical development which took place in a German prison camp during the first world war.

The four original musical works – three for Helmut Kallmann's main instrument, the piano, and one for solo voice – come from one of Dr Kallmann's teachers at the University of Toronto, Richard Johnston, and from three composers who have worked closely with Dr Kallmann – John Weinzweig in the early days of the Canadian League of Composers; R. Murray Schafer in the Ten Centuries Concerts series in Toronto in the mid-1960s, for which Dr Kallmann provided not only many program suggestions but in a few cases musical arrangements as well; and Clifford Ford in the Canadian Musical Heritage Society. In Johnston's 'Homage,' the middle *larghetto* section is based on the seventeenth-century *Prose de la Sainte Famille*, about which Dr Kallmann writes in his *History* (pp. 22-4). The title of Weinzweig's piece utilizes the siglum of the National Library of Canada, CanOn. Schafer's work for solo voice is an example of 'acoustic ecology'; in a letter to the editors the composer wrote that, when the work is heard in the intended outdoor environment of a Canadian mountain lake, the solo singer addresses each of the elements in turn, and echoes 'bring the voice back so that at times we do not know who the real singer is.' Ford takes as his source-tune a song by a composer of nineteenth-century Canada whose life and work have been a special research interest of Dr Kallmann's.

Biographical and analytical writings on Canadian composers are displayed in several facets: a series of preparatory notes by the late George Proctor for his projected study of Violet Archer's life and work; a description by F.R.C. Clarke of a hitherto unexamined major manuscript by Healey Willan; and the text and a personal commentary by Istvan Anhalt for his new vocal work, *Thisness*.

Patricia Kellogg outlines the CBC's record of fifty years of commissioning Canadian composers, while Ronald Napier narrates the history of the country's 'umbrella organization' for music, the Canadian Music Council.

Critical appreciation is exemplified in the essays of Walter Kemp (examining masses by three composers in relation to current liturgical criteria), Kenneth Winters (commenting on a selection of recordings from the modern Canadian music repertoire), and Geoffrey Payzant (expanding on work already published in his study of the musical thought of Glenn Gould).

We hope Helmut Kallmann will be pleased with this retirement gift. At the same time, it is appropriate that he is also a contributor. His bibliography of his own writings is included, through the conspiratorial co-operation of his senior staff at the National Library of Canada Music Division.

The editors are grateful to all the contributors; to Patricia Wardrop, who has expertly prepared the index; to Margaret Parker, Associate Editor of University of Toronto Press, whose keen judgment in editorial detail has been invaluable to us; to John Fodi, who has copied the musical examples for three of the essays; to Mabel Laine of the *Encyclopedia of Music in Canada* organization, Toronto, and Guy Huot of the Canadian Music Council, Ottawa, for assistance with the illustrations. We also warmly thank the following individuals and organizations who have facilitated the publication in various ways: Rodney Anderson; Floyd S. Chalmers, C.C., and M. Joan Chalmers; Ferdinand Eckhardt; Arthur Gelber, O.C.; Michael Koerner, O.C.; the Canadian Association of Music Libraries; the Institute for Canadian Music, Faculty of Music, University of Toronto; Manon Ames of the Faculty of Humanities Word Processing Centre, McMaster University; the National Library of Canada; and University of Toronto Press.

J.B.
F.A.H.

MUSICAL CANADA

BEVERLEY CAVANAGH

The Transmission of Algonkian Indian Hymns: Between Orality and Literacy

A fundamental problem presents itself to the researcher who seeks to comprehend an Indian hymn tradition. In view of the extensive publication of hymn-books in both historical and contemporary periods, does one regard the task as a musicological source study of written variants? Or, on the other hand, since hymns are frequently sung from memory or varied in performance, should one begin from the premises posited by folklorists for oral transmission? The answer is clearly both.

In virtually any society there are instances in which both oral and written elements play a role in the maintenance and development of a single tradition. The religious domain, I would speculate, may involve many such instances where ritual and belief are transmitted orally but written documents are often created to record doctrine and dogma. At all events, hymn singing most certainly falls on the line between orality and literacy. It is likely that in the case of such traditions the balance and indeed the very tension between orality and literacy must be understood before the meaning of the participants' experience can be understood.

Walter J. Ong, in writing about the fundamental difference between oral and written cultures, contends that

> writing makes 'words' appear similar to things because we think of words as the visible marks signaling words to decoders: we can see and touch such inscribed 'words' in text and books. Written words are residue. Oral tradition has no such residue or deposit. When an often-told oral story is not actually being told, all that exists of it is the potential in certain human beings to tell it. We (those who read texts such as this) are for the most part so resolutely literate that we seldom feel comfortable with a situation in which verbalization is so little thing-like as it is in oral tradition.[1]

He discusses at length the power of sound in an oral culture and, hence, the power of either spoken or sung words: 'In a primary oral culture, where the word has its existence only in sound, with no reference whatsoever to any visually perceptible text, and no awareness of even the possibility of such a text, the phenomenology of sound enters deeply into human beings' feel for existence, as processed by the spoken word. For the way in which the word is experienced is always momentous in psychic life.'[2]

However, there are few primary oral cultures in the modern world; there are rather oral cultures with elements of literary culture and literary cultures with elements of oral culture. This is the premise from which I have proceeded in the following study of hymn-books and oral transmission processes in Algonkian Indian languages.

The premise is somewhat at odds with many other studies of Christian hymnody in North American native cultures. These seem to have been influenced by two assumptions which bear scrutiny. The first is that the subject of Indian hymnody is a sub-category of missionization.[3] Where the singing of hymns was assumed to be a practice which was directed by Euro-American Christian missionaries, it is generally viewed as a derivative of a written tradition. The assumption that native hymn singing was controlled exclusively by clergy must now be challenged, however, by new data of several types:

1 analyses of differences in the perception of Christianity by native parishioner, missionary, and anthropologist;[4]
2 reports that hymns themselves are regarded as symbols of Indian identity;[5]
3 ethnographic evidence which documents intra-cultural performances of hymns, often within the framework of traditional ritual or belief.[6]

The second assumption which appears to underlie earlier studies of hymnody relates to our concept of the significance (symbolic value) of a 'hymn' itself. Unlike a folk-song, for example, it has a certain iconic value. It is my impression that we regard a hymn as a thing intact and that we are perhaps more resistant to the notion of hymnody as a process than we are to the idea of oral transmission in secular contexts. A hymn-book, for example, may be viewed as a practical tool for the teaching and performance of the repertoire, or it may be regarded as a sort of icon which encompasses the tradition. The actual contexts and uses to which hymn-books are put have rarely been examined. The view taken in this paper is that such publications are but one element in a process of transmission which has both oral and written aspects. In the first part of the paper, various factors affecting hymn transmission are outlined. In the second part, the structures of several hymn-books are examined and written and performed variants of selected hymns are compared.

Data for this study were collected during field work, primarily in the Naskapi community of Utshimashits (Davis Inlet, Labrador) and secondarily in the Montagnais communities of Sheshashit (Northwest River, Labrador), Sept Iles, and Mingan, Quebec. Comparative material from other Algonkian-speaking communities[7] was also consulted. In particular, I am indebted to Franziska von Rosen for access to material which she collected while working with Micmac in New Brunswick. While the examples are specific, some of the same basic patterns occur in the contexts of other non-Indian hymn traditions. I therefore hope that this way of examining hymnody may have some wider applicability.

FACTORS AFFECTING THE TRANSMISSION OF HYMNS

Although a musical tradition such as hymnody was introduced to Algonkian Indians as a tool of missionization, its subsequent development in each community was shaped by the social fabric and cultural norms of the locale. With regard to the transmission of hymns, the influence of the following factors must be carefully considered: the historical development of Christianity in specific areas; the contemporary social contexts for hymn singing; and the interpretation of hymns by Innu (the Naskapi-Montagnais word for *person*, used to identify native people) and non-Innu.

Historical development

First, historical events demonstrate that it is fallacious to assume that hymnody has been maintained and directed only by the clergy among Eastern Woodlands Indians. There are reports, for example, that the earliest converts among the Montagnais accepted the message of the first Jesuit missionaries (Father Le Jeune, Father Anne-Marie, and Brother Burel) only when the Christian doctrine was validated by a native religious vehicle – the dream. Particularly influential was Charles Meiachkauat, the chief at Tadoussac (site of the first mission), who recounted his personal experience as follows: 'En l'année 1639, étant un jour dans le bois j'ai eu une étrange vision, je vis un homme vêtu comme nous et qui me dit: "Quitte tes anciennes façons de faire, prête l'oreille à ces gens-là et fais comme eux. Puis quand tu seras instruit, enseigne à tes compatriotes." Je ne sais si c'était la voix du Grand Capitaine du ciel, mais je voyais et concevais de grandes choses.'[8] Furthermore, the contact between Indian and missionary was sporadic, not continuous, in many remote areas. In Labrador, for example, Jesuit priests were sent to Ferryland on the South coast of Labrador as early as 1627, but from the mid-eighteenth century until 1784, Roman Catholicism was outlawed, and the stiff penalties for harbouring a priest or permitting him to say Mass on your property involved the destruction of any building where Mass was celebrated.[9]

Although there were no missions in northern Labrador in the early nineteenth century, the range of nomadic travel was quite extensive, and contact between missionaries on the south coast of Labrador and northern Indians is documented (for example, W.G. Gosling reports the arrival in 1844 of Naskapi-Montagnais Indians at the Moravian mission in Hopedale, where they reported they had been baptized by Roman Catholic missionaries on the south coast of Labrador).[10] In 1836 the Hudson's Bay Company established a trading post in Hamilton Inlet, and from this time on it was common for the more northerly Indian bands to travel to Hamilton Inlet in the summer to trade with the Hudson's Bay Company and profess their faith. For the Mushuau Innu or Barren Lands Indians of Northern Labrador, this practice continued until a mission was established there in 1927. It was the Indians of Davis Inlet, not Roman Catholic church authorities, who pressed for a priest in their community. The letter, which initiated the idea of a mission in Davis Inlet was dictated to John Keats by Chief Joseph Rich in March 1925. After explaining that hunting was poor and that Rich could therefore not go to Northwest River that summer, Keats wrote: 'He wants to know if you are coming to Davis Inlet either next summer or the following summer, and if so, if you would write him through me, of the date you are about to get here, he says he will tell the Nescauppy Indians that you are coming so they can be here when you arrive. He would like for you to send him some "Singing Books" (Indian).'[11] The recipient of the letter, Father Edward O'Brien, became transient priest to the Labrador Indians, a position he held for twenty-five years. During this time he worked with the Hudson's Bay Company to provide relief for the near destitute families in this area. In fact, the majority of the papers in O'Brien's collection concern the desperate economic plight of the Indians. In the face of such critical circumstances, Joseph Rich's request for 'singing books' is a significant indication of the high priority given to this type of musical activity during this period. Furthermore, the fact that there was no mission at Davis Inlet until a resident priest was appointed in 1952 indicates that hymnody had flourished in this area without the direction of clergy. Both the nomadic annual cycle of the Indians and the transient nature of the missions suggest that until that time Christian traditions had largely been sustained internally, by the Indians themselves, with only occasional direction by clergy.

Contemporary social contexts for hymn singing

Not only did Indians often maintain the hymn tradition intra-culturally, but they frequently did so in contexts other than the Mass. Again, the Naskapi community of Davis Inlet will serve as an example.

With the founding of the mission there in 1952, and particularly with the construction of a larger church in the mid-1960s, important changes occurred in the context which sustained hymnody. In the village setting, Mass is celebrated on Sunday morning and there are shorter services each evening. The mission house was used for movies and court cases until 1984, when the band council built a new hall to remove these activities from the church. The physical layout of the interior is not unusual. Wooden chairs in the nave face a simple wooden pulpit and altar, an unused harmonium and the host sit to one side, and large hand-painted posters decorate every wall. For some prayers and sung items other than the Ordinary of the Mass, texts are projected on the back wall by means of an overhead projector.

In 'nutshimits' or 'the country,'[12] however, the space used for Christian ritual is the same as that used for the daily routine, a canvas tent where more traditional Indian ways predominate. In this context, the use of space is radically different than in the mission in that the people turn out towards the walls of the tent to pray. Although this is not always done when hymns are being sung, one singer explained, 'you turn outward if you really want to pray with the song.' Implicit in this explanation is the fact that, while Tshitshe Manitu (God) may be symbolized within the nave of the church, the Manitua (or spirits) of the Indian world surround us, separated from us by the tent wall. This is consistent with Algonkian beliefs documented elsewhere. We are reminded, for example, of Adrian Tanner's interpretation of Cree hunting rites, which often involved 'sacred objects' which have a sheet-like or membrane quality: 'This feature is found in rites in which the actor uses the membrane to communicate with the spirit world, a world which is represented as being on the other side.'[13] The evidence is there in the shaking tent (an inversion of the hymn-singing tent since in the former the spirits are inside and the people outside the tent wall) as well as in the traditional frame drum, whose membrane sometimes reveals spirits only to the singer and the sound of whose snares is sometimes described as spirit voices. In some places there are taboos about viewing the underside of the drum since the spirits of the instrument reside there.

In addition to different physical spaces, the different contexts of country and mission also require different roles for the participants. Although in relation to the country setting one singer commented that 'when the weather was bad, people would stay in the tent and listen to the old men sing hymns,' most evidence suggests a fairly egalitarian gender division. In the Davis Inlet mission, however, a small group of women have assumed leadership status.[14] One of these women sits on the parish committee which chooses the hymns for worship and initiates the singing in the course of services. She is consistently regarded as the star singer and the most knowledgeable person regarding Indian hymns. I shall return to this matter of increasing specialization later.

The usage of hymn-books in these two contexts is interesting. In both, performances imply that hymn-books function as mnemonic devices within an oral tradition. Words are changed into local dialect; this involves not simply the switch from 'l' to 'n' dialects,[15] but more complex changes. For example, the refrain 'Nutem innuts' (we the Indians) is changed in Davis Inlet to 'Missiue innuts' (the Barren Lands Indians, that is, a reference to the local people). The stanza structure in printed sources is often not parallel to the performed strophes of a hymn. In 'Nituashim,' for example, the melodic strophe repeats for every two lines of the four-line stanzas. In 'Ueshkats . . . ' the fourth line of the first stanza is repeated as a refrain in subsequent verses. In 'Shash papinu' the irregular stanza structure of the printed verse bears no relationship to the two- or three-phrase melody; in fact, one melodic repetition includes the last line of one stanza and the first of the next. Finally, unless the performer knows the proper text underlay, it is virtually impossible to fit the printed text to the tunes.

In both Davis Inlet and Mingan, multiple copies of hymn-books are not used during Mass and other mission services. In Davis Inlet texts are projected on the wall, as mentioned above. In Mingan, on the other hand, the lead singer or singers carry hymn-books and mimeographed texts with them to the service, and the congregation joins the singing for refrains and other parts of the hymns which are well known. The stanzas, however, are often performed by the lead singer alone. Paradoxically, virtually every family possesses one or more hymn-books, which are always taken into the country, and are well used. In one instance, for example, a singer claimed that she was unable to tape her favourite hymns because those pages had come loose and fallen out of her hymn-book. Mimeographed collections of favourite hymns are often mass produced locally. In Davis Inlet a large proportion of the hymns in the mimeographed anthology were new, so possibly the clergy recognized that hymns were learned in the family context and found this a useful medium for introducing new music to the parish. In fact, however, the acceptance of new hymns cannot be dictated by the clergy. For example, the old hymn-book *Aiamieu kie nikamu* remains more popular in the Naskapi-Montagnais communities than the new *Sheshus nashatau*, even though the church authorities dislike its outmoded theology. One of the reasons for its popularity is the fact that many Naskapi-Montagnais claim that the old hymns were composed entirely or in part by Indians. Local demand was sufficiently strong that a new edition of the earlier book has recently been issued. The popularity of this particular book clearly affects repertoire. So, of course, does the value placed on specific hymns within the collection. This aspect is difficult to assess, but is an essential factor in the transmission process.

The interpretation of hymns by Innu and non-Innu
The same hymn in the same social context can signify something quite different to clergy and parishioner, to native and non-native, and the concepts which underlie such interpretations have a considerable influence on repertoire choice.

In Davis Inlet, one of the resident missionary nuns described an incident in which a teacher who had come from England insisted that all native children speak only English in class and in daily conversation. When they reacted by 'speaking more Indian,' the teacher punished them. The children protested by running around the school-house for an hour singing the hymn 'Missiue innu.' Later, when one of the girls in the class was cleaning the house, she said, 'This is an ENGLISH house!'[16] The missionary frequently referred to 'Missiue innu' as the Indian national anthem and used it regularly in school assemblies. The anthem analogy was possibly suggested by the march rhythm of the refrain and by text lines such as these:

> The barren ground tribes,
> Those who wanted to be Christians,
> They help each other,
> So they can do well on this earth.
>
> You flew toward me,
> Caribou and beaver,
> Only hunting in the winter,
> You never tired,
> You walked over the country
> You walked over the Davis Inlet.

As the sister explained, the notion of Indianness was a proud feeling relating to an ideal concept, almost the stereotypic one of man in touch with nature in a desolate land. Her selection of hymns for use in the school was often influenced by similar considerations.

In contrast, Naskapi hymn interpretations usually offered a different perspective. In reference to 'Shash papinu,' for example, lead Naskapi singers emphasized that all the activities of life in the country were mentioned:

> When I'm walking, when I am tired,
> When I am sad, when I cry,
> When I am sick, and when I am hungry,
> Help me Jesus

or

> Great Spirit [came] on earth,
> In order to feed Jesus and Mary,
> and to clothe them.
> Help me to be a good hunter
> for all my hungry children.

The women explained that, for a period of time, this hymn was used once a year in the mission house, just before the villagers made their annual trek into the interior and during their stay in the country. The objects associated with 'Indian' life were regarded differently from those in the text of 'Missiue innu,' discussed above. The mention of hunting, in particular, was felt to relate to actual hunting success. The hymn functioned in a manner analagous to 'dream songs,' in which the use of the song actually unleashes power to effect change in one's life. Other hymn interpreters shared this concern with the power of hymns.[17] For example, 'E petshimut piishum,' the refrain of which begins 'When the sun goes down, we ask you to take care of us, Mary,' 'must always be sung at sundown,' according to one singer. Another type of interpretation did not imply the power of hymns but suggested a quality of immediacy and an emphasis on 'Indianness.' 'Stimauenimitin Pinamen,' for example, is dedicated to Saint Philomen, but in Davis Inlet Pinamen (Philomen) is sometimes regarded as an Indian princess who was abused by the chief of the tribe.

What is striking about these two styles of hymn interpretation (that is,

Innu and non-Innu) is that they share an emphasis on 'Indianness' but at the same time the symbology is different. While one text was glossed as a representation of Indian life, the other was described as if it was a form of Indian life. This difference is akin to Clifford Geertz's distinction in *The Interpretation of Cultures* between 'models for' and 'models of' reality.[18] That is, the data suggest that the missionaries regard hymns, prayers, and other patterns of Christian worship as 'models for' an idealized Indianness, while at least some Indians view the same patterns (as they view more traditional cultural forms) as 'models of' actual Indian experience. This distinction is basic in understanding the historical development of the tradition – in particular its contrasting form within the contexts of the village and the country.

The 'models for/models of' dichotomy also serves to explain at least some of the factors influencing repertoire choice and social usage, in particular, the increasing specialization of a few participants in the mission context. The whole notion of 'star culture bearers' is distinct from that of mere 'culture bearers' in a fashion somewhat parallel to the 'models for/models of' distinction. That is to say, 'star culture bearers' become representatives or symbols of a tradition particularly at a point where the tradition says something *about* Indian life but is not integrally governing it. Thus they, like the mission hymns, might be seen as models for reality.

Like many transcultural traditions, then, this one is not valued consistently. Some unravelling of the intra-cultural interpretations would, in such cases, appear to be a necessary preliminary to the study of oral transmission since both choice of repertoire and singing style are affected. Before returning to this matter, however, let us examine the role of hymn-books.

THE PRODUCTION, DISTRIBUTION, AND USE OF HYMN-BOOKS

The historical data presented above indicate that while hymn-books were valued commodities for Christian Indians, who regarded them as important tools for maintaining the tradition, they were not prerequisites for the development of Algonkian hymnody. In order to determine the role which they did play in the transmission process, one must examine the contents of representative publications, collect data regarding the use of hymn-books, and compare the printed music with performed versions of the same hymns. (Ideally, unpublished, hand-copied anthologies in private collections should also be studied, but although I have seen a number of these, none were available for detailed analysis.)

There are a number of differences between books published by Protestant denominations and those produced by the Roman Catholic church. In part, of course, these differences relate to language, the Protestant-English and Catholic-French dichotomy being obvious. In addition, however, there seems to be a difference in philosophy between the two groups. The Methodist hymn-books of Peter Jones, a Chipewyan minister, for example, seem to be directed towards clergy or bilingual parishioners who would be familiar with the English-language hymns from which he translated texts and which he printed on pages facing the Indian versions. The Methodist practice of indicating Common Metre or Long Metre was observed, but no tune references were indicated and no musical notation included. The order of the hymns followed that of the *Methodist Hymn Book*. So it was the English publication rather than local practice or the compiler's creativity that to a large extent dictated the form and content of the publication.

French Catholic sources are somewhat different. First, they are bilingual only in cases where two or more Indian languages are incorporated (see, for example, Vetromile's *Indian Good Book*, 1856, in various dialects of the Abenaki confederacy, but also containing some Montagnais hymns and prayers; see also Cuoq's *Tsiatak nihonon8entsiake*, 1865, in Iroquoian and Algonkian languages). The language selection suggests that the books were designed for Indian parishioners and reflected the needs of missions which served natives of more than one tribe. Furthermore, the translations often depart radically from the French or Latin sources.

In most publications music for Latin hymns and liturgical items is printed in chant notation. Even for the Ordinary of the Mass, no texts were ever standardized, probably because of the bewildering plethora of local dialects. Example 1 illustrates the range of variability between two of the same chants as published in Prévost's *Nikano masinaigan* (1885) and *Aiamieu kie nikamu* (1947). In the former the Indian translation begins after a Latin incipit. Both adhere to the chant contour although note repetitions are adjusted to accommodate the text translations. The Sanctus texts have some words in common (evident once one adjusts to the differences between the two orthographies), but the differences are extensive. Local practice seems, once again, to be reflected. Some translations were done with great care for the Latin text underlay; in the case of the popular 'Veni Creator Spiritus' (Example 2), for instance, the fidelity of the textual meaning seems to be secondary to ligatures and syllabic grouping.

Until the 1940s, tunes with 'airs' designated in French were rarely printed. There are a few anomalies. In Cuoq's *Tsiatak*, for example, a tune

The Transmission of Algonkian Indian Hymns 13

Example 1 Parallel Ordinary movements, transliterated from: a/ Prévost, *Nikano masinaigan* (1885), page 2, and b/ *Aiamieu kie nikamu mishinaigan* (1947) 247

Example 2 Transcription of a performance by the Davis Inlet congregation, compared with the *Liber Usualis* version. The Innu text may be translated as: Come, Good Spirit. Rejoicing a lot in you, and in the Father and the Son, from whom you come, Good Spirit.

in chant notation is headed with a French air title. However, the refrain structure of this melody, in which a line repeats with open then closed cadences, reinforces a secular connection. Like the Latin items, hymns with the same French tune reference have idiosyncratic texts in different publications (except, of course, where one hymn-book was an expansion or reworking of another one). Because of dialect differences, it seems that texts rarely circulated in the oral tradition but were usually composed anew by the clergy or parishioners in each community. (There may be some exceptions to this tendency, as illustrated by the text variants of hymns to the cantique 'Bénissons à jamais' discussed below.)

There have been some historical changes in the content and organization of Algonkian hymn-books. Although early books were occasionally illustrated (for example, Vetromile included elaborate borders and line drawings), twentieth-century publications tend to make more extensive use of illustrations, often photographs, to enhance their message. Particularly noteworthy in this regard is the Oblate Fathers' book *Sheshus nashatau* (1975), which includes photographs of Indians engaged, for the most part, in traditional activities such as fishing or hunting. As mentioned above, until the 1940s, tunes for the airs were rarely published. (Prévost's *Nikano masinaigan*, which Banks lists as having music throughout, contains only chant. This rather slight volume prints the 'Asperges,' 'Messe royale,' 'Messe du second ton,' and 'Messe des morts,' the last with several additional items at the end.) The appearance of the *Saulteux Hymnal* in 1942 thus marked a new style of hymn-book, since it contained both texts and tunes.[19] In 1971 the Bishopric of Moosonee followed suit with the *Cree Hymnal*,[20] and some other communities began adding tunes to their local compilations of hymns; an example is Rev. Père Adrien Derveau's *Recueil de cantiques montagnais* (1960, revised 1983),[21] an anthology which advertises itself as 'A Chipewyan hymn book for the Keewatin and Mackenzie Districts.'

It is difficult to say what the inclusion of tunes in these recent books means in terms of social usage. It could imply a loss of vitality in the tradition; if tunes are no longer known, they must now be written down so that they can be retaught. It could imply a redirection of the anthologies to the clergy or an increase in musical literacy on the part of the parishioners. The photographs in *Sheshus nashatau*, on the other hand, would seem to be easier to interpret as an obvious move towards a more popular format. Other possible steps in this direction, however, do not seem to have been favoured. The language distribution, for example, has not changed appreciably either in post-1940 publications or in the oral tradition (I have statistics only for the Labrador community of Davis Inlet).

TABLE 1
Language distribution of tune references

	Laverlochère and Garin (1847)	Cuoq (1865) (Algonkian hymns only)	*Saulteux Hymnal* (1942)	*Cree Hymnal* (1971)	Davis Inlet[a]
Total tune references	25	20	177[b]	149[c]	192
French	19	16	159	135	170
Latin	5	4	13	9	17
English	1	—	5	5	5

a Naskapi oral repertoire
b Plus twelve tunes for which there is no designated air
c Plus one tune for which there is no designated air

Table 1 indicates that items derived from Latin sources have decreased slightly in percentage but still constitute between 5 and 10 per cent of the collections, while English tunes comprise 2 per cent and French the remainder.

The appearance of published sources with printed tunes for vernacular chansons as well as chant enables us for the first time to study the tradition of Indian hymnody from two perspectives: the oral and the written. This is one instance where the old and sometimes unpopular questions of diffusion, and the distributional studies these questions imply, would seem to be productive, especially if the results were interpreted in the context of the historical and ethnographic data presented at the outset of this paper. Before investigating the dissemination of tunes and texts, however, let us examine the contents and organization of the three aforementioned hymn-books containing musical notation.

Historically the earliest and geographically the central collection of the three is the *Saulteux Hymnal*. The preface credits Conrad Latour's *Recueil de cantiques* as the main tune source and also cites Bouhier's *300 Cantiques* and Blanchin's *Recueil de cantiques d'Ottawa* as sources. A cross-check with Latour revealed sixty-one titles in common; however, not all are exact reproductions. Some tunes (see, for example, 'Au sang qu'un Dieu' or 'Chantons, Joseph') duplicate every detail, including tempo and expressive indications. Others have minor editorial changes (for example, in 'Dieu seul adore' the placement of a rest was corrected and in 'C'est dans tes bras' the tempo indication was changed, probably to be consistent with the rest of the publication), and in some cases the change is more substantial. 'Dans cette étable,' to cite one example, is transposed and contains melodic variation which creates uneven phrases. Since the hymns in *Saulteux* have all been hand-copied, it is impossible to tell which were taken from which source. Changes such as transposition, however, are unlikely to be accidental, and where this occurs one might assume that other changes were also intended; a likely hypothesis is that changes were sometimes made to reflect local versions of the tunes. The representation of irregular metres and phrases such as that in 'Dans cette étable' would be consistent with performance practice in many contemporary Indian communities. There is some further evidence to indicate that some hymn tunes may not have been copied from published collections but rather transcribed from local performers. In some, especially heterometric ones, the placement of bar-lines in relation to melodic motives is inconsistent (see, for example, the chorus of 'Mamakatc inakamikat,' p. 28, or compare the stanza and refrain of 'Kin, ki nickiinan,' p. 60). In other instances, metre changes without an indicated change of time signature may also indicate a transcription rather than a duplication of a published tune (see, for example, 'Meno-Manitowiian,' p. 88, in which the second line has a measure of 7/8 and one of 3/4 in a 4/4 context). If these indicators may be interpreted as evidence of local practice, this hymn-book is indeed a valuable source for the study of transmission processes.[22]

Recueil de cantiques montagnais lacks the earmarks of a professional edition. In fact, it resembles the commonplace handwritten anthologies with their occasional errors and collage-like composition. My copy, for example, has an 'Act of Consecration' in English printed sideways on page 11 underneath the Indian text for the hymn above; there are three different spellings of St Basil, and hand-printing is combined with typing in some of the texts. Different coloured pages are used to separate the hymns according to subject-matter. The musical notation appears to have been rather carelessly done, unlike that in the *Saulteux* collection, where little could obviously be attributed to scribal error (Example 3). The

Example 3 Two instances of possible scribal error in Derveau, *Recueil de cantiques montagnais* (1983)

Derveau collection lists Bouhier's *300 Cantiques* first as a musical source and also acknowledges Latour, the St Basil *Recueil anglais* (40th edition, 1935), Saurin's *Recueil de prières et cantiques* (1895), and a mimeographed *Recueil du Scolasticat St-Joseph*. Unlike the *Saulteux* collection, this one indicates the source for each hymn; furthermore, several sources (for example, Lebret, Air Breton, St-Hyacinthe) not acknowledged in the preface are cited for specific hymns. It is interesting that among the 'Idées directrices de ce recueil,' we find the following objective: 'Réunir les cantiques les plus chantés, dans nos vieux recueils montagnais, et *y ajouter quelques inédits*' (emphasis added). The unpublished hymns could be those taken from the mimeographed anthology cited above. But, in fact, many hymns have no source indicated. Again, these may be transcriptions of local variants, but even if one makes this assumption, one can rely less on these variants because of the unreliability of the musical notation.

The *Cree Hymnal* shares with *Saulteux* and Derveau the fact that it is compiled from other sources. In this case, the sources are not credited even though the musical notation and French titles were generally photocopied for the new edition. In all cases the Cree text in syllabics is either added to or used as a replacement for the original text (see Examples 1a and 8b). In some instances, double-stave music (treble and bass clefs) was cut in half, with only the two parts on the treble stave reproduced (see, for example, 'Adeste Fideles'). One chant melody ('Isti sunt') and two vernacular ('Dieu très bon' and 'Seigneur soit avec nous') appear to be handcopied. From the type-face one can deduce that Latour's collection was the main source, but seven additional cantiques were used. (A few, such as the English source for 'Creation' which prints guitar chords, appear only once.) One very interesting example is the hymn listed as 'Reviens pécheur' (p. 230): the music is duplicated from the *Saulteux Hymnal*, not from the hymn called 'Reviens pécheur' but from a Communion hymn which has no tune reference, 'Mi sa jikwa, Jesus' (p. 206). (See Examples 4 and 5.) (A reference to 'Reviens pécheur' does occur in the *Cree Hymnal*, but with another tune altogether; this is discussed further below.) This is interesting as a rare instance of a published Indian-language hymn-book serving as a source for a new Indian-language publication. The texts are not the same. (The *Saulteux* tune was cut and pasted into shorter lines; some misalignment of the staff lines is evident at these points, and in one instance a rest was cut off.)

The degree of overlap among the tunes in these collections and those in the Davis Inlet repertoire, while hardly conclusive evidence, is an indication of song diffusion. Predictably, there is more overlap between any two

Example 4 a/ *Saulteux Hymnal* (1942), p. 206; b/ *Cree Hymnal* (1971), p. 230.

230

E kichi ayamianiwat
mechi tayan
Reviens Pécheur.

Example 5 Indian hymns with tune references to 'Reviens pécheur' (see also Example 4): a/ transcription of a performance by Mani Shan Nui and Charlotte Gregoire, Davis Inlet, 1982 (collection and transcription by the author); b/ the Goudimel tune as reproduced in the *Saulteux Hymnal* (1942) 312. Derveau uses the same tune with the slight variant shown in measure 6.

geographically contiguous sources than between those separated by greater distance (Table 2). That is to say, over twice as many tunes are shared by *Cree* and *Saulteux* or by Derveau and *Saulteux* than by *Cree* and Derveau or Naskapi and Derveau. The only anomaly is the slightly larger overlap between the Naskapi repertoire and that of the more remote Saulteux (22) than that of the culturally and geographically closer James Bay Cree (17). There are nineteen tune references common to three of the four sources and six common to all four ('Bénissons à jamais,' 'Ça bergers,' 'Reviens pécheur,' 'Le voici l'agneau si doux,' 'Souvenez-vous,' and 'Venez divin Messie').

The group of tunes shared by all four or by three of the four sources is especially central to the tradition. Although we do not have tunes for earlier periods or other areas, the fact that numerous tune references to these titles occur in many nineteenth- and early twentieth-century collections corroborates this and suggests their longevity within the oral tradition of Algonkian hymnody. The nature of the musical differences evident among the extant tunes, however, suggests that a number of complex

TABLE 2
The overlap in tune references among contemporary Indian hymn-books and performances indicated by the number of common tune references between any two of the four sources

	Davis Inlet[a]	*Saulteux Hymnal* (1942)	*Cree Hymnal* (1971)
Saulteux Humnal	22		
Cree Hymnal	17	39	
Derveau: *Recueil*	19	38	18

a Naskapi oral repertoire

factors have affected the transmission process. In some cases (for example, 'Il est né') where a tune has remained popular within French tradition, little variability is seen among the Indian sources. In other cases, (for example, 'Reviens pécheur' and 'Venez divin Messie') cantiques have remained popular in both French and Indian traditions but many different tunes have been associated with the air. 'Reviens pécheur' is especially interesting in this regard: in a study of texts and tunes associated with this title, Claude Rozier published fourteen tunes, none of which resemble the three different ones in the small number of Indian collections examined.[23] There seems to be no question of 'tune family' relationships or modular borrowing among them. In fact, this particular air title seems to convey no information about the tune which may be used in a given community. The Indian versions retain, for the most part, the symmetrical metres and phrases of the French sources. This suggests that different tunes were borrowed rather than a common one adapted or recomposed.

In other cases, the variants demonstrate change customarily found in an oral tradition. Some predictable elements of song loss, through memory failure or creative change, are found in this sample. The pattern of song loss or change is not consistent, however. As shown in Example 6, Montagnais, Naskapi, and Micmac versions of the tune of the well-known noel 'Ça bergers' vary at the beginning, but the final line is strictly maintained in all cases. On the other hand, 'Shuk tshinaskumitin' begins in a similar manner in Naskapi, Montagnais, Chipewyan, and Saulteux versions, but the ending is individualized in each. In two cases, 'Uenisk' and 'Espishian,' the refrains of cantiques are excised to constitute independent tunes. It is interesting that, in the case of 'Uenisk' the refrain is used in isolation among the Naskapi-Montagnais while a two-section stanza with refrain sandwiched between the sections is retained further

west among the Saulteux (see 'Ondas,' in *Saulteux Hymnal*, p. 200). In accordance with the theories of Philips Barry, there is some evidence that tunes which exhibit substantial loss or change have been maintained in the repertoire longer. 'Ni stimauenimitin,' for example, a hymn that Davis Inlet people claim to have learned quite recently from Montagnais on the lower North Shore, is identical to printed versions of the air 'Louez soit à tout moment.'

Some hymn tunes associated strongly with the country context have proved particularly elusive to trace. For this repertoire group, the cantiques referenced in hymn-books are rarely found in French collections. In some cases tunes bear some resemblance to cantiques with different names (for example, 'Brûlant d'amour' shares with 'Au fond des brûlants abîmes' the narrow-ranging motion around the tonic in the first two phrases and the descent to the seventh of the Dorian mode in the two penultimate phrases). The evidence is too slight, however, to posit 'tune family' relationships for any groups of tunes.

From the point of view of oral transmission, 'Shuk tshinaskumitin' (Example 7a) is one of the most interesting of the group of tune references in all four sources. Gastoué[24] attributes the French text, 'Bénissons à jamais,' to the early eighteenth-century production of Grignon de Montfort. It appears rarely in nineteenth- and twentieth-century cantique collections I have seen thus far, but frequently in Indian hymn-books. Contemporary tune-books contain two distinct melodies and, in view of the fact that texts with different stanza and line lengths (Example 8) appear with this air designation in earlier collections,[25] it seems likely that two or more tunes have been used historically. Three versions of one tune occur in recent oral and written sources. This modal melody exhibits several features associated with a rather long process of oral transmission. The variants begin fairly consistently but the end of the stanza is mark-

Example 6 *opposite* Indian hymns based on the French noël 'Ça bergers assemblons-nous': a/ from Pellegrin, *Poesies chrétiennes* (1701), as quoted in E. Myrand, *Noëls anciens de la Nouvelle France* (Quebec: Dussault and Proulx, 1899) 74; b(i)/ from the *Saulteux Hymnal* (1942) 34, transposed up 2 semitones; b(ii)/ from Derveau, *Recueil de cantiques montagnais* (1983) 50; c/ transcription of a Naskapi variant sung by Agathe Piwas, Davis Inlet, 1982 (collection and transcription by the author); d/ transcription of a Micmac variant sung by Mildred Millea, Big Cove, 1985 (text from *Elnointoasimgeoel Alasotemagan*, Big Cove Cultural Centre, n.d., 26) transposed up 6 semitones (collection by F. von Rosen, transcription by the author). (Round parentheses are used for syllables printed in hymn-books but not articulated in performance. Square parentheses are used for extra syllables added in performance but not printed in the hymn-book used by the singer.)

24 Beverley Cavanagh

Example 8 Texts with the same air designation but with different refrain structures, line lengths, and poetic metres from Laverlochère and Garin, *Catéchisme, recueil de prières et de cantiques* (1854) 63, 74

edly different. The Naskapi-Montagnais version is similar to the Saulteux both in the retention of the c/c-sharp ambiguity and the descent to the flat seventh in line two of the refrain. (Differences in barring probably reveal more about the perceptions of the transcribers than about the accent structure, although one might argue that these differences reveal that the metric structure is ambiguous in performance.)

Text-tune relationships are sometimes quite confusing. The new *Cree Hymnal*, for example, includes a 'Bénissons à jamais' hymn in which the first line of the refrain reverses the word order of a variant in the *Saulteux*

Example 7 *opposite* Indian hymns based on one of the cantiques referred to as 'Bénissons à jamais': a/ transcription of a variant sung by Mani Shan Nui, Davis Inlet, 1982 (collection and transcription by the author); b/ from the *Saulteux Hymnal* (1942) 150, transposed down 3 semitones; c/ from Derveau, *Recueil de cantiques montagnais* (1983) 9, transposed down 5 semitones

Example 9 A Naskapi adaptation of the tune 'Tous n'est que vanité': a/ cantique from Ernest Gagnon, *Cantiques populaires du Canada français* (Quebec: n.p., 1906); b/ transcription of a performance in Davis Inlet, 1982 (collection and transcription by the author)

Hymnal. Furthermore, the *Cree Hymnal* uses the tune of the second of the two cantiques mentioned above, while the *Saulteux* uses the first. Texts in French and Indian sources are not consistent; nor are any two parallel in meaning. Words and phrases repeat among the Indian versions in a sort of modular fashion, again possibly indicating a long process of oral transmission. (Even the Iroquois version in Cuoq has a word with sounds like the opening of the Algonkian refrain.)

Taped variants collected by members of the Sound-Producing Instruments in Native Communities (SPINC) Research Group at Queen's University allow certain insights into the performed tradition, insights which printed variants cannot disclose. Some of these changes in performance reflect the musical context of traditional Naskapi-Montagnais genres such as the 'puamut nikamuna' (dream songs). Regular metres are often altered to indigenous rhythm/accent structures (see, for example, 'Eukun sheshakat' in relation to 'Tout n'est que vanité,' Example 9). Repeated notes are usually inflected microtonally upward (see, for example, 'Missiue innuts'). Form is regarded as a circular shape; hence stanza endings may be disregarded as the performer may stop in the middle of the tune.[26] A nasal vocal style which some singers associate with the country context is often adopted. Finally, textural practices may imitate local traditions. Although among the Naskapi-Montagnais monophony is the norm, in the lower North Shore community of Betsiamites, where French influence is syncretised, hymn singing in two parts is customary.

CONCLUSIONS

In view of the complexities of history, ethnography, and interpretation, what, in fact, can the study of hymn-books tell us about the tradition of hymnody in Algonkian Indian communities? How do they fit into the transmission process? On the other hand, how do the historical and ethnographic data help us interpret variability in the published and performed versions of hymns?

The evidence presented suggests that hymn-books, at least in the late nineteenth and the twentieth centuries, did not so much dictate the tradition as reflect it. Even the recent publications were put together in a manner which reflects local practice and local selection. Performance practice reinforces the view that Indian hymnody was to a large extent an oral tradition in which hymn-books functioned as mnemonic devices. The books were clearly not prerequisites for hymn singing, although they were valued commodities in most Indian households. Variability in performance reflects the local contexts, both linguistic and musical.

From a broader historical perspective, however, dismissing variability as a function of regionalism is inadequate. Certain kinds of variability demand interpretation. Circular forms, nasal singing style, rhythmic flexibility, and microtonal inflection occur most often in conjunction with hymns which are favoured in the country context and/or hymns which are interpreted intra-culturally as 'models of' rather than 'models for' reality. This sort of interpretation and the associated musical style are similar to the traditional dream song repertoire. In performance and interpretation, both traditions are closer to Ong's 'primary oral culture' than to a literate one. Hence, although an important vehicle for the maintenance of the hymn tradition is the written word, the dynamics of transmission are often rooted in 'orality.' At the very least, it should be recognized that transmission processes vary in accordance with usage and native philosophy.

CLAUDE BEAUDRY

Catalogue des imprimés musicaux d'avant 1800 conservés à la bibliothèque de l'Université Laval

Il est notoire que la ville de Québec conserve en ses murs le plus ancien fonds de musique imprimée au Canada.[1] Ces institutions et communautés religieuses telles l'Hôpital général, le Monastère des Ursulines, le Monastère des Augustines de l'Hôtel-Dieu, le Séminaire de Québec et l'Université Laval se partagent, en plus d'une importante collection de manuscrits musicaux anciens, ce précieux corpus, témoin le plus manifeste de l'activité musicale à Québec tout au long de son histoire, tant sous le régime français qu'après la conquête de 1760. A cet égard, la bibliothèque de l'Université Laval n'est pas en reste et conserve une bonne part de ce patrimoine musical imprimé dont la notoriété n'est certes pas étrangère aux résultats des premières investigations du Dr Helmut Kallmann au début des années cinquante, à l'époque où la bibliothèque de l'Université se confondait avec celle du Séminaire.

A l'occasion du lancement du projet du *Répertoire international des sources musicales* (RISM),[2] aussi dans les années cinquante, cette collection de musique a été l'objet d'un premier catalogue[3] dressé avec grand soin par M. Lucien Brochu, alors bibliothécaire à l'École de musique de l'Université Laval. Ce catalogue chronologique, qui n'a jamais été publié, a fourni les données pour l'insertion de la collection dans le RISM.

BUT

Le but du présent catalogue est double: d'abord, il s'agit de publier pour la première fois la liste complète et exclusive des imprimés musicaux d'avant 1800 et autour de cette date, conservés dans la section des livres rares de la bibliothèque de l'Université Laval. En effet, bien qu'une bonne partie du contenu de ce catalogue soit signalée dans le RISM, il n'en reste pas moins que ces titres sont dispersés à travers des milliers d'autres, et dans un répertoire composé de plusieurs volumes. Il n'est donc pas vraiment possible, à partir du RISM, de reconstituer la collection de l'Université Laval, et d'avoir une idée précise de son envergure et de son contenu. L'autre objectif poursuivi vise à dissiper une ambiguïté concernant la localisation mentionnée dans le RISM au sujet de certains documents de ce fonds. C'est qu'au cours des années soixante, la bibliothèque de l'Université Laval s'est détachée de celle du Séminaire de Québec pour devenir une entité indépendante, à l'occasion du déménagement de l'Université sur le campus actuel. Il y eut alors un partage des collections anciennes, dont celles de musique, entre ces deux institutions, avec comme résultat que certaines localisations du RISM, attribuées avant ce partage, sont maintenant erronées. Par exemple, *Octo cantica Divae Mariae Virginis* ... (Paris: Ballard, 1641) d'Artus Aux-Cousteaux est localisé à l'Université Laval dans le RISM, alors qu'en réalité l'ouvrage est conservé au Séminaire. Plus concrètement, les documents signalés 'C Qu' ou 'C Qul' (pour Canada, Québec, Université Laval) dans le RISM et qui ne figurent pas dans le présent catalogue, sont normalement conservés au Séminaire de Québec.

CONTENU

Les documents de cette collection peuvent être regroupés, grosso modo, en trois catégories: il y a d'abord les ouvrages liturgiques (antiphonaires, graduels, etc.) dont le plus ancien remonte à 1640; ensuite, les ouvrages datant du régime français (oeuvres musicales et traités sur la musique) depuis 1667; enfin, les publications postérieures à la conquête de 1760 dont l'origine est pour la plupart britannique et dont la plus grande partie a été reliée en recueils factices par leurs propriétaires, les familles Desbarats et Sheppard, au cours du XIXe siècle. Ces volumineux et nombreux recueils, dont trente-sept sont conservés à l'Université Laval, contiennent en majeure partie des oeuvres vocales (chant et piano), des oeuvres pour piano ou clavecin, ainsi que des oeuvres orchestrales arrangées pour piano ou pour ensemble de chambre avec piano. Il n'existe pas de partitions au sens moderne du mot pour ces arrangements. Par contre, chaque partie instrumentale est reliée en recueil. Malheureusement, beaucoup de ces parties sont perdues (ou sont peut-être dans d'autres bibliothèques?), de sorte que pour la plupart des arrangements pour formation de chambre le matériel n'est pas complet. Nous avons retenu de ces recueils les oeuvres antérieures à 1800 et également celles publiées autour de 1800, étant donné que la plupart des éditions anglaises de cette période ne sont pas explicitement datées.

Ces recueils étant constitués de publications distinctes reliées ultérieurement, ils ne sont pas paginés de façon continue. Exceptionnellement, quelques volumes ont été paginés à la main après avoir été reliés; dans ce cas, la première page des pièces signalées est indiquée. Quelques-uns de ces volumes comportent également un titre (p. ex. *Basso no 1*), une date ou un numéro inscrits à la main. Ces informations sont indiquées, le cas échéant.

MÉTHODOLOGIE

Le présent catalogue reprend une bonne partie des données de la liste originale de M. Brochu, avec son aimable autorisation. Il exclut cependant les titres qui ne sont pas localisés à l'Université Laval, et inclut quelques ouvrages qui n'avaient pas été répertoriés à l'époque. L'arrangement chronologique de cette liste, conçu en fonction de l'insertion dans le RISM, a aussi été écarté, car il se prêtait moins bien à la consultation. Pour la même raison, nous avons rejeté tout arrangement plus ou moins arbitraire par catégories d'oeuvres ou de documents, pour privilégier le simple ordre alphabétique auteurs-titres. Les différentes éditions d'un même titre (p. ex. les antiphonaires) ont été, par contre, classés chronologiquement sous ce titre. Les oeuvres de Clementi ont été mises en ordre d'opus, afin de pouvoir mieux les identifier. Les oeuvres de Haydn et de Pleyel ont été regroupées par genres, celles de Haydn étant identifiées selon le catalogue Hoboken[4] et celles de Pleyel d'après le catalogue Benton.[5]

Lors de la transcription bibliographique des oeuvres retenues, la page de titre a été recopiée intégralement, à l'exception de certains éléments qualificatifs jugés superflus qui ont été remplacés par des points de suspension, et des majuscules qui ont été systématiquement éliminées, sauf pour les noms propres évidemment, à l'image du RISM. Les oeuvres en plusieurs parties et les recueils ont été détaillés de façon à fournir le maximum d'informations. Pour faciliter le repérage et l'identification des ouvrages signalés, l'indice de classification de la bibliothèque de l'Université Laval a été inscrit sous chaque titre. La référence au RISM a également été indiquée, s'il y a lieu, sauf pour les ouvrages de musique liturgique, cette catégorie d'imprimés n'ayant pas été répertoriée par le RISM. Les ouvrages cités (sauf ceux de musique liturgique) qui n'ont pas été signalés dans le RISM portent la mention 'non signalé dans le RISM.' On en dénombre dix-sept. Tous ces titres, sauf un (La Feillée, *Nouvelle méthode* ... 1782), ont été publiés autour de 1800, ce qui expliquerait leur exclusion du RISM. Il y a également trois titres qui sont signalés dans le RISM, mais sans la mention de localisation à l'Université Laval; ces derniers sont notés 'non localisé C Qul dans le *RISM*.'

La rédaction de ce catalogue a permis de révéler un aspect fort intéressant de cette collection: parmi les 144 imprimés cités, 19 sont des 'unica,' c'est-à-dire qu'il ne subsisterait, pour chacun de ces imprimés, qu'un seul exemplaire connu et identifié dans le *RISM*, soit celui de l'Université Laval. Ces titres sont mentionnés de façon spéciale par un astérisque précédent la référence au *RISM*.

Il est à souhaiter que cette modeste contribution à la bibliographie musicale canadienne mette en lumière une collection historique jusqu'ici trop mal connue; puisse ce catalogue devenir un instrument de référence utile aux chercheurs et à tous ceux qui s'intéressent à cette tranche de notre patrimoine national.

Abrégé de l'antiphonaire romain ou vespéral pour tous les jours de l'année ...
  Avignon, chez J.J. Niel ... , 1780. 592p., 17 × 10.5 cm. (Ornement à la page de titre.) BQT 4385 1780

ALEMBERT, JEAN LE ROND D' (1717-83) *Elemens de musique théorique et pratique, suivant les principes de M. Rameau, éclaircis, développés et simplifiés par M. d'Alembert ... Nouv. ed., revue, corrigée et considérablement augmentée.* A Lyon, chez Jean-Marie Bruyset ... , 1762. xxxvi, 236p., 10 pl. (musique), 19.5 × 12.5 cm. ML 3815 A367 1762. *RISM* B6, p. 78

Antiphonarium juxta breviarium romanum, ex decreto sacro-sancti Concilii Tridentini. Pii V Pont. Max. jussu antea editum, et Clementis VIII auctoritate recognitum ...
  Lutetiae Parisiorum, typis Joannis Henault ... , 1670. (Ex typographia Clementis Gasse, 1669). 456, clxxxiip., 44 × 29 cm. (Deux pages manquent au début. Ornement à la page de titre.) BQT 4385 1670

[Antiphonarium romanum ...] La page titre manque. [1671], 500, cxciip., 27 × 20 cm. BQT 4385 1671

Antiphonarium juxta breviarium romanum ex decreto sacro-sancti Concilii Tridentini, Pii Pont. Max. jussu antea editum, et Clementis VIII auctoritate recognitum ...
  Parisiis, Sumptibus & Typis Ludovici Sevestre ... , 1683. 424, clxviiip., 45 × 29 cm. Gravure à la page de titre. (A la fin, six *Alleluia* manuscrits ajoutés.) BQT 4385 1683

Antiphonarium romanum, nova et certissima notarum editione modulatum juxta breviarium, ex decreto sacro-sancti Concilii Tridentini ... Parisiis, apud Joannem de La Caille ... & Robertum, J.B. de La Caille ... , 1689. 7, 351, cxxxvip., 20 × 13 cm. BQT 4385 1689

Antiphonarium juxta breviarium romanum ex decreto sacro-sancti Concilii Tridentini, Pii V Pont. Max. jussu antea editum, et Clementis VIII auctoritate recognitum ...

Parisiis, apud Ludovicum Sevestre ... , 1715. 424, clxviiip., 47 × 32 cm. (Ornement à la page de titre. A la fin, *Benedicamus Domino* manuscrit.) BQT 4385 1715

Antiphonarium juxta breviarium romanum ex decreto sacro-sancti Concilii Tridentini, Pii V Pont. Max. jussu antea editum, et Clementis VIII auctoritate recognitum ... Parisiis, apud Claudium Joan. Bapt. Hérissant ... , 1725. 424, clxviiip., 47 × 31 cm. (Gravure à la page de titre.) (Ex typographia Ludovici Sevestre, 1726.) BQT 4385 1725

Antiphonarium romanum juxta breviarium sanctae romanae Ecclesiae decreto sacro-sancti Concilii Tridentini restitutum, Pii V Pont. Max. jussu antea editum, Clementis VIII et Urbani VIII auctoritate recognitum ... *editio nova prioribus longe elegantior, necnon mendis quae in prioribus irrepserant accurate expurgata.* Lugduni; typis Amati de La Roche; & vaeneunt apud Petrum Bernuset ... , 1781. viii, 556, cciip., 50 × 32 cm. (Ornement à la page de titre.) (2 exemplaires.) BQT 4385 1781

ARNE, MICHAEL (1741-86) *Bacchus and Mars, sung by Mr. Arrowsmith, at Vauxhall Gardens, composed by Mr. Arne* ... London, printed by Longman & Broderip ... [ca 1799]. 4p., 32.5 × 24.5 cm. (Ex libris Miss Desbarats (?), sans titre, sans numéro ni date.) M 1 A11 S549 M987 3. *RISM A/I/1, p. 87 [A1495

ASTOR, W.H. *A Spanish air, with variations for the piano forte, by W.H. Astor* ... London, printed by Astor & Co., at their Music Warehouse ... [ca 1800]. 6p., 32.5 × 24.5 cm. (Ex libris Miss Desbarats (?), sans titre, sans numéro ni date.) M 1 A11 S549 M987 3. (Non signalé dans le *RISM*.)

BEMETZRIEDER, ANTON (1743-1817) *Nouvel essai sur l'harmonie, suite du Traité de musique, dédié à Mgr le Duc de Chartres, par M. Bemetzrieder.* Paris, Onfroy, 1779. 286p., 20 cm. MT 50 B455 1779. *RISM* B6, p. 133

BERNIER, NICOLAS (1665-1734) *Mottets à une, deux et trois voix avec symphonie, et sans symphonie au nombre de vingt six. Dédiez à Monseigneur le Duc de Bourgogne, composez par Mr. Bernier* ... *Gravé par H. de Baussen. Première partie* ... A Paris, chez l'autheur ... , Ballard ... , 1703. 254p., 39.5 × 28 cm. (Reliure armoriée.) M 1999 B 528 M922 B189. *RISM* A/I/1, p. 281 [B2088

BÉTHIZY, JEAN LAURENT DE (1702-81) *Exposition de la théorie et de la pratique de la musique suivant les nouvelles découvertes par M. de Bethizy. Seconde édition corrigée & augmentée par l'auteur.* A Paris, chez F.G. Deschamps, 1764. 331, 60p., 20 cm. Errata. ML 3815 B562 1764. (Non localisé 'C Qul' dans le *RISM*.)

Brunettes ou petits airs tendres, avec les doubles, et la basse-continue; meslées de chansons à danser. Recueillies et mises en ordre par Christophe Ballard ... Paris, Christophe Ballard, 1703-04. 2 vol. 16cm. M 1730 B189 B895 M799

CAMPRA, ANDRÉ (1660-1744) *Mottets à I. et II. voix, au nombre de neuf, avec la basse-continue; Le pseaume In convertendo, à grand choeur & symphonie; Et un autre motet, à la manière italienne, à voix seule, avec deux dessus de violons. Par Monsieur Campra. Livre troisième.* A Paris, chez Christophe Ballard ... , 1703. 132p., 36 × 25 cm. (Vignette à la page de titre. Reliés avec Campra: *Motets, livre premier.*) M 2018 C199 B189. *RISM* A/I/2, p. 36 [C691

– *Motets. à I. II. voix au nombre de neuf, avec la basse-continue; Le pseaume In convertendo, à grand choeur & symphonie; et un autre motet, à la manière italienne, à voix seule, avec deux dessus de violons; par monsieur Campra, livre troisième, nouvelle édition.* De l'imprimerie de J.-B.-Christophe Ballard ... , 1717. 132p., 34 × 24 cm. (Vignette à la page de titre.) M 2018 C199 M917 B189 3. *RISM* A/I/2, p. 36 [C692

– *Motets à I. II. et III. voix avec la basse-continue, par monsieur Campra ... Livre premier, quatrième édition.* A Paris, chez Christophe Ballard ... , 1710. 111p., 36 × 25 cm. (Vignette à la page de titre.) M 2018 C199 B189. *RISM* A/I/2, p. 36 [C686

– *Motets à I. II. et III. voix avec la basse-continue; par monsieur Campra ... Livre premier, nouvelle édition.* De l'imprimerie de Jean-Baptiste-Christophe Ballard ... , 1733. 111p., 39 × 24.5 cm. (Vignette à la page de titre.) M2018 C199 M917 B189. *RISM* A/I/2, p. 36 [C687

– *Motets I. II. III. voix et instruments avec la basse-continue ... par M. Campra ... , livre second, nouvelle édition.* [ca 1710]. 128p., 36 × 23.5 cm. (Page de titre incomplète.) M 2018 C199 M917 B189 2. *RISM* A/I/2, p. 36 [C690

– *Motets à I. II. et III. voix, et instruments avec la basse-continue ... , par M. Campra ... Livre second, nouvelle édition.* A Paris, chez Christophe Ballard ... , 1711. 128p., 36 × 25 cm. (Vignette à la page de titre. Reliés avec Campra: *Motets, livre premier.*) M 2018 C199 B189. *RISM* A/I/2, p. 36 [C690

Cantus diversi ex graduali romano, pro singulis solemnitatibus, dominicis, festis et feriis per annum. Lemovicis, ex typographia Joannis Bardou ... , 1729. 192p., 16cm. (Suivi de *Trois méthodes faciles pour apprendre le plein-chant*, 79p., *Table du plein-chant et Index cantus*, 2p., *Privilège du Roy*, 3p., *Quinque missae pro majoribus festis*, 84p.) M 2148 L42 1729

CARRÉ, RÉMY (1706-?) *Le maistre des novices dans l'art de chanter, ou règles générales, courtes, faciles, et certaines, pour apprendre parfaitement le plein-chant ... par frère Rémy Carré ...* Paris, chez le Breton ... , 1744. xii, [54]p. (Il manque 1f., et les pages i-lxxxiv, pagination supplémentaire.) BQT 4621 C314 1744. *RISM* B6, p. 208

CHERUBINI, LUIGI (1760-1842) *The favorite overture to Lodoiska, composed by Cherubini, arranged as a duet for the piano forte, by F. Mezger ...* London, printed by Clementi, Banger, Hyde, Collard & Davis ... [ca 1800]. 17p.,

34 × 24.5 cm. (Ex libris Miss Desbarats, vol. 65, p. 27.) M 1 A11 S549 C4472 1. (Non signalé dans le RISM.)

CLARKE, JOHN (1770-1836) *Thou dear native land. Poetry by John Stewart, esqr., composed with an acct. for the piano forte, by Dr John Clarke of Cambridge* ... London, printed by Clementi & Co ... , [ca 1800]. 7p., 33 × 24.5 cm. (Ex libris Miss Desbarats, vol. 1, p. 67.) M 1 A11 S549 M987 2. (Non signalé dans le RISM.)

CLEMENTI, MUZIO (1752-1832) [Opus 12] *Four sonatas for the piano forte and one duet for two piano fortes composed & dedicated to Miss Glover by Muzio Clementi. Op. XII*... London, printed by Muzio Clementi and Comp ... [ca 1800]. 49p., 33 × 24.5 cm. (Contenu: sonata I, p. 2-13; sonata II, p. 14-21; sonata III, p. 22-31; sonata IV, p. 32-42; duetto, p. 42-49. Ex libris Miss Desbarats, vol. 3, 1818, p. 43.) M 1 A11 S549 C4472 2. RISM A/I/2, p. 156 [C2820

— [Opus 22] *Three sonatas for the piano forte, or harpsichord, with accompaniments for a flute and violoncello dedicated to Miss Anna Maria Carolina Blake, by Muzio Clementi. Op. XXII* ... London, printed by Goulding, Phipps & D'Almaine ... [ca 1800]. 23p., 32.5 × 24.5 cm. (Contenu: sonata I (ré majeur) p. 2-9; sonata II (sol majeur) p. 10-17; sonata III (do majeur, 'La chasse') p. 18-23. Ex libris Miss Desbarats (?), sans titre, sans numéro ni date.) M 1 A11 S549 M987 3. *RISM A/I/2, p. 161 [C2921

— [Opus 38] *Twelve waltzes for the piano forte, with an accompaniment for a tamburino & triangle, composed by Muzio Clementi. Op. 38* ... London, printed by Muzio Clementi & Co ... [ca 1800]. 25p., 33 × 24.5 cm. (Contenu: fa maj.; si bémol maj.; ré maj.; sol maj.; mi bémol maj.; do maj.; sol maj.; do maj.; si bémol maj.; mi bémol maj.; la maj.; do maj. Gravure à la page de titre. Ex libris Miss Desbarats, vol. 3, 1818, p. 147.) M 1 A11 S549 C4472 2. RISM A/I/2, p. 167 [C3049

— [Opus 39] *Twelve waltzes for the piano forte, with an accompaniment for a tamburino & triangle, composed & dedicated to Mrs. Mayhew, by Muzio Clementi. Op. 39* ... London, printed by Muzio Clementi & Comp ... [ca 1800]. 25p., 33 × 24.5 cm. (Contenu: do maj.; la maj.; fa maj., 'The echo'; fa maj., 'How d'ye do?'; do maj.; sol maj.; mi bémol maj.; sol maj; do maj.; fa maj.; si bémol.; mi bémol maj. Gravure à la page de titre de Bowman. Ex libris Miss Desbarats, vol. 3, 1818, p. 125.) M 1 A11 S549 C4472 2. *RISM A/I/2, p. 167 [C3055

COSTELLOW, THOMAS *Three easy divertimentos for the piano forte, composed & inscribed to the young ladies at Miss Caley's boarding school, Walthamstow, by T. Costellow* [ca 1800]. 6p., 32.5 × 24.5 cm. Divertissement no 3. Contenu: March; Waltz; March; Sweet Robin. Ex libris Miss Desbarats (?), sans titre, sans numéro ni date.) M 1 A11 S549 M987 3. *RISM A/I/2, p. 237 [C4246

DIBDIN, CHARLES (1745-1814) *Death alive. Written & composed by Mr. Dibdin, & sung by him with the greatest applause in The Wags.* London, printed & sold by the author, at his music warehouse . . . [ca 1790]. 4p., 32.5 × 24.5 cm. (Ex libris Miss Desbarats (?) sans titre, sans numéro ni date.) M 1 A11 S549 M987 3. *RISM* A/I/2, p. 400 [D2767

Epitome antiphonarii, seu vesperale pro dominicis et festis . . . Gratianopoli, apud Petrum Faure . . . , 1741. 502, iv, [16]p., 16.5 × 10 cm. (Ornement à la page de titre.) BQT 4385 1741

Epitome antiphonarii romani seu vesperale pro dominicis et festis in quo continentur antiphonae, psalmi, capitula . . . Editio prima . . . Venetiis, apud viduam Joannis-Nic. Galles . . . , 1766. 566p., 17cm. M 2149 V4 L42 1766

Epitome gradualis romani seu cantus missarum dominicalium et festivarum totuis anni, juxta usum romanum, a D. de la Feillée revisum, auctum & emendatum . . . Parisiis, apud Joannem herissant . . . , 1749. 564p., 16cm. M 2148 L42 1749

Epitome gradualis romani, seu cantus missarum dominicalium & festivarum totuis anni. Ed. secunda . . . Venetiis, apud viduam Joannis-Nic. Galles . . . , 1773. 370, clxxivp., 17cm. M 2148 L42 1773

Epitome gradualis romani seu cantus missarum dominicalium et festivarum totius anni, juxta usum romanum; a Dom. de la Feillée, revisum, auctum & emendatum. Pictavii, apud Franciscum Barbier, 1791. 606p., 18cm. M 2148 L42 1791

GELINEK, JOSEPH (1758-1825) *Maience walse with variations for the piano forte, by Gelinek* . . . London, printed by Clementi & Co . . . , [ca 1800]. 10p., 33 × 24.5 cm. (Ex libris Miss Desbarats, vol. 1, s.d., p. 193.) M 1 A11 S549 M987 2. *RISM* A/I/3, p. 204 [G1360

GERBERT, MARTIN (1720-93) *De cantu et musica sacra a prima Ecclesiae aetate usque ad praesens tempus. Auctore Martino Gerberto* . . . Typis San-Blasianis, 1774. 2v., ill., xxxvpl. (graph., fac-similés), 26cm. (Vignette à la page de titre. *Missae in coena Domini,* 112p., à la fin du vol. 2.) ML 3002 G362 1774. *RISM* B6, p. 358

— *Scriptores ecclesiastici de musica sacra potissimum. Ex variis Italiae, Galliae & Germaniae codicibus manuscriptis collecti et nunc primum publica luce donati a Martino Gerberto, monasterii et congreg. S. Blasii in Silva Nigra abbate, S.Q.R.I.P* . . . . typis San-Blasianis, 1784. (3v., front., ill., (mus). graph., tables, 25 cm.) ML 170 G362 1784. *RISM* B6, p. 359

Graduale romanum juxta missale ex decreto sacro-sancti Concilii Tridentini, Pii V. Pont. Max. jussu editum, Clementis VIII. primum, nunc denuo Urbani Papae Octavi auctoritate recognitum . . . Parisiis, impensis Societatis typographicae librorum Officii ecclesiastici jussu Regis constitutae, 1640. 463p., 45cm. M 2148 L4 1640

Graduale romanum juxta missale, ex decreto sacro-sancti Concilii Tridentini, Pii V. Pontificis Maximi jussu editum, et Clementis VIII. primum, nunc denuo Urbani Papae Octavi auctoritate recognitum... Lutetiae Parisiorum, sumptibus & typis Ludovici Sevestre ..., 1694. 396, cxlviiip., 45cm. M 2148 L4 1694

Graduale romanum, juxta missale sacro-sancti Concilii Tridentini et S. Pii Quinti Pontificis maximi authoritate editum... Parisiis, apud Christophorum Ballard ..., 1697. 429, cliip., 21 cm. M 2148 L4 1697

Graduale romanum, juxta missale, ex decreto sacro-sancti Concilii Tridentini, Pii V. Pontificis Maximi jussu editum; et Clementis VIII. primum, nunc denuo Urbani Papae Octavi auctoritate recognitum... Lutetiae Parisiorum, apud Ludovicum Sevestre ..., 1720. 360, cxlivp., 45cm. (A la fin: 2 *Kyrie Roïal & C* manuscrits.) M 2148 L4 1720

Graduale romanum, juxta missale, ex decreto sacro-sancti Concilii Tridentini, Pii V Pont. Max. jussu editum; et Clementis VIII primum, nunc denuo urbani Papae Octavi auctoritate recognitum... Lutetiae Parisiorum, apud Cl. Joan. Bapt. Hérissant ..., 1732. 360, cliip., 47.5 × 30.5 cm. (Ornement à la page de titre. Ex typographia Lud. Sevestre.) M 2148 L4 1732

Graduale juxta missale romanum, ex decreto sacro-sancti Concilii Tridentini, Pii V. Pont. Max. jussu antea editum, et Clementis VIII. et Urbani VIII. auctoritate recognitum... Lugduni, typis Amati de la Roche ..., 1782. 368, cxix, xxivp., 21 cm. M 2148 L4 1782

GRESHAM, WILLIAM *The cypress wreath. A song from Rokeby, written by Walter Scott esqr., composed and inscribed to Miss Elizabeth Scott Haden of Streatly by William Gresham...* London, printed & sold by Preston... [ca 1800]. 9p., 33 × 24.5 cm. (Ex libris Miss Desbarats, vol. 1, p. 9.) M 1 A11 S549 M987 2. *RISM* A/I/3, p. 342 [G3835

GRÉTRY, ANDRÉ-ERNEST-MODESTE (1741-1813) *Mémoires ou essais sur la musique par le citoyen Grétry.* Paris, Impr. de la République, [1797]. 3v., musique, 20.5 cm. (Une réimpression de la 1ère éd. de 1789, avec 2 volumes additionnels. Liste des oeuvres dramatiques mises en musique par l'auteur de ces essais, v. III, p. 469-73.) ML 410 G834 A3 1797. *RISM* B6, p. 379

HAYDN, JOSEPH (1732-1809) [Symphonies, arr.] *Haydn's grand symphonies, composed for Mr. Salomon's concerts, and arranged for five instruments, viz: two violins, a german flute, a tenor and a violoncello: with an accompaniment for the piano forte ad libitum. By J.P. Salomon...* London, printed for the proprietor Rt. Birchall... [ca 1800]. 75p., 34.5 × 26 cm. Partie d'alto. (Contenu: *symph.* nos 1-3, Hob. I: 97, 93, 94, p. 1-19; *symph.* nos 4-6, Hob. I: 98, 95, 96, p. 20-37; *symph.* nos 7-9, Hob. I: 104, 103, 102, p. 38-57; *symph.* nos 10-12, Hob. I: 99, 101, 100, p. 58-75. Ex libris Miss Desbarats, vol. 9: *Viola*, 1ère partie.) M 179 H415 S989 B617 Alto. *RISM* A/I/4, p. 241 [H4082

- Partie de violoncelle. Pagination multiple. (Contenu: *symph.* nos 1-6, Hob. I: 97, 93, 94, 98, 95, 96; *symph.* no 12, Hob. I: 100. Ex libris Miss Desbarats, *Basso no 1.*) M 1 A11 S549 C447 2
- Partie de piano. Pagination multiple. (Contenu: *symph.* no 7, Hob. I: 104, p. 1-10. Ex libris Miss Desbarats, vol. 43: *piano forte no 2.*) M 179 H415 S989 B617 Piano
- [Symphonies, arr.] *Grand symphonies composed by Joseph Haydn, and arranged for five instruments, viz: two violins, a german flute, viola & violoncello; with an accompaniment for the piano forte (ad libitum) by John Peter Salomon* ... London, published by R. Birchall ... [ca 1800]. 27, 15, 14p., 34.5 × 26 cm. Partie d'alto. (Pagination multiple et incohérente.) (Contenu: *symph.* nos 1-3, Hob. I: 85, 83, 90, p. 1-14; *symph.* nos 4-6, Hob. I: 92, 51, 91, p. 15-26; *symph.* nos 7-9, Hob. I: 48, 64, 88, p. 1-15; *symph.* nos 10-12, Hob. I: 82, 80, 73, p. 1-14. Ex libris Miss Desbarats, vol. 9: *Viola*, 2e partie.) M 179 H415 S989 B617 Alto. *RISM* A/I/4, p. 242 [H4083
  - Partie de piano. Pagination multiple.
    (Contenu: *symph.* nos 8-9, Hob. I: 64, 88, p. 11-27; *symph.* nos 10-12, Hob. I: 82, 80, 73, p. 1-27. Ex libris Miss Desbarats, vol. 43: *Piano forte no 2.*) M 179 H415 S989 B617 Piano
- [Symphonies, arr.] *Dr Haydn's symphonies arranged as quintettos for a flute, two violins, tenor and violoncello with an adaptation or thorough bass for the piano forte, by Dr. Hague* ... Book I. London, printed & sold by Preston ... [ca 1800]. 45p., 34.5 × 26 cm. Partie d'alto (Contenu: *symph.* nos 1-3, Hob. I: 66, 69, 74, p. 1-11; *symph.* nos 4-6, Hob. I: 44, 63, 75, p. 12-22; *symph.* nos 7-9, Hob. I: 70, 41, 71, p. 23-33; *symph.* nos 10-12, Hob. I: 47, 77, 53, p. 34-45. Ex libris Miss Desbarats, vol. 9: *Viola*, 3e partie.) M 179 H415 S989 B617 Alto. *RISM* A/I/4, p. 241 [H4080
  - Partie de violoncelle. (Contenu: *symph.* nos 1-3, Hob. I: 66, 69, 74, p. 1-11; *symph.* nos 4-6, Hob. I: 44, 63, 75, p. 12-23; *symph.* nos 7-9, Hob. I: 70, 41, 71, p. 25-35; *symph.* nos 10-12, Hob. I: 47, 77, 53, p. 36-48. Ex libris Miss Desbarats, vol. 8: *Violoncello.*) M 179 H415 S989 B617 Violoncelle
  - Partie de piano. (Contenu: *symph.* nos 1-3, Hob. I: 66, 69, 74, p. 1-23; *symph.* nos 4-6, Hob. I: 44, 63, 75, p. 24-43; *symph.* nos 7-9, Hob. I: 70, 41, 71, p. 44-59; *symph.* nos 10-12, Hob. I: 47, 77, 53, p. 60-79. Ex libris Miss Desbarats, vol. 43: *Piano forte no 2.*) M 179 H415 S989 B617 Piano

HOOK, JAMES (1746-1827) *The careful wife. Comic hunting song sung by Mrs Mountain in The Lyric Novelist*, composed by Mr. Hook, written by Mr. Cherry. London, printed & sold by Preston at his wholesale warehouses ... [ca 1800]. 3p., 32.5 × 24.5 cm. (Ex libris Miss Desbarats (?), sans titre, sans numéro ni date.) M 1 A11 S549 M987 3. *RISM* A/I/4, p. 385 [H6501

— *Down in the valley the sun setting clearly. A favorite rondeau sung by Mrs. Bland, in the comic opera of The Soldiers return as performing with great applause at the Theatre Royal Drury Lane, composed by Mr. Hook* ... London, printed & published by Goulding, Phipps, D'Almaine & Co ... [ca 1800]. [4]p., 32.5 × 24.5 cm. (Ex libris Miss Desbarats (?), sans titre, sans numéro ni date.) M 1 A11 S549 M987 3. RISM A/I/4, p. 386 [H6511

— *Guida di musica. Being a complete book of instructions for beginners on the harpsichord or piano forte, entirely on a new plan, calculated to save a great deal of time & trouble both to master & scholar. To which is added twenty-four progressive lessons in various keys, with the fingering marked throughout. Composed by James Hook. Op. 37* ... London, printed by Muzio Clementi & Co., [ca 1800]. 25p., 25.5 × 36 cm. (Titre gravé.) MT 252 H781 op. 37. (Non signalé dans le RISM.)

— *Hither, Mary, hither come. A favorite song sung by Master Phelps with universal applause at Vauxhall Gardens, composed by Mr. Hook* ... London, printed & sold at A. Bland & Weller's Music Warehouse ... [ca 1800]. 4p., 32.5 × 24.5 cm. (Ex libris Miss Desbarats (?), sans titre, sans numéro ni date.) M 1 A11 S549 M987 3. RISM A/I/4, p. 402 [H6867

HYLER, G. *Sweet Marianne. A favorite song. The words by E. composed by G. Hyler* ... London, printed by Goulding, Phipps, D'Almaine & Co ... , [ca 1800]. 3p., 32.5 × 24.5 cm. (Ex libris Miss Desbarats (?), sans titre, sans numéro ni date.) M 1 A11 S549 M987 3. *RISM A/I/4, p. 458 [H8049

Hymnes et proses de l'Eglise, nouvellement mises en vers françois qu'on a notées pour faciliter à les mieux chanter sur le chant des latines, où l'on a ajouté plusieurs cantiques aussi notés ... A la Rochelle, Chez Pierre Mesnier ... , 1693. 110p., 15.5cm. M 2149.2 H996 F814 1693

Iesus, Maria. Preces quae dicuntur 25. nocte cujuslibet mensis, in Aede institutionis parisiensis Oratorii Domini nostri Iesu Christi infantiae sacrâ. Parisiis, ex officina Roberti Ballard, 1653. 24p., 22cm. M 2150.3 I22 1653

In festo vitae interioris Domini nostri Iesu-Christi. [Paris, Robert Ballard, 1668]. 47, 24p., 14cm. Titre de départ. (Page de titre manque.) M 2148.3 J58 1668

JANSEN, L[OUIS?] *Kreith's celebrated twenty-four airs and waltzes, composed & arranged as solos for the german flute, with a piano forte accompaniment (ad lib) by L. Jansen. Book I* ... London, sold by Clementi & Co ... [ca 1800]. 9p., 33 × 24.5 cm. (Ex libris Miss Desbarats, vol. 1, s.d., p. 163.) M 1 A11 S549 M987 2. (Non signalé dans le RISM.)

KELLY, MICHAEL (1762-1826) *When pensive I thought of my love. Sung by Mrs. Crouch in the opera of Blue Beard. Composed by Michael Kelly.* London, printed for Corri Dussek & Co ... , [ca 1800]. 3p., 33.5 × 26 cm. (Ex libris Sheppard, vol. 6, 1824.) M 1 A11 S549 C4472 3. RISM A/I/5, p. 20 [K309

KIRCHER, ATHANASIUS (1601-80) *Athanasii Kircheri . . . musurgia universalis, sive ars magna consoni et dissoni in x. libros digesta . . .* Romae, ex typographia haeredum Francisci Corbelletti, 1650. 2v. (reliés), front., ill. (musique), pl. (dépliantes), tables, diagrs., 33.5 cm. (Vignette à la page de titre.) ML 100 K58 1650. *RISM* B6, p. 449

KOTZWARA, FRANZ (1730-91) *Kotzwara's Battle of Prague. Adapted for two performers on one piano forte, by W.B. de Krifft . . .* London, printed by Muzio Clementi & Co . . . , [ca 1800]. 15p., 34 × 24.5 cm. (Ex libris Miss Desbarats, vol. 65, s.d., p. 47.) M 1 A11 S549 C4472 1. *RISM* A/I/5, p. 70 [K1123 [Ce William de Krifft a complété une oeuvre inachevée de Kotwara: *Siège de Québec*, sonate pour piano, violon, violoncelle et timbale ad libitum. Londres, Bland, 1792.]

LA FEILLÉE, FRANÇOIS DE (ca 1780-?) *Méthode nouvelle pour apprendre parfaitement les règles du plain-chant et de la psalmodie, avec des messes & autres ouvrages en plain-chant figuré & musical, à voix seule & en partie . . . Seconde édition considérablement augmentée, revue & corrigée, par M. de la Feillée . . .* A Poitiers, & se vend à Paris. Chez Jean-Thomas Hérissant . . . , 1754. viii, 572p., 17 × 10 cm. BQT 4621 L162 1754. *RISM* B6, p. 470

– *Nouvelle méthode pour apprendre facilement les règles du plain-chant et de la psalmodie; avec des messes & autres ouvrages en plain-chant figuré et musical . . . , par M. de La Feillée, ecclésiastique. Nouvelle édition, revue, corrigée, & augmentée par un ecclésiastique, élève de M. de La Feillée . . .* A Poitiers, chez Jean-Félix Faulcon & François Barbier . . . , 1782. viii, 611p., 18 × 10 cm. BQT 4621 L162 1782. (Non signalé dans le *RISM*.)

LATOUR, T . . . (1766?-1837) *Del Caro's hornpipe, with variations, calculated for the use of young performers, on the piano forte, by T. Latour.* London, printed by Clementi & Co . . . [ca 1800]. 3p., 32.5 × 24.5 cm. (Ex libris Miss Desbarats (?), sans titre, sans numéro ni date.) M 1 A11 S594 M987 3. (Non signalé dans le *RISM*.)

LEWIS, MATTHEW GREGORY *Say not that minutes swiftly move. A new song, the words by Mrs. Robinson, the music by Mr. Lewis . . .* Liverpool, printed & sold by H. Hime . . . , [ca 1790-1800]. 3p., 33 × 24.5 cm. (Ex libris Miss Desbarats, vol. I, s.d., p. 153.) M 1 A11 S549 M987 2. *RISM A/I/5, p. 330 [L2312

MARCHAND, LOUIS (1669-1732) *Pièces choisies pour l'orgue de feu le grand Marchand . . . Livre premier . . .* A Paris, chez Me Boivin . . . [ca 1740]. 23p., 23 × 30 cm. (Contenu: *Plein-jeu*, p. 2; *Fugue*, p. 4; *Trio*, p. 6; *Basse de trompette*. p. 8; *Quatuor*, p. 10; *Tierce en taille*, p. 12; *Duo*, p. 14; *Récit*, p. 16; *Tierce en Taille*, p. 18; *Basse trompette ou de cromorne*, p. 20; *Fond d'orgue*, p. 21; *Dialogue*, p. 22.) M 7 M315 B685. *RISM* A/I/5, p. 413 [M470

MARTINI (SCHWARTZENDORF), JEAN-PAUL-EGIDE (1741-1816) [*Messe pour choeurs, solistes et orchestre par Martini*] ... La page de titre manque [ca 1800]. 256p., 33 × 25 cm. (Edition gravée.) M 2010 M386 M584. RISM A/I/5, p. 446 [M1011
- *Martini's grand ouverture to Henry the Fourth adapted for the harpsichord or piano forte, with an accompaniment for the violin* ... London, printed by Muzio Clementi & Co ... [ca 1800]. 11p., 32.5 × 24.5 cm. M35 M385 H518 M994. RISM A/I/5, p. 449 [M1078
  - (Ex libris Miss Desbarats (?), sans titre, sans numéro ni date.) M 1 A11 S549 M987 3. RISM A/I/5, p. 449 [M1078
MONTÉCLAIR, MICHEL PIGNOLET DE (1667-1737) *Principes de musique. Divisez en quatre parties. La première partie contient tout ce qui appartient à l'intonation. La IIè ... tout ce qui regarde la mesure et le mouvement. La IIIè ... la manière de joindre les paroles aux nottes et bien former les agréments du chant. La IVè ... est l'abrégé d'un nouveau système de musique, par lequel l'auteur fait voir qu'en changeant peu de choses dans la manière de notter la musique, on en rendroit l'étude et la pratique plus aisées. Composez ... par Mr. de Montéclair* ... Se vend à Paris, rue St-Honoré, à la Règle d'or, 1736. 133p., 35.5 × 27 cm. (Catalogue des ouvrages de l'auteur p. 2.) MT 853 M773 1736. RISM B6, p. 594
MORIN, JEAN-BAPTISTE (1667-1745) [*Premier livre de motets de monsieur Morin, à I. et II voix avec basse-continue.*] Paris, Christophe Ballard, [1748]. 125p. 36.5 × 22 cm. (La page de titre manque.) M 2018 M858 M917. RISM A/I/6, p. 22 [M3666
MOZART, WOLFGANG-AMADEUS (1756-91) *A favorite sonata composed by A. Mozart, adapted for the piano forte, with an accompaniment for a violin, by P.A. Kreusser. Op IV* ... London, published & sold by the editor ... [ca 1800]. 15p., 32.5 × 24.5 cm. (Transcription de la *sonate* K. 381 écrite pour piano 4 mains. Ex libris Miss Desbarats (?), sans titre, sans numéro ni date.) M 1 A11 S549 M987 2. RISM A/I/6, p. 210 [M6728
- *Favorite duet for two voices composed by M. Mozart* ... London, printed by J. Dale ... [ca 1800]. 3p., 32.5 × 24.5 cm. (Contenu: 'Away with melancholy.' Ex libris Miss Desbarats (?), sans titre, sans numéro ni date.) M 1 A11 S549 M987 3. (Non signalé dans le RISM.)
NICKS, G. *Tell! Ah! tell me is it love, sung with great applause by Miss Bolton, composed with an accompt. for the piano forte, by G. Nicks* ... London, printed by Clementi & Co ... [ca 1800]. 4p., 33 × 24.5 cm. (Ex libris Miss Desbarats, vol. 1, p. 105.) M 1 A11 S549 M987 2. (Non signalé dans le RISM.)
NIVERS, GUILLAUME-GABRIEL (1632-1714) *Traité de composition de musique par le Sr. Nivers, Me compositeur en musique, et organiste de l'église S. Sulpice de*

Paris. A Paris, chez l'autheur proche S. Sulpice et Robert Ballard ... 1667. 18 × 12 cm. MT 40 N735 1667. (Non localisé 'C Qul' dans le RISM.)

PERCIVALL, G.A.F. *E'er Laura met my ravish'd view. Written by W. Kendall, composed by G.A.F. Percivall* ... London, printed by Clementi & Compy ... [ca 1800]. 5p., 33 × 24.5 cm. (Ex libris Miss Desbarats, vol. 1, p. 83.) M 1 A11 S549 M987 2. (Non signalé dans le RISM.)

— *Strephon and Lucy, duet for two voices, the poetry by Chatterton, composed by G.A.F Percivall* ... London, printed by Clementi & Co ... [ca 1800]. 7p., 33 × 24.5 cm. (Ex libris Miss Desbarats, vol. 1, p. 22.) M 1 A11 S549 M987 2. (Non signalé dans le RISM.)

PLATTS, MARTIN *Martin Platts' periodical collection of popular dances, waltzes, etc, with proper figures for the piano forte, harp or violin*. Published monthly by Messrs. Clementi & Co ... [ca 1800]. 4p., 33 × 24.5 cm. (Ex libris Miss Desbarats, vol. 1, p. 155.) M 1 A11 S549 M987 2. *RISM A/I/6, p. 514 [P2601

PLEYEL, IGNACE (1757-1831) [Duos, violon et piano, Benton 5940] *Fourteen favorite sonatinas for the piano forte or harpsichord with an accompaniement for a violin ad libitum, composed and humbly dedicated to Her Highness the Duchess of Wirtemberg by Ignace Pleyel. Book I* ... London, printed by Muzio Clementi & Co ... [ca 1800]. 29p., 33 × 24.5 cm. Partie de piano. (Ex libris Miss Desbarats, vol. 3, 1818, p. 175.) M 1 A11 S549 C4472 2. RISM A/I/6, p. 645 [P4590

— [Duos, violon et piano, Benton 5941] *Twelve easy & favorite sonatinas for the piano-forte or harpsichord, with an accompaniment for the violin ad libitum, composed by Ignace Pleyel. Book II* ... London, printed by Muzio Clementi & Co ... [ca 1800]. 30p., 33 × 24.5 cm. Partie de piano. (Ex libris Miss Desbarats, vol. 3, 1818, p. 207.) M 1 A11 S549 C4472 2. *RISM A/I/6, p. 652 [4681

— [Quatuors, arr., Benton 3452] *Pleyel's German hymn with [6] variations* ... Glasgow, printed & sold by John McFadyen ... [ca 1800]. 3p., 32.5 × 24.5 cm. Version pour piano. (Ex libris Miss Desbarats (?), sans titre, sans numéro ni date.) M 1 A11 S549 M987 3. RISM A/I/6, p. 664 [4897

— [Quatuors, arr., Benton 3356] *Trois quatuors de Mr Ignace Pleyel, tirés de l'oeuvre dédié à Sa M. le Roi de Prusse. Arrangéae pour clavecin ou piano-forte avec accompagnement de violon et basse, par Mr. Lachnitt* ... (1ère suitte). London, printed by Longman & Broderip ... [ca 1788]. 29p., 32 × 24.5 cm. (Contenu: *quatuor I*, ré min.: allegro agitato, adagio non troppo, rondo; *quatuor II*, sol maj.: allegro, rondeau; *quatuor III*, la maj.: allegro non troppo, romance, rondo. Partie de piano. Ex libris Miss Josette Desbarats, 1810, vol. 64.) M 179 P727 C744 L856. RISM A/I/6, p. 601 [P3895

— [Quatuors, arr., Benton 3357] *Trois quatuors de Mr. Ignace Pleyel, tirés de l'oeuvre dédié à Sa M. le Roi de Prusse. Arrangéae pour clavecin ou piano-forte,*

Catalogue des imprimés musicaux 43

avec accompagnemens de violon et basse, par Mr. Lachnitt. 2 suitte ... London, printed by Longman & Broderip ... [ca 1788]. 12p., 33.5 × 25 cm. (Contenu: *quatuor I*, fa maj., p. 2-4; *quatuor II*, ré maj., ré min., p. 6-8; *quatuor III*, do maj., p. 10-12. Partie de violoncelle. Ex libris Miss Desbarats, vol. *Basso no 1*, 1822.) M 1 A11 S549 C447 2. *RISM* A/I/6, p. 602 [P3907

- [Quatuors, arr., Benton 4739] *Trois quatuors de Mr. Ignace Pleyel, tirés de l'oeuvre dédié à Sa M. le Roi de Prusse. Arrangéae pour clavecin ou piano-forte, avec accompagnemens de violon et basse, par Mr. Lachnitt.* 4 suitte ... London, printed by Longman & Broderip ... [ca 1789]. 7p., 33 × 25 cm. (Contenu: *quatuor I*, fa maj., si bém. maj., fa maj., p. 2-3; *quatuor II*, sol maj., p. 4-5; *quatuor III*, mi bém. maj., p. 6-7. Partie de violoncelle. Ex libris Miss Desbarats, vol. *Basso no 1*, 1822.) M 1 A11 S549 C447 2. *RISM* A/I/6, p. 603 [P3920

- [Quatuors, arr., Benton 4725] *Trois quatuors de Mr. Ignace Pleyel arrangéae pour clavecin ou piano-forte avec accompagnemens de violon et basse par M. Lachnitt.* 6th Suitte ... London, printed by Muzio Clementi [ca 1800]. 26p., 32.5 x 25 cm. (Contenu: *quatuor I* do maj., p. 1-8; *quatuor II* sol maj., p. 10-15; *quatuor III* si bémol maj., p. 17-26. Partie de piano. Ex libris Miss Desbarats, vol. 37. 1822, p. 59.) M 1 A11 S549 C447 1. *RISM* A/I/6, p. 598 [P3849
  - Partie de violoncelle. (Ex libris Miss Desbarats, vol. *Basso no 1*, 1822.) M 1 A11 S549 C447 2

- [Quatuors, arr., Benton 3748] *Three quatuors by Ignace Pleyel performed at the professional concert Hanover Square arranged for the piano forte or harpsichord with accompaniments for the flute & violoncello by Muzio Clementi* ... 9th suitte. London, printed by Clementi, Hyde, Collard and Davis ... [ca 1800]. 46p., 32.5 × 25 cm. (Contenu: *quartetto IV*, 3 mvts, si bém. maj., fa maj., si bém. maj., p. 2-19; *quartetto V*, 2 mvts, sol maj., p. 20-32; *quartetto VI*, 3 mvts, do maj., fa maj., do maj., p. 33-46. Partie de piano. Ex libris Miss Desbarats, vol. 37, 1822, p. 87.) M 1 A11 S549 1. *RISM* A/I/6, p. 606 [P3953
  - Partie de violoncelle. (Ex libris Miss Desbarats, vol. *Basso no 1*, 1822.) M 1 A11 S549 C447 2

- [Quatuors, arr., Benton 4034.5] *Trois quatuors de Mr. Ignace Pleyel arrangéae pour clavecin ou piano-forte avec accompagnemens de violon et basse par Mr. Lachnitt.* 10 suitte ... London, printed by Muzio Clementi ... [ca 1800], 23 p., 32.5 cm. (Contenu: *trio I*, mi bémol maj., p. 2-9; *trio II*, ré maj., p. 10-16; *trio III*, fa maj., p. 17-23. Partie de piano. Ex libris Miss Desbarats, vol. 37, 1822, p. 135.) M 1 A11 S549 C447 1. *RISM* A/I/6, p. 606 [P3956a

- [Quatuors, arr., Benton 4743] *Trois quatuors de Mr. Ignace Pleyel arrangéae pour clavecin ou piano-forte avec accompagnemens de violon et basse par Mr. Lachnitt.* 13th suitte ... London, printed by Longman & Broderip ... [ca 1800]. 25p., 32.5 cm. (Contenu: *quatuor I*, do maj., p. 1-5; *quatuor II*, ré maj., p. 6-16;

44 Claude Beaudry

quatuor III, mi bémol maj., p. 17-25. Partie de piano. Ex libris Miss Desbarats, vol. 37, 1822, p. 161.) M 1 A11 S549 C447 1. *RISM* A/I/6, p. 600 [P3876

– Partie de violoncelle. (Ex libris Miss Desbarats, vol. *Basso no 1*, 1822.) M 1 A11 S549 C447 2

– [Symphonies concertantes, arr., Benton 1245] *Pleyel's celebrated concertante as performed with the greatest applause at the Pantheon and Hanover Square Concerts, adapted for the harpsichord or piano forte, with an accompaniment for a violin.* London, printed by Longman and Broderip ..., [ca 1800]. 9p., 32 × 24.5 cm. (Contenu: en mi bémol maj.: allegro assai, andante grazioso, menuetto, trio, adagio espressivo, rondo. Partie de piano. Ex libris Josette Desbarats, vol. 64, 1810.) M 179 P727 C744 L856. *RISM* A/I/6, p. 639 [P4503

– [Symphonies concertantes, arr., Benton 1253.5] *No 21 Pleyel's celebrated concertante, arranged as a duett for two performers on one piano forte, by Mr. Latour* ... London, printed & sold at Bland & Wellers music warehouse ... [ca 1800]. 17p., 34 × 24.5 cm. (Ex libris Miss Desbarats, vol. 65, p. 63.) M 1 A11 S549 C4472 1. *RISM* A/I/6, p. 655 [P4728

– [Symphonies concertantes, arr.] *Pleyel's celebrated second concertante, as performed with the greatest applause at the Nobility's Concerts for the harpsichord or piano forte with accompaniments for the violins tenor and bass adapted by M. Lachnith* ... London, printed by Longman and Broderip ... [ca 1800]. 19p., 32.5 × 25 cm. (En si bémol maj., deux mouvements. Partie de piano. Ex libris Miss Desbarats, vol. 37, 1822, p. 35.) M 1 A11 S549 C447 1. (Non signalé dans le *RISM*.)

– Partie de violoncelle. (Ex libris Miss Desbarats, vol. *Basso no 1*, 1822.) M 1 A11 S549 C447 2

– [Trios, violon, violoncelle et piano, Benton 4602] *Twelve grand sonatas for the piano-forte, with accompaniments for a violin & violoncello, in which are introduced a variety of Scotch airs and favorite pieces. Composed by Ignace Pleyel. In four books. Op. 14* ... London, printed by Clementi & Co ... [ca 1800]. 7p., 34 × 25 cm. Partie de violoncelle. (Contenu: *sonata I*, do maj., sol maj., do maj., p. 2-3; *sonata II*, sol maj., do maj., sol maj., p. 4-5; *sonata III*, si bém. maj., fa maj., si bém. maj., p. 6-7. Ex libris Miss Desbarats, vol. *Basso no 1*, 1822.) M 1 A11 S549 C447 2. *RISM* A/I/6, p. 591 [P3757

– [Trios, violon, violoncelle et piano, Benton 3567] *Three sonatas for the piano forte, with accompaniments for the violin and violoncello, dedicated to the King of Naples, composed by Ignace Pleyel. Opus 24, 2d book* ... London, printed by Clementi & Co ... [ca 1800]. 36p., 32.5 × 25 cm. (Contenu: *quartetto I*, 16th suitte, sol maj., p. 2-12; *quartetto II*, 16th suitte, la maj., p. 13-25; *quartetto III*, 16th suitte, la bémol maj. et fa maj., p. 26-36. Partie de piano.

Ex libris Miss Desbarats, vol. 37, 1822, p. 189.) M 1 A11 S549 C447 1.
*RISM A/I/6, p. 605 [P3935]
– Partie de violoncelle. (Ex libris Miss Desbarats, vol. *Basso no 1*, 1822.) M 1 A11 S549 C447 2

Pontificale romanum Clementis VIII Primum; nunc denuo Urbani VIII auctoritate recognitum. Romae, typis Vaticanis, 1645. 602p., 42 × 28 cm. Tranche dorée ciselée. Page de titre gravée. BQT 4436 1645

Processionale Ecclesiae rothomagensis. Religiosissimi Archipraesulis Francisci II, Normaniae Primetis jussu recognitum et editum de consensu venerabilis capituli. Rothomagi, apud societatem Typ. Librorum Officii Ecclesiastici, 1645. 376, cxip., 15 × 23.5 cm. Rubricae generales processionalis, ordo ad faciendam aquam benedictam, Proprium de tempore, Commune Sanctorum, Tropi seu Versus dicendi in Laudibus tridui ante Pascha. BQT 4458 1645

Processional ou sont contenus les offices communs & particuliers, avec quelques grandes messes à l'usage des religieux & religieuses de l'ordre de S. François. Et une petite méthode au commencement pour apprendre le plain-chant. A Paris, chez Edmé Couterot . . . , 1694. 160, cciiip., 19 × 12 cm. M 2154.4 F7 P963 1694

Processionale usibus ac ritibus sanctae romanae Ecclesiae accomodatum . . . Nova editio . . . Luteciae Parisiorum ex officina Petri-August. Le Mercier . . . , 1707. 244, xxxviii, 70p., 17 × 10 cm. BQT 4458 1707

Processionale romanum juxta breviarium sacro-sancti Concilii Tridentini et S. Pii Quinti Pontificis maximi authoritate, editum; cujus antiquus Ecclesiae cantus gregorianus è puro fonte romano elicitus, accuratè notatur. Luteciae-Parisiorum, Typis & Sumptibus Joan.-Bapt.-Christophori Ballard, christianissimi regis musicae monotypographi, nec-non ejusdem majestatis capellae notatoris, 1723. 192, [xxxiv]p., 20.5 × 13.5 cm. (Ornement à la page de titre.) BQT 4458 1723

Psalterium romanum sacro-sancti Concilii Tridentini decreto restitutum. Ex breviario romano nuper restituto, à Clemente VIII & Urbano VIII Pont. Max . . . quae omnia recens accuratius ordinata sunt jussi S.D.N.P. Alexandri VIII. Parisiis, Sumptibus Sevestre, 1680. 463p., 46.5 × 31 cm. (Gravure à la page de titre.) BQT 4379 1680

Psalterium romanum sacro-sancti Concilii Tridentini decreto restitutum, ex breviario romano nuper restituto à Clemente VIII & Urbano VIII Pont. Max . . . quae omnia recens accuratius ordinata sunt jussu S.D.N.P. Alexandri VII. Parisiis, apud Ludovicum Sevestre . . . , 1692. 473p., 48 × 31 cm. (Ornement à la page de titre.) BQT 4379 1692

Psalterium romanum sacro-sancti Concilii Tridentini decreto restitutum, ex breviario romano nuper restituto à Clemente VIII & Urbano VIII . . . Omnia recens accuratius ordinata sunt juxta S.D.N.P. Alexandri VII. Parisiis, apud

Franciscum H. Muguet ... , 1723. [xx], 473p., 47 × 30 cm. (*Tota pulchra est*, motet en plain-chant, manuscrit transcrit et enluminé à l'intérieur de la couverture, daté de 1768. Ornement à la page de titre.) M 2149.2 P8 L4 1723

Psalterium romanum sacro-sancti Concilii Tridentini decreto restitutum, ex breviario romano nuper restituto à Clemente VIII & Urbano VIII Pont. Max ... quae omnia recens accuratiûs ordinata sunt jussu S.D.N.P. Alexandri VII. Parisiis, apud Ludovicum Sevestre ... , 1725. 473p., 47.5 × 30.5 cm. (Ornement à la page de titre.) BQT 4379 1725

Psalterium romanum sacro-sancti Concilii Tridentini decreto restitutum ex breviario nuper restituto, a Clemente VIII et Urbano VIII Pontificibus Maximis ... quae omnia recens accuratius ordinata sunt jussu S.D.N.P. Clementis XI. Lugduni, apud Petrum Valfray ... , 1730. 498p., 50 × 32.5 cm. (Ornement à la page de titre.) BQT 4379 1730

Psalterium romanum sacro-sancti Concilii Tridentini decreto restitutum, ex breviario nuper restituto, a Clemente VIII et Urbano VIII Pontificibus Maximis ... , omnia recens ordinata sunt jussu S.D.N.P. Clementis XI. Lugduni, apud Petrum Valfray ... , 1730. 497p., 45 × 30 cm. (Ornement à la page de titre.) BQT 4379 1730

Psalterium romanum, sacro-sancti Concilii Tridentini decreto restitutum, ex breviario nuper recognito auctoritate Clementis VIII et Urbani VIII Pont. Max ... , quae omnia recens accuratius ordinata sunt jussu S.D.N.P. Clementis XI. Lugduni, typis Amati Delaroche ... , 1764. 512p., 49.5 × 32 cm. (Gravure à la page de titre.) 3 exemplaires. BQT 4379 1764

Psalterium romanum sacro-sancti Concilii Tridentini decreto restitutum, ex breviario nuper restituto, à Clemente VIII et Urbano VIII, Pontificibus Maximis. Parisiis, Sumptibus Societatis Bibliopolarum, 1776. 497p., 50 cm. (Gravure à la page de titre.) (Ex Typographia Petri Valfray.) BQT 4379 1776

RAMEAU, JEAN-PHILIPPE (1683-1764) *Démonstration du principe de l'harmonie, servant de base à tout l'art musical théorique & pratique ... par Monsieur Rameau.* A Paris, chez Durand ... [et] Pissot ... , 1750. xxiii, 112, xlviip., planches, 20cm. ML 3815 R171 1750. (Non localisé 'C Qul' dans le *RISM*.)

— *Nouveau système de musique théorique ... , pour servir d'introduction au Traité de l'harmonie; par monsieur Rameau ...* De l'imprimerie de J.-B.C. Ballard ... , 1726. viii, 114p., 2 tables (dépliantes), 26 × 20.5 cm. (Relié avec Rameau: Traité de l'harmonie.) MT 50 R172 1722. *RISM* B6, p. 683

— *Traité de l'harmonie réduite à ses principes naturels; divisé en quatre livres ... Par monsieur Rameau ...* De l'imprimerie de Jean-Baptiste-Christophe Ballard ... , 1722. xxiv, 432, 17p., 26 × 20.5 cm. (Relié avec Rameau: Nouveau système.) MT 50 R172 1722. *RISM* B6, p. 685

ROMBERG, BERNHARD HEINRICH (1767-1841) *Three duets, for two violoncellos; composed & dedicated to Frederick Rousseau, by Bernard Romberg.*

London, printed by Clementi, Banger, Hyde, Collard & Davis ... [ca 1800]. Opus 9, 24p., 33 × 24.5 cm. (Ex libris Miss Desbarats, vol. 3, 1818, p. 237.) M 1 A11 S549 C4472 2. *RISM A/I/7, p. 233 [R2427

ROSQUELLAS, P. *Pot-pourri for the violin obligato, with accompts for two violins, tenor, violoncello, flute, hautboys, horns & bassoon; composed & dedicated to his friend M.R. Lacy, By P. Rosquellas ... Op. 5*. London, printed for the author by Clementi & Co ... [ca 1800]. 5p., 35 × 26 cm. Partie de violoncelle. (Ex libris Miss Desbarats, vol. 8: *Violoncello*.) M 179 H415 S989 B617 Violoncelle. (Non signalé dans le RISM.)
- Partie d'alto. (Ex libris Miss Desbarats, vol. 9: *Viola*.) M 179 H415 S989 B 617 Alto
- Partie de premier violon. (Ex libris Miss Desbarats, vol. 43: *Pianoforte no 2*.) M 179 H415 S989 B617 Piano et violon.
- [*Rosquellas' Spanish guitar tutor*. London, Clementi and comp., ca 1800]. 38p., 33.5 × 26 cm. (La page de titre, les pages 3 à 16 et 27 à 36 incl. manquent.) (Contenu: *From thee Eliza I must go*, p. 18; *Ah! me twas an emblem of love*, p. 20; *Singing never gain'd a Maid*, p. 22; *A Spanish patriotic song*, p. 25. Arranged with an acc. for the Spanish guitar by Rosquellas. Ex libris Miss Sheppard, vol. 6, 1824.) M 1 A11 S549 C4472 3. (Non signalé dans le RISM.)
- *Second concerto for the violin with accompts for two violins, tenor, violoncello, flutes, hautboys, horns & bassoons; composed & dedicated by permission to ... Duke of Cambridge, by P. Rosquellas ... Op. 6*. London, printed ... by Clementi ... [ca 1800]. 5p., 35 × 26 cm. Partie de violoncelle. (Ex libris Miss Desbarats, vol. 8: *Violoncello*.) M 179 H 415 S989 B617 Violoncelle. (Non signalé dans le RISM.)
- Partie d'alto. (Ex libris Miss Desbarats, vol. 9: *Viola*.) M 179 H 415 S989 B617 Alto
- Partie de premier violon. (Ex libris Miss Desbarats, vol. 43: *Pianoforte no 2*.) M 179 H415 S989 B617 Piano et violon

ROSS, JOHN (1763-1837) *A duet for two performers on the piano forte, in which are introduced for subjects of the slow and last movements, Scotish airs, composed & dedicated to Miss Gordon, by John Ross ... Op. 26* ... London, printed by Clementi, Banger, Hyde, Collard & Davis ... [ca 1800]. 25p., 34 × 24.5 cm. (Ex libris Miss Desbarats, vol. 65. p. 1.) M 1 A11 S549 C4472 1. *RISM A/I/7, p. 231 [R2709
- *O strew the sweet flower as altered from the old Scottish ballad by John Rannie, composed by Mr. Ross, organist of St. Paul's Aberdeen* ... Printed for the author, by Longman, Clementi & Co ... [ca 1800]. 3p., 33 × 24.5 cm. (Ex libris Miss Desbarats, vol. 1, p. 79.) M 1 A11 S549 M987 2. RISM A/I/7, p. 250 [R2691

[ROUSSEAU, JEAN-BAPTISTE (1671-1741)] *Chants religieux et civiques pour les fêtes décadaires*. Paris, Rondonneau, [1798?] 36p., 16cm. M 2115 R864 1798

ROUSSEAU, JEAN-JACQUES (1712-78) *Dictionnaire de musique, par J.J. Rousseau* ... Paris, chez la Veuve Duchesne ... 1768. ix, 548 (i.e. 556)p., 14pl., 26.5 × 20.5 cm. (Vignette à la page de titre. Les chiffres 473-80 sont répétés dans la pagination.) ML 108 R864 1768a. RISM B6, p. 720

- *Dictionnaire de musique, par J.J. Rousseau.* Paris, chez la Veuve Duchesne, 1768. xii, 547p., 20 cm. ML 108 R864 1768. RISM B6, p. 720

- *Dictionnaire de musique par J.J. Rousseau.* [Paris], de l'Imprimerie de la Société littéraire-typographique, 1785. 2 vol., 15 × 10cm. (Collection complète des oeuvres de J.J. Rousseau, tomes 17-18.) PQ 2030 1783 17-18. (Non localisé 'C Qul' dans le RISM.)

ROUSSIER, PIERRE-JOSEPH (1716-90) *Mémoire sur la musique des Anciens, où l'on expose le principe des proportions authentiques, dites de Pythagore & de divers systêmes de musique chez les Grecs, les Chinois & les Egyptiens. Avec un parallèle entre le systême des Egyptiens & celui de Modernes. Par M. l'abbé Roussier.* Paris, Lacombe, 1770. xxix, 251, 20p., 27cm. ML 162 R867 1770. (Non localisé 'C Qul' dans le RISM.)

SHIELD, WILLIAM (1748-1829) *The post captain sung by Mr. Incledon at the Theatre Royal, Covent Garden, and in his new entertainment call'd Variety, composed by Wm. Shield, musician in ordinary to his Majesty. The words by Mr. Rannie.* London, printed by Goulding & Co ... [ca 1800]. 4p., 32.5 × 24.5 cm. (Ex libris Miss Desbarats (?), sans titre, sans numéro ni date.) M 1 A11 S549 M987 3. RISM A/I/8, p. 74 [S3251

The heaving of the lead, a favorite song sung by Mr. Incledon in Hartford Bridge, composed by W. Shield. [London], printed by Longman and Broderip ... [ca 1798]. 4p., 32.5 × 24.5 cm. (Ex libris Miss Desbarats (?), sans titre, sans numéro ni date.) M 1 A11 S549 M987. RISM A/I/8, p. 63 [S3002

[?] [*The sportsman's rhapsody. A favourite hunting song sung by Mr. Lyon.* Printed for & sold by James Aird, Glasgow, ca 1800]. [2]p., 33 × 24.5 cm. (Ex libris Miss Desbarats, vol. 1, s.d.. La page de titre manque.) M 1 A11 S549 M987 2

STEIBELT, DANIEL (1765-1823) *Grand concerto for the harp with accompaniments. Composed & dedicated to Madam Krumpholtz by D. Steibelt.* London, printed by Clementi, Banger, Hyde, Collard & David [ca 1800]. 5p., 35 cm. Partie de premier violon. (Ex libris Mrs. P. Sheppard, 1823.) M 1 A11 S549 C4472 6. (Non signalé dans le RISM.)

- *A grand concerto for the piano forte with accompaniments composed & dedicated to Madam Krumpholtz, by D. Steibelt* ... London, printed by Clementi, Banger, Hyde, Collard & Davis ... [ca 1800]. 23p., 33 × 24.5 cm. (Ex libris Miss Desbarats, vol. 3, 1818, p. 15.) M 1 A11 S549 C4472 2. RISM A/I/8, p. 174 [S4831

– *Three sonatas for the piano forte, composed by D. Steibelt. Op. 51* . . . London, printed by Clementi, Banger, Hyde, Collard & Davis . . . [ca 1800]. 21p., 33 × 24.5 cm. (Contenu: *sonata I*, p. 2-7; *sonata II*, p. 8-13; *sonata III*, p. 14-21. Ex libris Miss Desbarats, vol. 3, 1818, p. 95.) M 1 A11 S549 C4472 2. *RISM A/I/8, p. 187 [S5083

STEVENSON, SIR JOHN ANDREW (1761-1833) *Ah! say, lovely Emma, a canzonet with an accompaniement for the harp or piano forte, composed by Sir John A. Stevenson Mus. D* . . . Dublin, published by F. Rhames . . . [ca 1800]. 3p., 33 × 24.5 cm. (Ex libris Miss Desbarats, vol. 1, p. 134.) M 1 A11 S549 M987 2. *RISM A/I/8, p. 240 [S612

Tendresses bacchiques, ou duo et trio melez de petits airs, tendres et à boire, des meilleurs auteurs; avec une capilotade, ou alphabet de chansons à deux parties; recueillies et mises en ordre par Christophe Ballard . . . Paris, Christophe Ballard, 1712-18. 2 vol., 16cm. M 1578 B189

WEIDNER, T.C. *Three favorite airs, with variations for the german flute, with an accompaniment for the violoncello obligato composed & dedicated to William Broomhead, esqr. by T.C. Weidner.* London, printed by Clementi, Banger, Hyde, Collard & Davis . . . [ca 1800]. 20p., 33 × 24.5 cm. (Ex libris Miss Desbarats, vol. 1, p. 230.) M 1 A11 S549 M987 2. (Non signalé dans le RISM.)

ERICH SCHWANDT

Musique spirituelle (1718): Canada's First Music Theory Manual

Historians writing about seventeenth- and eighteenth-century Canada are concerned with that relatively small inhabited area of the St Lawrence Valley which was the heart of New France. They seem to focus their attention almost exclusively upon military manoeuvres, Indian massacres, English sieges, trade and commerce, and the harsh climate. Yet anyone who has read *Les Annales de l'Hôtel-Dieu de Québec*[1] will have discovered that, notwithstanding the exploits of soldiers, sailors, trappers, explorers, and entrepreneurs, the country was also being civilized: intellectual, spiritual, and artistic excellence was being fostered at the Hôtel-Dieu and at the Monastery of the Ursulines of Quebec. The compilers of the *Annales*, which document the period from 1639 to 1716, were witnesses to the importance of the fine arts in their own everyday occupations of healing the sick, treating the wounded, and educating their patients in the mysteries of the faith, for in addition to their knowledge of medicine, these dedicated women were skilled in painting, sculpture, architecture, embroidery, poetry, and music; they cultivated these arts as important and nourishing parts of their everyday lives.

The Augustinians of the Mercy of Jesus established their hospital – the Hôtel-Dieu – in Quebec City in 1639. The order was a cloistered one and followed the rule of Saint Augustine. Hospitallers were obliged to perform their offices in choir; thus liturgical music – plainchant and contemporaneous figural music such as the *petit motet* – was of great importance not only to the monastery but to the community as well. The populace of Quebec attended Mass, vespers, and other services at the monasteries and surely found the music they heard spiritually uplifting. Unfortunately, the documents – printed and manuscript music which they used and which has survived to the present – are few in number[2] and give us only an imperfect idea of what must have been a very rich and varied musical life. The references to music scattered throughout the *Annales* record only musical events of special significance; however, the daily routine must have included much interesting music. It would seem that in addition to plainchant the music of many contemporary French composers was performed regularly in the monasteries of Quebec, for the surviving copies of printed music are often worn to shreds.[3]

The woman responsible for the *Annales* in its final form was Mère Marie-Andrée Duplessis de Sainte-Hélène (1687-1760), a highly educated and intelligent religious of the order of Saint Augustine.[4] Her family arrived in Canada in 1689, leaving the two-year-old Marie-Andrée with her maternal grandmother at Chevreuse in the Île-de-France. We know little of her education, yet it must have been excellent, and literature and music were certainly part of her studies. Marie-Andrée joined her family in Canada in 1702 and five years later became a hospitaller.

Working from notes and documents assembled by Mère Jeanne-Françoise Juchereau de Saint-Ignace (1650-1723), who was an eyewitness to many important historical events in seventeenth- and early eighteenth-century Canada, Mère Marie-Andrée de Sainte-Hélène did further research and then wrote the history of the monastery from its foundation in 1639 to about 1716. Her literary style is an engaging one – at times the *Annales* reads like an exciting historical novel – and her account of the activities of the monastery and of Quebec during those years is a fascinating and important historical document.

Her major literary effort, and the one which has assured her a place among Canadian historians, was the *Annales*. However, she also wrote knowledgeably about music, and her *Musique spirituelle où l'on peut s'exercer sans voix* (1718), which is the subject of this essay, may be regarded as the first treatise on the theory and practice of music to have been undertaken in North America.

Musique spirituelle is preserved in the author's holograph at the archives of the Hôtel-Dieu.[5] Mère Marie-Andrée's object in writing it was to amuse and at the same time to edify her readers, who were, of course, her sisters in religion at the Hôtel-Dieu. The treatise is allegorical: in it the elements of music and the various aspects of proper performance are compared with the joys of monastic life, stressing prayer, obedience, charity, and the other virtues. Because the treatise takes a knowledge of contemporary French performance practice on the part of readers for granted, the manuscript can help to fill many gaps in our knowledge of music and the musical life of Quebec's monasteries in the early eighteenth century.

The work is composed of seven chapters, each of which is approximately 250 words in length and centres around two or three elements of music or aspects of its performance. These are first defined briefly and then made the basis of comparison with appropriate elements or aspects of the spiritual life. The chapters are ordered like a sight-singing manual, beginning with the most basic information and proceeding to more complex matters. (The sight-singing manuals owe not a little to the catechism in their method of presenting information. Reversing the procedure, Mère Marie-Andrée makes the arrangement of a music treatise serve as the basis for a 'catechism' of the most important parts of the monastic life.) The contents of the treatise may be summarized as follows:

1 the scale; the three clefs; transposition (by change of clef);
2 the accidentals and their effects;
3 the staff; the notes and their values; their arrangement into measures;
4 the *agréments du chant*;
5 singing in tune; chords and arpeggios; fugues;
6 rests; the symphony (i.e., improvised or composed preludes);
7 tempo and *mouvement*; the *notes inégales*; the conductor's role.

It is interesting that each chapter of this allegorical treatise proceeds just as logically and clearly as any contemporary manual of singing. While some of Mère Marie-Andrée's comparisons may seem a little far-fetched, she consistently focusses on all the most important elements of contemporary French performance practice, not forgetting *le bon goût*. For example:

One must sing in tune in order to sing well. The biggest voices are not always the most agreeable ones. 'Singing in tune' in our spiritual music is the ability to do everything properly, and at the right moment.

The measures in our spiritual music are the days of our lives, which, to be complete in the sight of the Lord, ought to be passed in a perfect regularity, omitting nothing in all the good works one performs, and accompanying every action from the heart ...

In ordinary music there are twelve different time signatures. The beauty of the music depends on observing the quality of movement that each signature indicates. Thus, if one goes quickly when one ought to go slowly, or slowly when one ought to go quickly, the Motet will be spoiled, for its beauty lies in its being well performed. It is vital to observe the signature which tells you how the music goes. The signature in our spiritual music is obedience: the more obedient one is, the better one sings. There is nothing easier than living an orderly life, and nothing as pleasant as following the precepts of our constitutions. For example (and to keep to our comparison), one ought to sing:

In choir: *lentement, posément et gravement.*

At the hospital: *vîte*, that is, *fervement*.
In the parlour: *legerement* and as if in passing.
At recreation: *gayement et gracieusement*.

The Superior conducts all this music. She sets the tempo. She calls for transpositions, provides accompaniments, furnishes the symphonies, and beats time. Provided that one is careful to follow her directions and to respond to the slightest cue, the concert will be so harmonious that it will charm every observer. It will delight God Himself, and will move Him to prepare substantial and rich rewards for the souls who have made the best progress in this science. I exhort you all to apply yourselves to it with all your heart, so that you may merit such a reward.

What the manuscript reveals to us directly about the musicianship of Mère Marie-Andrée de Sainte-Hélène (and by extension, about her sisters in religion) is that she had a command of contemporary French musical practices. This suggests that the monastery must have had copies of French musical treatises (such as those by L'Affilard, Dupont, and Berthet) in its library at that time, as well as a good collection of French sacred music in printed copies and manuscript. No theoretical documents are extant, but they may have been lost in the disastrous fire of 1755. At any rate, it seems unlikely that Mère Marie-Andrée de Sainte Hélène was relying entirely on her memory of what she had studied and read in France more than seventeen years before she wrote the work.

Although *Musique spirituelle* is an allegorical treatise, it displays Mère Marie-Andrée's understanding of music and its aesthetics; moreover, it shows her commitment to the idea that music has the power to move the passions and to inspire and elevate the mind, even if it is performed silently and 'sans voix.' Her approach is a far cry from the contemporary musical instruction at Boston and other centres in New England, where 'music' was synonymous with the singing of metrical psalms to very few well-known tunes such as 'St David' and 'Old Hundredth.'

In 1720 Thomas Symmes started the New England 'singing war' by calling for a return to singing the metrical psalm-tunes by note rather than by rote. The 'singing war,' as Charles Hamm has pointed out,[6] was a confrontation between the literate urban people, who preferred literal performance of the psalm-tunes from musical notation, and rural non-literate, folk who were content with an oral tradition. The published directions for learning to read the notes of the tunes associated with metrical psalms that appeared in the course of the 'singing war' are reduced to the lowest common denominator, being geared to the needs of musical illiterates.

In 1721 John Tufts published a few psalm-tunes in 'sol-fa' (a notation using letters instead of notes) together with a very elementary discussion of pitch and metre.[7] His *Small Book Containing 20 Psalm Tunes with Directions How to Sing Them* (for the use of 'Children, and People of the Meanest Capacities') has been called 'the first American musical text-book.'[8] In the same year (1721) Thomas Walter published his *Grounds and Rules of Musick Explained*, which was a collection of several psalm-tunes harmonized in three parts, employing conventional notation.

The 'singing war' of New England, which eventually led to an indigenous sacred folk music tradition, had no counterpart in New France. In Quebec contemporary French sacred music was performed as a matter of course, and from time to time served as a model for the gifted amateur composers of the monasteries who imitated its style. In addition, the principles of this music could, since they were common knowledge, be used as the basis for an elegant allegory: *Musique spirituelle*, Canada's first theoretical treatise, a complete transcription of which follows.

Musique Spirituelle où l'on peut s'exercer sans voix
A l'usage des Religieuses hospitalieres de la misericorde de Jesus
Par une religieuse du même ordre
Premiere édition
A Québec. Au monastere de l'hôtel-Dieu. 1718
avec permission

A la Reverende Mère Marie Madeleine de la Nativité, Religieuse hospitaliere de la misericorde de Jesus de l'hôtel-Dieu de quebec.
Ma reverende Mère:

Le Zele que vous faites paroître pour les sciences et le desir que j'ay de vous obliger, m'ont fait naitre l'envie de composer ce petit traité à vôtre honneur et gloire. Je vous le dedie avec plaisir ma reverende Mère quoy que je suis persuadée que vous n'y verez rien que vous ne sçachiez deja, et que vous êtes plus sçavante dans la pratique que je ne le suis dans la theorie, ce qui fait que je m'estimerois heureuse de recevoir des leçons de vous, aussy n'ay-je pas prétendu vous instruire, mais seulement vous divertir et vous donner en même tems une marque de l'attachement sincere et de la tendre amitié avec laquelle j'ay l'honneur d'être tres respectueusement,

Ma reverende Mère
Vôtre tres humble et tres obeissante servante
Sr M.A.D.S.L.N.
[Soeur Marie-Andrée Duplessis de *Sainte-Hélène*]

PREFACE

Comme la musique est une chose tres agréable, et qu'il y a nombre de personnes qui l'apprennent avec plaisir malgré ses difficultées, je croy qu'il se trouvera plusieurs ames Religieuses qui s'appliqueront avec joye a l'étude d'une musique qu'il est beaucoup plus avantageux de sçavoir que la musique ordinaire; c'est pourquoy je leur presente ce petit ouvrage ou je fais rapporter la pratique des plus solides vertus a la methode dont on se sert pour bien chanter.

Je compte du moins que les personnes qui manquent de voix et qui ont bonne volonté s'exerceront plus volontiers dans cette musique que dans celle de Campra, et que celles qui avec la bonne volonté ont encore de la voix auront quelque plaisir de voir les convenances qui se trouvent entre les deux manieres de chanter.

APPROBATION

de Monsieur de la Colombiere grand archidiacre et vicaire general du dioceze de québec, Conseiller au Conseil superieur de la meme ville et superieur des religieuses hospitalieres de l'hotel-Dieu.

Ayant lû un ouvrage intitulé musique spirituelle, non seulement nous n'y avons rien trouvé de contraire aux reigles et aux agreements de l'art de chanter, mais nous jugeons qu'il sera tres utile, et tres salutaire a toutes les Religieuses de ce monastere de le lire, de l'etudier, et de le pratiquer. C'est a quoy nous les exhortons.

Fait a québec le vingt huitieme november 1718.

J La Colombiere, superieur

Musique Spirituelle où l'on peut s'exercer sans voix
A l'usage des Religieuses hospitalieres de la misericorde de Jesus

AVANT PROPOS

Il y a trois clefs dans la musique que l'on nomme C sol ut, G re sol, F ut fa; on y chante par B mol par B car et par Diaise; la gamme sert a connoitre en quoy l'on chante. La musique est composée de mesures remplies de notes de diferentes valeurs pour marquer le tems, ces notes sont posées sur cinq lignes droites tirées sur du papier.

On y met plusieurs agréments qui donnent au chant beaucoup de grace; comme des points, des accents, des coulez, des ports de voix, des tenuës, des balencements, des aspirations, des feintes, des pincez, des tremblements subits, des cadences batuës et soutenuës, des soupirs, des silences et autres.

On trouvera par comparaison dans ce livre les rapports que l'on fait trouver entre la musique et la pratique de la vertu.

CHAPITRE PREMIER
La gamme, les clefs et les transpositions

La Gamme. C'est la regle et les constitutions dont l'étude est necessaire pour pratiquer constamment les excellentes vertus propres de nôtre état, telles que sont l'amour de Dieu et du prochain, la dénuëment de toutes choses, la purété de corps et d'ame, l'humilité, l'assiduité a la priere, l'assujetissement de nôtre volonté a celle de Dieu, et l'exacte regularité.
La clef de G ré sol qui sert aux dessus. C'est l'oraison, qui éleve l'ame au dessus de toutes les choses de la terre et qui l'unit a Dieu même.
La clef de C sol ut qui sert aux tailles. C'est la direction par laquelle on apprend les secrets merveilleux de la vie spirituelle pour s'avancer dans l'aquisition de toutes les vertus ce qui se rapporte a la vie illuminative.
La clef de F ut fa qui sert aux basses. C'est la lecture qui instruit des moyens de corriger ses vices, et ses deffauts; et de couper jusqu'a la racine les plus legeres imperfections ce qu'on appelle vie purgative.

Dans la musique ordinaire les trois clefs sont egalement necessaires; dans la nôtre pourvu qu'on sçache et qu'on possede bien la premiere on peut se passer des deux autres.
Les transpositions. C'est lorsque pour des oeuvres loüables et saintes et par l'ordre ou avec la permission des superieurs on change l'heure de l'oraison, on differe d'aller trouver son directeur, et on remet sa lecture a un autre tems.

CHAPITRE DEUXIEME
Du B car, du B mol, et du Diaise

Le B car qui laisses la clef naturelle. C'est la vie mixte ou l'on est continuellement occupé dans des actes de charité, de devotion, de patience, de misericorde, de desinterressement, de douceur et de modestie.
Le B mol qui fait baisser la voix d'un demy ton. C'est la vie cachée et contemplative ou l'ame s'exerce dans des vertus peu estimées des gens du siecle, mais fort precieuses aux yeux de Dieu; ces vertus sont la pauvreté, le mepris du monde, l'abstinence, la mortification, l'oraison, le silence et la retraite.
Le Diaise qui fait élever la voix d'un demy ton. C'est la vie active ou l'on

pratique avec éclat, la liberalité, la débonnaireté, la generosité, la force, la prudence, la ferveur, et le Zele des ames.

CHAPITRE TROISIEME
Du papier, des lignes, des mesures, des notes et de leur valeur

Le papier. Le papier de nôtre musique, c'est le tems sur lequel nous traçons toutes les actions de nôtre vie; il s'écoule et se perd sans que nous y fassions beaucoup d'attention, mais il n'en sera pas de même de nos oeuvres. Quoy que nous semblions les oublier il viendra un moment ou toutes nos pensées, nos paroles et nos actions bonnes et mauvaises se presenteront a nous, pour nous accompagner au jugement de Dieu, a fin d'y être pesées au poids du sanctuaire, Dieu veüille qu'elles ne soient pas trouvées trop legeres, et que leurs voix flechisse plutot sa misericorde que d'irriter sa justice.
Les cinq lignes. C'est nos cinq voeux dont la fidelle observation renferme tout la perfection religieuse.
Les mesures. C'est les jours, qui pour être pleins devant le seigneur doivent être passez dans une parfaite regularité sans rien omettre de tout le bien que l'on peut faire, accompagnant toutes ses actions de l'esprit interieur qui en est l'ame, et qui les rends méritoires pour l'eternité.
Les notes. C'est les vertus, dont la pratique est tres harmonieuse aux oreilles de Dieu.
La valeur des notes. C'est l'amour divin, qui donne le prix a toutes les vertus, selon qu'il est plus ou moins ardent.
Les points. C'est la pureté d'intention qui releve l'excellence des bonnes oeuvres et qui anoblit les plus petites actions.

CHAPITRE QUATRIEME
Des agréments du chant

Les accents. C'est les paroles douces et obligeantes qui entretiennent la charité.
Les coulez et les ports de voix. C'est lors qu'on joint deux vertus comme la patience a la douceur, la mortification a l'oraison, la charité a l'humilité, ainsy des autres.
Les tenuës et les balencements. C'est le perseverance et la longanimité qui fait soutenir lontems sans ennuy les travaux que l'on a entrepris pour Dieu.
Les aspirations. C'est les bons desirs, qui anime a la poursuite de la vertu.
Les feintes. C'est les addresses dont on se sert pour cacher ses bonnes oeuvres sous le voile de l'humilité.

Les pincez. C'est la soumission de jugement qui fait cesser promptement les pratiques les plus saintes des que les superieurs n'en permittent plus l'usage.

Les tremblements subits. C'est le plaisir que l'on ressent quand on apprend quelque chose qui est a la gloire de Dieu, où a l'avantage du prochain.

Les cadences batuës et soutenuës. C'est la joye solide et constante dont on joüy en s'aquittant de tous ses devoirs; ce qui rend la vertu facile et luy donne un lustre et un éclat qui la fait aimer a toutes les personnes qui la voyent pratiquer avec tant d'allegresse.

Les syncopes. C'est les veilles que l'on passe dans l'exercice de l'hospitalité ou de la priere parce qu'on joint la nuit au jour pour aimer servir et loüer Dieu sans interruption.

CHAPITRE CINQUIEME
Des roulements, des accords et du guidon

Les roulements. C'est des évenements ou il arrive que l'on a occasion de pratiquer presque toutes les vertus, et comme la flexibilité de la voix se fait admirer et qu'elle flate beaucoup l'oreille, de même dans cette musique la fidelité a suivre les inspirations et a profiter de tout pour s'avancer est charmante et si profitable qu'avec cela on peut devenir sainte en fort peu de tems, et parvenir a un tres haut degré de perfection.

La justesse. On doit encore chanter juste pour bien chanter, les plus grandes voix ne sont pas toujours les plus agreables. La justesse dans nôtre musique c'est la discretion qui fait tout faire a propos.

Les accords. C'est quand on a la paix avec Dieu, avec le prochain et avec soy-même.

Les fugues. C'est lors qu'on perd quelque chose de son repos pour servir et obliger le prochain, ce qui est quelquefois plus agreable a Dieu qu'une profonde paix.

Le guidon. C'est la vigilance qui ne laisse rien oublier, et qui fait prevoir sans inquietude tout ce que l'on doit faire.

CHAPITRE SIXIEME
Des silences et de la simphonie

Les mesures de silence. C'est les jours que l'on passe dans la retraite.

Les demies mesures. C'est les fêtes ou l'on a plus de tems qu'a l'ordinaire pour vaquer a Dieu.

Les soupirs. C'est les confessions ou le souvenir des fautes que l'on a comises excite dans l'ame la componction, et la fait soupirer amerement

pour le regret qu'elle conçoit de ses frequentes rechutes.
Les demy soupirs. C'est les oraisons jaculatoires dont l'usage est tres utile pour entretenir la ferveur et la presence de Dieu.
Les quarts de soupirs. C'est les regards amoureux qui l'ame jette vers le Ciel, avec un grand desir d'y aller.
La simphonie. C'est la sainte Communion dont la frequentation donne une merveilleuse vigueur a la vie devote, et nourrit l'ame bien disposée, d'une viande celeste et divine qui la fortifie admirablement pour accomplir avec courage tous les desseins de Dieu.

CHAPITRE SEPTIEME
De la maniere d'observer les mesures

Il y a dans la musique ordinaire douze differentes mesures, et l'agrément du chant depend du mouvement qu'on luy donne, de sorte que si l'on va vîte quand on doit aller lentement, et lentement quand on doit aller vîte, cela disgracie beaucoup un motet parce que la beauté d'un cantique est d'estre bien exprimé, il faut donc exactement observer la marque qui fait connoitre la maniere dont on doit suivre la mesure. Cette marque dans nôtre musique est l'obeissance, plus on est soumise, mieux on chante, rien n'est plus aisé que de vivre dans l'ordre, et rien n'est plus aimable que de se conformer a ce qui nous est prescrit dans nos constitutions, par exemple pour ne point sortir de nôtre comparaison on doit chanter:
Au choeur: lentement, posément et gravement.
A l'hopital: vîte, c'est a dire fervemment.
Au parloir: legerement et comme en passant.
A la recreation: gayement et gracieusement.

Les tems inégaux. C'est les travaux extraordinaires d'une communauté.

C'est la superieure qui regle toute cette musique et qui luy donne tel mouvement qu'il luy plait, elle fait les transpositions, elle met les accompagnements, elle ajoute la simphonie, elle bat la mesure, et pourvû que l'on soit bien attentive a executer ses ordres et ses moindres signes, le concert sera si harmonieux que non seulement il charmera les hommes, mais il fera les delices de Dieu même, et l'engagera a preparer de grandes et de riches recompenses pour les ames qui se seront renduës les plus habiles dans cette sçience a laquelle je vous exorte de vous appliquer de toutes vos forces pour les meriter.

finis coronat opus

LUCIEN POIRIER

La fortune de deux oeuvres de Jean-Jacques Rousseau au Canada français entre 1790 et 1850

On a étudié l'influence de la pensée de Voltaire au Canada français au lendemain de la Conquête;[1] par contre, on s'est peu arrêté jusqu'à maintenant à Jean-Jacques Rousseau. Rares sont, en effet, les mentions du nom dans les ouvrages sérieux récents relevant de l'histoire, de la littérature ou de la musique du Canada et plus proprement du Québec.

Le fait peut étonner, si l'on considère la pluralité des domaines couverts par la pensée du philosophe genevois (le social, le politique, l'éducation, la musique et le théâtre, pour ne nommer que ceux-là), la rigueur de la morale qu'il expose, susceptible de trouver des sympathisants dans une société où la sollicitude du clergé se fait pressante, et le degré de faveur que connurent les écrits sur l'éducation, par exemple, au tournant du XVIIIe siècle, principalement dans les pays germaniques.[2]

Bien sûr, la diffusion de la pensée présuppose l'accessibilité aux textes. Or, les ouvrages imprimés de Rousseau ne font pas défaut au Québec, à la fin du XVIIIe et au début du XIXe siècle. Le *Catalogue of English and French Books in the Quebec Library* de 1808 (p. 40) précise que les oeuvres complètes de cet auteur se trouvent à la Quebec Public Library, fondée en 1779 par le gouverneur Haldimand.[3] Par ailleurs, la présence de la collection complète des oeuvres dans l'édition de l'Imprimerie de la société littéraire-typographique de Paris parue au début des années 1780 et l'existence de trois exemplaires anciens du seul *Dictionnaire de musique*, à la bibliothèque de l'Université Laval, en fournissent d'autres éléments de preuve.

Ceci étant dit, la question se pose de savoir s'il y a trace au Bas-Canada d'une connaissance de la musique et des écrits sur la musique de Rousseau, et d'un reflet de celle-ci dans des documents historiques canadiens. Un survol des principaux imprimés, comprenant la presse, et l'examen d'un cahier de notes de cours conservé aux archives du Séminaire de Québec, permettent sans ambage de répondre par l'affirmative à cette interrogation. Le présent article rassemble certains résultats d'investigation sur le sujet, portant sur la période 1790-1850 environ; la ville de Québec sert de lieu témoin principal. Comme les faits observés convergent vers deux oeuvres de Rousseau, c'est sous l'étendard de leurs titres que seront présentés et discutés les plus marquants d'entre eux. Dans l'ordre chronologique de première édition européenne figurent: *Le Devin du village* (1753) et le *Dictionnaire de musique* (1768).

LE DEVIN DU VILLAGE

De toutes les pièces scéniques de Rousseau écrites entre 1740 et 1770 l'intermède *Le Devin du village* reste, malgré ses dimensions modestes et la simplicité de son caractère et de sa musique, l'oeuvre qui allait consacrer son auteur à la fois comme librettiste et musicien.

Comme l'a écrit Daniel Heartz: 'However slight the work, its message was deeply felt and pertinent to those social stirrings that made Rousseau such a prophet to his own and later times: the triumph of rustic simplicity and virtue over higher-class corruption and venality.'[4] Le musicologue américain précise que le succès de l'intermède fut immédiat, dès sa première représentation devant la cour de Fontainebleau, le 18 octobre 1752, et durable, puisqu'il tint l'affiche durant environ soixante ans en France et qu'on lui fit aussi bon accueil à l'étranger.[5] La partition gravée fut publiée à Paris en 1753; d'autres éditions suivront jusqu'au lendemain de la mort de Rousseau survenue en 1778.

Helmut Kallmann, et après lui de nombreux auteurs,[6] ont pressenti l'existence d'un rapport entre *Le Devin du village* de Rousseau et *Colas et Colinette ou le Bailli dupé* de Joseph Quesnel (1746?-1809), probablement 'la première oeuvre lyrique avec musique originale écrite en terre canadienne (et fort probablement en Amérique du Nord).'[7]

L'étude comparée des deux textes donne entièrement raison à ces auteurs. L'emprunt à peine déguisé des noms de personnages est à prime abord frappant: les Colin et Colette de Rousseau deviennent les Colas et Colinette de Quesnel; le 'bailli dupé' se substitue en quelque sorte au devin du village lorsqu'il tente de tromper le jeune Colas par le faux propos suivant: 'Sais-tu que je suis un peu *devin*, moi?'[8] Derrière le masque des noms d'emprunt, les personnages de Quesnel célèbrent, comme ceux de Rousseau, la supériorité de la simplicité rustique et la vertu des gens ordinaires sur les personnes de haut rang, selon l'expression de Daniel Heartz: les intrigues insoupçonnées des premiers mènent à la déroute et à l'humiliation des seconds.[9] Des similitudes au niveau de l'action rapprochent encore davantage les pièces de Rousseau et de

Quesnel: la brouille des deux amoureux, l'épreuve du personnage masculin par son amie, l'épisode du ruban au chapeau, le mépris des richesses et la réunion des fiancés. On notera toutefois que Quesnel a donné une caractérisation plus grande à ses personnages en opposant langage châtié et familier.

Le rapprochement entre Quesnel et Rousseau ne relève pas que de l'étude philologique. Un compte rendu de la représentation de 'l'Opera François' de Quesnel à Québec, paru dans *La Gazette de Québec* du 31 janvier 1805, en autorise l'élan:

Le dialogue, les chansons et la Musique, sont, comme nous l'apprenons, de la composition de Mr. Quesnel, et comme production coloniale, elle possede un mérite infini. Il arrive rarement que la poësie et la musique soient composée par la même personne.

Ce fut l'union de ces deux arts qui donna aux Operas de *Rousseau*, une supériorité sur ceux de ses contemporains; et excita sur l'audience une émotion de sympathie la plus puissante.

Comme le suggère cet extrait, Rousseau servit de modèle à l'auteur de 'la premiere piece de ce genre qui a été écrite et représentée dans cette Province'[10] non seulement en ce qui touche à la composition littéraire mais aussi à la musique. De fait, les deux partitions répondent à la caractérisation qu'a donnée Daniel Heartz de l'intermède de Rousseau: 'A folklike simplicity of tone pervades the whole.'[11]

On peut, de manière encore plus significative, mettre en évidence le lien qui unit Quesnel à Rousseau, et plus spécifiquement *Le Bailli dupé* au *Devin du village*. Quesnel réfère, en effet, explicitement à la partition de Rousseau, lorsqu'il met dans la bouche de Colas, 'chantant sans être apperçu,' le premier vers d'une chanson suivi d'un énigmatique '&c.,' à la fin de la scène III du premier acte de *Colas*. L'air est celui de Colette, à la scène VIII de l'intermède, dont on peut trouver la musique au numéro 15 des *Airs principaux du Devin du village*, gravés et réunis à la fin du tome 15 de la *Collection complete des oeuvres de J.J. Rousseau*, publié à Paris en 1783 (Figure 1).

Ironie du sort, l'emprunt à Rousseau plaçait Quesnel dans une situation absolument semblable où s'était trouvé l'auteur du *Devin* lui-même, cinquante ans plus tôt. On sait que, pour avoir fait siens 'trois seuls morceaux dans le Devin du village,' Rousseau fut accusé de pillage et soupçonné de n'être pas le compositeur de la musique de sa pièce.[12] L'affaire n'alla pas si loin à Montréal et à Québec, et Quesnel ne souffrit jamais d'atteinte à sa réputation et à son mérite de son vivant, relativement à cette affaire.

Figure 1 Planche X des *Airs principaux du Devin du village*, dans le tome 15 de la *Collection complete des oeuvres de J.J. Rousseau* publié à Paris en 1783 (photographie Paul Laliberté, du Service des ressources pédagogiques, Université Laval)

Les questions d'authenticité semblent de toute manière avoir été une préoccupation bien secondaire de nos auteurs, à la fin du XVIIIe siècle et au début du XIXe. La même chanson 'Allons danser sous les ormeaux' est là pour l'attester. L'auteur du *Nouveau Recueil de cantiques à l'usage du diocèse de Québec* (Québec, 1819), attribué à l'abbé Jean-Denis Daulé (1765-1852), recommande de chanter les neuf strophes de la pastorale 'Bergers par les plus doux accords' (p. 354-5) 'sur le majeur de l'Air: *Allons danser sous les ormeaux*,' sans faire référence à Rousseau ou à Quesnel, les deux auteurs qui, il est permis de le croire, ont contribué le plus au succès de la chanson en terre canadienne. La mélodie porte le numéro 189 des *Airs notés* (Figure 2); la basse, par contre, diffère de celle de Rousseau.[13] On est donc en droit de se demander si Daulé ne l'aurait pas empruntée à Quesnel.

Que Daulé ait emprunté l'air (et peut-être l'harmonie) au *Bailli dupé* de Quesnel plutôt que directement au *Devin du village* est suggéré par le fait que certains 'airs notés' de cantiques correspondant aux paroles de chansons pour lesquelles Rousseau a écrit de la musique sont sans ressemblance aucune. Il en est ainsi de: 'Quand on sait aimer et plaire' (no 6 des *Airs principaux du Devin du village* et no 21 des *Airs notés* de Daulé); 'Dors mon enfant,' romance de Berquin (nos 61 et 62 des *Consolations des misères de ma vie* de Rousseau, collection posthume de 95 airs, romances et duos publiée par M. Benoît en 1781, et no 83 des *Airs notés* de Daulé); 'Mon coeur charmé de sa chaîne' (no 48 des *Consolations* et no 68 des *Airs notés*);

Figure 2 No 189 des *Airs notés* du *Nouveau Recueil de cantiques* attribué à Jean-Denis Daulé (Québec, 1819), dit 'sur le majeur de l'AIR: *Allons danser sous les ormeaux*' (photographie Paul Laliberté, du Service des ressources pédagogiques, Université Laval)

'Tendre(s) fruit(s) des pleurs de l'aurore,' paroles de Bernard (nos 15 et 60 des *Consolations* et no 159 des *Airs notés*). Si Daulé avait connu la musique écrite par Rousseau sur ces mêmes paroles et sur d'autres, on imagine mal qu'il eût pu ainsi faire fi d'airs qui firent un temps la gloire de l'auteur du *Contrat social*.[14]

Pour en revenir à la partition de l'intermède de Rousseau et à l'intérêt qu'elle a suscité au Canada français, au cours de la période étudiée, signalons qu'après avoir fait l'objet de référence précise dans le récit 'Les Petits Souliers' de Hegesipes Moreau,[15] elle donna lieu à quelques représentations par les Amateurs canadiens de Québec, entre le 16 mai et le 4 juin 1846.[16]

Le retard mis par les comédiens canadiens à présenter cette production – retard en ce que venant près de trente ans après l'époque de gloire que connut le *Devin* à Paris et cinquante ans après les premières représentations en Amérique – peut s'expliquer par la répugnance des Canadiens à se réclamer de l'auteur de la lettre à d'Alembert sur les spectacles (1758) qui a fourni les munitions aux opposants du théâtre, le clergé particulièrement, dans les premières décennies du XIXe siècle.[17] Que les condamnations de Rousseau aient perdu de leur caractère de menace, quelques années avant les représentations du *Devin* à Québec, est en tout cas bien mis en lumière dans le passage suivant d'une lettre anonyme publiée dans *Le Canadien* du 16 mai 1838:

Nous ne nous attendions assurément pas à ce que les courtes remarques que nous fîmes dans notre feuille de vendredi dernier, à l'occasion de la représentation théâtrale de la veille, pussent avoir l'effet de renouveler, pour peu que nous y fussions disposé, la fameuse discussion qui s'éleva dans le siècle dernier entre Rousseau et Dalembert. Mais que le lecteur se tranquillise, telle n'est pas du tout notre intention. Nous laisserons 'l'Ami des Bonnes Moeurs' procéder ex-parte, attendu que tous les peuples civilisés ont prononcé jugement sur les plaidoyers de ces deux fameux avocats et que le nouvel athlète ne réussira vraisemblablement pas à faire infirmer ce jugement. L'éloquence entraînante du Philosophe de Genève a bien pu ouvrir le sein maternel aux enfants, mais il n'a pu fermer les théâtres.

Le nombre apparemment élevé de représentations du *Devin* en 1846 laisse croire que la pièce reçut bon accueil, malgré l'absence complète de comptes rendus dans la presse de l'époque. Par contre, une information tardive de Nazaire LeVasseur (1848-1927) apporte un témoignage précieux sur le degré de fidélité aux intentions de l'auteur que le directeur musical d'alors, Napoléon Aubin (1812-90), assura à cette occasion: 'M. Napoléon Aubin ... dirigeait la représentation. Devant cet opéra inachevé, M. Aubin n'hésita pas. Il compléta lui-même la partition, soli, choeurs et orchestre. C'était la première audition de l'oeuvre au Canada.'[18]

On ne sait de quelle édition de l'oeuvre Aubin fit usage. Quoi qu'il en soit, LeVasseur paraît indiquer hors de tout doute qu'il fit en son temps au niveau de la partition ce qu'un bibliothécaire avait réalisé avant lui pour les musiciens de l'Opéra de Paris, 'il compléta.' Si l'on se rapporte à une note infrapaginale dans l'édition de 1835, on y lit en effet ce qui suit:

On croit communément que la musique du *Devin du village*, telle qu'elle s'exécute maintenant à l'Opéra, a, depuis Rousseau, subi de grands changements dans la partie instrumentale; nous avons pris sur ce point des informations certaines, et voici le fait dans son exacte vérité. L'accompagnement du récitatif se réduisant, dans la partition, à une basse chiffrée sans l'emploi d'aucun autre instrument, et celui du chant n'en offrant presque point d'autre que deux parties de violon avec la basse, on a jugé que la partition ne pouvoit rester en cet état de simplicité, pour être exécutée dans une salle aussi vaste que celle de l'Opéra. M. Lefebvre, bibliothécaire de cet établissement, a fait avec autant de goût que de réserve les *remplissages* que cette circonstance nécessitoit. Il a coupé tous les repos du récitatif par des accords confiés aux différens instrumens, mais constamment fournis par la basse telle que le compositeur l'a donnée. Pour le chant, il en a, dans les mêmes vues, complété les parties d'orchestre dont l'effet, sans ce complément, pouvoit paroître trop faible. Les amateurs ont généralement applaudi à ces changemens; cependant il reste à savoir si les effets harmoniques ainsi renforcés, en altérant les rapports établis par le compositeur entre le chant et l'accompagnement, n'ont pas détruit cette *unité* qu'il fait avec raison valoir, et dénaturé jusqu'à un certain point son ouvrage. Ce qu'il y a de certain, c'est qu'il s'est fortement prononcé lui-même contre tout changement de cette espèce dans une note que l'éditeur de sa musique posthume nous apprend avoir été trouvée écrite de sa main, et conçue en ces termes: 'DANS TOUTE MA MUSIQUE je prie instamment qu'on ne mette aucun remplissage partout où je n'en ai pas mis.'[19]

L'indication est précieuse, car elle signale une manière en tout point conforme à la pratique des Romantiques, plus soucieux de pleine sonorité que de respect des intentions du compositeur.

LE *DICTIONNAIRE DE MUSIQUE*

Le *Dictionnaire de musique* de Rousseau est un ouvrage aussi fondamental pour les historiens de la musique que l'est *Émile* pour les éducateurs. La préface de l'ouvrage, datée du 20 décembre 1764, définit et retrace comme suit l'origine du livre: 'C'est ici moins un Dictionnaire en forme, qu'un recueil de matériaux pour un Dictionnaire, qui n'attendent qu'une meilleure main pour être employés. Les fondemens de cet Ouvrage furent jettés . . . à la hâte, il y a quinze ans, dans l'Encyclopédie . . . Blessé de l'imperfection de mes articles, à mesure que les volumes de l'Encyclopédie paroissoient, je résolus de refondre le tout sur mon brouillon, & d'en faire à loisir un ouvrage à part traité avec plus de soin.'[20] Puis, après avoir raconté les circonstances pénibles qui l'ont 'forcé de donner en si mauvais état un Livre [qu'il aurait] pû mieux faire' l'auteur dit espérer 'que les vrais Artistes & les hommes de génie y trouveront des vues utiles dont ils sauront bien tirer parti.'[21]

Nous ignorons le nom des 'Artistes et hommes de génie' qui, à Québec, surent tirer parti du *Dictionnaire* de Rousseau, peu de temps après sa parution en 1768. Mais le fait est incontestable, il s'est trouvé des maîtres de musique pour en assimiler le contenu et en faire la matière d'un enseignement sérieux, tout au moins dans les dernières années du XVIIIe siècle. La confirmation nous en est donnée par un manuscrit conservé aux

Archives du Séminaire de Québec sous la cote ASQ M-241. En voici une brève description.

Le document est un cahier mesurant 16 x 38,6 cm, contenant 539 pages dont il manque les pages 150 à 190, constitué de notes personnelles de cours sur la musique, la grammaire, la géométrie, la politique, la philosophie, la physique, la chimie, la logique. Même si le verso de la couverture porte la mention de 'Pierre Boisvert fils d'Eustache,' l'attribution du cahier est faite à Pierre Bédard, sur la foi d'une inscription figurant sur la couverture, côté recto. Futur député et membre de la Chambre d'Assemblée, celui qui allait fonder *Le Canadien*, avant d'être nommé juge à Trois-Rivières, Pierre Bédard (1763-1829), étudia au Séminaire de Québec de 1780 à 1788.[22] Le cahier de notes qu'il a rédigées selon toute vraisemblance sur les bancs de cette institution nous offre une vue précise des matières d'enseignement au Séminaire de Québec, à un moment de sa formation qui ne se trouve cependant pas précisé.[23]

D'après ce recueil, il ne fait pas de doute que Rousseau jouit d'une faveur particulière dans l'étude de la philosophie et de la musique. Pour cette dernière discipline, le *Dictionnaire* tient lieu de livre de référence unique. La preuve en est donnée aux pages 140 et 141 (Figure 3), où non seulement le nom de Rousseau se trouve cité à plus d'une reprise, mais encore le titre de l'ouvrage, accompagné d'indications précises, comme par exemple, vers le tiers de la page 140: 'les 1er chifres ecrits au dessus de l'accord marque la page du Dic. de musique de Rousseau le 2d marque la portée [*recte*: le système].' Ainsi, le dernier accord du quatrième fragment d'un système qui en compte cinq réfère, à l'aide des chiffres '20,2,' à la page 20 du *Dictionnaire*, 2e système.

Les sujets abordés se présentent comme dans Tableau 1. Après le numéro de la page, nous indiquons la vedette donnée par Bédard ou, en son absence, nous en plaçons une entre crochets. Cette liste détaillée établit nettement la place accordée aux questions relatives à la *règle de l'octave*, que Rousseau définit comme suit: 'Formule harmonique publiée la première fois par le sieur Delaire en 1700, laquelle détermine, sur la marche diatonique de la Basse, l'Accord convenable à chaque degré du Ton, tant en Mode majeur qu'en Mode mineur, & tant en montant qu'en descendant' (p. 413). On peut même constater (Figure 3, p. 141, 1er système, 6e accord) que la discussion faite par Rousseau sur le sujet de la faute que constitue l'accord de sixte sur le 6e degré a fait l'objet d'une étude visant à assurer la correction de l'accord dans le sens prévu par Rousseau: 'L'accord de Sixte, dont on Accompagne la sixième Note en montant, est une faute qu'on doit corriger, & que pour Accompagner régulièrement cette Note, ... il n'y a qu'un seul Accord à lui donner,

Figure 3 Extrait (p. 140–41) du cahier manuscrit de notes de cours de Pierre Bédard, conservé aux Archives du Séminaire de Québec (ASQ M-241)

savoir selui de Septième ... renversée d'un Accord de Sixte-ajoutée sur la Tonique' (p. 414).

La constatation de l'importance accordée aux *règles de l'accompagnement* dans le cahier de notes de Bédard, comme en font foi les définitions et exercices portant sur des points comme la règle de l'octave, la basse fondamentale, les accords, la liaison des accords, les cadences, est d'un enseignement très riche. Il s'en dégage qu'à une époque où commence à

TABLEAU 1
Table des sujets musicaux du cahier de notes de Pierre Bédard

Page
- 38 Succession des tons – Le cromatique – La Dominante d'un ton – Pour passer d'un mode à un autre – La liaison des accords – Characthère des modes
- 39 [Proportions mathématiques]
- 82 [Physique du son: diagrammes et proportions]
- 95 Règle de l'octave en mode majeur
- 140 Règle de l'octave
- 141 Règle de l'octave – Noms des accords
- 142 Règle de l'octave – cadences
- 144-7 [Sons, cordes, intervalles exprimés sous forme de rapports mathématiques et en diagrammes]

se répandre, à Québec comme ailleurs, un enseignement de type élémentaire, vulgarisé par des manuels souvent connus sous le titre significatif de *Principes de musique*,[24] une institution comme le Séminaire de Québec s'en tient strictement à une forme d'enseignement de la musique connue en France, dans le courant du XVIIIe siècle, sous le nom d'Accompagnement, débouchant assez naturellement sur la Composition.[25] Le passage de l'une à l'autre forme d'apprentissage est bien mis en évidence dans l'extrait qui suit de la lettre de Denis Diderot (1713-84), contenue dans les *Reflexions sur les leçons de musique* du fameux pédagogue français Anton Bemetzrieder (1743-1817), dix ans après la parution du *Dictionnaire de musique* de Rousseau:

Dans les leçons particulieres, ainsi que dans les Ecoles publiques, on débute par les accords de la régle de l'octave; l'Eleve les écrit en partition; on les lui fait retourner en tout sens: sous un chant, on lui fait poser la basse; au-dessus d'une basse, on lui fait écrire un chant. Dans une partition on lui fait remplir, tantôt un violon, tantôt la quinte, tantôt les cors, tantôt une voix, & tantôt une flûte; enfin on donne une phrase de chant, qu'on nomme *motif*; l'Apprenti Compositeur, sans dessein & sans intention, l'étend, la varie à l'infini; arrange les notes à deux, à trois, à quatre & à cinq parties; il fait plus, il fait une fugue à autant de parties que l'on veut. Sa mémoire lui fournit aussi des idées; il en fait une ariette, un motet, un duo, un choeur, une ouverture, &c, & le voilà passé Maître Compositeur.[26]

Nous n'avons pas la preuve que Pierre Bédard ait jamais poussé jusqu'à la composition son apprentissage de la musique, en suivant pas à pas le

Dictionnaire de musique de Rousseau. Il en va autrement de Charles Sauvageau (1807-49) qui, comme le prouve le manuel publié à Québec en 1844 à l'imprimerie de Napoléon Aubin, son beau-frère et futur directeur de la première représentation du *Devin du village* en terre canadienne, connaissait le *Dictionnaire* de Rousseau.

L'article XVI (p. 12) des *Notions élémentaires de musique, tirées des meilleurs auteurs et mises en ordre par Chs. Sauvageau* nous renseigne sur ce point. Il traite d'un sujet jadis cher à Jean-Jacques, l'expression. Sauvageau, le violoniste, cite le *Dictionnaire*[27] pour faire valoir la supériorité du violon sur les autres instruments, en raison de l'*'Expression* plus variée & plus universelle' qu'on en peut tirer, écrit-il, à la suite de Rousseau.

Ce témoignage à lui seul ne traduit pas une influence persistante et profonde de la pensée et de l'enseignement de Rousseau, vers le milieu du XIXe siècle, ainsi que nous en avons été témoins, quelque cinquante ans plus tôt au Séminaire, lieu où Sauvageau professe au début des années 1840. Sa musique, par contre, pourrait constituer un excellent sujet d'étude sous cet aspect,[28] mais c'est là une question qui sort du cadre restreint de nos propos actuels. Si nous nous en tenons au passage cité plus haut, qu'il suffise, en guise de conclusion, de rapporter une coïncidence curieuse: un Canadien emprunte à Rousseau sur le sujet même qui avait poussé le philosophe suisse, au siècle précédent, à se tourner vers la musique du Canada et de ses premiers habitants, connue, déclare Rousseau, grâce au père Mersenne.[29] 'On trouvera dans tous ces morceaux,' écrit l'auteur du *Dictionnaire de musique*, 'une conformité de Modulation avec notre Musique, qui pourra faire admirer aux uns la bonté & l'universalité de nos règles, & peut-être rendre suspecte à d'autres l'intelligence ou la fidélité de ceux qui nous ont transmis ces Airs.'[30] Ces remarques ne devraient-elles guider toute recherche sur les raisons qui ont poussé quelques-uns des meilleurs musiciens canadiens de la fin du XVIIIe siècle et de la première moitié du XIXe à se faire disciples de Jean-Jacques Rousseau ou du moins à nous apparaître tels?

NANCY F. VOGAN

Music Instruction in Nova Scotia before 1914

Music instruction in Nova Scotia has a long and varied past; folk traditions, individuals, institutions, and social, economic, and political factors have all influenced its development.

From the earliest days of colonization, the church was associated with instruction in music. When Father Fléché first came to Port Royal in the early 1600s, he began teaching the Micmacs how to sing the simplest parts of the Roman Catholic service.[1] This marked the first stage in a long-standing tradition of instruction in music, primarily Gregorian chant, by members of Roman Catholic orders in Nova Scotia. Later, these orders provided extensive instruction in secular music as well.

Music also played an important role in the various Protestant denominations. St Paul's Anglican Church, established shortly after the founding of Halifax in 1749, had a choir in its early years and installed a pipe organ by the 1760s. St Matthew's Church, where 'dissenting Protestants' worshipped, used the custom of 'lining-out,' a type of rote teaching of the congregation employed in many Presbyterian churches. Until 1873 the only musical instrument allowed in this church was a cello known as the 'kirk fiddle.'[2]

The introduction of singing schools, a tradition inherited from England and the American colonies, greatly assisted the development of choral music in the Protestant churches. Classes were given by singing masters who 'taught the rudiments of musical notation and singing, thus enabling their pupils to help with the musical part of the church service.'[3] However, most singing masters operated independently from the church; some also taught violin, flute, and piano, 'instruments very popular at dances and parties.'[4] Singing schools in Nova Scotia prior to 1800 include one in Liverpool begun by Amasa Braman in 1777, and another begun by Reuben McFarlen in Halifax in 1788. Some instruction may have been given earlier than this, particularly by itinerant clergy. For example, the early American hymn-tune composer and editor of *Urania or a Choice Collection of Psalm Tunes, Anthems, and Hymns*, Rev. James Lyon, visited Nova Scotia as a Protestant missionary in the 1760s. Rev. Jacob Bailey, a Loyalist clergyman who became the first rector of the parish church in Annapolis Royal, provided music instruction for his congregation. In 1789 he wrote to a fellow clergyman: 'Pray inform my kinsman that two years ago not a person in Annapolis ventured to sing in public, but they have now attained to great perfection. The best families have joined to encourage it, and we have for more than a year performed Psalmody in all its parts ... For your amusement I have enclosed the hymns we sang last Easter and New Year's Day, for the people here expect that I should compose hymns [i.e., write hymn texts] as well as sermons.'[5] During the nineteenth century, singing schools became more numerous in many areas of the province, particularly Pictou County with classes being held in a variety of locations, including schoolhouses, community halls, churches, and even farmhouse kitchens. This tradition continued into the early years of the twentieth century.

Instructional material usually consisted of tune-books published in the United States, but there is evidence to suggest that Stephen Humbert's *Union Harmony*, first published in Saint John, New Brunswick, in 1801, may also have been used. These publications contained instructions on the rules of good singing and music theory, as well as many sacred selections, usually in several vocal parts, and some included a few secular works as well. The growing popularity of the singing school movement inspired the Pictou printer and bookseller James Dawson to compile and publish *The Harmonicon* in the 1830s.[6]

Although many of the singing masters were itinerants who moved frequently from place to place, some of them were primarily self-taught musicians who saw a need for music instruction in their own areas. Such was the case with Andrew Mackay of Elmfield near Pictou, who devoted more than sixty years of his life to teaching sacred music. He learned music from his father, who had been trained in Scotland, and began to conduct singing schools at a young age. He held classes five nights a week in the schoolhouses of various communities, to which he travelled either on foot or by horse and wagon. He was usually paid a dollar per night for sessions that lasted thirteen weeks. Instead of using books, he wrote the music on the backs of sheets of wallpaper and hung these on the board for all to see.[7] In Halifax singing classes were offered by several individuals; these included the printer and musician Jacob Cunnabel, who had studied music in the United States and then returned to his native province, and Arnold Doane, a native of Barrington, Nova Scotia, 'who stayed in London for postgraduate studies in music on his return voyage from the Australian gold fields, and then settled in Halifax where he has been given credit for laying the foundation of the musical taste of his day in the capital of Nova Scotia.'[8]

In addition to instructional singing classes, numerous philharmonic societies were formed; these groups were sometimes associated with churches, but there were secular organizations as well. In addition to the groups established in Halifax, singing societies were founded during the 1830s and 1840s in other areas, including Lunenburg, Pictou, and Antigonish. Halifax had several music organizations, one of the major ones being the Harmonic Society, founded in 1842 with the objective of 'the improvement of its Members in the higher departments of Sacred Music, Vocal and Instrumental.' Regulations stated: 'As during its Meetings there will be no opportunity for receiving elementary instruction, some previous knowledge of Music is absolutely necessary, as a qualification for Membership.' The society was for men only; regulations stated that members could invite 'such Ladies as are capable of assisting at the Concerts,' but that all such invitations 'shall be given for the Season only.'[9] On the first Tuesday of every month members had the privilege of introducing a guest, either a 'Non-resident or a Lady.' Their programs included selections from major choral works including Handel's *Messiah* and Haydn's *Creation*. This organization was later succeeded by the Orpheus Club.

Military and town bands were active during this period, as were a few small orchestras. They were not limited to the larger centres; smaller garrison towns, such as Annapolis Royal, benefited greatly from the presence of military musicians. Retired military personnel often became active in the musical life of the community and were sometimes invited to an area to teach and direct performing groups. In the mid-1800s the newly formed Musical Society of Antigonish hired a retired bandmaster who 'gave music lessons to children and adults, formed a band, and arranged music for them.'[10] In 1849 a group of Yarmouth machinists from a local factory purchased brass instruments and advertised for a band director. This led to the formation of the Acadia Brass Band, the forerunner of the Yarmouth Citizens' Concert Band which is still in existence.[11]

From the earliest days of the province there were opportunities for people to study music privately, especially in Halifax. At first, much of this instruction was provided by military men, who 'taught others during their long periods of waiting for military action. As early as 1761 ... Halifax residents could study German flute, violin, French horn, oboe, and bassoon.'[12] During the nineteenth century the piano became very popular, particularly because these instruments were manufactured in the city. By the middle of the nineteenth century many of the music teachers in Halifax were from Europe. They included 'Senor Louis G. Casseres, an excellent pianist and voice teacher who was appointed pianist to Lieutenant-Governor the Earl of Mulgrave; Prof. E. Jeans, violoncellist from London, who augmented his income by repairing and tuning organs and pianos; and Mr. E.C. Saffrey, prominent in the Harmonic Society, who attempted to raise the level of musical knowledge by occasional lectures at the Temperance Hall.'[13]

In addition to instruction given by independent teachers operating out of their own studios, music was also taught in many private schools, several of which were church-affiliated institutions. Among those established by Protestant denominations was the Grand Pré Seminary in Wolfville, founded by the Baptists in 1858, which in 1860 became the Acadia Ladies' Seminary. The Mount Allison Ladies' College, opened by the Methodists in 1854 in Sackville, New Brunswick, also attracted many students from Nova Scotia. Music played an important role in curricula at both these schools. Several Roman Catholic orders established schools which have become noted for their music. The Sisters of Charity, for example, arrived in Halifax in 1849 and began to teach young girls shortly thereafter. In 1873 they founded Mount St Vincent Academy, which has played an important role in the musical life of Halifax. The order of the Sisters of the Sacred Heart, also founded in Halifax in the mid-nineteenth century, established the Academy of the Sacred Heart in 1852. At the turn of the century, this convent school was described as follows: 'All the usual branches of Ladies' education may be obtained here and it is needless to say that the moral as well as the secular training of the rising generation is equally cared for. Music is an important item ... There are eleven pianos in use in the building.'[14] The Sisters of the Congregation of Notre Dame from Montreal established several convents in the Maritimes. These included Mount Saint Bernard in Antigonish, founded in 1883, which later became affiliated with Saint Francis Xavier University, and Holy Angels Convent, founded in Sydney in 1885. The three sisters sent from Montreal to Sydney included Sister St Helen of the Cross, who taught music, so there was a music department at Holy Angels from the outset. Among institutions dedicated to educating young men, St Anne's College, founded at Church Point in 1890, offered both vocal and instrumental music instruction. A college band gave its first performance in 1893 and played an important role in the St Cecilia Society.

During the latter decades of the nineteenth century, citizens in Halifax felt a growing need for a non-denominational conservatory of music in the port city. This led to the establishment in 1887 of the Halifax Conservatory of Music, which was associated with the Halifax Ladies' College and later became affiliated with Dalhousie University. The first director of the school was Charles Porter, a graduate of the Leipzig Conservatory who had come to Halifax to assume the post of organist at St Matthew's Church. He remained director of the conservatory until 1900, when he decided to turn his attention to a business career in Halifax. An impressive list of instruments and subjects taught was cited in the bulletin for the early years of the conservatory; it included various orchestral instruments, piano, voice, organ, and theory. Some conservatory students went on to post-graduate training at the New England Conservatory in Boston, and many went to Berlin or Leipzig.

Music was also included in the program of studies at the School for the Blind in Halifax shortly after it opened in 1871. The offerings were soon expanded to include instruction in voice, piano, and various other instruments as well as the theory of music. A piano-tuning division was later opened, and a pipe organ was installed in the auditorium. Several graduates of this school pursued further studies in music, particularly in Leipzig and Berlin.

References to the teaching of music in the public schools of Nova Scotia can be found shortly after 1800. It was not until the second half of the century, however, that significant progress was made in this field. Music was introduced as a subject for students at the provincial Normal School in Truro shortly after it opened in 1855; for many years a new music teacher was appointed annually. During the 1860s music teaching was reported in the schools of Lunenburg, Shelburne, Lockeport, Pictou County, and Advocate Harbour. There were also sessions given for teachers in the Yarmouth area. The Lunenburg County inspector described the common attitude: 'Although not scientifically taught, [vocal music] is practised in every school in the county with but few exceptions, and wherever practised is attended with happy effects, both as a safety-valve for exuberant spirits, and a pleasing and judicious relaxation from the drier duties of the school.'[15]

More formalized instruction began in the Halifax schools when Jacob B. Norton, a native of Boston, was hired by the Halifax School Commissioners to train schoolchildren to sing. The *Acadian Recorder* in 1867 noted this appointment and commented: 'Knowing of the success of Professor Norton during the past year in the practice of his profession we congratulate the commissioners on having obtained the services of so efficient a teacher.'[16] Norton adopted the tradition of an annual public examination in music; one of the first was held in July 1868. Over 1500 pupils were assembled in the Temperance Hall, with school officials and parents in attendance. The examination was extensive, covering many aspects of music rudiments. An observer commented: 'To see some of the boys and girls transpose from one key to another, proved that they not only had a smattering of rudiments, but that they thoroughly understood them; and not until the transposition of the minor scale, could the competitors be cut down to the number of prizes.'[17] This event was followed by a special evening concert which featured students in a large chorus accompanied by a regimental band. At a similar event in 1870 the students made a presentation to Norton at the conclusion of the exercises; in his reply Norton made reference to the lack of a suitable music book for the students and announced the recent publication of a text by himself and a colleague from Boston. This work, entitled *The Dominion Songster for Schools, Classes and the Family Circle*, was dedicated 'to the children of the public schools throughout the Dominion'[18] and contained an extensive collection of song material, including a few compositions by Norton himself.

As the population of the schools increased, it became more and more difficult for Norton to provide adequate instruction for all the pupils. He approached the board about this matter, stating: 'If the teachers would qualify themselves to teach the rudiments, as in some parts of Germany and the United States they are compelled to do, then the Music Teacher with such assistance could attend all the departments in the city without so much hard labour.'[19] Despite the fact that this issue was left unresolved, Norton continued to receive support from the school authorities, who frequently commended him for his work with over 3400 children. However, when the board found itself in financial difficulties a few years later, it decided to abolish the position of Teacher of Music and informed Norton that his services would no longer be needed.

Although the position was not reinstated until after the first world war, interest in music instruction in the Halifax schools did not end with Norton's departure. However, owing to the strong feeling that music instruction should be in the hands of the classroom teachers, authorities stated that all teachers should show some ability to conduct singing in the common schools with at least the 'simplest musical notation' – the tonic sol-fa. This method of teaching music became popular in many areas of the Maritime provinces during the last two decades of the nineteenth century, thanks largely to Rev. James Anderson, a Presbyterian minister at Musquodoboit Harbour. In fact his interest in this movement eventually led him to leave his charge and devote his full time to music. He wrote numerous articles on this approach for teachers' periodicals, travelled to various points in the Maritimes giving instruction in tonic sol-fa, and taught special summer school classes. He also gave classes at the Summer School of Science, a voluntary interprovincial organization established in 1887, which held annual sessions in a different Maritime centre each summer; teachers who completed the requirements there were awarded certificates from the Tonic Sol-fa College in London. Instruction was given at regional teachers' institutes throughout the province by Anderson and by various individuals who had been trained by him. One of his pupils, Ada Ryan from Halifax, published a textbook based on this method which was used in Nova Scotia schools for several years.[20] In the fall of 1891 Anderson was appointed by the government of Nova Scotia to provide instruction in tonic sol-fa in the schools throughout the province. His work was well received by teachers and school authorities who commented: 'We find fault with only one feature in the flying mission of Mr. Anderson. Instead of half a year, Mr. Anderson should have been kept at work for a whole year at the very least.'[21]

Throughout the 1890s education authorities became more emphatic in their recommendation that all children in the lower grades be given instruction in vocal music and urged teachers to use tonic sol-fa in their classrooms: 'Every pupil (excepting of course those known to be organically defective as respects music), should be able to pass an examination in vocal music before promotion to a higher grade ... Teachers musically defective may comply with the law by having these lessons given by any one qualified.'[22] Despite this strong recommendation, there was no marked improvement in school music instruction in the province prior to 1914, although in a few areas such as Cape Breton music did receive considerable attention. The report of a teachers' institute held in North Sydney shortly after the turn of the century stated that 'a remarkable demonstration of the successful musical education of the public school pupils of North Sydney and Sydney Mines was given.'[23] An editorial in the *Journal of Education* declared that one teacher, Professor Chisholm, had 'put these towns in advance of any others in the Province in this respect' and further stated that 'those who cannot sing should take up other professions than that of teaching in our common school grades, and those who can sing should be better trained than our minimum now requires.'[24] This program in Cape Breton, however, was short-lived.

Another important factor in the development of music in various parts of Canada has been the role played by women's organizations, and Nova Scotia has been no exception in this. The Ladies' Musical Club established in Halifax in 1905 played an active part in the musical life of the city for many years. The club at first followed a study plan as outlined by the

American National Federation of Music Clubs, but it soon broke this affiliation and developed its own programs of study. It also established performing groups for its members, including an all-ladies' orchestra. For many years the club's meetings were held at the School for the Blind, and students from the school were invited to attend the musical presentations. The club took an active interest in the public schools as well, offering monthly concerts by members and lobbying the school board regarding the appointment of a singing teacher. It later sponsored a series of music competitions for the schools which were forerunners of the music festivals of today.

In the years leading up to the first world war there was a conscious attempt to develop a sense of patriotism in the entire population, particularly the young, and music played an important role in this effort. Patriotic selections were sung in the classroom, in assemblies, and at various community events. One of the most important of these celebrations was Empire Day, which was initiated by the Dominion Educational Association at a meeting in Halifax in 1898. A resolution was put forward that one day of the school year should be 'devoted to the cultivation of feelings of loyalty and attachment to our country.'[25] The school day immediately preceding 24 May was chosen, and for many years schoolchildren throughout the Dominion were assembled for patriotic observances on this date. These programs usually concluded with the massed singing of 'God Save the Queen' and other patriotic selections including 'The Maple Leaf Forever' and 'Rule Britannia.' 'My Own Canadian Home,' written and published in Saint John, New Brunswick, in 1890, was also frequently included.

Feelings of loyalty and attachment to country were encouraged in many aspects of life, including church, community, and school activities, and manifested themselves not only in pride in the country but also in pride in the cultural heritage of that region. By the turn of the century Nova Scotians had begun to establish a sense of confidence in their own musical traditions, including opportunities for the serious study of music, which led Hugo Talbot to state in the preface to his publication *Musical Halifax*: 'We may flatter ourselves that (judging from the number of prominent musicians educated entirely in Halifax) a musical education can be obtained here unsurpassable in the Dominion.'[26]

MARIA CALDERISI BRYCE

John Lovell (1810-93): Montreal Music Printer and Publisher

To Montrealers and their visitors the name Lovell has long been synonymous with the *Montreal City Directory* (1842-1978). Now in its fourth generation of family ownership and management, Lovell Litho & Publications Inc. publishes little other than related directory products, for example, *Criss-Cross* (a street directory) and the *Red Book* (a telephone index). But the directory proper was the firm's last link with the long, fruitful, and often turbulent career of its first publisher, John Lovell.

The 1842 and 1843 editions were actually published by Lovell & Gibson together with Robert W.S. Mackay, the compiler. After a hiatus of eighteen years John Lovell resumed publication and proceeded to expand and improve the service to his constituents over the next thirty years. But the directory was just one of the amazing variety of products which rolled from the hand- and steam-powered presses of what became the largest printing establishment in nineteenth-century Canada. No subject was too grand, too scientific, too romantic, or too humble. Some evocative and tantalizing titles, drawn from the retrospective national bibliography,[1] are: *The Mysteries of Montreal: Being Recollections of a Female Physician* by Ch. Führer (1881), *Protection and Free Trade* by John Maclean (1867), *On Crime and Insanity* by Joseph Workman (1877), *The Renewal of Life by the Swedish Movement-Cure* by David Wark (1869), *The Heiress of Myrtle Grove: An English Tale Founded on Facts* by a Montreal Lady, A.E.B. (1870), *Manuel de piété: ou Recueil de prières et de pratiques* by Mathurin Bonnissant (1872), and *Histoire du Canada et des canadiens sous la domination anglaise* [by M. Bibaud] (1878).

The above sample, however, hardly begins to reflect the even greater breadth of activity which engaged Lovell from 1835 to Confederation. During that time he founded and published, or printed, no fewer than twenty-four newspapers and periodicals:[2] English and French, scientific and juvenile, literary and legal, religious and commercial – there appears to have been no limit to his vision and capacity. And sheet music, hymnbooks, and other musical works took their places along with pamphlets, government papers, the first Canadian textbooks, and maps in the steady flow of job printing and publishing which as early as 1867 kept 150 people employed at an impressive array of specialized machinery.[3]

In an effort to understand why a busy, committed, and successful craftsman and enterprising businessman made the special effort it must have required to produce the relatively few music publications that he did, I have sought out personal and business archives without success. This is not surprising, since the Lovell plant built in 1842 burnt down in 1885.[4] A few scattered items in the Public Archives of Canada – receipts, a stock offer, a couple of letters about his textbook series, another turning down a manuscript which he did not consider a good financial risk – helped fill out a picture of the man. However, there was nothing directly pertinent to music publishing, such as the market for music, contacts with composers, the cost of music type, and special training for music typographers. The mechanics themselves remain a mystery. There could not have been more than one music typographer in Montreal during the 1840s who not only knew how to lay out a page of music but did so with considerable skill.[5] Did Lovell perhaps share his typesetter with other printers? Eusèbe Sénécal's music publications are uncannily similar to Lovell's, not to mention those of *La Revue canadienne* and *La Minerve*.

Conversations with his descendants merely evoked amazement that John Lovell had had anything to do with publishing music, nor do the scant biographical accounts reveal even the slightest clue to his personal involvement with the subject. The discursive *Reminiscences of Seventy Years* (1908)[6] by Lovell's wife, Sarah, contain many references to music, including descriptions of family singsongs. But Sarah, who was herself musical, did not marry John until 1849, long after he had begun to publish music. The closest we come to a direct connection is a letter from Susanna Moodie, the acclaimed author of *Roughing it in the Bush*, acknowledging the receipt in Belleville of the piano which she had obviously asked Lovell to choose for her.[7]

Perhaps his own memoirs would have revealed something. But given the content of the autobiographical sketch written at the request of the editor of the *American Dictionary of Printing and Bookmaking*[8] and published in a pamphlet entitled *John Lovell and the Bank of Montreal* in 1892,[9] it is doubtful that he would have entered in any detail into a facet of his publishing career which was neither dramatic nor lucrative. No trace has been found of the publication or of a manuscript of an autobiography, nor has the biographical sketch which E.B. Biggar, the journalist and author of

Canada, a Memorial Volume (1889), was planning to publish yet come to light. A letter from Sydney R. Bellingham dated 19 October 1898[10] replying to Biggar's request for biographical data outlines in some detail events during 1837 and also certain aspects of Lovell's career in the 1850s and 1860s, but it refers the prospective biographer to Robert Lovell, the son who managed the business, for further information.

In any case, here is a brief résumé of the eventful life of a most enterprising and courageous businessman who was deeply devoted to his country and to the dissemination of knowledge about its resources, whether physical, intellectual, or artistic.

John Lovell was born on 4 August 1810 in Harbour Hill, near Bandon, County Cork, Ireland. With his parents and seven brothers and sisters, he arrived in Montreal on his tenth birthday. His father worked as agent and manager of a farm in Muskinongé for about three years, and shortly after the family's return to Montreal John began an apprenticeship with the printer Edward Vernon Sparahawk, the owner and editor of the *Canadian Times*. By the time Sparahawk sold his shop in 1825, young Lovell had learned enough of the craft to be kept on by the new owners, who soon sold out to Ludger Duvernay. (Duvernay would gain fame – or notoriety – as publisher of *La Minerve* (1826-99), the voice of the French-Canadian patriots, suffering imprisonment and exile during the troubled thirties for his outspoken journalism.) But times continued to be bad for the shop, and in 1827 Lovell accepted a good offer of employment from the *Montreal Gazette*, where he remained until 1831. That year he went to Quebec to work as a parliamentary printer, but cholera broke out there and he returned to Montreal in the summer of 1832. He became shop foreman of *L'Ami du peuple de l'ordre et des lois* (1832-40), where *The Irish Advocate* was also printed for its owners. Increased tensions between the French-Canadian majority and British-Canadian minorities resulted in the formation of several defensively narrow 'national' societies. In 1835 John Lovell bought *The Irish Advocate* and began his business career at the height of a period of economic depression and political unrest.

When the rebellion finally erupted into arrests and armed resistance in November 1837, Lovell closed his shop[11] and reported for active service in the Montreal Cavalry, which he had joined five years earlier as a volunteer militiaman. Around this time, he granted permission to one of his employees, a certain Cinq-Mars, who had a wife and nine children in dire need of sustenance, to borrow a small hand press and a few cases of type in order to print and sell small handsheets. Although Cinq-Mars had promised to print only translations from the English papers, martial law being in force, his patriotic tendencies apparently led him to go beyond this, and Lovell's office and equipment were seized. Lovell was indignant that his loyalty could have been in doubt, seeing that he had risked his life in the important battle at Saint-Charles; he later received an apology from the attorney general.

A graphic account of Lovell's role at Saint-Charles is given in Sidney Bellingham's letter, already mentioned.[12] As accompanying magistrate to Colonel Wetherall's forces sent to disperse a body of rebels collected at Saint-Charles, Bellingham agreed to carry a despatch through enemy lines. Previous despatches to nearby government forces had been intercepted, and it was obvious that reinforcements would be needed to carry out the mission. Lovell volunteered to accompany his fellow-Irishman.[13] Their adventure has all the elements of an exciting, somewhat Gothic tale: a dark night, tired horses, a ferry crossing, frightful weather, deception, and daring. The picture created here of young Lovell is that of a vigorous, courageous, bilingual, and enterprising loyalist with a strong belief in the righteousness of his government's actions. The battle which followed was the turning point in the rebellion, and to Lovell was given the honour of cutting down the 'Cap of Liberty' which the rebels had attached to a high pole as a sign of their defiance. Both men were offered, and refused, a monetary reward for their bravery.

Details about Lovell's publishing career from its resumption in 1838 with *The Literary Garland* to his death in 1893 must be gleaned from the nature of his publications themselves (which often included advertisements of his plant and services), from official documents, newspaper reports, and the occasional letter or receipt in archival collections. His vigour and aggressiveness had obviously extended to business and political contacts. By 1854, Mr Bellingham remembers,[14] he was 'a wealthy and successful printer, owning large printing establishments at Toronto, Montreal and Quebec. He printed all the Parliamentary Papers.' But Lovell had a falling-out with John A. Macdonald and was ousted from his printing privilege. Bellingham goes on to describe Lovell's enterprising recovery and 'ambitions to connect his name with the history of Canada' which led to the publication of *Lovell's Canadian Dominion Directory for 1871*. The preparation of this enormous volume of 2562 pages was beset by financial intrigue and other difficulties.

John Lovell's stormy position on copyright, the reprint industry, tariffs, and free trade is well documented in George Parker's book, *The Beginnings of the Book Trade in Canada*.[15] I have neither the competence nor the space to treat adequately this exciting chapter of our publishing history, with its accusations of piracy and opportunism, and protestations against fuzzy legislation and inept negotiators. I should like, instead, to proceed to Lovell's activities as a music printer and publisher.

Lovell was not the earliest music printer in colonial Canada,[16] but he was the only one who published in all three formats – periodicals, sheet music, and books – and in both square and round notation. All of his work was type-set, a method seldom used after the introduction of engraving and lithography, both of which were infinitely more suitable for music printing. Furthermore, he was the only printer who concentrated on Canadian composers and writers.

He began music publishing within the pages of *The Literary Garland*, edited by his brother-in-law, John Gibson, who became his partner in 1842.[17] It was the longest-lived magazine in British North America, beginning publication in December 1838 and continuing until December 1851. Put into the context of Lovell's activities during the 1837 rebellion, the venture becomes even more amazing. That Lovell went to considerable trouble and expense to solicit and pay for quality material by Canadian authors is documented by Susanna Moodie in the letter already cited and in several of her publications. Mrs Moodie was a regular contributor to the magazine and acclaimed Lovell as 'one of the first and most successful pioneers in establishing a national literature in the Canadian colonies.'[18]

From the beginning, with few exceptions, each monthly issue of forty-five to fifty octavo pages included a piece of music, varying in length from one and a half to three pages. While Lovell may have been a music lover, he did not presume to take on the responsibility for the music pages of his journal. On the last page of the first issue he announced: 'It affords us much gratification to state the Musical Department of the *Garland* has been generously undertaken by a gentleman of the highest professional celebrity, who has furnished us with a favourite Waltz of the 1st or Royal Regiment, hitherto unpublished. This will prove a most delightful science of harmony and song.'[19] The 'gentleman' mentioned is later identified as W.H. Warren, a piano teacher, organist, and composer, whose original works and arrangements of pieces by well-known European composers make up just over half of the 135 pieces published over thirteen years. Among the other Canadian composers represented in the *Garland's* music pages were Joseph Maffré, Charles Sauvageau, Francis Moodie, and J.S. Dunbar Moodie, Susanna's husband. The music is all quite simple and is written for piano solo or voice and piano, obviously meant to be performed by subscribers of little musical experience on the increasingly ubiquitous pianos and melodeons in middle-class homes. It is clearly and generously laid out in what soon became recognizable as Lovell's typographical style.

John Gibson's death in 1850 coincided with an increased infiltration of foreign magazines which, because of much larger circulation, could be sold more cheaply. In an editorial in the December 1850 issue, Mrs E.L. Cushing, who took over as editor after Gibson died, pleaded with the *Garland*'s readers for their continued patronage, but to no avail. The decreased circulation necessarily led to a decrease in quality, more reprints, and less-experienced writers, and the decision was taken to discontinue publication with the December 1851 issue.

The only other periodical which contained music and was definitely printed by John Lovell was *The Snow-Drop; or, Juvenile Magazine* (1847-53) edited by Mrs Cushing and Harriet Cheney. The first series contained simple articles on nature, stories, and puzzles, but no music. With a change of publisher in 1850, and a new series, the editors proudly announced the inclusion of 'simple airs, accompanied by appropriate words ... A love of harmony is so desirable in young persons, and can be so easily cultivated, that we are happy to encourage the taste by furnishing this additional attraction to our pages.'[20] Thereafter, each monthly issue included a page of extremely simple music, but the magazine ceased publication in June 1853 without warning or explanation.

In 1840 Lovell printed the first known piece of sheet music in Canada. *The Merry Bells of England* by J.F. Lehmann, a choirmaster from Bytown (now Ottawa), is a single folio, comprising a simple but elegant title page displaying a variety of type, and one and a half pages of music for voice and piano with the first stanza underlaid, the second and third occupying the bottom half of page three. The layout and type of the music pages are identical to those in *The Literary Garland* except for the longer line of type, and the title page is a hint of the cover designs to come during the succeeding years leading up to Confederation. No sheet music between 1840 and 1847 has as yet been discovered, but the piece called *The Cathcart Polkas* by Henry Schallehn, printed by Lovell & Gibson in 1847, more than makes up for the lapse. Its glorious title page was offered as an example of what the printers were capable of in *Specimen of Printing Types and Ornaments, in Use at the Printing Office of Lovell & Gibson*.[21] This 118-page catalogue is a further indication of Lovell's commitment to excellence and of the expense he was prepared to assume to achieve, and to advertise, that excellence. Besides the cover to *The Cathcart Polkas* on a fold-out page, it includes three lines of melody from 'The Jersey Waltz' of unknown origin as a sample of the firm's music type and layout.

Twenty-five pieces of sheet music printed by John Lovell (or Lovell & Gibson, Montreal) have been found to date, all of them predating the early 1860s. Only one states explicitly 'imprimé et publié par John Lovell.' It is assumed that for all the others Lovell merely performed a printing service, either for the composer or, as in several cases, for other Canadian publishers who did not have a print shop capable of producing music.

L'Incantation de la Jongleuse by Ernest Gagnon
Photograph courtesy of the National Library of Canada

Souvenir de Venise by Ernest Gagnon
Photograph courtesy of the National Library of Canada

They represent a consistently high quality of music typography, but it is obvious from the more complex and ambitious works by Ernest Gagnon, such as the violin part from *L'Incantation de la jongleuse*, that the method had its limitations. And although some of the covers are extremely elaborate, others are restrained and simple. An example of middle-of-the-road elegance is *Souvenir de Venise*, also by Ernest Gagnon.

Lovell's music books and pamphlets are the most natural extension of his 'normal' stock output. Of the twenty-seven known titles,[22] twenty-one are sacred. These, though, range from English and French Protestant collections to English, French, Latin, Iroquois, and Algonkian Catholic hymnals, besides other liturgical works. Although Lovell was a member of the Church of England, he had many friends among the Catholic clergy, and needless to say, was fully bilingual.

To continue on a personal note, Lovell was also the father of ten children (all six sons went into the publishing business, four in the United States), a companionable husband who travelled extensively with his wife both in North America and in Europe, and an informed participant in current affairs. He never engaged in the retail trade or entered active politics, yet his position in the community and his wide circle of friends and business acquaintances would have added weight to his opinions, which he was seldom loath to express. For all his pugnaciousness and aggressiveness – evident in some of his pamphlets and articles[23] – he had a gift for recognizing and fulfilling the changing needs of his countrymen. In his eighty-third year he was attempting to raise money for his largest publishing venture ever, an eleven-volume set to be called 'Lovell's Gazeteer and History of Canada' which he expected would cost $200,000 to prepare: 'If undertaken, 110 editors will be employed on it, to ferrit [sic] out, *on the spot*, the history of every place having a name in Canada, from the landing of the *first white man* to the present time.'[24] He died five months later on 1 July 1893 without realizing this ambitious work.

The following lists of Lovell's music imprints will illustrate that he was not only the largest, most prolific printer in Canada in the nineteenth century, but also the most versatile and imaginative. Most important, however, he encouraged Canadian writers and composers to take their rightful places in our published legacy.

MUSIC IMPRINTS OF JOHN LOVELL FROM 1840 TO 1888

In two chronological lists, the following titles represent the known and reported Lovell imprints[25] in libraries and private collections. A location siglum[26] is given for those items not held at the National Library of Canada, indicating the copy examined. If the location is followed by an asterisk, that item was not seen personally by the writer but was described over the telephone by a staff member of the holding library. Unseen or 'lost' items are so indicated.

A dimension is given for each book or pamphlet to help the reader to visualize the physical item. This was not done for the sheet music since in the first place there is little variance (between 30 and 33 cm), and secondly many of the pieces are bound in albums and have been cropped.

Sheet music

1840

The Merry Bells of England. Song, by J.E. Carpenter. Composed, and respectfully dedicated to Major Daniel Bolton, R.L., Bytown, by J.F. Lehmann. Montreal: Printed by John Lovell, in the Office of the Literary Garland, Saint Nicholas Street. 1840 [3]p. (One of two earliest known sheet music publications; an extremely simple design but fine and elegant.)

1847

The Cathcart Polkas. Composed expressly for a ball given by the Countess Cathcart, performed by the Band of the Second Battalion Rifles, on the 10th Feb. 1847 and most respectfully dedicated to Her Ladyship, by Henry Schallehn. Montreal: Printed by Lovell & Gibson, St. Nicholas Street, 1847. 7p. QLB.* (Extremely elegant title page with a variety of lettering and the royal emblem at head of title.)

1847 or 1848

The Assembly Waltzes. Dedicated to the Ladies of Montreal. By H. Schallehn. Published by Mead, Brothers & Co., Notre Dame Street. Lovell & Gibson, Printers, St. Nicholas Street. [9]p. [1847-8?]. (Simpler but also very elegant title page printed in blue ink and delicately enframed music pages; signed and dated by owner: 'May 12th '48.')

Cellarius Waltz by H. Schallehn. (Skeletal description by private owner indicates Mead Brothers & Co. as publisher and Lovell & Gibson as printer; probably published same year as preceding piece.)

1848

Marche de la St. Jean Baptiste. Composée pour le piano forte, et très respectueusement dédiée au Président et aux membres de la Société St. Jean Baptiste de Montréal, par J.C. Brauneis. Montréal: De l'imprimerie de Lovell & Gibson, Rue St. Nicolas, et à vendre chez les libraires, 1848. [3]p. QMM/Music. (Elaborate cover with leafy corners; at head of title: small emblem of the rising sun behind mountain and cloud, surrounded by maple leaves and motto 'rendre le peuple meilleur.')

The Montreal Bazaar Polka. Composed and respectfully inscribed to Miss M. U[?]M . . . , by J.C. Brauneis. [Lovell & Gibson, 1848?] [3]p. QMM/Music. (Title page blank except for large bold title; all other information in caption title; attributed imprint and date based on similarity to previous piece.)

1858

La Prière des anges. Dédié à Son Eminence Monseigneur l'Archevêsque de Québec, par Ch. Wugk Sabatier. Propriétaire: A. Busch. Montréal: Des presses à vapeur de John Lovell, Bureau du 'Canada Directory,' Rue St. Nicolas, 1858. 11p. QMBN. (Copyright notice on verso of title page: 'Entered according to Act of Congress, A.D. 1858, by J. Schuberth & Co., in the Clerk's Office of the District Court of the Southern District of New York.')

Stadaconé. Danse sauvage pour piano. 'Le laid, c'est le beau . . . ' Victor Hugo. Par Ernest Gagnon. A Québec: Chez J. & O. Crémazie; J.T. Brousseau; A.H. Verret; et M. Carey. A Montréal: Chez J.W. Herbert, & Cie. Montréal: Des presses à vapeur de John Lovell, Bureau du 'Canada Directory,' Rue St. Nicolas, 1858. 8p.

1859

Les Echos du sanctuaire. Morceaux sacrés, composés par Ernest Gagnon. No. 1 *Ave Maria.* Montréal: Imprimé par John Lovell, Bureau du Canada Directory. Rue St. Nicolas, 1859. [8]p. QMBN. (Caption title: 'Ave Maria. Solo pour voix de *Baryton* ou *Contralto*, avec Choeur *ad libitum*.')

Form Riflemen Form! A patriotic song, by H. Prince. Montreal: Published by Henry Prince, 1859. John Lovell, Printer, St. Nicholas Street. [6]p. (At head of title: 'To the Volunteer Force of Canada,' probably referring to the additional militia companies being formed in the late 1850s.)

La Montréalaise, chant d'union. Dédié à tous les canadiens amis du progrès et de l'union. Musique de Charles Wugk Sabatier. Paroles de Felix Vogeli. Montréal: Des presses à vapeur de John Lovell, Bureau du 'Canada Directory,' Rue St. Nicolas, 1859. [4]p. (Verses 2 to 7 and chorus on last page; dated 'Montreal, 4 Novembre 1859'; stirring and patriotic text encourages French and English collaboration.)

Un Soir à bord. Quadrille, sur des airs populaires canadiens et français. Composé, et dédié à Pierre Fortin, Ecuyer, Commandant de 'La Canadienne,' par Ernest Gagnon. Montréal: Des presses à vapeur de John Lovell, Rue St. Nicolas, 1859. [7]p.

Therefore with Angels & Archangels, &c. The Sacramental Doxology. Montreal: J.W. Herbert & Co., 1859. Printed by John Lovell. [3]p.

1860

Les Couleurs du Canada. Bouquet offert à la Société St. Jean Baptiste de Montréal, le 24 juin 1858, par M. De Puisbusque. Musique d'Octave Peltier, dédiée aux élèves du Collège de Montréal de 1860. Colophon: Montréal: Des presses à vapeur de John Lovell. [1860?] [3]p. QMBN. (Title only on first page; dedication and author/composer information in caption; and printing details at foot of last page.)

Grande Marche Canadienne. Composée expréssément pour la Procession et dédiée à Son Altesse Royale le Prince de Galles par Charles W. Sabatier. Exécutée par la Bande de Prince. Montréal: Des presses à vapeur de John Lovell, Bureau du 'Canada Directory.' Rue St. Nicholas, 1860. [3]p. QMBN

Souvenir de Venise. Grand nocturne pour piano. Composé, et dédié à Théophile Hamel, Ecr., artiste peintre, par Ernest Gagnon. Montréal: Des presses à vapeur de John Lovell, Rue St. Nicolas, 1860. 11p. (Long runs in thirty-second notes and multiple leger lines accentuated the rigidity of type-set music; but a virtuoso display by the music compositor.)

1862

Le Bon Vieux Temps. Quadrille, sur des airs populaires, composé pour le piano par Joseph A. Defoy. Montreal: Imprimé et publié par John

Lovell, Rue St. Nicolas 1862. [7]p. QMBN. (Besides the often-used beaver on maple log emblem under the arched title, the extremely rich border includes the British coat of arms at each corner and several musical instruments along each side.)

L'Incantation de la jongleuse. Nocturne pour violon, avec accompagnement de piano, par Ernest Gagnon. Des presses à vapeur de John Lovell, Rue St. Nicolas, Montreal. [1862] 4p. and part. (At head of title: 'Hommage à M. Paul Létondal, artiste-musicien'; reviewed in *L'Echo du cabinet de lecture paroissial*, 15 March 1862, as a new publication.)

Sancta Maria, Succurre Miseris! Solo pour soprano, tenor ou baryton, composé et respectueusement dédié à Sa Grandeur Monseigneur l'Évèsque de Montréal, arrivant d'Europe; par son très humble et très obéissant serviteur Chs. Wh. Sabatier. (Quelques jours seulement avant sa mort! ...) Montréal: Imprimé par John Lovell, Rue St. Nicholas, 1862. [4]p. QMBN

Undated[27]

La Belle Canadienne polka. Par Charles Vilbon. [colophon] Imprimé par John Lovell, Rue St. Nicolas, Montreal. [5]p. QMBN. (Cover in pink paper, as in *L'Incantation de la jongleuse.*)

La Frontière. Chant national. Paroles de Jean Baptiste Bonhomme, musique de Guillaume Fleury d'Eschambault. Montreal: Des presses à vapeur du Canada Directory, Rue St. Nicolas. [3]p. (A new edition of the *Canada Directory* was published by Lovell in 1857; this imprint was a form of advertisement. An extremely defensive, anti-annexation text, reacting to a speech by Franklin's grandson at a recent congress in Montreal in which he suggested that there was only one people in America and that a border no longer existed between the two countries; succeeding stanzas show how the French-Canadians have maintained and guarded that border in spite of their treatment by the English Canadians.)

Nos jours de gloire. Chanson canadienne par Guillaume Fleury d'Eschambault. Montréal: De l'imprimerie de John Lovell, Rue St. Nicolas. [3]p. (Elaborately embellished lettering and small beaver on maple log. Poor quality paper. Words recall past glories such as Carillon and Chateauguay and offer hope that such days may come again.)

La Patrie avant tout. Chant dédié aux miliciens canadiens. Paroles de Ovide Dufresne. Musique de J.U. Marchand, organiste. [3]p.

QMBN. (No imprint or colophon, but type style, ornamentation, and layout suggest a Lovell work. First stanza speaks of the homeland being menaced by strangers and a call to defend and protect it to the death if necessary.)

Snow Shoe Galop. Composed expressly for the Montreal Snow Shoe Club, and respectfully dedicated to Miss Charlotte G. by Charles Emery St. Clair. Montreal: Published by J.W. Herbert & Co., 131 & 133 Notre Dame St. Printed by John Lovell, St. Nicholas Street. [6]p. QMBN. (Unusual title page layout: all lettering printed on the diagonal, stark and heavy, with small illustration of snow shoe race in progress in upper left quadrant.)

The Snow Shoe Tramp. A song of the North West. By Alfred Bailey. Music by Harold F. Palmer. Respectfully dedicated to the Snow Shoe Clubs of Canada. Montreal: Published by J.W. Herbert & Co., 131 & 133 Notre Dame St. Printed by John Lovell, St. Nicholas Street. [3]p. QMBN. (At head of music: 'As sung by the Members of the Aurora Snow Shoe Club of Montreal.' Arranged by Geo. W. Herbert.)

Books and pamphlets

1848

A Collection of Original Sacred Music. Arranged in full score with organ or piano forte accompaniment by F.H. Andrews, fourteen years organist of the Chapel of the Holy Trinity, Quebec. Montreal: Printed by Lovell and Gibson, St. Nicholas Street, 1848. 89p. 30 cm. QMM/Music.

A Selection from the Psalms of David for Morning and Evening Service. Together with chants and responses, edited by Major George Talbot. The music, arranged in score, in four parts, with accompaniment for the organ or piano-forte by W.H. Warren, organist of Christ's Church, Montreal. Montreal: Printed and published by Lovell & Gibson, St. Nicholas Street, 1848. 97p. 29 cm.

1851

Répertoire de l'organiste ou Receuil de chant-grégorien à l'usage des églises du Canada, dédié à sa grandeur l'illustrissime et reverendissime Monseigneur Ignace Bourget, Évêsque de Montréal, par J.B. Labelle, Organiste de l'église paroissiale de Notre-Dame de Montréal.

Montréal: De l'imprimerie de John Lovell, Rue St. Nicolas, [1851]. 128p. 32 cm. QMBN. (Date is take from the *imprimatur* and *avant-propos*; elaborate title page displays many varied types and flourishes enclosed by a simple double-ruled border with embellished corners.)

1860

Business Guide to the City of Montreal. With a Collection of Popular Songs. Montreal: Printed by John Lovell, St. Nicholas Street, 1860. 49[1]p. 16 cm. QMM/Lande. (An exemplary piece of advertising, not only for the paying subscribers whose full-page ads occupy the recto and are backed by a song containing both words and melody, but also for Lovell himself, who proudly proclaims his responsibility at the foot of each page, besides giving himself a double page ad on pp. 42-3.)

Kaiatonserase. Tsiok8e, hetsise8anenton ne Ra8enniio. Tiotiaki: Tehoristorarakon John Lovell, 1860. 132p. 18 cm. OTU.* (Music in square notation pp. 97-127; cover title reads: *Kaiatonserase, ou Vade-medum du chantre iroquois*; translation attributed to the Rev. James Brown.)[28]

1862

Cantiques à St. Joseph. Dédiés à la jeunesse canadienne, suivis de pieux exercices en l'honneur du même saint et des saints anges. Montréal: Imprimé par John Lovell, Rue St. Nicolas, 1862. 176p. 16 cm. QQLa.* (Music on pages 151-73: fifteen 'Motets à Saint Joseph.')

Chants évangéliques pour le culte public et pour l'édification particulière, à l'usage des églises du Canada. Avec musique à quatre parties. Montréal: Imprimé par John Lovell, 1862. 198p. 18 cm. QQLa.* (A French Protestant hymnal; preface is signed by L.E. Rivard, who was the compiler of the work and the composer of some of the hymns.)[29]

1864

Antiphonarium romanum juxta ritum sacrosanctae romanae ecclesiae. Marianopoli: Joan. Lovell typographus, Via S. Nicolai, MDCCCLXIV. 612, lviiip. 23 cm. (Square notation throughout, as in all the other Latin titles in this list.)

Graduale romanum juxta ritum sacrosanctae romanae ecclesiae. Marianopoli: Joan. Lovell typographus, Via S. Nicolai, MDCCCLXIV. 508, lxxvip. 23 cm. QQLa.*

Ienenrinekenstha kanesatakeha, ou Processional iroquois à l'usage de la mission du Lac des Deux Montagnes. [Tiotiaki: Tehoristorarakon John Lovell, 1864.] 108p. 18 cm. (Attributed to Jean-André Cuoq, priest of Saint-Sulpice. OONL copy lacks cover, which bears above imprint given in Pilling.)[30]

1865

Cantus ex graduali et antiphonario romano ordinarii facultate recognito desumptus. Marianopoli: Ex typographia J. Lovell, Via S. Nicolai, MDCCCLXV. 115, xliii, [3]p. 22 cm. (Four pages of text of a smaller size, 19 cm., tipped in between unpaginated imprimatur and index.)

A Help to Country Congregations in the Diocese of Quebec. Being the embodiment of the experience of a clergyman, who for many years trained and conducted a choir. Montreal: Printed by John Lovell, St. Nicholas Street, 1865. 40p. 17 cm. OTMCL*

Tsiatak nihonon8entsiake onk8e on8e akoiatonsera, ionterennaientak8a, teieri8ak8atha, iontaterihonnien-nitha, iontateretsiaronk8a, iakentasetatha, iekaratonk8atonkentisonha oni. Kahiaton oni tokara nikareenake erontaksneha. Kaneshatake tiakoson. *Le livre des Sept Nations, ou Paroissien iroquois,* auquel on a ajouté, pour l'usage de la mission du Lac des Deux-Montagnes, quelques cantiques en langue algonquine. Tiohtiake: Tehoristorarakon John Lovell, 1865. 460p. 19 cm. (Translation attributed to Jean-André Cuoq.)[31]

1867

Antiphonarium romanum juxta ritum sacrosanctae romane ecclesiae. Editio secunda, revisa et castigata. Marianopoli: Joan. Lovell typographus, Via S. Nicolai, MDCCCLXVII. 611, lviiip. 22 cm. OTREC*

Graduale romanum juxta ritum sacrosanctae romanae ecclesiae. Editio secunda, revisa et castigata. Marianopoli: Joan. Lovell typographus, Via S. Nicolai, MDCCCLXVII. 508, lxxxvip. 23 cm. QQLa*

Messe royale et messe du second ton. Montréal: Imprimé par John Lovell, Rue St. Nicolas, 1867. 8p. 22 cm. QMBN

1872

A Help to Country Congregations, being the embodiment of the experience of a clergyman, who for many years trained and conducted a choir in the Diocese of Quebec. 2nd edition. By request. Montreal: Printed by John Lovell, St. Nicholas Street, 1872. 43p. 17 cm. NSWA*

1873

Excerpta è cantibus liturgicis superiorum auctoritate recognita. Mariae immaculatae. Secunda editio. Marianopoli: Joan. Lovell, typographus, Via S. Nicolai, MDCCCLXXIII. 412, xxviii, xip. 21 cm.

Ocki aii masinaiganikikinohamagan, ou Nouveau syllabaire algonquin. Moniang: Takwabikickote endatc John Lovell, 1873. 64p. 15 cm. (*Haec dies* and *vidi acquam* in square notation with Ojibway-Algonquin text underlaid pp. 56-58. Translation attributed to Jean-André Cuoq.)[32]

1874

The Musical Miscellany: containing a choice selection of songs with music. County of Haldimand. April, 1874. O.L. Fuller, Montreal, publisher. Montreal: John Lovell, printer, 23 & 25 St. Nicholas Street, 1874. 32p. 22 cm.

1876

Bohrer's Automatic Piano Hand-Guide. Its construction, purpose and uses: together with numerous testimonials from the leading conservatories and most distinguished pianists and piano professors of Europe. Montreal: Lovell, 1876. 28p. 22 cm. (Both guides were reported to have been located at QQLa but could not be found there or at QQS. Bohrer was Mrs Lovell's piano teacher.)

Le Guide-mains automatique Bohrer. Sa structure, son but et son emploi: accompagné de nombreuses attestations des principaux conservatoires, des pianistes et des professeurs les plus distingués de l'Europe. Montréal: Lovell, 1876. 28p. 22 cm.

1877

Church Hymnal. Compiled and arranged by a committee appointed by the Bishop of Montreal. Rouses Point, N.Y.: John W. Lovell, publisher; and sold by John Lovell, Montreal, 1877. 585p. 21 cm. QMM/Music. (Committee statement and preface dated: 'Rouses Point, 21st Nov. 1877'; index to tunes: 579-85.)

1878

Cérémonial des soeurs des SS. Noms de Jésus et de Marie. Hochelaga, Montreal. Montréal: Compagnie d'impression et de publications Lovell, 1878. 33p. 23 cm. QMBN*

1879

A Pocket Song Book for the Use of the Students and Graduates of McGill College. Compiled and published by a student in arts. Montreal: Lovell Printing & Publishing Company, 1879. 34[2]p. 17 cm. QMM/Archives.* (This songbook contains the first known printing of *Alouette*.)[33]

1886

Church Hymnal. Compiled and arranged by a committee appointed by the Bishop of Montreal. Montreal and Rouses Point, N.Y.: Lovell Printing and Publishing Company, 1886. 578p. 21 cm. QMM/Music. (Committee statement dated: 'Montreal, 4th Dec. 1874.')

1888

The Office of Tenebrae. Transposed from the Gregorian chant into modern notation, by Rev. James A. McCallen, S.S., St. Patrick's Church, Montreal. Montreal: Printed by John Lovell & Son, 23 & 25 St. Nicholas Street, 1888. 142p. 25 cm. DCU-H.* (Another printing with identical title page has 88 [1]p. ACU.*)

Ordo ad visitandas parochias aliaque excerpta e pontificali romano. De licentia illustr.imi ac rev.imi DD. Fabre, Episcopi Marianopolitani edita. Marianopoli: Apud Fabre & Gravel, Bibliopolas, M.D.CCC.LXXXV. Colophon: Marianopoli, ex typis J. Lovell & Filiorum. 99p. 17 cm.

A Little Fantasy on J.P. Clarke's Ballad "Summer and Winter"

to Helmut

Clifford Ford

© Clifford Ford 1986

A Little Fantasy on 'Summer and Winter'   99

15.2.86

CARL MOREY

Orchestras and Orchestral Repertoire in Toronto before 1914

The nineteenth century was the century of the orchestra. Most of the repertoire that is still heard in our concert halls was composed and most of the great orchestras of today were established between the beginning of the nineteenth century and the outbreak of the war in Europe in 1914. However, despite the importance of orchestral developments in Europe and even in the United States, it was only slowly and with difficulty that the orchestra and its repertoire were established in Toronto. To be sure, Toronto had an active musical life, but it revolved around singing by both choirs and soloists. An instrumental ensemble was seldom more than an adjunct to voices, so that the development of an orchestra was inhibited throughout the nineteenth century. In 1892 Augustus Vogt, outstanding choral director and church organist that he was, could lament at length in the columns of the *Mail* about the fortunes of orchestral music, 'which is almost entirely absent from the city, not only in fact but also in consideration, so taken up it is with church music.'[1] Nevertheless, by 1900 Torontonians had heard a number of fine orchestras and a fair amount of symphonic literature, and if they still lacked an orchestra of their own, that would soon be remedied.

The instrumental ensemble that always did have a secure status in the city was the band, and it was important in both the social and musical life of the young city. Military bands were present in York (later Toronto) from the day Simcoe got off his ship in the bay in 1793 to establish his new town. In addition to their obvious obligations to the militia, the bands also functioned as social purveyors of dance music at balls, or as the core of whatever instrumental group could be mustered for the oratorios that were the mainstay of local large-scale performance activities from the middle of the century. Bands, therefore, were the instrumental ensembles most likely to be heard in Toronto. Their activities can be summed up by the advertisement that appeared in the *Globe* for a Promenade Concert in St Lawrence Hall, to be directed by Adam Maul: 'The Band will perform a selection of favourite pieces and arias from the most celebrated Operas, after which Dancing will commence.'[2] Winter concerts in halls and summer concerts in parks and private gardens provided a steady supply of light classics, and the tunes of operas and their overtures were best known to the local citizens through arrangements for wind band. Many local musicians appeared as conductors of band concerts, among them St George Crozier, J.D. Humphreys (who was better kown as a singer), Carl Peiler, Holt, John Carter (the organist at St James' Cathedral), and John Bayley. Italian opera provided an endless source of material, although occasionally something special, such as Beethoven's overture to *Egmont*, might appear. When a farewell concert was given in 1869 for Stoeckel, the bandmaster of the 29th Regiment, the composers represented on the program included Mendelssohn, Verdi, Rossini, Weber, Johann Strauss and Donizetti.[3]

From the end of the 1870s, the famous bands of the United States began to visit Toronto on a regular basis, and while they brought much light music, they also brought a high technical level of playing and sometimes more substantial programming than the local bandmasters offered. Patrick Gilmore brought his band many times after 1879, the last visits in 1895 and 1896 being conducted by Victor Herbert, as good an indication as any of the musical standards of such a group. The band included in its repertoire Wagner's overture to *Tannhäuser* and the *Ride of the Valkyries*, and the first movement of Schubert's 'Unfinished' Symphony; it appeared with vocal soloists for such pieces as the quartet from *Rigoletto* and the sextet from *Lucia di Lammermoor*; and it played at concerts of the Philharmonic Society to accompany the choir in excerpts from oratorios. Later on, Liberati, Creatore, and Duss brought their bands. When the Band of the Grenadier Guards visited in October 1904 for six concerts, the music at the matinee on 19 October was all by Wagner, and other visiting bands served up similar fare of popular, and often contemporary, classics.

The most famous of the visiting bands was that of John Philip Sousa, who first visited the city in 1893 just a year after the Sousa Band's first concert. Like all bands of the period, Sousa's played excerpts from the operas of Wagner, Bizet, and Mascagni, as well as older favourites. In 1907 the band introduced Richard Strauss's *Til Eulenspiegel* to the city. Sousa was ill on that occasion, and the band was directed by a former Toronto resident, the cornet soloist, Herbert L. Clarke.[4] Clarke also conducted in 1909 when the program included the prelude and Liebestod from *Tristan und Isolde*, as well as a piece by Rachmaninoff with the intriguing title

Prelude: Crime and Punishment.[5] By this time, however, orchestras had become a regular part of musical life in the city, and a local orchestra had even been successfully launched. Although bands retained their popular appeal, by the turn of the century they no longer figured as a kind of ersatz orchestra for the musical community.

The early excursions into instrumental repertoire by various concert societies in the city were erratic, and for some time orchestral music was chiefly in the hands of visitors, the first notable ones being the Germania Musical Society. The society was made up of a group of twenty-three young musicians from Berlin who, with a combination of self-interest and missionary zeal, decided both to make their fortunes in America and at the same time to improve the musical quality of the New World. From 1848 until they disbanded in 1854, they played hundreds of concerts in the United States and Canada, introducing much orchestral music for the first time.[6] Several of their members were to become major figures in the musical life of the cities where they eventually settled. The society first played in Toronto at the Royal Lyceum on 28 June 1850, when the program consisted of miscellaneous works, such as *Variations Burlesques on Carnival of Venice* for bassoon and the *Railroad Galop*, but also the overtures to *Zampa* by Hérold and *Der Freischütz* by Weber, and the wedding march from Mendelssohn's *Midsummer Night's Dream*. The public was urged to attend this performance with the assurance that it would be 'far superior to almost anything of this kind that has previously visited Toronto.'[7] They played four concerts in all and added to their local repertoire Weber's *Jubilee Overture* and the overtures to Mendelssohn's *Midsummer Night's Dream*, Flotow's *Alessandro Stradella*, Rossini's *William Tell*, Mozart's *Die Zauberflöte*, and Beethoven's *Fidelio*. From the point of view of the addition of significant works, the most novel selection was the scherzo and finale from Beethoven's *Fifth Symphony*. Mindful of their local audience, the Germanians also performed a 'Musical Panorama of Broadway, New York, a grand descriptive Potpourri, in which some Canadian Melodies will be introduced.'[8] The Germania Musical Society returned in June, 1852, but except for a few more overtures they added nothing more to the major symphonic repertoire other than to repeat the excerpts from Beethoven's *Fifth*.

It was twenty years before another comparable orchestral group appeared in the city, and that was the famous orchestra of Theodore Thomas, which appeared at the new Shaftesbury Hall on 3 October 1873. Thomas first took his orchestra on tour in 1869, the inauguration of what was to become a legendary pioneering series that crossed the continent. The program in Toronto included the *Leonora Overture No. 3* by

Beethoven, the Weber-Berlioz *Invitation to the Dance*, the Andante from Mozart's 'Jupiter' Symphony, the second *Hungarian Rhapsody* by Liszt, the overture to *Tannhäuser*, and Johann Strauss's *Wiener Blut*. There were also some vocal solos, and Vieuxtemps's *Fantasia on Slavonic Airs* for violin and orchestra. The review in the *Mail* was the occasion for the anonymous writer to deliver a homily on orchestral music, a commodity still somewhat foreign to Toronto audiences.

The grandest and most elaborate works of the great masters are written for full orchestra, because it was only through such a medium that men like Beethoven and Mozart could convey to the world an approximate idea of their inspirations. Orchestral playing carries the listener directly into the region of abstract musical emotion . . . A popular love for the orchestra is almost certain evidence of popular progress in music, and to foster this love in our midst should be the aim of the wealthy and influential, by doing all in their power to encourage the frequent visits of first-class instrumental societies.[9]

It might be observed as too typical of the city to look to the importation of foreign performers rather than to the development of a local instrumental society, although it must also be noted that even by 1900 Toronto had a population of only about 200,000, whereas the prominent eastern-US cities all had populations several times that.

Toronto also had to learn concert manners, and the above review goes on to report an unfortunate incident that required Thomas to instruct in behaviour as well as repertoire: 'The overture had scarcely been begun, when a disturbance was created by the arrival of a number of persons who had either the misfortune or the bad taste to arrive late. Theodore Thomas very properly signalled his band to cease playing, and did not allow them to recommence till quiet had been restored.' Although the newspaper reviews give no hint of it but rather indicate that there was a good audience and that the concert was a great success, the evening became legendary in some minds because of the poor attendance and the meagre receipts. The embarrassment of the event would be recalled years later when a visit by Thomas and his orchestra was received with enthusiasm.[10]

The amateur Rochester Philharmonic Orchestra from across Lake Ontario visited in 1881 under their conductor, Henry Appy, with a program that consisted mostly of miscellaneous violin and cello solos, although they did play the overtures to *Dinorah* and *William Tell* and the Allegro and Scherzo from the *Symphony No. 4* by Niels Gade. Apparently the attendance at the Friday night concert was small, no doubt because most of the city was busy welcoming home a local hero, the world-famous sculling champion Ned Hanlan. A good audience was guaranteed for the Saturday matinee by the announcement that 'Mr. Edward Hanlan, Champion Sculler of the World, will occupy a box.'[11]

If Toronto had been cool to the Theodore Thomas Orchestra and the Rochester Philharmonic, the response to the announced visit by Leopold Damrosch and his Grand Symphony Orchestra in December 1882 was so great that an extra performance had to be added.[12] The programs included such things as Berlioz's *Rakoczy March* and two Hungarian dances by Brahms, but Damrosch also played the overtures to *Oberon* and *Tannhäuser*, as well as Beethoven's *Leonora Overture No. 3* and a piece by Wagner only a few months old, the 'Prelude to his new opera Parsifal.' Beethoven's *Fifth Symphony* and the funeral march from the *Eroica* were played, and two symphonic poems by Liszt, neither of which was identified by name. When Damrosch and his orchestra returned a few months later in May 1883, advertisements for the two concerts carried an approach to marketing that would be more familiar a century later: 'Arrangements have been made with the Grand Trunk Railway by which return tickets will be issued at a fare and a third for parties of eight or more who show tickets for these concerts. They may order seats by telegraph or mail.'[13] The major work was again Beethoven's *Fifth Symphony*. There were also soloists this time, the soprano Martinez, the mezzo-soprano Sofia Scalchi, and the great Venezuelan pianist Teresa Carreno. There were arias from *Mignon*, *La Cenerentola*, *Le Nozze di Figaro* ('Voi che sapete'), *Aïda*, *Tannhäuser* (Elizabeth's prayer), *Der fliegende Holländer* (Senta's ballad), and a duet from *Semiramide*. The orchestra also played the overture to *Tannhäuser*, the prelude to Act III of *Lohengrin*, and the 'Forest Murmurs' from *Siegfried*. Carreno was the soloist in the *Hungarian Fantasy* by Liszt, and at the second concert she joined forces with the young Toronto pianist and pupil of Liszt, Waugh Lauder. Together they played Schumann's *Andante and Variations*, opus 46, for two pianos and orchestra.

For the remaining years of the nineteenth century and well into the twentieth, visiting orchestras came to the city regularly and were largely responsible for the gradual introduction of the great orchestral repertoire. They often appeared in conjunction with local choral societies, whose abilities and ambitions now far exceeded the quality of the instrumental collaboration they could expect from Toronto players. Carl Zerrahn, one of the original Germanians of forty years before, returned with his Boston Festival Orchestra in November 1890 for two concerts with Herbert Torrington's Philharmonic Society. It was also under the auspices of the Philharmonic Society that Theodore Thomas returned to the city in June

1891 with a program that included the now familiar *Fifth Symphony* of Beethoven as well as the *Piano Concerto in E Minor* by Chopin with Rafael Joseffy as soloist. The Theodore Thomas Orchestra, under its founder and – from 1905, when it was the Chicago Orchestra – under Frederick Stock, became regular visitors, both in their own concerts and in conjunction with choral societies. It should be understood that whenever orchestras visited as guests of choruses, they always played instrumental pieces and usually gave a concert or two devoted to orchestral music in addition to accompanying the choir.

In the next few years, the Theodore Thomas Orchestra gave the city performances of such works as Dvorak's *Symphonic Variations* and Liszt's *Piano Concerto in A Major* with Busoni as soloist (December 1892), Dvorak's *Symphony 'From the New World,'* Smetana's *The Moldau*, and Tchaikovsky's *Variations*, opus 55 (March 1895), Tchaikovsky's *Sixth Symphony*, Smetana's *Sarka*, and Brahms's *Variations on the Chorale 'St Anthony'* (January 1896). After the 1895 concert one reviewer recalled for his readers the disastrous first appearance of the orchestra in 1873 but reported that on this occasion 'three thousand people attended' at Massey Hall.[14]

Walter Damrosch brought the New York Symphony Orchestra to Toronto in 1892, and that orchestra too appeared on numerous occasions. The Pittsburgh Symphony Orchestra came regularly from 1903, first under Victor Herbert and after 1905 under Emil Paur. The orchestras of Cincinnati and Boston and the New York Philharmonic under Josef Stransky also played from time to time.

One of the more interesting visitors over a short term was Anton Seidl, who had been Wagner's assistant at Bayreuth and had been brought to America to succeed Leopold Damrosch as conductor of the German repertoire at the Metropolitan Opera in New York. In November Seidl brought to Toronto an unidentified orchestra probably made up of his players from the Metropolitan, since a disastrous fire in the opera house had caused the cancellation of the 1892-3 season. The program for 23 November, however, was not at all operatic, and Seidl finally added Beethoven's *Sixth Symphony*, the 'Pastoral,' to Toronto's still limited experience of those works. When he returned in April 1893, Seidl was officially conducting the Metropolitan Opera Orchestra and had a group of singers with him, so he was able to perform the Wagnerian repertoire for which he was so noted. The first concert was devoted entirely to Wagner and included the overture and bacchanale from *Tannhäuser*, with chorus, the prelude and Act II duet from *Lohengrin*, the prelude and Liebestod from *Tristan und Isolde*, and the prelude and glorification from *Parsifal*, as well as orchestral and vocal excerpts from *Die Walküre, Die Meistersinger*, and

Siegfried. The second performance on 22 April was more varied and included *Les Préludes* by Liszt and the 'Flower Maiden' scene from *Parsifal*. When Seidl returned in October 1896 with a popular program the audience was very small and a matinee performance had to be cancelled. The chief novelty was the *Piano Concerto in G Minor* by Saint-Saëns, with Julia Rive-King as soloist, the first of that composer's works to be heard in Toronto.

Over the next decade, up to the outbreak of the war in 1914, the orchestral repertoire heard in Toronto slowly expanded. The establishment of a permanent Toronto orchestra in 1907 altered the situation significantly, but visiting orchestras continued to make important contributions. Among the Beethoven symphonies, the *Fifth* was the only one to have repeated hearings. After Seidl's introduction of the *Sixth* in 1892, Damrosch added the *Seventh* (1892), and Victor Herbert the *Third* (1903) and *Eighth* (1904), and Paur conducted the *Ninth* with the Mendelssohn Choir in 1906. The same composer's piano concertos were seldom heard: only No. 4 in 1896 with Joseffy as soloist with the Buffalo Symphony Orchestra, and No. 5 in 1905 with Paur as soloist. Brahms was also slow to have a hearing. After Thomas introduced the *Variations* in 1896, it was several years before the symphonies were heard. Damrosch conducted the *First Symphony* in 1907, and Paur performed it in 1910, but it was Frederick Stock with the Theodore Thomas Chicago Orchestra who played the other major orchestral pieces: the *Academic Festival Overture* in 1908, the *Second Symphony* in 1912 and the *Fourth Symphony* in 1914. He also conducted the *German Requiem* in 1908 with the Mendelssohn Choir.

Gradually other works that have since become standard were heard: the three last symphonies and *Romeo and Juliet* of Tchaikovsky, Berlioz's *Symphonie fantastique* (Damrosch 1907), Franck's *Symphony in D Minor* (Stock 1908), and Schumann's *Symphony No. 4* (Cincinnati Orchestra under Vander Stucken 1903). There were also works now regarded as curiosities, such as Raff's *'Lenore' Symphony* (Damrosch 1892) and *'Im Walde' Symphony* (Thomas 1904), and Goldmark's *'Rustic Wedding' Symphony* (Damrosch 1907). Two conductors led works of their own: Paur his *Symphony 'In der Natur'* in 1909, and Stock his *Symphony in C Minor* in 1910.

It is difficult to remember now how seldom Mozart was played until fairly recently. Paur conducted excerpts from *König Thamos* in 1909, but it was the new Toronto Symphony Orchestra under Welsman that performed the *Symphony in E Flat* in 1911. Richard Strauss, by contrast, was gaining a popularity similar to Wagner's. Victor Herbert conducted *Don Juan* in 1904, and Paur played the love scene from *Feuersnot* in 1906. Stock added *Tod und Verklärung* and the *Serenade* for wind instruments in 1908 (the latter on a program with Hugo Wolf's *Italian Serenade*), and the Dance of the Seven Veils from *Salome* in 1909. In the same year Paur introduced the authentic version of *Til Eulenspiegel*, two years after the Sousa Band had played it.

Along with Strauss, the other contemporary composer who was well represented was Edward Elgar. His *Cockaigne Overture* was conducted by Herbert in 1903. Paur added *Sea Pictures* in 1905, Stock *Enigma Variations*, and Damrosch the *Symphony in A Flat* in 1909. The *Introduction and Allegro* was heard under Stock in 1914.

Although the quartets of Debussy and Ravel became popular in the city, the orchestral music was not to be heard for many years. Stock played the *Prélude à l'après-midi d'un faune* in 1909 with great success and it was subsequently heard from time to time. The Toronto Symphony Orchestra played the *Petite Suite* in 1913. Only the *Mother Goose Suite* represented Ravel in a performance under Damrosch in 1913. Stransky conducted Dukas's *Sorcerer's Apprentice* in 1914. It was not until after 1918 that what might generally be called 'modern' music began to be heard with anything like regularity, and even then such works were more likely to be heard at chamber music concerts than at orchestra concerts.[15]

Among the visiting orchestras, two from Europe should be noted. On 15 March 1901, Hans Winderstein conducted two concerts with the Leipzig Philharmonic Orchestra. Not to be confused with the famous Gewandhaus Orchestra, this ensemble had been founded by Winderstein expressly to give 'popular' concerts, popular in the sense not of repertoire so much as of audience. They played the usual overtures, as well as the *Fifth Symphony* of Beethoven, Tchaikovsky's *Concerto No. 1 in B Flat Minor* for piano, and Saint-Saëns' *Concerto No. 3* for violin. On 25 April 1912, one of the greatest conductors of the day, Arthur Nikisch, directed the London Symphony Orchestra in a concert that included Tchaikovsky's *'Pathétique' Symphony*.

If foreign orchestras finally established much of the major symphonic repertoire, Toronto had to assume its own responsibility for such repertoire if it was to flourish as a musical community. It did so only slowly and with difficulty. Occasions in the nineteenth century when instrumental music was performed by local musicians were sporadic, and the record of activity is scanty. Attempts to establish a musical society began at least by the mid-1830s, when 'the gentlemen Amateurs of the Toronto Musical Society will perform several vocal and instrumental pieces of music.'[16] Such groups were the principal concert organizations for at least the next fifty years and specialized in mixed programs of songs, glees, and instrumental solos, chiefly fantasias and variations.

The first organization to be formed with somewhat higher ambitions was the Toronto Philharmonic Society, which, under the name Toronto Choral Society, had its first organizational meeting on 7 April 1845.[17] The accepted format was adhered to, but under the musical direction of James Paton Clarke[18] the short-lived society did include the beginnings of symphonic repertoire in the city. They played a number of overtures, including *Der Freischütz* by Weber, *La Muette de Portici* and *Fra Diavolo* by Auber, *Semiramide*, *Il Barbiere di Siviglia*, and *L'Italiana in Algeri* by Rossini, *Zampa* by Hérold, *Prometheus* and *Coriolanus* by Beethoven, and notably *Don Giovanni* by Mozart. They also included in the opening concert, 26 December 1845, the *Symphony No. 36* by Beethoven – presumably the *Second Symphony*, opus 36. At the second concert on 29 January 1846, there is an even more ambiguous reference to '*Symphony, Grand*' by Beethoven. Mozart was almost never performed in the city throughout the century, and the overture to *Don Giovanni* would be noteworthy in itself, but at the concert on 23 April 1847 he was further represented by an unidentified symphony, as far as can be ascertained the only such work by Mozart played in the city until the early twentieth century. For this concert the instrumental group included the Band of the 81st Regiment, whose director was St George Crozier.

There is an intriguing reference to 'an efficient orchestra, which will be conducted in the Germanic style' at a concert given by Henry Schallehn in 1851, but there was no indication of what was conducted or of the size and quality of the instrumental ensemble.[19] At Schallehn's 6 March concert of the same year the program of oratorio excerpts was varied by a symphony by Beethoven, but positive identification is lacking. On 27 February 1854, the first and almost the only Haydn symphony to be given throughout the nineteenth century was the *Children's (Toy) Symphony*, although modern scholarship has demonstrated that even that was not by Haydn but by Leopold Mozart. The Philharmonic Society also included an unidentified symphony of Beethoven's at a concert on 25 April 1854. The same society gave a symphony by Andreas Romberg and the funeral march from Beethoven's *'Eroica' Symphony* at a concert on 27 February 1855. When St George Crozier conducted the Metropolitan Choral Society at a concert in 1858, he included the overtures to *Die Zauberflöte* and *Fidelio*. For the modern reader it is difficult to interpret a remark by the newspaper reviewer as to whether it indicates the high level of competence of the players or the indulgence of the listeners: 'The overtures, under the able conductorship of Mr. Crozier, were well executed, and the last being played at sight, a better proof of the proficiency of the orchestra could not be required.'[20]

The instrumental ensembles, excepting the military bands, had all been *ad hoc* groups assembled for particular concerts, usually in support of choral concerts in the same way the visiting American orchestras were often to serve in future years. It appears that the first attempt to gather players for rehearsal on a regular basis was made in 1867 by George Strathy, a prominent Toronto musician and professor of music at the University of Trinity College: 'New Musical Society. – We would remind the members of the musical profession, bands and amateurs who can perform on an orchestral instrument, of the meeting to-night, at 8 o'clock in the Mechanics' Institute, called by Dr. Strathy, with the view to forming a society for the performance of orchestral music.'[21] The society played sporadically at concerts, in 1869 as the Toronto Amateur Musical Union and in 1870 as the Toronto Musical Union and the Toronto Orchestral Union. With the latter name, it was conducted by J. Davenport Kerrison in 1873 at concerts that continued the modest repertoire of overtures and *potpourri*. Kerrison went to New York in 1874, and that seems to have ended the Orchestral Union. In 1880 the Toronto Opera Company Orchestra played at a couple of concerts, including one on 17 September 1880 that included Haydn's *'Surprise' Symphony*.

In 1881 there was yet another attempt to put the performance of orchestral music on a regular footing: 'Toronto Orchestral Association. – At a meeting held last week at the residence of Mr. Robert Marshall, King street West, it was decided to form an orchestral organization for the study and practice of orchestral works exclusively ... The studies of the Association are to be under the direction of Mr. Bayley, the talented bandmaster of the Queen's Own ... It is expected that eighteen or twenty will be present at the first rehearsal to-morrow evening.'[22] The Orchestral Society survived until the fall of 1881, but then it too disappears from the record.

Having been unsuccessful with his orchestra, Strathy took up the fight for orchestral repertoire at the piano. He organized the Toronto Pianoforte Players' Classical Club and for two years gave performances of great symphonic literature in arrangements for multiple players from three to twelve in number. In this way he was responsible for performances of Beethoven's *Second, Fourth,* and *Fifth* symphonies and the overtures to *Egmont, Die Zauberflöte, Prometheus, La Clemenza di Tito,* and *Semiramide,* among others. The performers were all young lady amateurs, more than likely Strathy's students.

Herbert Torrington, who had been a force in Toronto music since 1873, conducted an orchestral concert at the Horticultural Gardens on 9 May 1882 that far exceeded the ambitions of any previous local instrumental group. There were the usual miscellaneous pieces, but there were also movements (unspecified) from Mozart's *'Jupiter' Symphony*, the overture to *Oberon*, and the overture and ballet music from *Preciosa* by Weber. There was a performance of the *'Emperor' Concerto* played by Waugh Lauder, the first such work of Beethoven's to be heard in the city. The reviewer for the *Globe* on 10 May 1882, was puzzled by the concerto: 'Mr. W.W. Lauder then appeared in a concerto from Beethoven, which he had played in Leipzig and Weimar. Mr. Lauder is a most artistic manipulator of the piano, and to those who can appreciate and understand high class music, to hear him is a pleasure.'

The increased orchestral interest in Toronto, nourished by local musicians as well as the American orchestras that were beginning to appear, was probably the inspiration for a long article that appeared in the *Globe* on 23 April 1883, calling for the establishment of an orchestra.

> Mr. John Hague, to whose intelligent advocacy the cause of musical culture in Toronto owes much, has issued a circular containing a strong plea for the establishment of a local orchestral society. Symphony music is always attractive when well rendered, and the greatest musical want of Toronto at present is the material for a permanent association capable of rendering the works of the great masters in this department of art. This want has been keenly felt in connection with the performances of the Philharmonic and Choral societies, both of which have been compelled to depend largely on instrumentalists from outside places in Canada or the neighbouring States. A good local orchestra would be of great aid in the effective rendering of oratorios and cantatas, and would be the means of familiarizing the Toronto public with a class of music which is far from being as familiar as it should be.

Torrington pressed on with his attempts, although it was 1887 before he sought to establish an orchestra on a regular basis under the name Torrington's Amateur Orchestra. The high standard of the 1882 concert was never again realized, and although Torrington performed many major oratorios, the orchestral repertoire under his direction only occasionally rose above the trivial. He reorganized the ensemble in 1891 as the Toronto Orchestral School, but with no more substance. In 1893 the Toronto Permanent Orchestral Association was announced with $5000 guaranteed funding, and with Torrington as conductor.[23] Despite the apparent financial support, nothing more is heard of the association. When Torrington conducted an orchestra at the opening concerts of Massey Hall in June 1894, the reviews in the *Mail* were very critical of the low calibre of orchestral playing. By that time the visiting orchestras had provided opportunities to hear what first-class playing could be. Torrington continued with the determination that had made him the most prominent musician in the city, although that prominence was at least partly based as much on persistence as on artistry. In 1900 he was rehearsing at his College of Music the Toronto Orchestral Society, an organization formed 'to study the symphonies, overtures and other works of the great composers.'[24] The society's main function, it turned out, was to accompany student concerts at the college.

Through the 1880s other attempts to found an orchestra were made by the violinist Heinrich Klingenfeld and by the music dealer and bandmaster Thomas Claxton. What might have most justified high expectations was the Toronto Symphony Orchestra established by Francesco D'Auria in 1890. D'Auria was an outstanding musician with wide experience, but his enterprise, like the others, was underfinanced and lasted only a season with no significant contributions to repertoire. The name 'Toronto Symphony Orchestra' was taken up again for an organization to be conducted by Humfrey Anger in 1897 and by another under James Dickinson in 1901. Dickinson's group did give a public concert, but it was possibly the first organization to experience serious union problems. It was reported that 'several of its best players seceded at the last moment, on the ground, it is understood, that they could not associate on the same platform with non-union men.' Furthermore, 'the attendance was not encouraging.'[25]

As it turned out, the most promising event for the future of a Toronto orchestra was the opening in 1887 of the Toronto Conservatory of Music. As early as 1889 there was a rehearsal of a conservatory orchestra under Giuseppe Dinelli.[26] Bertha Drechsler-Adamson, a violinist of distinction, also conducted a string orchestra at the conservatory from about this time, and she was influential as both instrumentalist and conductor in establishing a high standard of ensemble playing. The turning point came in 1906, when the Toronto pianist Frank Welsman returned home from Europe and joined the teaching staff of the conservatory. It was reported that his condition for joining the conservatory was that a regular orchestra be formed with himself as conductor.[27] Until then the orchestra had been an amateur group functioning with the school, but during the winter the Board of Directors announced a new policy of engaging professional musicians for the conservatory orchestra and paying them for rehearsals.[28] On 11 April 1907 the Toronto Conservatory Symphony Orchestra was launched under Welsman's direction at Massey Hall. The choice of music for the first program was not auspicious, consisting as it did of various short popular pieces, three movements from Beethoven's *First*

Symphony, and an entr'acte from Schubert's *Rosamunde*. The conservatory's first graduate, J.D.A. Tripp, was the soloist in Liszt's *Hungarian Fantasy*. Newspaper reports were uniformly enthusiastic, and the orchestra never lost the support of the press. Indeed, over the next few years there always seems to be an element of surprise that Toronto has finally been able to assemble an orchestra on a regular basis. On 9 December 1908 the *Mail* could confidently state that 'the Toronto Symphony Orchestra has in less than three years accomplished marvels and hereafter it is an assured factor in the musical development of the city.' A couple of months later, on 20 April 1909, the *Globe* paid the orchestra the ultimate compliment when it found it equal to the choirs in the city: 'The audience dispersed with the elated conviction that Toronto has at last got an orchestra that has reached the standard of the excellence of our best choral societies.'

The first full season was launched in December 1907. The name still included 'Conservatory,' although a review in *Musical Canada* in January 1908 refers to the 'Toronto Symphony Orchestra.' In its November issue *Musical Canada* could note that the conservatory had retired from management of the orchestra and that it was henceforth to be managed by a citizens' committee. The change in management also brought about a change in policy in the seating arrangement. Mrs Drechsler-Adamson had served as leader of the first violins, a remarkable fact since prejudice against women playing in orchestras was then virtually total and would remain so for many years to come. No doubt Toronto simply did not have enough male players to be able to ignore the fine women players in town, especially someone of the quality of Mrs Adamson. With the season of 1908-9, however, Frank Blachford became the concertmaster, and although Mrs Adamson continued to share the first desk she fell before the policy of reorganization that placed women players on the inside row of the violins rather than in the outer row, where they were too obviously exposed to public view.[29]

At the concert of 9 April 1908 the orchestra established its credentials by having its first international guest, Vladimir de Pachmann, who was the soloist in Chopin's *Piano Concerto in F Minor*. The program also included the *Symphony in F*, opus 9, by Hermann Goetz. According to the list of musicians in the program at that concert, there were fifty-nine players. The outbreak of war in 1914 was effectively to end the activities of the orchestra just as it was establishing itself in the city with the same reputation that had previously been reserved for the choral organizations, but during those six seasons it contributed significantly to Toronto's knowledge of orchestral repertoire. The orchestra included in its concerts such works as Schubert's *Symphony in B Minor*, the *'Scottish' Symphony* of Mendelssohn, the *Third, Fifth, Seventh* and *Eighth* symphonies of Beethoven, the last three symphonies of Tchaikovsky, and Mozart's *Symphony in E Flat* and *Symphony in G Minor*. With the Elgar Choir of Hamilton it played Verdi's *Requiem*, and with the Sheffield Choir of England it performed Elgar's *Dream of Gerontius* in both Montreal and Toronto with the composer as guest conductor.

In the concerto repertoire the Toronto Symphony Orchestra made contributions that were distinctively different from what the visiting orchestras offered. Although the visitors sometimes brought distinguished partners for a concerto performance, the Toronto Symphony Orchestra's policy of having a famous soloist at each concert meant that for the first time Torontonians had a steady diet of concertos. Fritz Kreisler introduced Beethoven's violin concerto in 1910, to be followed by Eugène Ysaÿe in 1913 and Carl Flesch in 1914. Kreisler also played Brahms's violin concerto in 1913. Kathleen Parlow and Mischa Elman both played Tchaikovsky's violin concerto, as well as other works. Elman appeared with the orchestra in the Mendelssohn concerto and in Saint-Saëns' *Concerto in B Minor*, and Parlow played Bruch's *Concerto in G Minor*. Jan Kubelik also played the Mendelssohn concerto, and Efrem Zimbalist was the soloist in Lalo's *Symphonie espagnole*. Among the pianists, Wilhelm Bachaus performed Beethoven's *'Emperor' Concerto* in 1912. Josef Hofmann played Tchaikovsky's *Concerto in B Flat Minor* and Rubinstein's in D minor, the latter work also being the vehicle for the debut with the orchestra of the young Toronto pianist Ernest Seitz. Teresa Carreno played MacDowell's *Second Piano Concerto*. The orchestra had something of a *coup* when it obtained the Russian pianist Sergei Rachmaninoff just two weeks after his American debut. When Rachmaninoff appeared with the orchestra on 18 November 1909, he was the soloist in his own *Second Piano Concerto in C Minor*, a performance that inspired the reviewer next day in the *Globe* to write with unwitting irony, 'The concerto is a work that one would like to hear a second time.'

There were also frequent vocal soloists, of the same fame and calibre as the instrumentalists, who invariably sang opera arias: Johanna Gadski, Ernestine Schumann-Heink, Clara Butt, Emmy Destinn, Lillian Nordica, Alma Gluck, Louise Homer, and Leo Slezak.

In its issue of October 1914 *Musical Canada* announced that 'the promoters of the Toronto Symphony Orchestra have, in view of the present unfavourable conditions, decided to abandon the proposed concerts of the organization for this season.' Except for a couple of concerts to raise money for the war effort, the Toronto Symphony Orchestra was now defunct. It had, though, proved that Toronto could produce and support an orchestra of its own, and the memory of that accomplishment remained as a basis for establishing a new orchestra in 1923. By that time the domination of the city's musical life by the choral societies had waned, and the orchestra would finally take its place at the centre of Toronto's musical life.

ELAINE KEILLOR

Musical Activity in Canada's New Capital City in the 1870s

One hundred years before the Music Division of the National Library was established, Ottawa was adjusting to the fact that it was now the capital of a fledgling country called Canada whose domains 'from sea to sea' were still mainly empty wilderness. Writing in 1871, Charles Roger pointed out the rapid changes that had taken place:

All classes of the people are being more or less influenced by the great change which has come over Ottawa since the advent of the seat of Government. Fine shops, vying with those of Montreal or New York in the character of their goods have sprung up; societies for the improvement of knowledge in literature and science have been instituted; agreeable promenades have been constructed; terraces of superior dwellings have taken the place of wooden buildings without eaves-troughs or waterspouts, and all the banks are doing business in elegant and substantial stone structures.[1]

Nevertheless Roger went on to comment: 'Ottawa is, we repeat, making rapid progress, covering a space of three miles in length and about as many in breadth but having no good place of amusement – no theatre, nor any proper Music Hall, and a wretchedly ugly looking City Hall.'[2] Through the available newspapers of the 1870s, the *Ottawa Citizen* (OC) and the *Ottawa Free Press* (OFP), this 'rapid progress' can be traced, to show that a relatively thriving musical life existed in Ottawa by 1880.[3]

At the beginning of the decade music-making took place in ways already established by the end of the 1860s and typical of many Canadian communities of around 21,000 at the time. There were good fiddlers, such as the one Lett described in verse:

> From violin of Robinson Lyon,
> Who drew such music from its strings
> Scotch reels, strathspeys and highland flings,
> And Irish jigs in variation,
> As made one feel that 'all creation'
> Could scarcely match his wizard spell,
> 'Twas he that played the fiddle well![4]

Itinerant musicians roamed Ottawa's streets. In August 1872 an organ grinder and his monkey were being appreciated in Lower Town (*OFP* 22.9.1874). The *Ottawa Free Press* commented on two travelling musicians: 'A blind man led by a little girl ... are at present wandering through our streets ... The old man plays on the accordion and sings arias from various operas. The child accompanies him on what is known as the French fiddle, and she sings ... They draw a large crowd' (*OFP* 22.9.1874). A larger group playing for coins was Krieger's German Band from New York (*OFP* 28.8.1872). In 1877 the *Ottawa Free Press* noted the larger than usual number of itinerant musicians on the streets travelling in pairs such as a 'harper and violinist' (*OFP* 17.4.1877).

Another activity of earlier decades that had spawned music-making and musical appreciation in English-speaking areas of North America was the singing school. Professor Workman had one in the New Edinburgh schoolroom in Ottawa as late as 1869-70 (*OC* 31.1.1870). In September 1872 H.G. Tiepke announced the organization of an elementary singing-school class for gentlemen (*OC* 13.9.1872). Most if not all repertoire used in a singing class during the nineteenth century consisted of hymns and the occasional anthem. Thus, even though the singing school was largely a social activity rather than a religious one, it did have links with the churches, which instigated most of the events containing music in Ottawa in the early 1870s. The *Ottawa Citizen* reported the Congregational Church Soirée as having included readings, duets, and anthems by the choir led by the organist, Eliza Smith (*OC* 17.1.1871). Local musicians were requested to offer a selection at such events and also at similar evenings organized by the various patriotic societies: the St George's, St Andrew's, and St Patrick's societies and the Institut canadien français (French Canadian Institute).

The highlight of each year for each of these patriotic societies was the celebration of its patron saint. Early in the decade the selections chosen were specifically tied to the ethnic group involved. For instance, the contents of the St George's Day celebrations in 1870 had an overwhelming English flavour:

After the parade, the Christ Church choir under church organist, Mr. Fripp, performed. In the evening a Grand Concert was held at Her Majesty's Theatre with a medley of English Ayres played by Gowan's Band.

The Flag that Braved a Thousand Years;
England Yet by Mrs. Mike;
Fair Flora Decks, trio by Messrs. Brewer, Horsley and Timms;
Pianoforte solo by Miss Smith;
Death of Lord Nelson, by Mrs. Brewer;
Life's Burden, glee by Messrs. Horsley, Brewer and Rowe;
Flag of the Free, by Miss McCarthy;
Horse Flesh Banquet, comic ditty by Corporal Putman.

INTERMISSION

Band selections;
England, Europe's Glory, by Mr. Brewer;
Slave Ship, by Mrs. Miles;
British Navy, by Mr. Horsley;
Qui Vive, duet by Misses Brandhort and Armstrong;
The Gypsies' Laughing Trio, by Messrs. Horsley, Rowe and Brewer;
Sing Me an English Song, by Miss McCarthy;
My Story, it is true, by Corporal Putman   (OC 25.4.1870)

This type of exclusive viewpoint for each group rapidly broke down during the decade as Ottawans began to see their destiny in larger terms than just Irish, Scottish, English, or French-Canadian. Such changes could have been due in part to the growing presence of other ethnic groups such as Germans, but in any case it soon became the norm to see French-Canadian music and soloists included in the St Patrick's or St Andrew's Day presentations and Irish songs sung during St George's Day celebrations. The French Canadian Institute seems to have led the way, as their presentation on 6 December 1871 included the decidedly English farce *Box and Cox* along with Offenbach's operetta *Lischen et Fritzschen*, done in French (OFP 7.12.1871). The program of the St Patrick's Literary Association of Ottawa for 18 March 1878 was as follows:

Fantasia on Irish Airs – GGFG Band
Piano solo: *Campanella* (Wollenhaught) [i.e., Wollenhaupt] – Miss Scott
Song: *The Day When Ya'll Forget Me Thomas* – Mr. Brophy
Clarinet solo: Andante and Polacca – Clappe
Song: *The Angel Whisper* (Lover) – Miss Retter

Duet: *La rencontre des amis* – Mesdames Gelinas and Lapierre
Piano solo: *Le cri de délivrance* (Gottschalk) – Sig. Loredan
Song: *The Irish Oak* (Maugan) – Mr. Sinclair
Song: *The Angel's Serenade* (Brege) – Miss Carrier
Song: *When the Tide Comes In* (Millard) – Mr. O'Brien
Song: *Am I Remembered in Erin* (McGee) – Miss Daugherty of Toronto
Song: Rondo Finale from *Lilly of Kilarney* – Mme Gelinas
Song: *The Nightingale's Thrill* – Miss Bell (*OC* 12.3.1878)

BANDS

Most of these patriotic events had at least one band in attendance, and indeed, excepting only church music for those who attended religious services, band music had been for some time the most prevalent and influential form of music-making in Ottawa. The Bytown Amateur Band was active in 1842 and a brass band had been formed by Paul Favreau in 1844.[5] In the 1860s there were at least five bands in existence: the Ottawa Field Battery (organized 1855),[6] the St Patrick Brass Band, the band of the 100th Regiment, the Victoria Band, and the Canadian Band under George Sutherland.

In the early 1870s the band most frequently mentioned was that of the 60th Regiment under Signor Raineri. It had the honour of playing for the ball in the lobby of the Senate Hall of the Legislative Buildings on 25 February 1870 when Prince Arthur, the third son of Queen Victoria, was visiting Ottawa. The dance program was as follows:

1. Quadrille (Royal Boudoir)
2. Waltz (Hesperus Klange)
3. Galop (Strohfledel)
4. Lancers (Somebody's Luggage)
5. Waltz (Stella Colas)
6. Galop (Jongleur)
7. Quadrille (La Grande Duchesse)
8. Waltz (Venus Reigen)
9. Galop (Dominion State Ball)
10. Lancers (Echoes of London)
11. Waltz (Rhein Sagen)
12. Galop (Froh und Heiles)
13. Quadrille (La Perichole)
14. Waltz (Ben Lomond)
15. Galop (Flick and Flack)
16. Lancers
17. Waltz (Kate Kearney)
18. Galop (Hit and Miss)
19. Waltz (Frühlings Lieder)

(*OC* 26.2.1870)

The galop *Dominion State Ball* had been composed by Raineri especially for the occasion, and its entire edition was sold out by 28 February (*OFP* 28.2.1870). Because of the large crowd at this ball another room was opened where Gowan's Band provided the music. This band and the

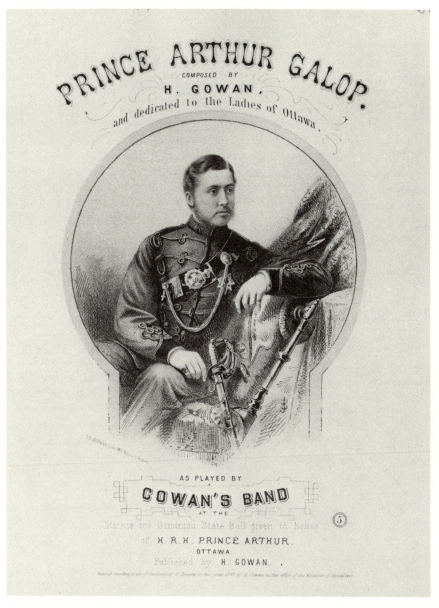

Prince Arthur Galop by H. Gowan
Photograph courtesy of the National Library of Canada

Gowans – James H., a carver and gilder, John, and Hunter, a flutist, who wrote the *Prince Arthur Galop* for this ball – had long played a role in Ottawa's musical life. An advertisement in the *Ottawa Citizen* stated: 'J. Gowan takes the opportunity of thanking the public for their patronage to his band for the last 12 years, and begs leave to state that he has on hand a first class Quadrille band, with a full number of performers' (OC 29.12.1869). This last reference is difficult to interpret. According to the *Ten-Cent Canadian Ball-Room Companion and Guide to Dancing*, a good dance band of the period would consist of four musicians to play piano, cornet, violin, and violoncello.[7] Nevertheless in 1871 this particular band was described as follows: 'Gowan's Band may soon defy the Dominion to produce its equal. It now numbers 18 or 20 performers, all capable of rendering their parts in first class style in any new piece of music at sight' (OC 8.9.1871). Probably the size of Gowan's Band varied according to the situation and the musicians available.

The Band of the 60th Regiment faded from the scene, but a new band, the Ottawa Brigade Garrison Artillery (OBGA), was organized by J.C. Bonner, its repertoire broadened to include operatic selections in addition to dance music and marches. This was duly noted in a review of one of their concerts:

Of course no one would look for perfection in such a short period of time; however a great deal of praise is due to the bandmaster, Mr. Bonner, for the efficient state at which the band has arrived, as well as for his laudable endeavour to introduce a superior class of music than is usually played by amateur bands. Of the two operatic selections the *Grande Duchesse* (Offenbach) was the best performed. About *Tancredi* (Rossini) there appeared to be a lack of confidence and not too strict attention to time on the part of the drum ... If we might make a suggestion it would be a more judicious use of the big drum, and a tenderer treatment at the hands of the performer. (OFP 24.1.1871)

In the following year the arrival of Frederic Temple Blackwood, first Marquess of Dufferin and Ava, meant major changes in the role of the governor-general and in the encouragement of music. Lady Lisgar, the wife of the former governor-general, Sir John Young Lisgar, had sponsored one musical concert on 27 May 1871, but Lord and Lady Dufferin encouraged music-making as well as theatre: 'In the evenings, after the opening of Parliament, the Dufferins held a series of balls in the oval room upstairs ... musical parties in the drawing room, and dinners ... for all officials and members of Parliament in their turn.'[8] A major musical decision in 1872 was the formation of the Governor-General's Foot Guards

(GGFG) Band. Since this was led by J.C. Bonner there were ramifications for the OGBA band. Eleven members retired in June (OC 5.6.1872), but an OGBA brass and string band performed a concert under William Cowan on 17 October 1872. By 1874 Signor Liberati was the leader, but when he left in 1876, eventually to become a leading cornetist at Atlantic Gardens, New York (OFP 21.10.1878), J.C. Bonner returned as bandmaster. In 1874 the OGBA band had thirty-two members (OFP 12.12.1874).

Meanwhile Bonner had created an effective GGFG band, starting off with sixteen musicians (OC 12.6.1872). By 1874 there were both fife and drum and brass bands (OC 7.5.1874), but there was also a smaller string band used for balls and banquets at Rideau Hall. The OFP reviewer reported that the String Band of the GGFG played the National Anthem 'very much out of tune' at the concert on 28 January 1874 (OFP 29.1.1874). As for instrumentation, only the programs of 1 August, 21 August, and 25 September 1877 give any indication of this by noting cornet, clarinet, piccolo, baritone, euphonium, horn, and althorn solos. The content of the GGFG's programs was similar to those of the OBGA, with operatic selections interspersed between dances and marches. By 1874 James Carter was the bandmaster, and a program under his direction given in August 1876 for the Scotch Games consisted of the following:

Quick March on Scotch Airs – Buchanan
Duet: Attila – Verdi
Waltz: Manola – Winterbottom
Grand Selection: Semiramide – Verdi [Rossini]
Quadrille on Scotch Airs – Hamilton
Galop: Queen Victoria – Hecker
Waltz: Dream on the Ocean – Gungrel (? Gung'l)
Overture: Nabucco – Verdi
Quadrille: The Busy Band – Hartman
Regimental March

(OFP 23.8.1876)

Carter resigned in July 1877, and Arthur A. Clappé, newly arrived from England, became bandmaster (OFP 1.8.1877), but when Clappé left to lead the Sarnia Independent Band, Carter returned to the GGFG (OFP 8.9.1879). Both the GGFG and OBGA bands gave regular concerts throughout the year. On winter evenings one of them would provide music for two hours in the building known as the Rink described below. In 1876 the GGFG band gave twice-weekly concerts for four to five months in the summer.

Besides these two active bands there were a number of others operating in Ottawa during the 1870s. In 1872 the Temperance Order organized a band consisting of twenty flutes, two piccolos, one bass drum, and seven snare drums (*OFP* 25.7.1872). By 1874 there was an Independent Cornet Band under the direction of L.T. Adams, but by 1876 it was known as the Ottawa City Cornet Band. After it collapsed a number of its members formed the Dragoon Guards Band (*OC* 7.6.1879). The Union Brass Band under H. Milton was giving weekly summer concerts in 1876 and later was called the Union Fire Band (*OC* 24.5.1878). The Loyal Orange Young Britons Band, a band for young people aged fifteen to twenty-one, conducted by James Brewer, came into existence in 1876 (*OFP* 21.3.1876). Judging from existing programs, these bands played basically march and dance music, as did another band conducted by Brewer, the Band of the Ottawa Field Battery, active by September 1876. In June 1878 this band had sixteen members (*OFP* 29.6.1878), but it dropped to fifteen under the leadership of James Elliott in 1879. Whatever the instrumentation, the program of 31 July 1879 consisted of a quick step, waltzes, and quadrilles interspersed with songs.

Some of the above bands used their repertoire to play for dances, but for most balls special quadrille bands were normally employed. Gowan's Band was most frequently called upon, but other popular groups were Sutherland's Celebrated Quadrille Band, also known as Sutherland's Brass and Quadrille Band, and Marier's Quadrille or String Band. Towards the end of the decade there were several quadrille clubs in Ottawa that met weekly to dance to their own specific quadrille band: the Eureka Quadrille Club had James Carter's String Band or Quadrille Band (*OFP* 29.1.1878), the Big Drum Quadrille Class and Boston Quadrille Assembly used Alex Brown's String Band (*OFP* 31.5.1878; *OFP* 12.8.1879), and the Star Quadrille Club danced to the strains of McGillicuddy's String Band (*OFP* 28.12.1878). Although precise instrumentation is not given for any of these bands, a listing of performers and instruments in the quadrille band which performed for the Public Schools concert at the Opera House in 1877 does survive: 'A quadrille band assisted in all the instrumental selections and ... was composed of William Cherry, first violin, William Cheney, jr., second violin, James Vandusen, double bass, John Ahearn, piccolo, James Barrett, cornet' (*OFP* 22.12.1877). This group does not correspond to the ensemble preferred by the author of the *Ten-Cent Companion*, but probably such bands varied considerably according to the available instrumentalists and the occasions.

There were other bands connected with religious institutions. In Ottawa the most prominent of these were the Roman Catholic organizations, particularly St Joseph's College Band, also known as the Ottawa College Band, led by Father Ballard. This band participated with the Cathedral Band under M. le Chevalier G. Smith and the Templeton Band under Mr Nare Roy in the procession greeting the new bishop, Duhamel, in October 1874 (*OFP* 28.10.1874). Another Roman Catholic band was that of the Christian Brothers School (*OFP* 26.6.1876). No indication of the repertoire used by these bands is given, but presumably it would not have included dance music, which was frowned upon by church leaders.

FACILITIES

These Ottawa bands performed on many different kinds of occasions. They were sometimes joined by bands from Hull, such as the Union Chaudière Company Band, which led the St George's parade on 18 January 1872, and the Chasseurs, who with the Chaudière and two Ottawa bands participated in a St-Jean-Baptiste Day parade (*OFP* 26.6.1876). As venues for the music-making of these bands there were the streets of Ottawa, parade grounds, the Rink, various assembly halls, and even excursion boats in the summer, but more formal concerts required proper facilities. Roger's comment quoted above pointed out Ottawa's lack of such facilities at the beginning of the decade. In 1856 Her Majesty's Theatre, seating 1000, had been completed, at a cost of $7000, and although it was still used occasionally in the early 1870s, its facilities were very limited and dilapidated. The most frequently used venue was the Rink, which was also known as the Ottawa Music Hall in the early 1870s. Not only was it used for skating in the winter or for dances (Lady Dufferin wrote: 'I danced a set of lancers and some other things with D.'),[9] but a temporary floor and risers were used for occasions such as local concerts or the visits of opera companies or minstrel troupes. In 1876 the collapse of some of the temporary galleries at a public school entertainment virtually ended the use of this facility for concerts, and the Rink was turned into a gymnasium by the end of the decade (*OFP* 13.5.1876).

The Gowans did much to rectify the dearth of facilities. In January 1869 a hall was opened in the same building as their business, 113-115 Sparks Street. Its popularity was noted: 'This popular resort is becoming a household word amongst our citizens, and is always associated with pleasant and interesting recollections or anticipations. The Hall and Gowan's Band are seldom idle and are ever prominent features to the entertainments of the city' (*OFP* 4.2.1871). In the *Ottawa Directory* of 1873-4, an advertisement stated that the hall was being enlarged to accommodate 1500 persons.[10] With the great success of this hall, Hunter Gowan apparently acquired higher ambitions and set out to provide the theatre whose absence had been noted by Roger. Gowan's Opera House, seating over 1000, and built at a cost of $35,000 with stage carpentry and scene painting by the staff of Booth's Theatre, New York, was opened at 136 Albert Street on 1 February 1875 (*OFP* 4.1.1875; 27.1.1875) with a performance of Balfe's *The Bohemian Girl* that was attended by the Dufferins: 'The great event of the day was the opening of the new theatre here – the first one at Ottawa. The house is really very nice, and the state box a comfortable and convenient one.'[11] Certainly this facility increased theatrical and musical activity tremendously during 1875 and 1876. The house rented for $60 a night (*OFP* 3.12.1875), but, perhaps owing to the economic depression from 1876 to 1879 and the drop in Ottawa's population from 25,471 to 23,789,[12] it remained dark for weeks at a time during 1877. By early 1877 the Gowans had started a local minstrel troupe and by July had left Ottawa to join 'a newly organized minstrel company of high merit' (*OC* 25.7.1877). The Opera House continued operations, but this advertisement appeared in 1878: 'Chancery sale of valuable building lots and Grand Opera House on the south side of Albert St. Final order for sale made in the cause of Heney vs. Gowan. Tues. 10 Sept. Known as Gowan's Grand Opera House, furnished with gas and water fixtures, drop-curtain, certain scenery, seats, furnace for heating ... ' (*OFP* 19.8.1878). Both this facility and Gowan's Hall – renamed St James' Hall in 1877, and then taken over by J.L. Orme and Son who moved to 113-115 Sparks Street in 1878 – continued to be regularly used (*OC* 6.5.1878).

In addition to these venues two others were added during the decade. In New Edinburgh the Music Hall was opened after $1000 was spent on 'a stone building in the rear of Mr. R. Blackburn's store, formerly used as a brewery' (*OFP* 19.2.1875). The Institut canadien français, 'a purely literary and musical institution ... established in 1852,' wanted better facilities for its productions and therefore erected an edifice on York Street at a cost of $20,000. It included a theatre that seated 1200 and had a stage and four private boxes arranged similarly to Gowan's Opera House (*OFP* 20.6.1877).

STAGE ENTERTAINMENT

In all the locales mentioned a wide variety of travelling artists entertained Ottawans during the 1870s. The most typical group was the minstrel company; some well-known ones had visited Ottawa/Bytown as early as 1850. In the 1870s Cool Burgess, considered pre-eminent in this field of entertainment, visited Ottawa at least six times; as manager of the Gaieté

Vaudeville Company on 30 May and 1 June 1871, as headliner on 8 December 1871 and 1-2 November 1872, with the Townsend Family on 20 September 1875, with his Grand Combination on 22-23 January 1878, and with the Spaulding Swiss Bell Ringers on 20 May 1879. Other popular groups were Whitmore and Clark's Minstrels and Brass Band, who appeared on 26-27 January 1871, 1 February 1872, 20 February 1874, and 18-19 February and 26 August 1875, and Skiff and Gaylord's Minstrels, who performed on 19 January and 4 November 1872 and 16-17 February 1874. The size of these companies varied from twenty performers in Hagar and Mudge's Minstrels and Burlesque Troupe to fewer than fifteen. The advertisement for Whitmore and Clark's mentioned the presence of three clog dancers, three song and dance men, a full quartet (presumably TTBB), and a brass band of twelve pieces led by T.J. Allan and including Herman Miller, trombone, and Thomas Maynard, violin (*OFP* 20.1.1871). A typical minstrel company evening would include instrumental solos on the banjo or the cornet interspersed with solo songs, choruses, dances, and comic skits delivered in black-face.[13]

Since some of these troupes appear to have originated in the southern United States there may have been actual black performers involved rather than just white ones in burnt-cork makeup. But whether this was so or not, there was also interest in the genuine music of the blacks, such as spirituals. The Jubilee Singers – consisting of Rev. Pollard, his wife, and Amy Taylor – performed on 25 August 1873. They were followed by the Wilmington North Carolina Jubilee Singers on 23-24 November 1874, the Original Tennesseeans on 14-15 October 1875, the Nashville Tennessee Coloured Jubilee Singers on 30-31 January 1877, and the Sheppard Jubilee Singers on 8 November 1877. Usually the reviewer would pick out a few particular songs for comment, but for the Tennesseeans, the 'most talented and interesting colored group that ever visited Ottawa,' most selections performed were listed:

Come along Moses; We will end this war; Arise, Shine, Give God the Glory; Jonah and the Whale; Moonlight on the Lake; Gathering Home; Swing Low, Sweet Chariot; Goin' to have meeting here tonight; Reign, Master Jesus, Reign; Hail! the Army, Hail; Gently down the stream of time; Hard Trials and Tribulations; What are the wild waves saying (duet); My Old Cabin Home; Poor Black Joe; The Old Ark is Moving; Why March on, you shall join the Victory; Keep a'Hinching Along; Rocked in the Cradle of the Deep; Away Across the Sea ... During the progress of the evening they sold a large number of their songs. (*OFP* 16.10.1875)

Presumably these presentations were basically choral, but other travelling groups would present a mixture of choral numbers and vocal and instrumental solos, interspersed with farces, readings, and comic sketches. Bob Butler's Original Pantomime and Humpty Dumpty Troupe of New York, which performed on 1-3 April 1875, even included clog dances and a performance of the Highland Fling (*OFP* 2.4.1875). The instrumental accompaniments for this group were provided by Gowan's Orchestra – essentially an expanded version of the band under Mr Littmann, formerly of New York – which often played works such as the overture to *La gazza ladra* or selections from *Guillaume Tell* by Rossini before and during intermissions of entertainments at Gowan's Opera House (*OC* 23.10.1874; *OFP* 24.1.1874). Occasionally instrumentalists shared the bill with these groups; for example, James Archer amazed Ottawans with his simultaneous performance on piano and tin whistle in the presentation of James Taylor's Comique Opera Company (*OC* 26.3.1874). On 22 July 1874 the Guy Family were accompanied by their Silver Hellicon Band and Orchestra, and the actors Mr John Murray and Miss Grace Cortlandt were accompanied by Leach's Metropolitan Company and orchestra (the week of 25 September 1876). Don Shelby's Novelty Troupe, 'complete with orchestra and brass band, composed of 10 solo players,' was much appreciated: 'Don Shelby's Troupe is a first class combination. Harry Bennett in his Irish vocalizations and witticisms, the Corellas in their grotesque acts, Niles and Evans in their European eccentricities proved themselves specialty artists far above the common' (*OC* 8.6.1878).

Although some of these visiting organizations had the word 'opera' in their name (such as the Liza Weber Burlesque Opera Troupe, 19 and 26 August 1871), they did not perform real operas or operatic selections. Nevertheless Ottawans had experienced opera in a theatrical setting apart from selections played by the bands and performed by local amateurs. In the late 1860s both Bateman's and Holman's Opera Troupes had performed Balfe's *The Bohemian Girl* (1843) while the Holmans also gave Offenbach's *La Grande Duchesse de Gerolstein* (1867), and *La Belle Hélène* (1864), and Balfe's *Statanella* (1858) and *The Enchantress* (1845) in July 1869. On 20-21 June 1871 the Grand English Opera Company with full chorus and orchestra presented Flotow's *Martha* (1847) and Auber's *Fra Diavolo* (1830). Another performance of *Martha* was given by the Italian Opera Troupe along with Donizetti's *Lucrezia Borgia* (1833) on 15-16 July 1872. It is doubtful that these works were performed complete because the presentation of Lecocq's *La Fille de Madame Angot* (1872) by Grau's Grand Opera on 26 October 1874 was described by a reviewer as the first full opera given in Ottawa.

The Holman English Opera Company returned to Ottawa to open Gowan's Opera House during the week of 1 February 1875 and performed *The Bohemian Girl*, Bellini's *La Sonnambula* (1831), *Fra Diavolo, La Grande Duchesse, Lischen and Fritzschen*, Rossini's *Cinderella* (1817), Donizetti's *The Love Spell* (*L'Elisir d'Amore*, 1832). It was admitted that the Donizetti, performed with the burletta *Black Eyed Susan*, was shortened in order for the Holmans to catch a train to Montreal. For most of the other performances a burletta or farce was included, indicating that the main work was probably presented in an abbreviated form. Nevertheless, for the first time Ottawans could appreciate opera in the proper surroundings and not on the make-shift stage of the Rink: 'The scenery was really beautiful, the dresses of the ladies and gentlemen of the Company gorgeous to a degree which few would expect a travelling company to be in possession of. The music incidental to the piece was ably executed by Mrs. Harriet Holman who is an able conductor, and to whom much of the success of the opera is due . . . Mr. Gowan's fine orchestra was present and played several choice selections between the acts' (*OFP* 4.2.1875). The Holmans did not travel with an orchestra but relied on Mrs Holman to play the score from memory on the piano. Although it seemed that Gowan's Orchestra did not join her in 1875, it did so on the Holmans' first visit in 1876 to perform Lecocq's *Giroflé-Girofla* (1874) and *La Fille de Madame Angot, La Grande Duchesse, The Bohemian Girl, La Sonnambula*, and Offenbach's *La Périchole* (1868) and *Barbe-bleue* (1866): 'We must not forget a meed of praise to Mrs. Holman, who so delightfully accompanied the opera on the piano nor to Gowan's orchestra which aided the lady therein so materially with so little prior practice' (*OFP* 21.1.1876). When they returned in November 1876 to give the first performances in Ottawa of Offenbach's *La Princesse de Trébizonde* (1869) and Balfe's *The Rose of Castille* (1857), that practice was continued: 'The music furnished by the Orchestra with Mrs. Holman presiding at the piano was of the first order' (*OFP* 10.11.1876).[14] In 1878 (16-19, 31 January, and 1-2 February), the Holmans returned and repeated several of the above operas, adding Wallace's *Maritana* (1845) and Offenbach's *Geneviève de Brabant* (1859).

A major event in Ottawa's musical life was the first presentation of Gilbert and Sullivan's HMS *Pinafore* (1878) by the Martinez English Opera Company of Boston on 20-21 January 1879. These performances were quickly followed by a local production on 23 April, the Fifth Avenue Opera Company's version on 26-27 June 1879, and one by Haverley's Juvenile Opera Company on 15-17 September 1879. In the *Ottawa Free Press* on 22 July 1879 there is a letter from a woman who complained that the whole family including herself were constantly going around singing whole family including herself were constantly going around singing 'snatches of *Pinafore*.' Its popularity encouraged W.H. Fuller to write a brilliant parody on current Canadian political themes, called *HMS Parliament*. Sung to the music of *Pinafore*, this piece opened in Montreal and arrived in Ottawa on 22 February 1880.

CONCERT REPERTOIRE

Selections from operas and operettas frequently appeared on the programs given by concert companies. A typical company was the Barnabee Concert Company of Boston – H.C. Barnabee, baritone, J. Winck, tenor, Mrs H.M. Smith, soprano, Miss A.E. Clark, contralto and accompanist, and Miss Persis Bell, seventeen-year-old violinist – who gave a program of operatic selections, ballads, and vocal and instrumental solos (*OFP* 30.11.1874). Such a mixed program was certainly the norm for North America and still existed to a degree in Europe, but it meant that large-scale instrumental works were rarely performed. There was a gradual trend towards the inclusion of what we would call standard repertoire in Ottawa in the 1870s. Seraphael, the English boy pianist appearing with Mrs Scott Siddons, performed a *Sonata in E Flat* by Beethoven and Thalberg's *Home Sweet Home* Variations (*OC* 4.5.1874). Arabella Goddard, a student of Kalkbrenner and Thalberg, performed Beethoven's *Sonata* opus 26, Handel's *Harmonious Blacksmith*, and shorter pieces, and there were selections by two singers and a violinist (*OFP* 29.1.1876). The violinist Camilla Urso included Tartini's *Devil's Trill Sonata* and an unaccompanied Bach *Gavotte* in a program assisted by three singers and a pianist (*OFP* 22.11.1878).

For a soloist to perform a whole evening was very rare indeed. One apparent example in Ottawa was Blind Tom (Thomas Bethune, 1849-1908), who performed on 11-14 November 1872, 9-10 November 1875, 12-13 February 1877, and 19 December 1878. Although he was reputed to be an excellent pianist with seven thousand pieces in his repertoire, the reviews seemed to indicate that he was a nineteenth-century showman in the style represented today by Borge and Liberace:

Tom accompanied himself on the piano in several tunes, singing *The Old Sexton*, *Rocked in the Cradle of the Deep* and also a piece of his own composition called *The Man What Plays the Banjo*. Tom's rendering of *Old Hundred* in which he introduced his imitation of the church organ was decidedly rich, and brought down the house ... Tom repeated the experiment of playing *Yankee Doodle* with the right hand, *Fisher's Hornpipe*, in the left hand and singing *Tramp Tramp* at the same time ... The performance closed with the imitation of the *Battle of Mannassas*. (*OFP* 10.11.1875)

Because of the strong Irish element in Ottawa society, Erin and the Brennans and Rosa d'Erina were great favourites. The latter was an Irish mezzo-soprano, pianist, and organist who did numerous one-woman presentations in Ottawa during the years 1872-6 as well as assisting at the occasional local concert.[15] A distinctive solo program was that of the harpist Aptommas on 15 September 1876, which included arrangements of Beethoven's *Moonlight Sonata* and pieces by Mendelssohn and Handel (*OFP* 16.9.1876).

The most demanding programs given in Ottawa were those of the Mendelssohn Quintette Club of Boston, founded in 1852. They gave one or two performances each year of chamber music, arrangements, and solos with their five or six musicians, occasionally joined by a local performer. On 25-26 April 1874 Professor E.J. Butler of the Ottawa Ladies' College joined them to play Haydn's *Trio in G* (*OC* 4.4.1874). In 1875 they included Wagner's 'Bridal Procession' from *Lohengrin* in their program, which the reviewer called 'very fresh and bold' (*OFP* 4.11.1875).

Like most Europeans, Ottawans became familiar with standard orchestral literature through piano reductions for from two to eight pianists. It was not until April 1893 that Ottawans heard a real orchestra – the New York Symphony Orchestra under Walter Damrosch – but in 1875 the Beethoven Quintette Club of Boston had performed the Andante and Allegro from Beethoven's *Seventh Symphony* (*OFP* 11.6.1875). Apparently this had been specifically requested. A few months earlier a review of the Boston Philharmonic Club, whose program included the overture to Rossini's *Tancredi*, horn, violin, and vocal solos, and Mozart's *Piano Quartet in G Minor*, stated: 'There was a very large and a very select audience ... It looks as though our citizens had finally come to the conclusion to show their appreciation of really first class talent, and by this means secure for Ottawa a better order of talent than we have hitherto been favored with ... Mozart's Quartet held the interest of the audience to the end although it was exceedingly long' (*OFP* 13.1.1875).

In Ottawa there was genuine pleasure when visiting artists such as the Holmans were both outstanding and Canadian. After a concert by Mrs Elena Waters that included the violinist Frantz Jehin-Prume and his wife, the mezzo-soprano Rosita del Vecchio, the reviewer stated that it 'drew the fullest house of any concert this season, which proves what we have always said, viz., that the people of Ottawa will go to hear first class music, rendered by first class artists' (*OFP* 19.4.1871). Jehin-Prume returned to Ottawa with Calixa Lavallée on 21 September 1875 and with Guillaume Couture on 6 March 1876. After recently completing three years of study at the Paris Conservatoire, Alfred De Sève appeared in Ottawa to an enthusiastic reception:

High art in Canada is so repeatedly represented to audiences by other than Canadians that it is both a relief and a gratification to chronicle an almost classical concert in which Canadians alone took part, and in such a manner as to win warm and repeated applause. Our French Canadian citizens are well known to possess among themselves musical talent little short of professional excellence, and it is no empty compliment to say that they are an important factor in the musical economy of this city. (*OFP* 13.2.1879)

Twice annually during the years 1875-8 the Shaughraum Company of the Academy of Music, Montreal, appeared in Ottawa but in spoken-drama productions rather than concerts.

In addition to concerts by touring artists there continued to be an ever-increasing number of programs by local musicians: 'The taste for music in Ottawa must be increasing rapidly when we can support three amateur concerts in one week at Gowan's Hall' (*OFP* 25.3.1874). Performances of touring artists served to raise the standard of programming and skills so that there was a decided evolution in the repertoire heard at concerts by local musicians during the 1870s. As for musical education, W.G. Workman (1841-1900) taught vocal music at the public and normal schools in Ottawa, and all the ladies' schools included music in their curricula. For instance, the Congrégation de Notre Dame offered piano at $30 per annum, harp at $50, guitar at $20, and organ at $40.[16] By March 1874 the increase in the number of students studying music at the Ottawa Ladies' College from 55 in 1873 to 122 (*OFP* 25.9.1874) brought about the decision to organize a conservatory affiliated with the college, under the directorship of Professor E.J. Butler (*OC* 9.3.1874). During the mid-1870s, movements of standard piano concertos appeared on the Ladies' College programs, replacing salon-type piano pieces. In 1876 all graduating students in piano were required to play the following repertoire: 'Bach's Prelude and Fugue in A flat, No. 17; Handel's *Harmonious Blacksmith*; Haydn's Sonata in E flat; Mozart's Fantasia and Sonata in C minor; Beethoven's Sonata Op. 26; Weber's *Polacca Brillante*, Op. 78; Schumann's *Kreisleriana*; Mendelssohn's *Capriccio* Op. 33, No. 3; Thalberg's Variations on *Home Sweet Home*; Chopin's Ballade in F minor and Liszt's Hungarian Rhapsody No. 1' (*OC* 22.8.1876).

Undoubtedly the use of such serious and demanding repertoire had come about with better teachers settling in Ottawa. In the latter part of the decade these included Signor P. Loredan, whose piano recital was reviewed as follows:

It is not too much to say that never since the visit of the talented late 'Gottschalk' has anything in the way of pianoforte playing been presented in Ottawa equal to Signor Loredan's performance on this occasion ... None ... has had the courage to give us as much of the high class of music as (Loredan) ... From the commencement of the *Andante* (Beethoven's *Appassionata* Sonata) to the conclusion of the *Presto* it was listened to with rapt attention and enthusiastically applauded. We no longer fear that Ottawa will be charged with a lack of appreciation of classical music. Times are changed since the occasion when poor Gottschalk walked off the stage of the old Theatre in disgust at the end of his recital because he saw that he could not be understood. (*OFP* 25.2.1878)

When Edward Fisher succeeded Butler as head of the conservatory he began to give regular organ recitals, which always included classical works by J.S. Bach and others rather than arrangements. The reviewer of his recital in 1875 pointed out that organ recitals were unknown in Ottawa before 1873 'due to the lack of outstanding instruments. Now there are two good Warren and Sons, Montreal, organs at Christ Church and St. Andrew's' (*OFP* 20.12.1875).

ORGANIZATIONS

Even before 1870 Ottawa had had large organizations for group music-making. H.R. Fripp had formed the Ottawa Choral Society in October 1865; by 1870 it was known as the Ottawa Philharmonic Society. On 25 January 1870 this group performed the entire first part of Haydn's *Creation*, plus a selection of secular choruses, duets, and solos (*OC* 20.1.1870). After the society collapsed, perhaps because Fripp left music to enter the civil service, a new organization, the Ottawa Choral Union, under the leadership of F.W. Mills, was formed in 1874 (*OFP* 15.9.1874). Their first concert on 22 February 1875 included selections from *The Creation*, performed by a chorus of 120 and an orchestra including E. Marley, first violin, John Hounsell, viola, J.W. Vandusen, bass, F.W. Harner and H. Pardon, flutes, P.S. Boucke, clarinet, Signor Liberati and H. Michaels, cornets, Signor Gorazzi, baritone, A. Harrison, tympani, and Mrs More, piano (*OFP* 24.2.1875). After Mills left the city without receiving his full conductor's fee, the choral union's attempt to restructure itself failed (*OFP* 24.11.1876), but by 1878 a new choral society had been formed under the leadership of Edward Fisher (*OFP* 4.2.1879). (Fisher moved to Toronto in 1879 and by 1887 had founded the Toronto Conservatory of Music.)

Meanwhile there had been an attempt to revive a chamber music ensemble such as the Quintette Club formed in Ottawa in 1860 and consisting of John Mercer and J.H. Gowan, violins, Geo Sutherland, cornet, Alex Duff, flute, and Louis Fecht, piano (*OFP* 24.2.1875). W. Warren, who taught twenty-four lessons per quarter at $10 in piano, voice, harmonium, violin, English concertina, or cornet, announced a 'class for the practice of Classical Music, Vocal and Instrumental commencing on October 1, 1872' (*OFP* 25.9.1872). His efforts were eventually taken up by Arthur A. Clappé who formed the Musical Union. Their first concert – with four choruses (including *Come if You Dare* by Purcell and Wagner's *Pilgrim's Chorus*), vocal duets and solos, and a French horn solo by Mr Harze – was accompanied by a string quintet consisting of A. Marier, and H. Tasse, violins, E. Marier, viola, J. Marier, cello, and K. Marier, bass (*OFP* 11.2.1879). This instrumental group performed two overtures, Mozart's *Marriage of Figaro* and Clappé's *Adopted Child*. This society continued under the direction of Edgar Buck when Clappé left town. J.W. Harrison replaced Fisher as head of the conservatory in September 1879 and by December had launched a chamber music series that would include the first Canadian performance of Bach's *Concerto for Three Pianos* (*OC* 11.2.1880).

Thus by the end of the 1870s Ottawa had a substantial base of musical education, opportunities for group music-making, and a support system of music dealerships: J.L. Orme had been in existence since 1861 and remained exclusively a music store until 1929; H. & J. Gowan also handled instruments and music; and A. & S. Nordheimer opened an Ottawa branch on 2 January 1872. Moreover Ottawans had produced a surprising amount of original music – ranging from church music, songs, and piano pieces through band music to operettas – during the decade. John C. Bonner was the most prolific, with two songs, three marches, a waltz, a quadrille and lancers, and four galops, and was reported to be working on an opera based on a Canadian theme. Other operatic works were Tiepke's *Who Killed Cock Robin?* (1873), F.W. Mills's *The Maire of St Brieux* (1875),[17] Workman's *May Queen* (1876), Clappé's *The Adopted Child* (1878), and Gustave Smith's *L'ut dreze* (1879). The first performance of Mills's operetta took place at Rideau Hall in 1875, and Lady Dufferin commented: 'It is an operetta, written by Mr. Dixon ... and composed by Mr. Mills, the organist in Ottawa. The music is very pretty and the whole play excellent.'[18] When it was produced at Gowan's Grand Opera House there was a cast of seven principals, a chorus of thirty-six, and an orchestra under Mills (*OFP* 27.3.1876).

Probably the most ambitious composition was *Canada's Welcome*[19] by Clappé, with text by Frederick A. Dixon, written in honour of the new governor-general, the Marquis of Lorne and his wife, the Princess Louise, daughter of Queen Victoria. The score, begun in December 1878, was two hundred pages long and called for nine soloists (representing Canada, the seven provinces in union, and an Indian chief), a chorus, and 'the orchestra of not less than twenty-two different instruments (the most complete ever heard in Ottawa, and perhaps in Canada)' (*OFP* 25.2.1879). The long and generally complimentary review of the music and its performance in the *Ottawa Free Press* pointed out that the 'overture, in two movements, [was] based principally on Gounod's "Mirella"' and that a chorus bore resemblance to 'the style of the "Soldier's Chorus" [sic] in Gounod's "Faust"' but noted the composer's expertise in canonic writing and his gift for grateful melodies in the style of Dibdin, Shield, and Arne.

Looking back over the events of 1879, an article on 'Music in Ottawa' commented with pride: 'There are not wanting signs of great improvement in musical taste and exemplification in our city' (*OFP* 1.12.1879). Having developed creditable music-making facilities, Ottawans were also eagerly keeping abreast of new trends. Although saxhorns were common, the saxophone (patented in 1846) was not heard in Ottawa until Bertha and Ida Foy's Mirth and Mischief-makers gave two presentations at the Grand Opera House on 23 and 25 September 1878. In May of that same year the Edison Speaking Phonograph, on display at the Ottawa Exhibition, had created much interest (*OC* 16.5.1878). But probably the best hint of the future of transmitting sound was revealed in the review of a concert that took place in St James' Hall:

During the day the Dominion Telegraph Company connected the hall with their central office on Elgin Street and also with the manager's residence at the Chaudiere, there being three Blake transmitters placed in the concert room. A number of ladies and gentlemen, through the courtesy of Mr. Soper, were thus afforded an opportunity of enjoying the concert in the company's office, where a score of telephones had been brought into requisition ... The experiment was a success from every point of view, and as the use of the telephone is still in its infancy, it is difficult to predict the grand results it may lead to (*OFP* 26.11.1879).

Homage to Helmut

Homage to Helmut

Homage to Helmut

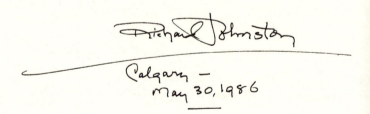

ROBERT DALE McINTOSH

Ships of the Fleet: The Royal Navy and the Development of Music in British Columbia

In its early years the colony of Vancouver's Island depended both economically and socially on the presence of the ships of the Royal Navy anchored on the Pacific Station in Esquimalt harbour. Engaged largely in hydrographic survey work and the establishment of the British 'presence' in the Pacific, the officers and men still found time to pursue those social activities which had formed so much a part of their lives before coming to the 'furthest west' on the coast which would become British Columbia. Most ships of the line had a band, some even an orchestra and dramatic corps, all supported, both morally and financially, by the officers who were often of the 'landed gentry' and attempted to maintain some of the cultural comforts of home while stationed on isolated colonial outposts.

There is little documentary evidence of these activities before the first newspapers were published in 1858, but Robert Melrose, a workman on Craigflower Farm, states in his diary that he attended 'a Splendid Theatre on board the Frigate "*Trincomalee*"' in October 1853,[1] a 'Grand Theatrical Opera' at the Naval Hospital in Esquimalt in September 1855, and another theatrical play and ball on board the HMS *President* in October of the same year.[2] Martha Beeton Cheney Ella, an early resident of Metchosin, was also present at the event of 1853 and reports that the 'cream' of Victoria's social set, including Mr and Mrs Langford, Mr and Mrs Skinner, and the 'Gentlemen from the Fort' were honoured guests.[3] Mrs Ella also attended a ball held at the fort in 1856 for which the Admiral's band[4] provided the music and notes that it was 'a very pleasant party' and 'kept up untill [*sic*] 4 o'clock in the morning.'[5] In his journal for 1859, A.T. Bushby describes a dinner on board HMS *Satellite*.[6] 'A bit before turning in,' he states, '[we] walked the deck with officer of the watch and listened to seamen singing in parts.'[7] Bushby, a musician of some ability, would have known good singing when he heard it. An 'amateur dramatic corps' of the *Satellite* performed at Cusheon's Naval and Military Theatre on Government Street in April 1860, and on the same program 'a selection of the most choice pieces of music [was] performed by the talented band of H.M.S. *Topaze.*'[8] The band of the *Topaze*, under the direction of F. Jarrett, was very popular in Victoria and played many concerts in the community while the ship was stationed there. At a concert on 24 February 1862 in which the band participated, a race-riot nearly broke out:

Soon after the doors were opened, complaint was heard from a number of gentlemen who had purchased tickets before coming to the theatre, at the presence in the dress circle and parquette of some twenty colored men, and at one time about fifty ticket-holders were congregated in the passage offering their tickets at half price or giving them away to acquaintances who chose to enter. Two or three gentlemen, who said they had purchased their tickets with the understanding that there were to be reserved seats for the colored population, remarked that they would request the parties who had sold them to return the money ... After a pretty free expression of opinion in a quiet way the dissatisfied parties withdrew.[9]

The fleet musicians were often made available to supplement local performers for special occasions. One such instance, was in February 1863 – a Grand Concert in Aid of the Lancashire Relief Fund, featuring a local orchestra under the direction of George Sandrie, with players on clarinet, trombone, and side drum provided by the *Topaze* band.[10] The group played the 'Il Trovatore Waltzes' (Mariott) and 'Lurline Waltzes' (D'Albert) as well as the 'Victoria Galop' composed specifically for this concert by Sandrie, in addition to his arrangement 'Selections from William Tell.'[11] The last appearance of the *Topaze* band before leaving the station was as part of a benefit for the popular singer Belle Divine, which was held in June 1863. On this occasion they played overtures to *Tancredi* (Rossini) and *Zampa* (Hérold), selections from *Il Trovatore* (Verdi) and *Les Huguenots* (Meyerbeer), and a selection of national airs. Belle Divine, who was 'in every respect a complete success,' favoured the audience with 'Happy Be Thy Dreams' (Thomas) and 'Come Where My Love Lies Dreaming' (Foster), obviously impressing the nearly all-male audience.[12]

There were several other ships on the Pacific Station at this time, and all appear to have had competent groups of musicians on board. Bands attached to the *Tribune, Ganges,* and *Sutlej*[13] provided many concerts both in the community and at Foster's Pier in Esquimalt while they were on that station.

The band of the *Sutlej*, under the direction of Joseph Bloom, was particularly in demand, as the following 'Letter to the Editor' of the

Colonist indicates:

> The Sutlej Band
>
> To the Editor of the British Colonist, – Sir, – I presume you are aware that the Sutlej Band performed on Foster's wharf, at Esquimalt, on Saturday Night ... for the benefit of the public. Now it must be obvious to everyone that the people of Victoria cannot enjoy the pleasure of listening to that excellent band in consequence of the distance, as they must either walk or incur the expense of five or ten dollars for a conveyance, and the times at present will not allow us to 'stand the press.'
>
> It is but seldom we have the opportunity of hearing such a band as the Sutlej Band, then why cannot it come to Victoria once a week or fortnight, and perform in front of the Government buildings, or on the renown [sic] Church Reserve, so that all, great and small, rich and poor, can have the chance of hearing some good music? It is a pity that so much breath should be wasted in discoursing classical music to the fishes and frogs in the bays and bogs of Esquimalt ... Can there be raised by subscription enough funds to defray the expense of an omnibus to bring the Sutlej Band to Victoria every Saturday or every other Saturday? And if this can be done will the Admiral permit the band to come? ...
>
> Yours very respectfully,
> C SHARP[14]

'C Sharp' must have succeeded in his aim, because the *Sutlej* band continued to be reported as taking an active part in musical affairs in Victoria until their last concert in September 1866, for the benefit of the local militia band, when they played the overture to *Semiramide* (Rossini), selections from *La Traviata* (Verdi), *Nachtlager in Granada* (Kreutzer), and *I Bengali* (Bousquet), the overture to *Alessandro Stradella* (Flotow), and selections from *Anna Bolena* (Donizetti).[15] With respect to this concert, a reviewer for the *Colonist* stated: 'The portion of the programme which was rendered by the H.M.S. Sutlej Band, it is almost superfluous to say, was executed in truly artistic style.'[16]

In addition to a fine band, the *Ganges* had a competent dramatic troupe, and the assistant paymaster on this ship, William K. Horne, composed what is generally considered to be the first composition from the west coast – 'The Vancouver Waltz' (1860).[17]

HMS *Hecate* was on the Pacific Station from 1861 until 1863 surveying the coastline of the island and, according to Lady Franklin, 'the choir at [St Paul's Naval Garrison Church] Esquimalt is always furnished by the "Hecate" men who indeed form a large portion of the congregation.'[18] At the same time HMS *Bacchante* was on the station, and the bandmaster,

Edmund Maguire, stayed on in Victoria after the departure of his ship, establishing himself as a free-lance musician and conductor of the Victoria Fire Department Band.[19] Later he and John Allen, who had come about the same time from San Francisco to lead the Victoria Theatre orchestra, established the Victoria Musical Society, which gave many concerts under a variety of names until Maguire left Victoria in about 1867.

Other ships on the Pacific Station in the mid-1860s included the paddle-wheel sloop *Devastation* (1861-4), which transferred six of its musicians to the *Sutlej* before the latter returned to England, and the corvette HMS *Clio* (1864-8), which provided several 'Naval Entertainments' consisting of both vocal and instrumental music while in port.[20]

HMS *Zealous*, which was on the Pacific Station from 1867 to 1872, had a fine band under the leadership of Henry Gunther, as well as an amateur dramatic corps,[21] both of which entertained at many concerts while in port, including some outdoor performances at Foster's Pier, Esquimalt.[22] Apparently not all naval bandsmen were happy with their lot, however, for in 1868 the *Colonist* reported the desertion of both the bandmaster and a bandsman from HMS *Pylades*.[23]

In July 1869 the French flagship *L'Astrée* anchored off Esquimalt, and its band was described as 'one of the finest that has visited here since the days of the Ganges [i.e., 1858-60].'[24] Several concerts were given on Foster's Pier, and a subscription was begun to bring the band to Victoria,[25] but the ship was called to San Francisco before this could be accomplished.

After 1870 the significance of the fleet musicians in the musical life of Victoria diminished. By this time there were a number of professional musicians residing in the city, and various local bands and orchestras under the leadership of such men as William Haynes (who came to BC as a bandmaster with the Royal Engineers in 1859) and Charles Schaffer (who left Victoria in 1877 under mysterious circumstances involving bills unpaid and monies owing) provided much local entertainment. However, a few naval bands visited Victoria in the last quarter of the century, including those of HMS *Repulse* (1873-6) and the *Triumph* (1879-82 and again 1885-8). The calibre of local Victoria musicians had increased to such an extent by 1880 that the bandmaster of the *Triumph* used this advertisement in an attempt to entice some of them to join his forces: 'WANTED: Musicians for the Band of H.M.S. Triumph, Esquimalt. Must be good performers and of good character. Apply on Board.'[26] The conductor of the *Triumph* band on its second tour of duty on the station was Antonio Agius, who left the Royal Navy in 1887 and was approached by the local militia to take over direction of the Garrison Artillery ('C' Battery) Band, a post which he held until 1889.

HMS *Swiftsure*, which today lends its name to Victoria's most prestigious sailing event, was posted to the Pacific Station in 1882[27] and possessed a fine orchestra, band, and dramatic corps. On 21 August 1883 members of the ship's company, assisted by several 'lady amateurs' of Victoria, presented what appears to have been an outstanding performance of Gilbert and Sullivan's *HMS Pinafore*,[28] followed about a year later by a performance of the same work in conjunction with the Tivoli Opera Company of San Francisco.

The leader of the *Swiftsure* band and orchestra was H.E. Loseby, a violinist and composer of some note. In 1889 he offered his services as a private teacher of the violin and other stringed instruments in Victoria[29] and organized many local concerts involving both the ship's personnel and local performers, at one of which his songs 'Golden Hours' and 'Love's Longing' and his cornet solo 'Victoria!' were performed.[30]

HMS *Nymphe* was on the Pacific Station from 1890 until 1895, involved in hydrographic survey work on the coast of Vancouver Island. In June 1895 the ship was in Nanaimo harbour, bound for Campbell River to do a resurvey of Menzies Bay. Officers and men from the ship attended a production of *HMS Pinafore* performed by the Nanaimo Operatic Company on 11-12 June of that year. So enchanted were they by the performance of Aggie Glaholm in the character of Josephine that they were inspired to name Josephine Flat, south of Menzies Bay, in her honour.[31]

Among the last of the 'musical' ships of the Royal Navy to visit Victoria in the nineteenth century was HMS *Warspite* (1890-3 and 1899-1902). There were evidently some fine musicians on board, and these performers, owing to the kindness and interest of Rear-Admiral Charles Frederick Hotham, were frequently allowed to perform at concerts in Victoria, either as soloists or in ensembles with Victoria musicians. In fact the bandmaster, Mr Laffey (a violinist of some repute), elected to remain in Victoria as a professional musician when the flagship departed.

The facilities of the Pacific Station were transferred to the Canadian Navy in 1910, and for the next thirty years the influence of the naval establishment on musical activity in the province was minimal. With the formation of the Royal Canadian Naval band of HMCS Naden (the Naden band) in 1940, however, many fine wind musicians, largely recruited from overseas, came to the west coast. The presence of these musicians immediately became evident in the musical community of Victoria, and personnel from the band were everywhere in evidence, from pit to podium, in local musical productions. From the inception of the present Victoria Symphony Orchestra in 1941 Naden musicians played key roles in its development (in 1943 the orchestra included twenty-three players from Naden), and this co-operative effort resulted in a considerable degree of stability and expertise in the wind sections.

The establishment of the Canadian Forces School of Music at Naden in 1954 further enhanced musical activity at the base, and with the amalgamation of the Canadian forces in 1968 the Naden band was one of only two groups to be retained in the permanent forces.

It can be seen from this short survey that the influence of the naval base at Esquimalt on the development of music on the west coast has been profound. The first musical performances heard in the colony of Vancouver's Island were provided by Royal Navy personnel; the first musical composition indigenous to British Columbia was written by a naval officer; musical performances by naval bands inspired local performers to perfect their craft; and many naval musicians remained in British Columbia after their tour of duty was over, teaching, performing, and directing local ensembles. There is no doubt that musical activity on the west coast would have been less rich, and much slower to develop, had it not been for the influence of our cousins from across the sea.

GILLES POTVIN

Maurice Ravel au Canada

A partir de la dernière décennie du XIXe siècle, l'Amérique du Nord commença à accueillir un nombre relativement imposant de compositeurs européens éminents qui effectuèrent la traversée de l'Atlantique pour venir aux Etats-Unis et parfois au Canada pour diriger leurs oeuvres ou participer à leur exécution. Parmi les plus célèbres, citons Tchaikovsky (1891), Dvorak (1893), Mascagni (1902), Richard Strauss (1904), d'Indy (1905 et 1921), Leoncavallo (1906), Mahler, Puccini et Elgar (1907), Saint-Saëns (1910), Prokofiev (1918), Milhaud (1922), Stravinsky (1925), Bartok (1927-8) et Ravel (1928). La venue de ces illustres visiteurs coïncidait avec une activité lyrique et symphonique qui connaissait un essor sans précédent aux Etats-Unis et, à un degré moindre, au Canada, ce qui pourrait expliquer le fait que peu d'entre eux vinrent au Canada alors qu'ils se trouvaient dans la république voisine.

Seuls Mascagni, Leoncavallo, Elgar, Prokofiev, Milhaud et Ravel s'aventurèrent au Canada. Vincent d'Indy y séjourna brièvement en 1921 mais Stravinsky n'y mettra les pieds qu'en 1937. On s'étonne que des compositeurs français comme Gounod et Massenet n'aient jamais effectué le grand voyage, compte tenu de la popularité dont jouissaient alors leurs opéras et oratorios, tant aux Etats-Unis qu'au Canada. Quant à Debussy, on sait qu'il a envisagé un voyage en Amérique lequel ne s'est jamais concrétisé. C'est finalement Maurice Ravel qui aura été le premier grand compositeur français à se produire au Canada en personne, lors d'une tournée nord-américaine qui se prolongea durant quatre mois au début de 1928. A l'itinéraire de cette tournée figuraient les villes de Vancouver, Toronto et Montréal où Ravel joua ses oeuvres au piano en plus d'accompagner une cantatrice dans ses mélodies. En cette année 1987 qui marque le cinquantenaire de la mort du musicien, il est tout à fait approprié d'évoquer les étapes canadiennes de cette tournée, d'autant plus que des

Canadiens y participèrent à titre d'interprètes et aussi au plan de l'organisation matérielle.

Arrivé à New York sur le *France* le 4 janvier 1928, le compositeur en repartit le 21 avril suivant sur le *Paris*. Dans l'intervalle, il traversa les Etats-Unis du Nord au Sud et de l'Est à l'Ouest, visitant une vingtaine de villes, dont New York, Boston, Chicago et Cleveland, où il monta au pupitre pour diriger ses oeuvres les plus célèbres comme *La Valse*, *Rapsodie espagnole*, *Le Tombeau de Couperin* et *Shéhérazade* avec la soprano Lisa Roma comme soliste. Dans les autres villes, il se contenta de jouer ses oeuvres au piano et d'accompagner la cantatrice.

La musique de Ravel ne connaissait pas en 1928 l'immense popularité dont elle jouit aujourd'hui. Ses oeuvres pour orchestre n'étaient connues au Canada que d'un petit nombre d'initiés qui avaient voyagé aux Etats-Unis ou en Europe ou qui en possédaient les rares enregistrements. Sa musique de chambre, ses oeuvres pour piano et ses mélodies avaient cependant trouvé ici quelques interprètes aussi audacieux que talentueux comme les pianistes Jean Blake Robinson (Mrs Walter Coulthard) à Vancouver, Alberto Guerrero à Toronto et Léo-Pol Morin à Montréal. Sa musique vocale avait aussi trouvé ici d'excellents interprètes en la personne de la mezzo-soprano Eva Gauthier et du baryton Victor Brault. Ce dernier avait même chanté les *Trois Poèmes de Mallarmé* à Londres sous la direction du compositeur. A Toronto, le *Quatuor en fa* avait été exécuté dès 1911 et Montréal l'avait entendu en 1920 joué par le Quatuor Dubois.

Le principal artisan de la venue de Ravel aux Etats-Unis et au Canada fut le pianiste français Elie Robert Schmitz (1889-1949). Féru de musique contemporaine, il avait organisé des concerts à Paris dès 1911 avec des collègues épris du même idéal. La guerre allait mettre fin à cette initiative mais Schmitz allait reprendre son activité aussitôt après l'Armistice. A la suite de ses récitals et conférences en Europe et en Amérique du Nord, il organisa en 1920 la Franco-American Musical Society qui devint trois ans plus tard la Pro-Musica Society dans le but de favoriser des échanges de musiciens, particulièrement de compositeurs, au niveau international. Doué d'un talent d'organisateur peu commun, Schmitz, aidé de sa femme, la pianiste Germaine Schnitzer, établit des chapitres de Pro-Musica dans de nombreuses villes d'Europe, d'Amérique et même d'Asie. C'est sous les auspices de Pro-Musica que des compositeurs comme Casella, Kodaly, Bartok et Nadia Boulanger vinrent en Amérique à cette époque.

Dès 1922, le couple Schmitz avait approché Maurice Ravel afin de l'intéresser à effectuer une tournée nord-américaine. Il avait refusé sous le prétexte qu'il n'était pas pianiste et qu'il ne prisait pas l'idée d'être exhibé comme dans un cirque. Des tentatives répétées ne furent pas plus heureuses. En 1926, Ravel se laissa finalement convaincre quand Schmitz lui offrit une garantie de $10,000 minimum pour une tournée de trois mois. "C'est beaucoup d'argent ça!" commenta le musicien, vraiment sceptique à l'idée qu'on voudrait payer cette somme pour le voir et l'entendre jouer du piano. Ravel confirma l'entente dans une lettre en date du 29 mai 1926.[1]

De retour à New York, Schmitz obtint une somme de $5000 des pianos Mason & Hamlin à condition que Ravel utilise ce piano en exclusivité. L'autre $5000 fut assuré par les chapitres de Pro-Musica. D'autres villes, dont celles du Canada, s'ajoutèrent par l'entremise de l'imprésario Lucy Bogue et de son associé canadien Bernard R. LaBerge.

La tournée projetée fut mise au point non sans difficultés. On découvrit en premier lieu qu'un agent britannique détenait une option englobant tous les pays de langue anglaise. Pour permettre à Ravel de jouer en Amérique du Nord, il fallut payer un dédit ($1200 selon Vivian Perlis, $1000 selon Madeleine Goss). Les organisateurs furent aussi aux prises avec des exigences assez curieuses de Ravel, notamment l'assurance qu'il disposerait d'une provision suffisante de Caporals, sa cigarette préférée, et d'une variété de vins de son choix. Tout fut finalement arrangé selon ses souhaits et c'est un Ravel souriant et détendu qui débarqua à New York au début de janvier, accompagné de nombreux bagages, dont une garde-robe contenant vingt paires de pyjamas, des douzaines de chemises et de costumes aux couleurs flamboyantes et pas moins d'une cinquantaine de cravates!

Ses débuts officiels eurent lieu le 15 janvier au Gallo Theater de la 54e rue. A ses côtés figuraient au programme le violoniste Joseph Szigeti, le harpiste Carlos Salzedo, un ami de longue date, la chanteuse Greta Torpadie et d'autres artistes, dont le Quatuor Hart House de Toronto qui avait été engagé pour jouer le *Quatuor en fa*. Il avait été convenu que Ravel se rendait auparavant à Toronto afin d'assister aux répétitions de son oeuvre. Harry Adaskin, second violon du quatuor, a évoqué cette première incursion du musicien en territoire canadien.

We went up to his room [at the King Edward Hotel] and he appeared in a longish and belted mauve jacket looking very chic with his white hair and bird-bright eyes. He was very slight, but had presence. He greeted us politely and with gravity in French, since he spoke no English, and we put up our music stands and began to play. Ravel made no remark, except in one spot where we made a slight ritardando. There he leaped up as if he'd been shot and said: 'Pas de retard.' Otherwise he said not a word until we had finished all four movements. Then he thought for a moment, and finally said – I think I can recall his exact words: 'Ce n'était pas comme ça que j'ai conçu le quatuor.' ('This was not how I conceived the quartet.') I don't know how my colleagues felt, but I felt awful. Finally Geza [de Kresz, first violin] said: 'Would you please tell us how you would like us to play it.' But Ravel promptly said: 'No. You play it with such conviction that any change would be unwise.' He was very calm and relaxed about the whole thing, offered us drinks, and then took us downstairs to a marvellous lunch, prepared for us by his friend the chef. During the meal he was chatty and friendly, and we got the feeling that he definitely did not want us to change anything – except that one retard, of course. Naturally he was quite right. We loved the work, we played it with confidence and assurance, and any monkeying with it now would spoil it.[2]

Adaskin précise que le *Quatuor* fut exécuté également à Albany, NY, ainsi qu'à Toronto, les organisateurs ne pouvant se permettre de faire suivre le quatuor dans toutes les villes où se produirait le compositeur.

RAVEL À VANCOUVER

Un mois après ses débuts à New York, Ravel arriva à Vancouver venant de Portland, Oregon. Il était accompagné de la chanteuse Lisa Roma. Il avait dans l'intervalle donné plusieurs concerts et dirigé des orchestres. Il avait visité Hollywood et rencontré des vedettes de cinéma comme Lionel Barrymore et Douglas Fairbanks. Malgré de longs trajets en chemin de fer, le compositeur semble être demeuré en excellente forme même s'il écrivit à Hélène Jourdan-Morhange: 'Je vois des villes magnifiques, des pays enchanteurs, mais les triomphes sont fatiguants.'[3]

Le concert était prévu pour le mardi, 14 février, au New Auditorium, angle des rues Georgia et Denman, sous les auspices de l'imprésario Lily J. Laverock. Dans les jours qui précèdent, la presse locale publia des articles substantiels annonçant l'événement. Le samedi 11, le *Vancouver Sun* publia une photo du compositeur sur deux colonnes accompagnée d'un texte titré comme suit: 'Ravel Visit Big Event in Music World':

A great and singular personality, Maurice Ravel of Paris, France's foremost composer, will appear as pianist on Tuesday, playing some of the most popular and beautiful of his own works for piano and accompanying Lisa Roma, dramatic soprano of the Philadelphia Grand Opera company, in some of his finest and loveliest examples of song. The event is unique in local annals for it is the first occasion on which a composer of so great prominence in the history of music has ever visited Vancouver. Minor composers, such as Rachmaninoff, have been welcomed here, but none who have made so profound an impress on the history of music as has Maurice Ravel ...

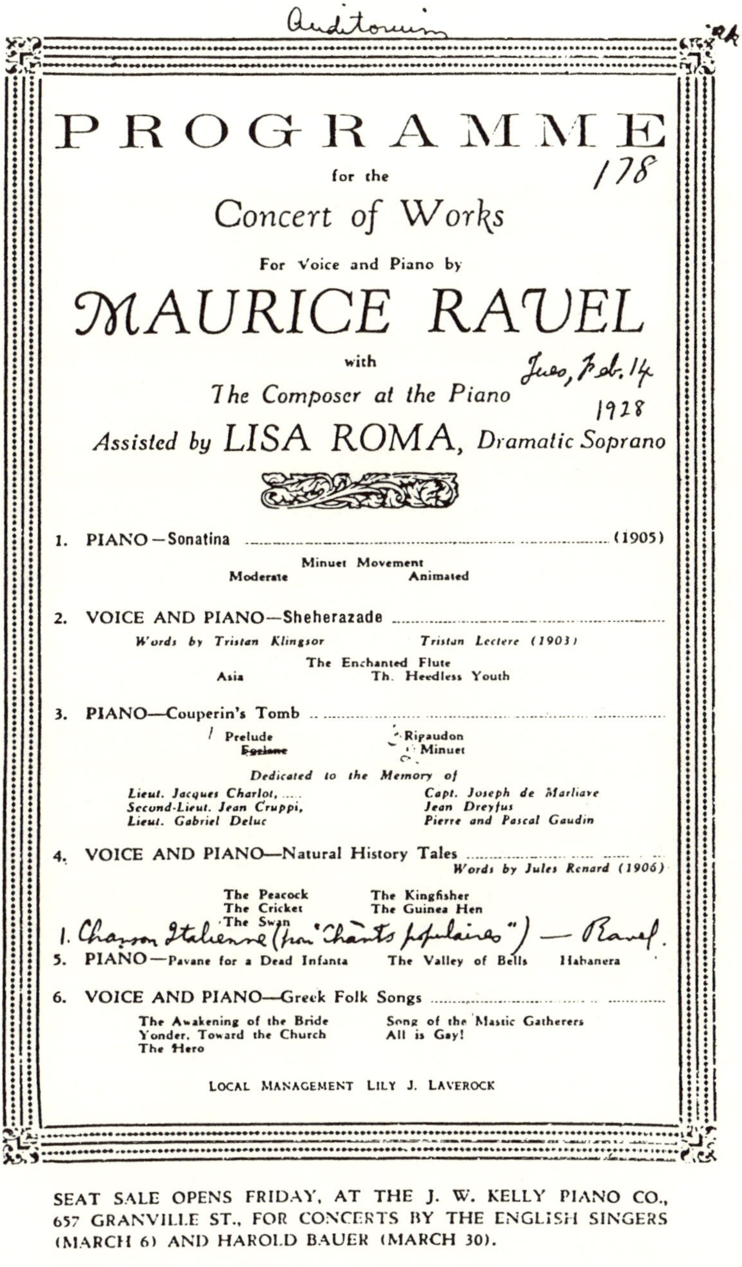

PROGRAMME

for the

Concert of Works

For Voice and Piano by

MAURICE RAVEL

with

The Composer at the Piano

Assisted by LISA ROMA, Dramatic Soprano

[handwritten: Auditorium / 178 / Tues, Feb. 14, 1928]

1. PIANO—Sonatina .... (1905)
   Moderate   Minuet Movement   Animated

2. VOICE AND PIANO—Sheherazade
   Words by Tristan Klingsor   Tristan Lectere (1903)
       The Enchanted Flute
   Asia   Th. Heedless Youth

3. PIANO—Couperin's Tomb
   Prelude   Ripaudon
   ~~Eglaue~~   Minuet
   Dedicated to the Memory of
   Lieut. Jacques Charlot,   Capt. Joseph de Marliave
   Second-Lieut. Jean Cruppi,   Jean Dreyfus
   Lieut. Gabriel Deluc   Pierre and Pascal Gaudin

4. VOICE AND PIANO—Natural History Tales
   Words by Jules Renard (1906)
   The Peacock   The Kingfisher
   The Cricket   The Guinea Hen
   The Swan

   [handwritten: 1. Chanson Italienne (from "Chants populaires") — Ravel]

5. PIANO—Pavane for a Dead Infanta   The Valley of Bells   Habanera

6. VOICE AND PIANO—Greek Folk Songs
   The Awakening of the Bride   Song of the Mastic Gatherers
   Yonder, Toward the Church   All is Gay!
   The Hero

LOCAL MANAGEMENT LILY J. LAVEROCK

SEAT SALE OPENS FRIDAY, AT THE J. W. KELLY PIANO CO., 657 GRANVILLE ST., FOR CONCERTS BY THE ENGLISH SINGERS (MARCH 6) AND HAROLD BAUER (MARCH 30).

Copie du programme du concert Ravel à Vancouver le 14 février 1928 conservé à la bibliothèque musicale de l'Université de la Colombie-britannique et obtenue par l'entremise de la Bibliothèque publique de Vancouver

Un autre texte, publié le lendemain dans le *Vancouver Daily Province* sous la signature de R.J. (sans doute Rhynd Jamieson) visait de toute évidence à familiariser le public avec le compositeur.

One of the most widely discussed of present-day composers will visit Vancouver this week. I refer to Maurice Ravel, the remarkable Frenchman whose inventive genius is the talk of the musical world. Owing to the interest which surrounds the appearance of this historic figure here I feel it necessary, in justice to the cause of modern music, to say something concerning Ravel and his art ... Ravel's visit to Vancouver is an event of more than passing note, and I trust for the sake of our musical progress the distinguished Frenchman will be welcomed by a great audience. It will be interesting to hear what he has to say and how he says it.

Ravel joua sa *Sonatine*, trois mouvements du *Tombeau de Couperin*, *Pavane pour une infante défunte*, *La Vallée des cloches* et *Habanera*. Il accompagna Lisa Roma dans *Shéhérazade*, *Histoires naturelles*, *Cinq Mélodies populaires grecques* et, en rappel, *Chanson italienne*. La distinguée compositrice Jean Coulthard assistait à l'événement et en a gardé un souvenir très vivace.

When we heard Ravel in 1928 it must have been in the horrible old Georgia Auditorium (which fortunately is no longer in use), a cavernous, arena-like space with very poor sound. Ravel was very slim and small, rather delicate looking. He played almost like a young child – very simple and no 'concert pianist' style at all. One piece I remember in particular was the *Pavane*; he played it very simply with almost no expression at all. He brought with him a French soprano ... who sang some of his songs which he accompanied in a similar manner; as I can remember, the soprano didn't have a particularly compelling voice. All this certainly did not appeal to the Vancouver audience who knew little or nothing about Ravel. They were there to hear a 'real concert pianist' plus a virtuoso singer. True, there was a small and very appreciative group present, but, to the great embarrassment of my mother and other musicians in her circle like Frederick Chubb and Mrs Della Johnson, the audience started going out in droves after the first couple of numbers. By the end of the concert there were fewer than fifty left. Audiences in those days really didn't know what they were missing. My mother took great pains to explain to my sister and me that Ravel was not a virtuoso but a *great* composer. I assume that [among] the critics would have been old "R.J." – R. Jamieson of the *Province* who, to give him his due, realized what a great treat this was. But Vancouver audiences enjoyed gossiping about the great scandal for many weeks after.

Dans l'ensemble, la réaction des deux quotidiens fut positive même si la musique de Ravel et son jeu au piano laissèrent les critiques quelque peu perplexes. Dans le *Province* R. Jamieson intitula son compte rendu: 'Maurice Ravel Heard In An Unusual Recital':

... a recital ... not likely soon to be forgotten by the large gathering of music-lovers who heard the artist. Here was a new experience for concert-goers who have been in the habit of listening to music of the old and more familiar school. The composer was given an enthusiastic reception. It was a 'trying' evening for the audience and while at times I could not but recall the compositions of some of the great immortals, I could not excape the conviction that the music of this modern genius was invested with craftmanship of a very remarkable nature. As a matter of fact this is one of Ravel's chief qualities; some indeed would say his supreme characteristic. Ravel obviously has no love of virtuosity for its own sake. His care for detail and occupation with perfection of workmanship are apparent on every page, in every bar, even in every chord. The man himself is very much like his music, elegant, precise, meticulous and thoroughly methodical. But the question arises. Does the music of this modern move the heart? Is it human in its appeal to the average listener? I am rather inclined to answer these questions in the negative.

Le compte rendu du *Sun* le même jour est signé J. Cheltenham et il avait comme titre: 'Ravel Program Enchants His Hearers Here.' Comme son collègue, il vanta les oeuvres du compositeur français, exprimant quelques réserves ici et là, notamment sur son jeu au piano:

The famous Frenchman was assisted by Lisa Roma ... Between them they presented a Ravel program which, while it provoked no riotous enthusiasm, at least had some ardent listeners and provided many moments of real enchantment ... A quality of passionate keenness was present in all his playing, and, though it more often suggested the glitter of a needle than the flash and sweep of a sword, it was always compelling and always effective enough to offset certain shortcomings in technique. It was, of course, a composer's exhibit, not a virtuoso's. This gave the occasion an unusual distinction, and while many of those present found a certain monotony of fragility and tenuousness in the music there were also to be found continual delights – atmospheres wrapping one round with the still ecstasy of Faery, rhythms seiing [sic] yet intangible, threads and sprays of melody, strange, poignant, fleeting ... one felt that at no time did Ravel the pianist achieve the full poetic and delineative wizardy of Ravel the composer as, for instance, it was certainly achieved when Enesco, the violinist, played the *Tzigane* here last month ...

Le séjour de Ravel à Vancouver n'a pas été, autant que l'on sache, marqué d'autres événements d'importance. On ne peut toutefois s'empêcher de citer la question qui terminait le compte rendu de R.J. dans le *Province*, 'What will the world think of Maurice Ravel ten years hence?' ('Que pensera le monde de Maurice Ravel dans dix ans d'ici?').

RAVEL À TORONTO

Après Vancouver, Ravel reparti pour les Etats-Unis afin de poursuivre une tournée exténuante et organisée de façon plutôt cahotique. L'itinéraire, établi sans trop tenir compte des distances, l'obligea à de longs parcours en train. Souvent il devait revenir sur ses pas afin de respecter l'itinéraire prévu. Chaque concert était généralement suivi de réceptions et autres activités sociales, sans compter les inévitables interviews. Le compositeur, dont on sait que la constitution n'était pas des plus fortes, résista cependant admirablement et semblait très heureux, si l'on se fie à la correspondance qu'il échangea continuellement avec ses amis et intimes. Dans sa lettre du 4 avril à sa marraine, Mme Fernand Dreyfus, écrite sur le train entre New York et la Nouvelle-Orléans, il lui fit part de son retour en avril et, non sans ironie, lui dit: 'Et je ne serai pas crevé comme on vous l'a dit, je ne me suis jamais mieux porté que durant cette folle tournée. J'ai fini par en découvrir la raison: c'est que jamais je n'ai mené une vie aussi raisonnable.'

En vue du concert de Toronto annoncé pour le jeudi, 22 mars, au Margaret Eaton Hall, Ravel et Lisa Roma arrivèrent en gare Union en soirée, dès le dimanche 18, venant de St Paul, Minnesota. Il fut accueilli par une délégation qui comprenait le consul de France, M. Rochereau de Sablière, et son fils; Ernest MacMillan, directeur du Toronto Conservatory; MM. Geza de Kresz, Milton Blackstone et Boris Hambourg du Quatuor Hart House, et quelques autres personnalités. Il accorda aussitôt une interview à Augustus Bridle, critique musical du *Toronto Daily Star*, qui la publia le lendemain:

Mons. Ravel is about the height of Napoleon. In a fawn hat and bulgy overcoat to match, a negligee striped shirt and tie en suite [sic] and straight iron-gray hair, he twinkles like a morning star, defiant of time, fatigue or place, or anything but the immediate business of seeing and hearing what life is every moment he is awake. Seated at a rotunda table, not caring who heard him talk French about music and life, he spoke through Boris Hambourg, excellent interpreter. He talked volubly and vividly. His eyes snapped with 'joie de vivre.' He twiddled all his fingers as he spoke, as though playing on a harp. Tuesday he would be motoring to Niagara Falls – to get a new theme for composition. Ah! Splendid ...

Dans ses réponses aux nombreuses questions du journaliste, Ravel exprima avec précision et concision ses vues sur divers sujets comme le nationalisme en musique ('Much of it is national. We are all minutely different. French are unlike Germans. Schoenberg and Stravinsky and de Falla and Rieti, all agree upon being opposed to romanticism but also to differ in themselves. I am myself keenly alive to the Group of Six in France'), sur la mélodie ('No, you can never kill melody; you only change its character'), sur le jazz ('Jazz is universal. We are all affected by it; all schools, all composers, Stravinsky, Schoenberg, de Falla – all of us. My own sonata I made to represent the workaday world on the piano – wheels and things – with the violin taking the melody about it'), sur l'inspiration ('Anything in nature is a subject for music. Skyscrapers, trains, dynamos, street cars are all as much material for music as mountains and clouds and seas'), sur l'influence réciproque entre compositeurs ('All composers are influenced by one another. There are certain tricks that we all share in common – with minute differences. We have our formulas just as the classicists had').

Au sujet de sa visite aux chutes Niagara le journaliste lui demande ce par quoi il s'attend à être le plus frappé: le bruit des chutes, les couleurs de l'eau ou l'immensité des cataractes. 'I am affected always by everything there is as I see it and hear it and feel it. It may be more color or mass, or motion or sound. It is all one. We moderns take it all in. We never know what may catch us next. A cloud or a foghorn or a pretty face or a crowd or a fire. All is life – for music just as it is for painting or literature.' Ravel ne semble pas avoir subséquemment commenté sa visite aux chutes Niagara. Il est sûr cependant que cette merveille canadienne ne lui a pas inspiré d'oeuvre. (Dans sa biographie de Calixa Lavallée, Eugène Lapierre rapporte que Ravel, en voyant les chutes, se serait écrié: 'Quel majestueux si bémol!' mais ne donne cependant pas la source de ce témoignage.)

Profitant de quelques jours de répit, Ravel rendit visite à Ernest MacMillan, directeur du Toronto Conservatory, qui l'avait accueilli à son arrivée. Carl Morey, l'actuel doyen de la faculté de musique de l'université de Toronto, se souvient que sir Ernest lui rappela beaucoup plus tard cette visite.[4] Ayant remarqué dans le bureau de MacMillan un buste de Bach (ou de Beethoven), Ravel lui aurait demandé pourquoi il n'y avait pas aussi un buste de Mozart! (A son arrivée à New York au début de janvier, Ravel avait déclaré aux journalistes: 'Pour moi, les plus grands musiciens sont Bach et Mozart.')

Présenté par le bureau Carleton Wix Associated, le programme du concert de Toronto (billets au prix unique de $2.20) était sensiblement le même que celui de Vancouver, sauf qu'il se terminait par le *Quatuor en fa* joué par le Quatuor Hart House, le compositeur se contentant de jouer le *Rigaudon* du *Tombeau de Couperin*. Dans la même semaine, le Massey Hall présentait deux célébrités, le pianiste Paderewski et le violoniste Fritz Kreisler, ce qui n'empêcha pas Ravel de faire salle comble.

Dans son édition du 22 mars, jour du concert, *The Globe* publia une photo du compositeur avec la mention 'world's greatest contemporary composer.' Le compte rendu du critique Lawrence Mason le lendemain ne laissa aucun doute quant au succès du concert:

A capacity crowd turned out in honor of the event . . . All were warmly applauded and encored while the central figure of the occasion received a veritable ovation. M. Ravel is not a virtuoso excutant and Miss Roma, though she sang the difficult music with artistic intelligence, did not display a voice of unusual beauty or distinction, so that the performing honors were easily borne off by our fine local ensemble. The Hart House players indeed were in particularly good form and brought out the peculiarly Gallic exquisitenesses of the Ravel quartet with quite ravishing deftness and felicity . . .

La réaction du critique qui signait 'Yenmita' dans *The Evening Telegram* du même jour (pseudonyme d'Edward W. Wodson) fut par contre assez bizarre, autant que son titre: 'No Heart in Ravel's Work – Synthetic But Pleasing':

Ravel himself has a personality – a gracious, gracefully exquisite sort of personality who might be a chemist or a renowned surgeon or a painter. His music is like himself. It is a matter of opinion of course; but you must forget that you ever knew, or thought you knew and liked or thought you liked if you are to listen to his songs and pianism and keep happy . . . Science, mathematics, and logic are gods to-day, the music is not composed but invented and devised by processes that are intellectually synthetic. The heart of it is gone. His playing, and Miss Roma's singing, ignored the emotions entirely. Of course it was Ravel's music, and since Ravel might have been a chemist, a surgeon or a painter, it is absurd to expect emotions in his work . . . To those who like modernistic music such as Ravel's Ravel's music is just what they will like. He had a splendid reception last evening from a large and distinguished audience.

Il reste à préciser que la première heure du récital Ravel, 8 h 30 à 9 h 30, fut transmise sur les ondes radiophoniques par la station CFCA du *Toronto Daily Star* sous les auspices de la T. Eaton Co. et de la Hambourg Concert Society. Des annonces à cet effet parurent dans la presse torontoise. Carl Morey souligne que la station CKAC de Montréal retransmit ce programme en se rattachant au poste torontois mais aucun des horaires radiophoniques parus ce jour-là dans la presse montréalaise n'en font mention.

RAVEL À MONTRÉAL

Après Toronto, Ravel et Lisa Roma repartirent pour les Etats-Unis, les étapes suivantes étant Chicago, la Nouvelle-Orléans, Houston, le Grand Canyon, Buffalo et, de nouveau, New York avant Montréal, étape ultime de cette extraordinaire tournée. Avant d'aller plus loin, il faut cependant rappeler un événement qui marqua cette tournée le 7 mars. Ce jour-là était celui du 53e anniversaire de naissance du compositeur et sa grande amie, la cantatrice canadienne Eva Gauthier, qui habitait New York, fit en sorte que cet anniversaire ne passe pas inaperçu. Le compositeur se trouvait fort heureusement dans la métropole américaine et une grande soirée en son honneur fut organisée à l'appartement d'Eva Gauthier.

Parmi les nombreux invités se trouvait George Gershwin, qui se mit au piano après dîner. Maurice Ravel fut totalement séduit par la musique de son jeune collègue américain. Il appert que Gershwin sollicita alors de Ravel la faveur d'obtenir des leçons de lui. Selon Eva Gauthier, Ravel aurait répliqué: 'Vous êtes maintenant un Gershwin de première qualité. Si vous étudiez avec moi, vous deviendrez un Ravel de deuxième qualité.' L'histoire, sous différentes formes, a fait le tour du monde depuis. Gershwin allait bientôt partir pour Paris et ce qu'il obtint de Ravel fut une lettre d'introduction pour Nadia Boulanger qui, elle aussi, lui fit une réponse dans le même sens que celle de Ravel.[5]

Organisé par l'imprésario Louis-H. Bourdon, le concert Ravel à Montréal prit place au théâtre Saint-Denis sur la rue du même nom, le soir du jeudi, 19 avril. Ce concert allait être le dernier de cette exténuante tournée et, par le fait même, l'adieu de Maurice Ravel à l'Amérique du Nord.

Le compositeur arriva le matin même à la gare Windsor et fut aussitôt interviewé par un représentant du quotidien *La Presse*. Un propos assez étonnant du musicien servit de titre à son article: 'Le Jazz N'Est Pas Destiné à Mourir, Il Survivra, au Contraire, et C'Est Par Lui Que Commencera La Musique Américaine.'

Petit et délicat, cheveux grisonnants, Maurice Ravel est d'une charmante urbanité ... M. Ravel – et il ne s'en cache pas – est un enthousiaste de la musique américaine. Il est très probable qu'il écrive une composition pour l'orchestre de Paul Whiteman. 'Le jazz,' dit-il, 'exerce aujourd'hui une très grande influence sur le monde et les compositeurs. C'est une musique qui est destinée à survivre et qui sera le point de départ de la musique américaine. Il est appelé à se transformer, à subir une évolution. Ce qui fait aujourd'hui sa popularité, c'est la force de son rythme ... ' Parlant ensuite des compositeurs modernes, M. Ravel ne cache pas ses préférences pour Stravinsky, de Falla et Vaughan Williams. 'Ce dernier,' dit-il, 'est vraiment un compositeur national. Son inspiration est vraiment anglaise. C'est une erreur de dire que l'art est universel. Au contraire, l'art est essentiellement national. Il s'inspire des légendes et des traditions d'un pays. Un artiste subit toujours l'influence de son milieu, de son pays natal.'

A Montréal comme ailleurs au cours de cette tournée, Ravel a rarement parlé de sa propre musique. C'était d'ailleurs son habitude d'être avare de commentaires sur ses oeuvres et sa façon de travailler. Mais il fit au journaliste montréalais une confidence qui ne manque pas d'intérêt. 'Parlant ensuite de sa propre musique, M. Ravel dit qu'il considère que son oeuvre ne commence qu'en 1920 avec sa *Sonate* pour violon et violoncelle. Il est à la fois heureux et surpris d'apprendre de la part de M. Louis-H. Bourbon que cette oeuvre a été exécutée à Montréal par son beau-père, le professeur J.-B. Dubois.'

Le samedi précédent, *La Presse* avait publié la photo du compositeur sur deux colonnes, accompagnée d'un article qualifiant Ravel

l'un des plus grands compositeurs et pianistes français de notre époque, le maître incontesté de la musique française moderne, inspiré par Chabrier et Debussy ... C'est là un événement artistique qui sort de l'ordinaire, car rares sont les compositeurs jouissant d'une aussi grande renommée mondiale qui soient venus faire connaître leurs propres oeuvres personnellement à la population de la métropole canadienne ... Maurice Ravel est assurément le plus grand auteur de musique moderne. Il est le prototype de la France artistique et s'il est adoré dans son pays, il est adulé partout ailleurs ...

Le programme de Montréal différait de ceux de Vancouver et de Toronto du fait que la chanteuse norvégienne Greta Torpadie remplaça Lisa Roma comme interprète des *Histoires naturelles* et de *Shéhérazade*. Cette dernière oeuvre fut substituée à la dernière minute à trois des *Cinq Mélodies populaires grecques*. Le compositeur joua sa *Sonatine* et les applaudissements du public l'incitèrent à revenir sur scène à trois reprises pour jouer successivement *Pavane*, *Rigaudon* du *Tombeau de Couperin* et *Habanera*. L'exécution du *Quatuor* fut cette fois confiée au Quatuor Dubois – Edgar Braidi et Lucien Sicotte, violon; Joseph Mastrocola, alto; Jean-Baptiste Dubois, violoncelle – qui en avait donné la première audition montréalaise le 6 avril 1920. Mais le clou de cette soirée fut l'unique présentation au cours de cette tournée de *Ma Mère L'Oye*, les cinq pièces pour piano à quatre mains que le compositeur interpréta en fin de programme avec le pianiste montréalais Léo-Pol Morin, qui avait été à Paris l'élève de piano de Ricardo Vines, le célèbre pianiste espagnol et ami du compositeur. Vines avait créé *Jeux d'eau*, la *Sonatine*, *Miroirs* et *Gaspard de la Nuit*.

Si tous les comptes rendus furent unanimes à qualifier d'événement ce concert, ils le furent aussi pour déplorer le fait qu'un public si peu nombreux s'y soit rendu, à commencer par Frédéric Pelletier dans *Le Devoir* du lendemain:

On pouvait croire que le théâtre Saint-Denis se remplirait hier soir pour entendre M. Maurice Ravel. Hélas, c'est à peine si la salle était au tiers remplie. Même en admettant que M. Ravel n'est pas un de ces virtuoses qui fascinent les foules par leur jeu prestigieux, il y avait là une occasion unique d'entendre des oeuvres renommées dans tout l'univers, avec l'interprétation et le sens que leur donne l'auteur ... Pour ceux qui font passer la musique avant celui qui la joue, qui s'intéressent à l'oeuvre et ne demandent pas autre chose qu'une présentation probe, intelligente, pour la goûter dans sa plénitude, le concert d'hier a dû être une jouissance sans pareille, mais il faut bien avouer que M. Ravel, qui sait manier son clavier avec une clarté parfaite et faire comprendre ses plus menues intentions, n'est pas un de ces pianistes dont l'exécution exerce son emprise sur les auditeurs ordinaires ...

Le critique anonyme, dont *La Presse* publia l'article le même jour, adopta un peu le même ton:

Toute solennité fut bannie par Maurice Ravel lui-même du récital que ce grand pianiste-compositeur donna hier soir au théâtre Saint-Denis devant un auditoire trop peu dense, mais combien sensible. Et cette absence d'apparat, la timidité ou la simplicité d'un artiste qu'on devait pousser chaque fois hors de la coulisse pour qu'il répondit aux applaudissements multiples de l'assistance, qui venait saluer du même pas nerveux et balancé jusqu'au même milieu du piano, une main dessus, et d'un même brusque mouvement de la tête et de la moitié du corps, toute cela couvrait déjà d'un grand charme une exécution primesautière, spirituelle et enjouée. Qui ne se souviendra toujours de cette soirée Ravel délicieuse entre mille autres? ...

La presse montréalaise de langue anglaise accueillit très favorablement le concert Ravel, même si H.P. Bell, dans le *Montreal Daily Star* ne semble pas avoir pris très au sérieux la musique de Ravel:

The Ravel Concert Was Happy and Informal – Every one who went to the Ravel concert on Thursday must have had a thoroughly pleasant evening, for the performers appeared to enjoy themselves as much as their audience. The proceedings began seriously enough, it is true, with Ravel's fine string quartet in F. The Dubois quartet ... put some of their very best playing into this, but the tone of a string quartet can scarcely be effective in a big space like the St. Denis theatre. After this overture the stage was rearranged a little and Ravel himself came into the middle of the picture and stayed there for the rest of the evening; a cheerful and smiling little gentleman, he made the centre of proceedings which were always interesting but never too serious ... The concert ended with "Ma Mère l'Oye" in its original form of a piano duet ... This was never meant to be taken seriously and Ravel took care to bring out all its humours, which made it a good climax to the jollities of the evening ... the proceedings, all through, gave one the feeling of being present not so much at a concert as at a small family party of engaging and accomplished people, who were trying over some new music.

Immédiatement après le concert de Montréal, Ravel repartit pour New York où il s'embarqua sur le *Paris* de la French Line le samedi 21 avril, à minuit. Il arriva au Havre six jours plus tard avec tous ses bagages et la somme de $27,000 qu'il avait gagnée au cours de cette tournée de quatre mois, durant lesquels il avait parcouru l'Amérique du Nord dans tous les sens.

Outre la correspondance échangée durant son voyage avec son frère Edouard et d'autres intimes, Maurice Ravel ne semble pas avoir tenu de journal et il n'a jamais publié de récit ou chronique de la tournée. On ne peut donc que spéculer sur les impressions qu'il a pu ressentir au cours de ce long périple, y compris les visites qu'il fit à Vancouver, Toronto et Montréal. Sa discrétion et sa modestie légendaires s'opposaient sans doute à l'expression publique de telles impressions. A son arrivée à Montréal, il avait pourtant déclaré au journaliste de *La Presse* que 'le Canada est un pays qu'il désirait connaître depuis longtemps, car c'est un coin de la France.'

Si les journaux de Vancouver et de Toronto, outre les comptes rendus habituels des concerts, semblent être demeurés silencieux après le départ du musicien, ceux de Montréal, notamment *Le Canada* et *La Patrie*, déplorèrent l'accueil réservé que lui fit la métropole du Canada. A titre de deuxième ville française du monde, Montréal aurait dû recevoir un musicien avec tout l'éclat et l'enthousiasme que méritait sa renommée. Dans *Le Canada* du 28 avril, Dominique Laberge écrivit:

L'événement artistique par excellence de la saison a eu lieu: ce fut la visite de l'éminent pianiste-compositeur et chef d'orchestre français Maurice Ravel. Il a donné un récital qui ne sera pas de sitôt oublié. Hélas! une pareille aubaine dont trop d'amateurs de musique se sont privés et qui vaut plus, comme le disait un confrère, que toutes les exhibitions du virtuosisme le plus remarquable, est chose plutôt rare à Montréal. Maintenant que l'événement est passé, nous ne pourrons plus broder sans fin de brillantes arguties sur le thème connu qui l'alimentait: 'Il faut prouver à Maurice Ravel que nous apprécions son art, son génie tout autant que nos voisins des Etats-Unis.' Nous n'avons plus à y revenir puisque le maître a passé et, pour plusieurs, comme une ombre fugitive... Nous ne savons pas quelle impression a gardé Maurice Ravel de sa visite à Montréal, mais il n'a pas dû être édifié par le nombre si mince qui est allé l'entendre. Il aurait été frappé par la grandeur de nos salles et se serait peut-être dit: 'Les Canadiens sont un peuple prévoyant, ils construisent grand... en prévision de l'avenir.'

Il ne faut pas s'étonner si Léo-Pol Morin fut celui qui trouva les mots et les expressions les plus senties pour situer cet événement historique dans sa perspective la plus juste et en dégager toute la portée. Dans un article de *La Patrie*, 'En marge du concert de Maurice Ravel' paru le 21 avril, il déplora lui aussi l'absence d'un public nombreux mais ne pu s'empêcher de poser des questions:

Mais l'avons-nous réellement aimé? Nos oreilles ont-elle entendu? Avons-nous saisi les nuances de ce beau, clair et harmonieux génie? La leçon de cet art si mesuré, si parfaitement équilibré et proportionné a-t-elle été comprise? Peut-être que non... Mais peu importe, cher Ravel, que vous soyez un virtuose de première, deuxième ou troisième dimension. Là n'est pas la question... Notre admiration a de plus hauts mobiles et de plus éternels. Ce que nous aimons en vous, c'est le créateur d'images vivantes, de pages aussi parfaitement belles que celles du *Trio*, de *Daphnis*, des *Jeux d'eau*, du *Gibet*, de *La Valse*, des *Chansons madécasses*, des *Sonates*, etc.

Le journaliste Dominique Laberge, dans son article du 28 avril dans *Le Canada*, avait souhaité le retour de Ravel, cette fois faisant entendre lui-même son oeuvre symphonique à la tête d'un orchestre. Son voeu ne se réalisa pas car la maladie qui allait l'emporter en 1937 commença à se manifester dès 1933, lui interdisant toute activité professionnelle. Mais sa célébrité mondiale avait atteint un sommet avec le *Boléro*, les deux *Concertos* pour piano et le cycle *Don Quichotte à Dulcinée*.

Si Maurice Ravel fut célèbre de son vivant, il l'est encore plus depuis sa mort. Au Canada comme partout au monde, son oeuvre jouit d'une exceptionnelle popularité et c'est avec fierté que son nom s'inscrit dans l'histoire des trois villes canadiennes qui l'ont accueilli.

KEITH MacMILLAN

Ernest MacMillan: The Ruhleben Years

RUHLEBEN

The German prison camp 'Ruhleben' for male British civilians during the first world war – stark, cheerless, crowded, noisy – would seem to have been the last place on earth for a young music student to prepare himself for entry into the demanding world of the professional musician, but that was the experience of Ernest Alexander Campbell MacMillan, virtuoso organist and church musician, in those agonizing years from 1914 to 1918. How that took place is the subject of this article, throughout which I refer to my father as ECM.

Picture Ruhleben as a moderate sized race-course, faced by three grand-stands underneath which, in peace-time, had been refreshment rooms, kitchens, offices, betting-booths and the other usual adjuncts of a race-track . . . eleven brick stables as well as an administration building. The stables were our original barracks: six men were allotted to each horse-stall . . . This was luxurious in comparison to the accommodation in the lofts above, where straw sacks were laid side by side at night and rolled up in the daytime, giving us a space in which to read, eat and meditate on our troubles. Each prisoner was supplied with one blanket (decidedly inadequate for winter nights), a straw sack to sleep on and a single basin for both washing and collecting rations. Many other requisites however could be bought at the canteen; prisoners who had money or received remittances from home were decidedly better off than those who depended on the small allowances provided by the British Government, but no one was altogether destitute.

This description is to be found in ECM's memoirs, as yet unpublished and from which much will be quoted in this article. Written in 1955-6, some forty years after the first world war, his account of the events of those

© Keith C. MacMillan 1987

Ernest MacMillan: The Ruhleben Years

years shows them to be still vividly clear in his mind at that time.

Ruhleben (literally 'peaceful life' – provoking many ironic jokes among the prisoners), on the western outskirts of Berlin, had been established in September of 1914. On 6 November four thousand Allied civilians, mostly British, were poured into its horse stalls, stables, and other buildings, there to live for the next four years. (At first the prisoners were confined to the immediate area of the grandstand and administration buildings on the one side of the track, but soon the race-track oval and its enclosed grassy space were also at the disposal of the prisoners, at least in the daytime, principally as sports field and strolling ground.)

All this should not conjure up lurid visions of the much more brutal prisoner-of-war and civilian concentration camps of Nazi Germany. Ruhleben, the first such civilian prison camp in modern times for enemy alien civilians, although damned by the Allies at the time as yet another German 'atrocity' and although spartan in its physical facilities, was far more leniently administered than those of the later war: 'Home Rule came into force today: i.e. the soldiers have no *direct* intercourse with the prisoners, and the captains rule the roost. Hope it turns out well – at any rate it is pleasant not to have a burly fellow hanging around ready to order you about.'[1]

THE PRISONERS

The 'captains' were British and were responsible, through the captain of the camp, to the German camp Kommandant. As long as they posed no disciplinary or other problems to the German authorities, and subject of course to the strictures of confinement, the prisoners could, and eventually did, take into their own hands the government of their lives and 'society.' The evolution of this closed community, from a rabble of men in November 1914 into a fully functioning and remarkably diversified society, with its own unique spirit and an active artistic, educational, sporting, and religious life – indeed one could say distinctive culture – was later traced in much detail by one of the prisoners, the Canadian sociologist and church musician J. Davidson Ketchum in his book *Ruhleben*.[2] Suffice it to say here that the prisoner population of Ruhleben embraced the gamut of society – merchant seamen, travelling salesmen and business representatives, clerics, artists, musicians, sportsmen, even Anthony Eden's brother, (Sir) Timothy – virtually all of them British, including eventually (though not until January 1915 and after) those from the British Dominions and the colonies who happened to be in Germany at the outbreak of hostilities: 'Almost every trade and profession was represented in Ruhleben and many prisoners displayed or developed unexpected talents. A prominent physicist was our one and only oboist in the camp orchestra ... as things became organised, the right man was usually found for the right place.'[3] Although England had declared war on Germany early in August of 1914, it was not until the approach of winter that the Germans and Allies both conceded that the war was to continue well into the winter at least. The Germans then decided to intern all enemy aliens, in the belief that the English had already done the same.

On that evening in November, when these hapless Britishers and others were marched through the barbed-wire gates, the buildings had little heat or electricity, no inside lighting, dangerously inadequate latrines, and scarcely any cooking facilities. Each prisoner had only what he had been able to carry: 'All were jammed together in a small stableyard ... Few had ever met previously; their only common bond was their British citizenship. The Germans for their part merely penned them up and left them to their own resources.'[4] At first the prisoners could not bring themselves to face the possibility of a long internment and so made few long-term plans to provide for a future as yet unknown. By the onset of winter, however, it had become evident that their release would not be soon, and some diversionary activities began to be organized. Among the most ambitious was the formation of a camp orchestra and choir, conducted by an enterprising amateur musician, Charles Adler, who managed to present a substantial portion of Handel's *Messiah*. Although the musicians in the camp felt that Adler's ambition had exceeded his grasp, nevertheless all admitted that his spirit and determination exerted a powerful influence on the morale of the camp and emboldened other musicians to more ambitious activity. By the end of the winter of 1914-15 the skeleton of most future camp activities had taken recognizable shape: 'A revue was staged on March 28. The Debating Society had already put on an excellent Mock Trial, and the concerts were growing more ambitious ... the Arts and Science Union was running two lectures a week on such topics as Dietetics, Heredity, Modern Greece, and the Renaissance in Italy ... the readjustment which is the key-note of this period [winter 1914-15] had been achieved. The men were at last ready to believe in their city, and so to make it real.'[5] Thus, when on 19 March 1915 young Ernest MacMillan, aged twenty-one, arrived at the camp, already in place was a functioning social and cultural structure into which he could step.

INTO THE CAMP

And step into it he did, although in ways which must later have astonished (and possibly dismayed) his Presbyterian father and family. Although very much the new boy, in age and in camp experience, he

Ernest MacMillan: The Ruhleben Years 167

quickly became involved in the life of the camp in general, and specifically in the production of a camp musical revue.

I began by tackling music of a light type, nor do I regret doing so. My first job was to write, arrange and conduct the music for a revue entitled *Don't Laugh*.

Our 'Review' of which I spoke in my last home letter, made a great hit, and five performances seem to have been insufficient, as there is every probability there will be at least one more . . . I had an orchestra of about 20 picked players and on the whole the music was quite fair. In my 'overture' I introduced all sorts of tunes which one hears around the camp, as well as the review songs.[6]

Don't Laugh was to prove an event of much significance in ECM's professional life, providing his very first conducting experience other than with a church choir, and he clearly enjoyed it, although, possibly prompted by his Presbyterian background, he professed some distaste for the popular type of melody: 'Some of the songs are quite clever and amusing, but I am anxious to be finished and done with the music, which is of the "popular" variety.'[7] Such forays into the popular field yielded other benefits however:

I gained valuable experience by directing variety shows, a Christmas pantomime and a special performance of *The Mikado* for which I had to evolve a new score – not having one in the camp. A conductor who can follow the unrhythmical eccentricities of a music-hall comedian can follow anybody – and some distinguished artists can be eccentric enough. Moreover most of the music for such shows had to be arranged and scored – if not actually composed – for the occasion; not every young musician has the opportunity of hearing his orchestrations played immediately after they are written. However I was glad when I was able to conduct symphonic concerts. We had a regular winter series of these.

Above all, he had a captive audience! But what was the background which the young musician brought with him as he entered this unlikely, impromptu, and very unsystematic musical training-ground?

EARLY YEARS

In his youth he had demonstrated prodigious powers as a budding musician. His father, a minister of the Church of Scotland in Canada, was even then becoming one of the Presbyterian Church's leading hymnologists, and his mother also was quite at home playing the piano. Little

Ernest very early gained considerable competence on the piano, and not much later on the organ. He made his first major public appearance at the age of ten on the wheezy instrument in the Massey Music Hall as a small item in the lavish and popular Festival of the Lilies of 1904.

The general unfolding of his life need not be detailed here, since it can readily be found in numerous short biographies[8] – his early studies with Alfred Hollins and Professor Niecks in Edinburgh, his Associateship of the Royal College of Organists at thirteen, his Mus Bac from Oxford and Fellowship of the RCO at seventeen, and church appointments in Canada and in Scotland. Even as an undergraduate in modern history at the University of Toronto (he was class president of 1T5) he became deeply involved in the musical life of the university, as founder and president of the University Musical Society, which organized many campus concerts (including one with members of the Toronto Symphony Orchestra) and as assistant university organist and choirmaster, not to mention his musical editorship of a new university hymn-book, which he shepherded through the Oxford University Press in 1912.

By mid-1914, therefore, although not yet twenty-one, he had already gained much practical experience in academic, church, and concert music on both sides of the Atlantic and was becoming experienced in the practical aspects of music publishing and concert management. Thus, thoroughly accustomed to working within organizations, he was developing a considerable aptitude for leadership. In this prewar period he also laid the foundations, in Canada, in Britain, and in the eastern United States, of a subsequent career as a recital organist.

In 1913 he became engaged to Laura Elsie Keith, whom he later married, though not till the last day of 1919. Approaching his age of majority and feeling the need to broaden his musical horizons, ECM decided to study composition and piano for a couple of years in Paris at the Conservatoire. He probably had in mind studying piano with Harold Bauer, whom he had admired for years and who was to be teaching at the Conservatoire. So off he went across the Atlantic (for the ninth time in his life) in June of 1914.

While settling into the Paris milieu in the summer of that fateful year, he was invited to join the family of a well-to-do American acquaintance, Antoinette Burgess, to attend the Wagner Festival in Bayreuth. The invitation was irresistible. They arrived there on 26 July to be plunged that same night into the opening of the *Ring* cycle. Through Mrs Burgess's connections the young Canadian was quickly introduced to some of the musical luminaries of Germany, such as Karl Muck (whom he had met previously in Boston), Siegfried Wagner, and Hans Richter.

Scarcely noticed by these ecstatic Wagnerites were the ominous events taking place in the chancelleries and army commands of Europe. On 28 July Austro-Hungary invaded Serbia; on 30 July (the night after Bayreuth's *Götterdämmerung*) Russia mobilized and two days later was attacked by Germany. On 3 August Germany declared war on France and invaded Belgium. Young Ernest, not quite twenty-one, had as yet no idea of the implications of all this for the course of his own life. In any case, being with a group of Americans to whom this European conflict was of remote concern, he was largely unperturbed by the rumblings of the militaristic volcano. Nor was there a British consul nearby to advise him. His American friends, however, suggested that he would be well advised to seek the advice of the American consul in Nuremberg, which he did, on 3 August. The next day England declared war on Germany, and ECM, as a British subject (all Canadians were British subjects in 1914), became an enemy alien, required to register with the Nuremberg police. He then returned to Bayreuth for the next three weeks to finish out the festival. Returning to Nuremberg he was informed that he must remain in the city until the international situation had clarified and report daily to the police. He followed these instructions for the next few months.

It was during this period of quasi-liberty that he got to know that venerable city well. He went to concerts and other musical presentations, made the acquaintance of a group of English musicians (whom he later encountered in Ruhleben), and wrote the first sketch of most of his *String Quartet in C Minor*, of which the third movement is inscribed 'August, 1914, Bayreuth' and the first two 'September, 1914, Nürnberg.'

By an unfortunate bureaucratic error, it was not until January that it was discovered that he had failed to comply with the provisions of 'das Kriegszustandgesetz,' the 'Defence of the Realm Act,' which required that enemy aliens should register. Apparently ECM's monthly reporting to the Nuremberg police was not sufficient (or, as ECM later speculated, the police might have mistaken Canada's 'Toronto' for Italy's 'Taranto'). In January, therefore, he was arrested, tried for this offence, and sentenced to nine weeks in the Nuremberg jail. This time was spent in virtual solitary confinement, although through the good offices of the American consul he had books and limited writing materials. Fortunately, as an organist he was exempted from the hard manual labour that was the usual lot of prisoners. He whiled away the time mostly by reading German literature, beginning with Goethe's *Wilhelm Meister*, 'which greatly enlarged my German vocabulary.'

Thus it was that, at the end of this sentence, on 19 March 1915, he was taken from the Nuremberg jail straight to Ruhleben.

His previous nine weeks in a city jail had doubtless prepared him in some measure for the spartan nature of his coming existence and, although dismayed at the prospect of a long sojourn under such conditions, he was heartened to find in Ruhleben many kindred spirits in science and art, in literature and drama, and above all in music.

CAMP MUSICAL ACTIVITIES

My own chief interest in camp activities lay first in musical, and then in dramatic ventures. A camp orchestra had already been organized when I arrived; most of the instruments belonged to the players but means were eventually found to buy or rent some of those we lacked – particularly pianos ...

The composition of the orchestra was never complete, and we had to cut our coat according to our cloth. Rarely was there more than one of each wood-wind instrument and there were no bassoons. Quentin Maclean proved most resourceful in filling in the missing parts on a harmonium. The brass section had also its gaps but there was a very fair body of strings.

In his memoirs he lists some of the musicians and their various attributes and subsequent careers:

Benjamin Dale, afterwards Warden of the Royal Academy of Music in London – one of the best musicians I have ever known;

Edgar Bainton, Director of the Conservatoire at Newcastle-on-Tyne and afterwards New South Wales Conservatorium in Sydney [Australia];

John Peebles Conn, later of Glasgow, taught me much in the matter of orchestral routine and, as concertmaster of the orchestra, saved me from disaster when I overlooked a change of tempo in the first orchestral concert I ever conducted;

Two of our best pianists were *William Lindsay*, who later settled in Minneapolis and taught on the faculty of the University of Minnesota, and *John Pauer*, afterwards with Dale at the Royal Academy of London;

Frederick Keel (known even in those early days as 'Daddy' Keel) was a fine singer and composer whose songs have by no means lost their popularity;

Charles Weber, former Kapellmeister at Chemnitz, later conducted the Carl Rosa Company with notable success;

Godfrey Ludlow, an Australian pupil of Leopold Auer, was our best solo violinist;

Quentin Maclean, then known by his middle name, *Morvaren*, was one of our younger musicians; under Straube, organist of the Thomaskirche in Leipzig, and

Max Reger he had already developed skill and versatility as organist and composer and was always ready to help in any capacity.

Yet another was Percy Hull, later to become organist of Hereford Cathedral, who was knighted in 1947.

Benjamin Dale, one of the English musicians whom ECM had already met in Nuremberg, became his closest friend, certainly during the camp years. Maclean in later years moved to Toronto, where he continued his career not only as a church organist (Holy Rosary and St Michael's College) but as an outstanding theatre organist (Shea's, formerly on Bay Street at Queen), being heard often over the CBC and other radio stations.

There were at least two other Canadian musicians in the camp, Harry Field ('Harry had lived for years in Germany and was not as young as most of us – indeed I believe he had at one time studied with Liszt'; Field had actually studied with Martin Krause, a pupil of Liszt) and also J. Davidson Ketchum, already mentioned, who conducted the camp's YMCA choir, mostly for their religious services.

Physically primitive and depressing though Ruhleben was, there was also in that dismal place the potential for an active, indeed lively, intellectual life: 'The Englishman must have his club; to meet this need various groups joined forces and, by means of modest subscriptions, had sheds or "lean-to's" erected at the sides of brick barracks. Here they could enjoy a measure of privacy and congenial company. I joined one such club, known as the "Corner House"; its membership consisted chiefly of artists, musicians and others interested in the arts.' Not only was there the Corner House, with its 'congenial company,' but also the Arts and Science Union already mentioned, a sort of Royal Society in microcosm. It organized various events, especially a continuing series of lectures and other such presentations. Three months after his arrival, for example, on 15 June ECM gave a lecture to the A & S Union on 'The Viennese Classicists' and in the following year a lecture to a kindred organization, the Historical Circle, on 'Milestones in Canadian constitutional development.' (Before leaving Canada he had completed three years of an honours course in modern history at the University of Toronto.) Over the coming years he and other camp musicians gave various lectures and lecture series.

There is a record of many other such ECM enterprises: a lecture on Debussy, probably some time in 1917, and on 30 April of that same year a lecture on 'A sketch of Russian music,' audience preparation for a program of Russian music, mostly 'modern,' to be given one week later. Just who was the guiding genius behind these presentations is not clear, but ECM had for some time been very interested in recent trends in Russian music, and in fact in late 1915 had been making a close study of some of the piano sonatas of Skriabin. We know of at least one other such lecture by ECM and its related concert of English music, mostly recent, including works by Delius, Elgar, and Cyril Scott.

Probably the most ambitious series was given throughout the month of May of 1917, when ECM and Dale gave ten illustrated lectures on the Beethoven symphonies – the first an introduction, each of the other nine being devoted to a particular symphony. In each, ECM would give an analysis of the work, which would be followed by a playing by himself and Dale of the entire symphony, probably piano four-hands. (What they did about the choral part of the ninth we can only guess.)

This also illustrates something of ECM's growth as a 'practical' and chamber music pianist – a good sight-reader with a good sense of ensemble. Indeed on many camp occasions he played the piano part in various piano quartets and quintets, a number of which he performed in later years in Canada with the Hart House Quartet and others. It is not clear just what pianos were available in the camp, although there was at least one (not always dependable) grand.

CAMP THEATRE

Nor was he involved only in music in the camp. On 8 March 1915 the first camp dramatic production had been given: Shaw's *Androcles and the Lion*, rehearsed and produced 'under fantastic difficulties.' Once started, however, and proving immensely popular, the dramatic productions increased in number and quality of presentation.

The variety and scope of these productions was astonishing, ranging as they did from Greek tragedy to farces like *The Brixton Burglary* and *The Private Secretary* ...

I began to take an interest in the theatre. Theatres had been taboo in our family during my early years ...

My brief histrionic career was chiefly devoted to female impersonations. This was not from choice, although I found it good fun at first and especially enjoyed playing Lady Bracknell in *The Importance of Being Earnest* [December 1915] ... My stage career included one production of my own – Shaw's *Fanny's First Play* [September 1916] – in which, faute de mieux, I allotted myself the part of Darling Dora ...

In 1916 we celebrated the three hundredth anniversary of Shakespeare's death by productions of *Twelfth Night* and *Othello* together with concerts of more or less authentic Elizabethan music.

Sketch of Ernest MacMillan as Lady Bracknell in *The Importance of being Earnest*, December 1915 (artist unknown)
Photograph courtesy of the National Library of Canada

ECM played in both the Shakespeare productions, Maria in *Twelfth Night* and a small part in *Othello*. It may be wondered from what source came so much printed material – books, plays, musical scores: 'A library, offering both light and heavy reading, was a great boon; most of the contributions came from Great Britain and especially from generous publishers while some of the prisoners contributed their share.' To what extent the library also supplied a wide range of musical scores we can only surmise. Among ECM's papers, now in the National Library of Canada, has survived a substantial amount of manuscript music – incidental music for camp dramatic productions, academic exercises, etc. – written on manuscript paper printed in Germany, some dated as of the second half of the war, from which it may be inferred that at least some manuscript paper was probably obtained from suppliers in nearby Berlin; and if manuscript paper could be so obtained, perhaps also were many scores and even instrumental parts of published chamber and orchestral works, especially German. This, however, is speculation. (During the second world war, ECM was a busy volunteer member of the YMCA War Prisoners Committee in Canada, among other things seeing to it that German prisoners on this side, and Canadian prisoners on the other, were supplied with musical materials of the kind for which he was so grateful in the first.)

But by 1917, 'the novelty of acting had begun to wear off and, although I accepted a few minor male roles, I was tired of being an actress. Besides I had more serious work to do. I was anxious, while I had the time, to work toward my *doctorate in music* at Oxford.' Of which, more later.

CONDUCTING AND ORCHESTRATING

It is as a conductor that Ernest MacMillan became most widely known in the full flight of his later career. This, too, sprang from roots first sprouted in Ruhleben: 'Last evening, being the *quatorze juillet* ... I conducted Bizet's suite *L'Arlésienne* (No. 1) and was much complimented thereon. Except for the Minuet the men did not play at all badly ... Dale at the piano is a host in himself. I also did the entr'actes etc. for the *Private Secretary* and the *Speckled Band*, and am beginning quite to fancy myself as a conductor! At least it is excellent experience which I should scarcely have had in ordinary circumstances.'[9] Some four months later he conducted his first all-orchestral concert: 'The assisting artist at my first concert was a fellow Canadian, Harry Field ... The concerto was the *Liszt E flat*, which he played with fine vigour and gusto.' On that occasion Field's professionalism was put to the test when the damper pedal stuck.

By the end of 1915 ECM had been put in charge of the music, scoring, rehearsing, and conducting of the camp pantomime, *Cinderella*, a production impressive enough that the American ambassador, James Gerard, came down from Berlin to see it. (In later years apparently ECM thought not too badly of it and included the overture, with its melange of first world war popular songs, in a Toronto Symphony Christmas Box concert at the close of 1944.) Two months later we see him sharing the orchestra podium with Charles Weber and conducting entirely from memory, a foretaste of his later conducting style. Also foreshadowing the future, on Palm Sunday of 1916 he conducted a concert which included the bass recitative, 'At Evening Calm,' No. 74 of the *St Matthew Passion*, which he had been studying for some months before. By then he had become, and was to develop further as, one of the camp's principal conductors, casting a speculative eye into a highly indefinite future: 'Since coming here, I have found that I have a natural talent for conducting which I should greatly like to develop; how, where and when remains to be seen. A virtuoso pianist I shall never be, though I think a year's practice would make me a fairly capable one.'[10] By early 1916 he had also made up his mind to resume his work in preparation for a some-day doctorate in music from Oxford (he had achieved the Oxford B MUS some five years earlier, at the age of seventeen), and so began writing fugues and other counterpoint exercises with the general idea of 'keeping his hand in': 'The difficulties of working at music in a prison camp are not inconsiderable, the chief being the lack of privacy.' The lack of privacy, and of silence, is a recurring theme in the correspondence and other accounts of Ruhleben's daily life. Sir Timothy Eden put the matter more unequivocally, speaking particularly of the first couple of years: 'For not one single instant during the whole of that time has any prisoner had the slightest privacy.'[11] In his letters and in his short diary ECM, like so many of his fellow prisoners, spoke constantly of the lack of privacy, of the constant noise of four thousand men moving about, talking, laughing, playing games, even playing the odd gramophone, mostly in comparatively confined spaces. Much of his reading he had to do under the bed-covers at night, with a flashlight. Score-study, not to mention composition which had to be done mostly by daylight, therefore required enormous concentration.

Yet another enemy of concentrated work was the soul-destroying psychological depression against which the prisoners waged a constant struggle in one way or another – not just from the gloomy uncertainty of their future, but a deep, enervating, psychological numbness which seemed at times to be beyond their will to dispel.

Sunday October 10th [1915]

Another of my blue days – & the deepest kind of blue at that. I wonder if some people can realize what utter depression is? It is by far the worst kind, too – the kind for which there is no special cause outside oneself . . . I can see nothing but gloom & wretchedness ahead of me . . . adjourned to the Corner House where everyone was engaged in making asinine & childish rhymes. Got disgusted & back to the barrack. Going to bed as sulky as I got up.[12]

The depths of these depressions were rarely expressed to their full in ECM's letters home, usually because he did not wish to convey the worst of these even to his fiancée, let alone to his family. Nevertheless these bouts of depression, or the apprehension of them, were a constant presence, to be lived with, to be wrestled with, and somehow to be overcome.

Thus, even though ECM would seem to have had all the time in the world for the major intellectual effort required by the exigencies of an Oxford MUS DOC, the psychological counterpressures demanded an enormous and constant effort of will to be withstood.

In resuming his work toward the degree, ECM was assuming, early in 1916, that he would have to await the war's end before he could sit for the examinations at Oxford. It was the intervention of a certain Dr Logie, who knew his way around Oxford, that encouraged him to explore the undreamed-of possibility of applying and being examined for the degree while yet in the camp. Dr Logie guided him in his petition to Oxford which, to his enormous surprise, was granted, of which fact he received formal confirmation in November 1917. Although for more than a year he had been working steadily on his counterpoint and other academic exercises, apparently using old Oxford exam sheets, from then on his work toward the degree took on new life, meaning, and vigour.

I plunged in headlong and, during the last year and a half of internment, did little else. For a long time I wrote a fugue a day as well as numerous exercises . . .

The requirements comprised the submission of a work for chorus and orchestra of specified length and character . . . I embarked on the composition of my 'exercise' – a setting of Swinburne's ode *England*. Subsequently some of my friends expressed surprise that a work of so patriotic a nature should have been passed by the German censors but in point of fact their only concern was that no military information could be transmitted by a musical code.

Meanwhile he was by no means neglecting other activities. He wrote home in early May 1916 that he 'was completing' the first version of his

String Quartet in C Minor. (It is curious that in his letters and memoirs no mention is made of a performance of this work, nor even of one or other of its four movements, since among the musicians in the camp there was an excellent string quartet headed by Godfrey Ludlow, and any new work by a fellow prisoner was readily given a performance. This early version was thus probably never played, possibly not yet completed at that time. Although in later years ECM always spoke of it as a 'student work,' he rewrote it, apparently in 1921; the Hart House String Quartet gave the premiere performance of it three years later. In 1967 it was recorded by the Amadeus Quartet and distributed world-wide, ironically, by the German company Deutsche Grammophon Gesellschaft.)

Throughout 1916 and 1917 he continued to conduct and compose (often incidental music for plays), to arrange, lecture, perform as pianist with other musicians, and to organize musical and theatrical events.

THE MIKADO

Probably the most ambitious of all the camp's theatrical productions was of Gilbert and Sullivan's *The Mikado*, presented at Christmas time, 1916. It was ambitious in more than the usual production sense. There was in the camp a copy of the libretto of the opera, but not of the score, which thus had to be reconstructed – from memory. ECM and four other of the camp musicians undertook this task under ECM's direction, the others being (as confirmed on the title page) A.G. Claypole, Ben Dale, W. Pauer, and Charles Weber. The orchestral score, which now resides in the National Library of Canada, is thus in several handwritings, but most of the work seems to have been that of ECM. The orchestration, of course, had to conform to the talent and instrumental resources of the camp, the orchestra being essentially single winds and brass, normal strings (but with two cello parts), and piano and harmonium. The entire musical production was in the hands of ECM, who also conducted all performances (apparently from memory): 'In the meantime, the "Mikado" keeps me from the blues, and I think it will not be at all bad. It was certainly rather heavy work scoring it, (the score is at least two inches thick) but there is a lot of fun in it, too ... There is a great pleasure to be gained, for me, conducting even an amateur orchestra. I haven't touched an organ for two years and a half, but I fear I shall find its colours pale mournfully before the richness of strings. Why didn't I learn the fiddle when I was ten?'[13] The production was given thirteen performances in December of 1916 and was an enormous success, not only within the camp but beyond; it played to the prisoners and to the German camp Kommandant and his staff and a

The cast and orchestra for *The Mikado*, December 1916–January 1917 (*2nd row, 4th from left*, Quentin Morvaren Maclean, Godfrey Ludlow, Ernest MacMillan) Photograph courtesy of the National Library of Canada

number of German visitors, and also to the American ambassador and retinue, who came down to the camp for a special presentation. The production was written up in the *Illustrated London News*, thus attracting much attention outside the camp, adding substantially to the awareness on the part of the British and Allied publics of the psychological resilience of the prisoners. ECM has said that this production was one of the very few cases in which D'Oyly Carte waived royalties and offered no objection to the production of an unauthorized score.

Perhaps it was these experiences in stage and musical drama which encouraged ECM to muse on the idea of opera as a possible future conducting career.

You know, I've a good mind to begin agitating for a Toronto opera company when I return – beginning in a modest way, but entirely a local venture. If we could find some Maecenas willing to finance the scheme as Beecham is doing in Manchester, it might turn out to be a huge success in the end. There is no end of good voices in Toronto, but of course you need experienced teachers and above all, money. Popular prices and all operas (and comic operas) in English ...

Ernest MacMillan: The Ruhleben Years

Besides I think there would be more public spirit at home now than before the war, and it ought to be directed into the proper channels when the war comes to an end.[14]

(Certainly in the late twenties he established the beginnings of an opera company. The Toronto Conservatory Opera Company's performances in the late twenties and 1930 of *Hänsel und Gretel*, Purcell's *Dido and Aeneas*, the North American première of Vaughan Williams's *Hugh the Drover*, and others were enthusiastically received, supported, and attended to capacity. Alas, however, the Great Depression and the following world war deferred for yet another couple of decades the development of opera in Toronto.)

THE DOCTORATE

But the steady work toward the Oxford MUS DOC occupied more and more of his available time and energy (even though from March of 1918 he was in charge of organizing all camp entertainments, no small responsibility).

You will probably have heard, long ere this, that I have passed my Mus.Doc. exams – or rather the one necessary exam. Dr. Logie was at the bottom of it; he incited me to commit the crime in the first place, and also drew up the petition. Said petition requested that I be allowed to try the first (theoretical) exam. here, and never for a moment did I expect more. However the Oxford authorities proved themselves exceptionally generous (the war seems to have revolutionized even Oxford!) and excused me the exam., allowing me the degree on the strength of an exercise alone. That was last November. During the following months I wrote an exercise between meals, sent it in about the middle of April – and apparently it passed ...

The exercise is a setting of Swinburne's ode *England*, which seemed a timely subject, though as a rule my feelings toward Swinburne are cool. I didn't set the whole poem and the result is somewhat unbalanced and occasionally scrappy, but I think a good deal of it would sound well. It is scored for a fairly large orchestra and eight-part choir. I have had several very nice letters of congratulation already (apparently there were notices in the English papers) ... That's all about that.[15]

'That' was by no means 'all about that.' Having been listed in the Oxford *Gazette* of 19 June, the notice of this feat was picked up by both the British and Canadian press, so that long before his return home half a year later his name was widely known, to the musical profession and public alike.

(His young sister Dorothy wrote, prophetically, on 25 June, 'Dear Doctor MacMillan – Oh the appalling dignity of it! I suppose you'll be a "Sir" next.') 'I celebrated the occasion last week by catching the "Spanish Grippe" and having to spend nearly a week in the *Schonungs-Barake* ... Some people have had really a very bad time with our pet epidemic ... However I daresay a week or so will see the last of it, and the depressed feeling it has spread over the camp will vanish like snow in April.'[16] The 'Spanish Grippe' was of course the outbreak of the deadly influenza epidemic which reached Canada in October of that year and which was to claim some twenty million human lives the world over before it abated.

HOPE AT LAST

From the correspondence it seems evident that it was not until late summer of 1918 that the prisoners dared to think that the war might be coming to an end. Little indications began to appear all about them, in the newspapers of course, but even in the camp itself: 'After the first year, most of us depended almost entirely for sustenance on parcels from home. Food became increasingly scarce in Germany owing to the blockade ... In the last two years, we were undoubtedly better fed than the majority of the German people. By the end of war it was not unusual to see some of our guards poking into swill-tubs to see if by chance anything edible had been discarded by their prisoners. Yet our parcels continued to arrive with almost unbroken regularity.' Some days before the signing of the Armistice the prisoners noticed that the guards had 'melted away' – they just went home. This left the prisoners not only unconfined but also unguarded against the starving and possibly hostile populace of Berlin. However, to the credit of the Berliners the Ruhlebenites were left in peace: 'With our own eyes we saw trains passing the camp carrying crowds of cheering workers into Berlin: the fact that Germany had lost the war was secondary to the general relief that it was over and that with it had passed the militaristic regime that had so long dominated the German people ... few of us felt any great personal resentment; certainly we had been better treated than prisoners in some military camps and much better than our friends at home had been led to believe.' Since it was obvious that arrangements would shortly be made for the prisoners' release and transportation to England, there seemed little point for individual prisoners to try to reach the United Kingdom on their own, so they stayed in their prison 'home' for the time being. Indeed, many made short excursions from the camp, mostly into Berlin, which, although carrying on with great difficulty, still maintained a modicum of cultural life.

The Great Day, then, came almost as an anticlimax. I remember that I was engaged in binding a book – my hobby for the moment – when a friend came in to tell me that the armistice had been signed. 'Oh!' I said, 'that's good,' and went on with my work ...

Restrictions on our movements were practically abolished and Berlin, which still had many attractions to offer, was at our doors. I heard a fine performance of *Fidelio* at the Charlottenburg Opera House and I confess that tears filled my eyes when, in the fifth bar of the overture, the two horns sounded their notes with perfect clarity and security. I had almost forgotten that horns could sound like that! Sitting behind me was a girl eating a baked potato which her escort had presumably brought with him as a special treat. Food was at a premium and the value of the mark was dropping like a stone down a well. Yet the Berliners had to have their music. On Busstag (Repentance Day) I attended a performance of Brahms' *Deutsches Requiem* and, though I doubt if the German people felt much repentance for their national sins, they too had suffered grievously and hearing Brahms' noble music under such conditions was impressive beyond words.

RELEASE

It was not until the last week in November that ECM entrained for Copenhagen, there to proceed further by boat to Leith, a suburb of his ancestral city of Edinburgh, to stay with the family of his adopted 'aunts,' Margaret ('Peggy') MacLean and 'Polly' Lothian, whose home, companionship, and good counselling had been the cornerstone of his early years in Edinburgh and who had been the staunchest of his UK friends and supporters while he was in prison and in the camp.

His former Edinburgh organ teacher, Alfred Hollins, in his autobiography, relates an incident of that time:

After the armistice MacMillan was released and sent back to Leith. He had a Sunday to spare, and I invited him to play the evening service. Although he had not touched an organ for over four years and it was much longer than that since he had last played St. George's organ, one would have thought he had been using it uninterruptedly all his life. For the opening voluntary he played from memory the slow movement of Mendelssohn's second sonata.

It must have been eleven or twelve years since he had studied it with me, and I was delighted to find that he had not forgotten a single thing I had taught him about registration etc ... During the collection he played the beautiful Adagio from Bach's Toccata in C, also from memory. His concluding voluntary was the St. Anne's Fugue.[17]

The *St Anne*, after four years away from the instrument!

ECM was to stay in Britain until mid-January 1919, partly waiting for transport home, but also in order to negotiate in London with the music publisher Novello for the publication of his by-then widely publicized *Ode – England* and also with Henry Coward, the conductor of the Sheffield Musical Union, for the première performance of the work, which took place on 17 March 1921 (it was performed again on 11 and 12 April in Toronto by the Toronto Mendelssohn Choir and the Philadelphia Orchestra, conducted by H.A. Fricker).

He reached home in Toronto about the end of January, widely regarded as something of a war hero (which always embarrased him, considering how he had spent those four years in comparative safety and some comfort compared with those who suffered, were wounded, and died in the muddy, hellish trenches). He was himself much more concerned about his feelings for his fiancée, with whom he was soon to be reunited, and hers for him, after a separation of four and a half years.

Their apprehensions were groundless; they quickly decided to be married as soon as he could establish a position and income to support a marriage and a family.

PREPARATION FOR A CAREER

During the months of April and May of 1919 ECM made a tour through the western provinces, giving organ recitals and lectures on 'My experiences in a German prison camp,' making the acquaintance of musicians by the score across the country and returning with an encouraging pocketful of money. In July he was appointed to the teaching staff of the Canadian Academy of Music (later amalgamated with the Toronto Conservatory), thus beginning his long career in teaching and educational administration, and in December he was appointed organist and choirmaster of the well-to-do Timothy Eaton Memorial Church, where he inaugurated a major series of organ recitals extending over several years, mostly of Bach, and from which vantage point he launched many major musical performances, including his renowned presentations of the *St Matthew Passion*.

With this solid foundation under his feet, and with the wide variety of musical experience and training he had undergone in Ruhleben, his long-delayed and eagerly anticipated career was about to begin.

And as the final block in the foundation of his future career, he and his long-time sweetheart and fiancée of more than six years were married, with his father officiating, at St Andrew's Presbyterian Church (now just across the street from Roy Thomson Hall), on the afternoon of 31 December 1919.

I was born nine months later.

CanOn Stride

John Weinzweig
(1986)

© John Weinzweig, 1986

CanOn Stride 185

186 John Weinzweig

CanOn Stride 187

GEORGE A. PROCTOR

Notes on Violet Archer

Invited by the editors to contribute to this volume, George A. Proctor had accepted and in mid-October of 1985 wrote to suggest the title 'Violet Archer and the *Gebrauchsmusik* ideal in Canadian music.' He was at work on a study of Violet Archer and her music for the series *Canadian Composers/Compositeurs canadiens*, and the proposed paper was an offshoot of that larger project. At Dr. Proctor's untimely death in December of that year, only a draft page of introduction for the article had been produced, but the Archer study itself was well advanced towards completion and at this writing is being prepared for publication.

Because of his prominence as a musician, a writer, and a bibliographer of Canadian music, and especially because of his many associations with Helmut Kallmann, the editors were reluctant to omit Dr Proctor from the company of contributors and decided with the kind permission of his estate to publish his working notes for the Archer study. These are rough notes made by Dr Proctor following a series of conversations with Violet Archer in 1984, and they appear here with only minor editorial changes and a change in the order of topics. A good deal of the material recurs in more developed form in the completed chapters of his book, but these notes do offer an interesting glimpse of its initial state and an illustration of his methods, besides illuminating the career, personality, and ideas of a distinguished composer. THE EDITORS.

EARLY LIFE

Violet Archer was born on 24 April 1913 in Montreal of Italian immigrant parents who had first come to Canada in 1912. In July 1914 her mother decided to visit her own parents in Como, Italy, and took Violet with her, leaving the father in Montreal, where he worked as a cook. Violet had two older brothers who had not yet emigrated to Canada, and the idea was that her mother would return to Montreal with all the children after having a visit with her family. The first world war broke out in September 1914, and the family could not get passage back to Canada. Violet, her mother, and her two brothers were forced to remain in Italy for five very hard years, living at first with Violet's mother's parents and then with an uncle. Food was scarce, as was money, since it took a long time for any funds sent by her father in Montreal to reach them. But these were formative years for Violet Archer: 'At age one and a half I am told that I was sensitive to musical sounds, especially the piano.' One of her cousins with whom she was living was given piano lessons, and Violet was extremely jealous. At the end of the war the family returned to Montreal to be reunited with the father, but it took a while to become readjusted to Canada. At this point Violet did not speak a word of English, and neither did her mother. Violet was very lonely.

Although Archer's parents were brought up in the Roman Catholic faith they had reservations about some of its dogmas and gradually turned towards the Waldensians, a sect of Italian dissenters which traces its history back to the twelfth century. Since the Waldensians held beliefs similar to the Presbyterians, it was natural that the Archers should attend the Presbyterian church upon coming to Canada. Violet's generation was then brought up as Presbyterians; in fact, the congregation to which her family belonged is still to be found in Montreal. Now part of the United Church of Canada, it is known as John Beckwith Memorial Church, after the nineteenth-century Englishman (not the composer) John Beckwith, who supported the Italian Protestants. Sunday morning service, Sunday school, evening service, mid-week prayer meetings, and youth groups were all important functions for the Archer household. Violet's parents were very devoted to their church, and the children followed suit without question. Violet also sang in the church choir with her brothers from the age of twelve.

When Archer was nine her parents bought her a piano, a very exciting event. Her musical studies revolved around the piano. At high school she became involved in performing background music for plays, no doubt valuable experience for her early professional role as a piano accompanist. Originally the Archer family lived near Montreal High School but later moved to the north end of the city. In spite of this Violet attended Montreal High, often traversing the distance by walking for an hour. Archer remembers that she was very independent in her youth and insisted on getting to places in the city by herself, even though she suspected that her mother followed her unobtrusively to make certain that she came to no harm.

The Archer family was a closely knit unit, and traditions from their Italian heritage formed an important part of family life. The pastor of their church arranged instruction in the Italian language, and Violet studied it until she was fourteen. Through this she got to know the literature. She remembers a sonnet by Dante which her mother taught her at the age of seven which she recited for the six-hundredth anniversary of the birth of the poet (Archer's memory for dates is remarkable). Archer was seventeen when she began studying at the McGill Conservatorium. Her father could not afford to send his children to university since he was a chef who, owing to the Depression, had been laid off by his employer. For good reason her father wondered how Violet ever hoped to make a living in music, but she was immovable. She got a full-time job as studio accompanist for the voice teacher Merlin Davies (Davies was a successful teacher in Montreal who taught into his nineties, one of his students being Alexander Gray of the University of Calgary). Davies was a dedicated Welshman who frequently gave concerts at the Verdun school for the medically handicapped, and Archer went along to play the piano. Archer never aspired to be a concert pianist even though her piano teacher encouraged her to do just that.

Archer's legal name is Violet Balestreri Archer, her surname being a literal translation of Balestreri, the original Italian surname of the family. The name Archer was added legally in 1940, principally for the benefit of the brothers, who had gone into the banking profession by that time. Archer acknowledges somewhat wryly that 'foreign' names were somewhat of a problem in 1940, but even today she sometimes has to spell "Archer." Archer credits her parents with creating a love of music in the home even though they were perturbed that she wanted to pursue music as a career. Both parents loved opera and took her to what performances were available in Montreal in the twenties. The first concert she remembers was a performance by Beniamino Gigli, the renowned Italian tenor who first performed at the Met in 1920. Archer's big disappointment in her early musical life was to miss a performance by Arturo Toscanini when he came to Montreal. Her parents left her at home this time because the performance would have kept her up too late. Archer's parents were quite strict in the upbringing of their children, a quality which Violet now appreciates and which she sees as being absent from most homes in the present day. She was permitted to speak only when spoken to and was sent to her room as punishment when she giggled out of turn. One senses that this discipline which was instilled in her as a child is to be found in the respect for order and tradition which one finds in her music. Archer's father played the clarinet and her mother sang around the house. She would often hum operatic tunes by Verdi and Puccini; when Archer now goes to the opera and hears these same tunes, she has a vivid recollection of her mother singing them around the house. Archer's eldest brother took voice lessons and her sister likewise studied the piano briefly. Her second brother liked music but never took lessons. All of the family liked listening to serious music, what Archer calls 'good stuff.'

PROFESSIONAL ACTIVITIES

Archer has been very active throughout her career as a contributing member to many professional organizations. She has been (and continues to be) a judge for young composers' contests and has organized Canada Music Week and International Music Day activities in Edmonton. At the same time she was chairperson of the theory/composition division at the University of Alberta Department of Music, all the while carrying a heavy teaching load. The young composers' contests which Archer has adjudicated over the years include those of the Canadian Federation of Music Teachers, PRO Canada, the Okanagan Festival, the Canadian Federation of University Women, the Banff Centre, the Canadian Broadcasting Corporation, and the National Federation of Music Clubs (US) as well as state contests in Oklahoma and Louisiana. Archer has often acted as the sole judge in these contests, but in many instance she was a member of a small jury. Very conscientious in her duty in this regard, Archer has always made it a practice of writing a critique to offer help and direction to the young composer. Passing judgment is not sufficient, in her opinion.

In recent years Archer has spent a great deal of time and energy promoting the activities of Canada Music Week in Edmonton. This special week takes place in the fall of each year and is promoted by the Canadian Federation of Music Teachers.

ARCHER ON COMPOSITION

'I have always investigated new music and new techniques. I studied Schoenberg's techniques on my own and have always exposed students to the twelve-tone school. I do not care to use the technique myself and I object to the "fanaticism" associated with it.' Archer says she is aware of all the turmoil in the world ('Heavens! it's awful') but she does not see any reason to express only the distorted and frantic side of life in art. She says that, although she can understand that Schoenberg and his followers lived through very distressing times, 'so have others, including myself, but I do not want to make these situations a constant theme in my musical expression.' Archer is aware there is a movement back to romantic stylistic elements, as in Rochberg, Stockhausen, and Schafer – 'I don't have anything against this, although I do not wish to follow it myself.' Similarly, Archer has studied electronic music and techniques but does not regard herself as an electronic composer. She feels she needs to be aware of new things. She is also interested in computer music and attended the 1981 international conference at North Texas. She found it 'fascinating,' but again does not wish to follow it herself.

Asked whether she views her works as falling in different style periods, Archer replied, 'Yes, I do.' In the early works she sees her music very much under the influence of modality à la Vaughan Williams (influence of Douglas Clarke). Her second style period was more chromatic, up to the time when she studied with Hindemith. The latter influenced her greatly and taught her to be less chromatic. The *Sonata No. 1* (1956) for violin and piano, *Sonata* (1956) for cello and piano, *Divertimento* (1949) for oboe, clarinet and bassoon, and *Trio No. 2* (1957) all show the influence of Hindemith, and 'I do not apologize for this.' In the early 1950s Archer sees more influence from the Schoenberg school. She became very much involved with the variation technique which she regards as one of the most important attributes of twentieth-century music and one of the most important contributions of Schoenberg.

Archer regards the *Cantata sacra* (1966) as a turning point in her stylistic development. It is more expressionistic and chromatic. However, Archer says that none of her works are serially organized and she is not interested in this. She acknowledges the use of tonality by assertion, such as can be found in *Cantata sacra*.

Archer is not inclined towards aleatoric music. Her work *Improvisations* (1973) for piano is not aleatoric; rather, it was just a fun piece which she wrote for a friend – written-down improvisations for the piano. 'I do not go in for aleatoric music because I feel I am wasting my time.' At the same time, however, Archer maintains that she has nothing against aleatoric music as such.

With regard to theatrical music Archer has great enthusiasm for opera. The main difficulty is the great cost of production. Her comic opera, *Sganarelle* (1973), has been produced twice – once at the University of Alberta (1974) and again at the Banff Centre in 1978. She is pleased that it has been mentioned in the book *Opera America*.[1] She is equally enthusiastic about her second opera, *The Meal* (1983), a serious opera which is awaiting its first production. Archer is mindful of the cost of large-scale productions (both operas are one-act chamber operas, so can hardly be classified as large-scale in themselves). She acknowledges that even works for chorus and orchestra have limited performance possibilities.

Of her many works only a few have received many performances – *Fanfare and Passacaglia* (1949) for orchestra, *Divertimento* (1957) for orchestra, and *Three Sketches for Orchestra* (1961). The *Sonata* (1970) for clarinet and piano has received so many performances that 'I have lost track,' to quote Archer, but the other sonatas are not performed much. The *Sonata* (1965) for horn and piano is performed infrequently and the *Sonata* (1973) for oboe and piano receives maybe two performances a year.

Archer likes very much to work with texts. 'Since I left high school I have been associated with choirs and the human voice. I adore texts and like working with them. I am constantly reading, especially poetry. If I had not gone into music, I would have gone into English because I favoured literature so much.' In her choice of texts she favours those with an optimistic or religious bent. She says that she is aware of the seamy side of life, but 'I do not want to expound on it.' She like texts with nature themes (e.g., *Landscapes*, 1950; *Daffodils*, 1972). She likes the poetry of the Canadian Dorothy Livesay, although some of the latter's works are 'rather expressionistic, and I am not interested in setting these.' Archer says that there is a certain kind of musical language suitable for expressionistic texts, and 'it is not my language.' Archer admires *Pierrot Lunaire* by Schoenberg (his best work, in her opinion) but is not interested in setting this type of poetry herself. Archer does feel a certain affinity towards Canadian poetry – e.g., Arthur S. Bourinot, A.J.M. Smith. She sees a tremendous variety in Canadian poetry. She has not made any settings of French-Canadian poetry (other than folk songs) because she has tried some and the results have sounded too much like Debussy, in her opinion. Archer is not interested in setting the recent poetry of Margaret Atwood or Irving Layton, who in their own ways are good poets but 'too sordid' to interest her for musical settings. (She has actually set some of the early poems of Layton.)

Archer was asked whether she liked to work on commission and whether she found it too confining. Her answer to these two questions was a prompt, 'Yes and no, respectively.' She said that she had to like the project but did not consider it a bad thing to have to work towards a deadline. She prefers to work on only one commission at a time; in fact, after a single experience of working on two at once, she says she would never do that again. She regards herself as fortunate in that all of her commissions have been felicitous.

ARCHER AS A PERFORMER

Archer was trained as a pianist and made her living initially as a teacher of piano and theory and a professional accompanist. She performed as a pianist (especially in the chamber works of Beethoven, Mendelssohn, Schumann, and Brahms), organist, and percussionist. She played percussion in the Montreal Women's Symphony under Ethel Stark for almost eight years. She studied timpani with Louis Decair of the Montreal Symphony. She was the percussionist in the MWS and so played all the percussion instruments except timpani in that orchestra. She feels she learned a great deal through this experience. The orchestra was quite accomplished and Ethel Stark (a student of Fritz Reiner at the Curtis Institute) was well respected. The culmination of this experience was a performance in Carnegie Hall, New York. Archer continued to play percussion during her two years at Yale (New Haven Symphony). As a composer she found the orchestral experience invaluable because she saw the orchestra from the inside, so to speak. This was not the end of her percussion performing career, for at the University of Oklahoma Archer played percussion in the Bartok *Sonata*. In view of this experience it is surprising that she has not written more for percussion. She says that she wrote six pieces for piano and timpani a long time ago, but they are not in her catalogue and she is not sure where they are.

Archer was a professional accompanist in Montreal in the 1940s in addition to being a teacher of piano and theory and writing arrangements for amateur song-writers. She also acted as a substitute organist but found this activity very hectic and nerve-wracking. During the period 1944 to 1947 when she also taught at the McGill Conservatorium she only had time to compose at five o'clock in the morning. Archer's only performing today is to play the piano 'to try out the stuff I write!'

ARCHER AS A TEACHER

'There is so much that can be learned by rethinking the old into the new ... anything without structure or direction is doomed to failure.'

Archer has definite ideas concerning her role as a teacher. She frequently indicates in conversation that teaching is a close second to her interests in composition. She has taught a wide variety of subjects, beginning in her early days with piano and theory. In her university teaching career she has taught every course in the theory/composition curriculum. She does have her preferences, which are for small group instruction (classes of fifteen and under) and counterpoint (both sixteenth-century and eighteenth-century). She also likes to teach advanced harmony and composition as well as analysis of twentieth-century music. She sees the latter as being invaluable for every music undergraduate student, but at the University of Alberta it is required only of composition majors. One does not have to talk with Violet Archer long before one realizes that she holds strong views on pedagogical matters. In fact, one would not think that she is retired to hear her discuss the multifarious issues which confront university music professors on a daily basis. For one thing Archer feels strongly that 'we need a five-year program for composers – four years is so little!' Performance majors make use of very little twentieth-century music – 'and I'm not afraid to be quoted on that!' Looking back on the succeeding generations of students that she has known over the past thirty years, Archer comments that she does not see a marked change in the quality of music student. Although she feels that entrance standards to university music schools should be higher, she does not think that they have changed appreciably over the years.

Archer also believes strongly in exposing young children to twentieth-century music. Her view is that children absorb twentieth-century sounds like languages. She sees nothing extraordinary in this, especially since she spoke three languages herself by the age of seven! (She spoke Italian at home, English at school, and French at play.)

I first came to know Archer through the Canadian Association of University Schools of Music (established in 1965; it has since been renamed the Canadian University Music Society). The meeting of 1967 brought together university music professors for the purpose of discussing standards in the various music programs throughout the country. As a member of the theory committee, Archer had a great deal to say on these matters. In all of her views she showed strong traditionalist leanings, no doubt derived from her own educational background. But the observer gleaned that she was doing more than copying her own mentors. Her beliefs were rooted in deep personal convictions which were the result of years of committed teaching.

Like her own mentor, Paul Hindemith, Archer has clear-cut ideas as to what each course should attempt to accomplish and she is very open about sharing these ideas with others. She believes strongly in the education of the 'complete' musician. Not only does she see very few jobs for the extreme specialist, she endorses the idea that the best-trained musician is one who has developed all aspects of the art of music – the performer must have experience in the compositional and historical aspects, and the composer must be able to perform on an instrument and know the interplay through time of the cause-and- effect relationship of musical styles. Similarly, in her view, the historian and teacher must have direct experience with the creative or compositional side of art. Not only does Archer stress the necessity of a well-rounded musical education, but she stresses that prospective teachers should develop the ability to teach subjects other than their specialties (Archer herself was called upon to teach Italian diction at North Texas, and she does not look upon that as a bad experience).

In the details of teaching composition Archer, as might be expected, has clearly defined views. She sees analysis of scores as being one of the most important aspects of the formal study of composition. Her concern is, 'What have the "greats" done?' with respect to melody, rhythm, and form. In her introductory composition course (now discontinued at the University of Alberta, much to her regret) she required each student to keep a detailed notebook which she graded at the end of the term. In the first-year composition course Archer studied exclusively twentieth-century scores with her students. Much emphasis was placed on analysis but also on writing simple melodies and two-part counterpoint. She then moved on to three-part counterpoint and the writing of chordal structures. In the latter she emphasized the writing of arbitrary, but analysable, chords. For twentieth-century counterpoint she used Ernst Krenek's *Studies in Counterpoint* (1940). One of her interesting classroom techniques was to devote ten to twelve minutes of each class period to the writing of an exercise in order to develop each student's ability to write quickly and write away from the piano. Archer does encourage students to work away from the keyboard but at the same time she does not object to their trying things out at the keyboard. She regards her own experience as a student of having to write examinations away from the keyboard as being a positive one and, accordingly, encourages her own students to do the same.

Archer is very strong on one point. She insists that her students become familiar with all styles and encourages them to work in an atonal style (and also twelve-tone). Archer sees the twelve-tone technique as only one of several possibilities and objects vehemently to the claims of Leibowitz and others that it is the only twentieth-century technique worth considering. Archer is not interested in what she calls 'paper music,' that is, music which is based on intricate mathematical calculations apparently devoid of any consideration of what she considers the sine qua non of music, the sound. Archer insists that each student should develop his or her own style. In the second year of composition studies she allows students the opportunity to go their own way but at the same time she continues to expose them to a variety of twentieth-century scores through analysis.

In addition to the writing and analysing of music in class, Archer is a strong believer in ear training. For this she draws once again on Paul

Hindemith, this time on his *Elementary Training for Musicians* (1946; rev. 1949), a text which is both basic and advanced and which has served well several generations of musicians. Archer herself is very much concerned with 'basics,' in her approach to both teaching and the creation of music. In this respect, and with respect, one might safely call her a conservative.

Archer has a realistic view of the present-day audience for contemporary music. She sees a slight improvement over her lifetime but does not think that there is a substantial audience for new music amongst the general public. Her analysis of the situation is that the average person does not respond well to contemporary music because the musical memory has not been developed. Since each successive sound which is heard is not retained, there is no feeling of anticipation on the part of the listener. And to Archer it is the feeling of anticipation which is the basis for genuine musical appreciation. Archer's solution to this dilemma is not for composers to return to tonal styles in the nineteenth-century sense, as Rochberg and others have done, but rather to educate the young listeners of tomorrow in the contemporary language of music, as R. Murray Schafer attempted to do in the 1960s. From her own experience with languages, she is convinced that the ability to feel comfortable with a language has to be developed at an early age (and Archer includes music as a language). As a corollary to this, she sees it as incumbent on the composer to write pieces which introduce contemporary idioms to the young person. It is especially demanding on the composer to produce something interesting within the technical limitations of the beginning or intermediate student.

VIOLET BALESTRERI ARCHER: A BIOGRAPHICAL CHECKLIST

Date of birth   24 April 1913

Formal education   L MUS (McGill) 1934, B MUS (McGill) 1936, ACCO (Associate, Canadian College of Organists) 1938, B MUS (Yale) 1948, M MUS (Yale) 1949; honorary D MUS (McGill) 1971

Periods of composition: 1 / the early period (the 1940s), 2 / the Yale years, 3 / teaching in the United States in the 1950s, 4 / return to Canada (1961), 5 / sabbatical (1972-3) and the first opera, 6 / recent works to retirement (1973-8), 7 / since retirement (1978-85)

1930-2   Professional accompanist for Merlin Davies, voice teacher in Montreal

1933 Began teaching career as private teacher of piano and theory.

1934 Studied composition with Claude Champagne during summers of her Bachelor of Music program (no composition was taught in B MUS program). Champagne followed the tradition of the Paris Conservatoire – formal grounding in the old masters (like Hindemith). Archer objected to writing traditional harmony – she heard dissonance from the beginning. She respected Champagne for his profound learning. 'Why do I have to write these silly minuets?' On her own Archer did write other things and brought them to Champagne, and 'he was patient.' Archer was one of four children in her family and had to work while studying in order to support herself.

1935 Continued summer studies with Champagne.

1936 Studied composition with Douglas Clarke (b. 1893), founder and first regular conductor of the Montreal Symphony Orchestra (1930-41). Worked mostly in small forms and traditional idioms, but Clarke did encourage her to write for orchestra. Clarke had been Archer's teacher in the B MUS program; in her third and last year she had been required to compose a work for orchestra and one for a cappella chorus (completely on her own, without instruction). It was following the writing of these exercises that Clarke agreed to accept Archer as a composition student. She continued to study with Clarke for four years, all of which was on scholarship. Clarke's approach was to give the student scores of contemporary music to study and to give a critique of works written by the student, but he would not suggest how to make modifications in a work. During this time Archer studied many works of Vaughan Williams and Gustav Holst (Clarke's teachers) as well as those of Debussy and Ravel. Clarke would bring back scores from England where he went every summer – he knew many of the composers personally. Archer attended every rehearsal of the Montreal Symphony; she became very much absorbed with the idea of writing for orchestra. Her first meaningful composition was orchestral (written in partial fulfilment of the B MUS degree).

1937-8 Continued studies with Clarke.

1939 Continued studies with Clarke. As a consequence of her own student experiences, Archer became convinced that, although a teacher cannot give creative talent to a student, he or she most certainly can give guidance on how to evaluate and work with ideas. Furthermore, Archer agrees with Hindemith that each person has some creative talent and this should be developed to the utmost (i.e., the performer should have some experience 'creating' music in order to know what he or she is performing). In all of her teaching Archer has stressed the mental process behind the music. She believes it is as important for the performer to understand this as for the composer. Archer also believes that the creative process in music parallels that of the other arts. 'Geniuses are few and far between, let's face it, but thinking habits can be formed with continuous practice. Teaching is a matter of unlocking the key to the composer's creative process.' Archer likes to teach adults as well as young people. 'First of all I am a composer, but close behind I am a teacher. Teaching to me is creative.'

1940   Archer became dissatisfied with her own knowledge and works and felt a great need for more guidance. She became interested in Bartok's piano music which she acquired at the International Music Store in Montreal, especially *Ten Easy Pieces* (1908). 'I had never heard anything like it.' In the meantime Bartok had emigrated to the United States (New York) in October 1940. The Montreal Women's Symphony Orchestra was established (conductor, Ethel Stark). Archer became a member of the percussion section; this provided further stimulus to her interest in orchestral writing.

1941   During 1941 Bartok was supposed to come to Montreal to perform with the Montreal Symphony Orchestra but was unable to get the required visa. At the suggestion of a friend who had studied at the Juilliard School in New York, Archer wrote to the *Musical Courier* to ask for help in contacting Bartok. The answer came back that Bartok could be reached through Boosey and Hawkes in New York.

1942   Archer accordingly wrote to Bartok in January 1942, told him what she had done to date and asked whether he would accept her as a student. (She now realizes her naivety in all of this.) Archer waited for a reply, received none, and had given up hope when a letter finally arrived in April. It was a handwritten letter from Bartok asking her to submit some of her music. Archer sent him 'some of my better things – piano preludes,' and after a few weeks she had another letter from Bartok in which he said he would be in New York in the summer and could teach her then. (Bartok was employed as a visiting assistant in music at Columbia University where he transcribed and edited the Parry Collection of 2600 discs of Yugoslav folk music which was housed at Harvard University. Bartok held this post from March 1941 to the end of 1942 at an annual salary of $3000.) Bartok's fee was $10 per lesson, which was a lot of money at the time. However, Archer was determined to study with him and made arrangements to get to New York from Montreal. Upon arrival Archer telephoned Bartok to arrange for her lesson. On the way to her lesson she got lost on the subway and ended up at the opposite end of New York to where Bartok lived (Archer arrived at the Woodlawn Cemetery, whereas Bartok lived in the Bronx). In Archer's words, 'I was almost in tears and I was scared. I went to the caretaker of the cemetery and asked if I could use the telephone. I called Bartok and he very understandingly gave me another appointment.' The next week Archer was more successful and thereafter had one lesson per week for the remainder of the summer. Archer describes her lesson in this way: 'He started off by dictating from the Steinway concert grand in his living room some Hungarian folk songs. He assigned me the task of making arrangements of some of these for clarinet and strings, which I still have. I had a difficult time with these because Hungarian folk tunes were so different and I had not had much background in harmonizing modal melodies. My final assignment was a theme and variations for string quartet.' Archer believes this to be important in that she sees variations as the technique of the twentieth century. She relates that she had no idea how dire was Bartok's financial position.

1943   Archer wrote to Bartok asking whether he would continue her lessons, but he replied that he was in the sanatorium at Saratoga Springs and could not. Archer sent Bartok a copy of Ernest Gagnon's *Chansons populaires du Canada* through Boosey and Hawkes. Partly as a result of her studies with Bartok, Archer has retained her interest in folk music to this day. When questioned as to how many other students Bartok had at the time when she studied with him, Archer replied that there were two: Tibor Serly and Jack Beeson. A publisher at Mercury (Feist), and a friend of the composer's, told Archer that he was surprised that she was able to study with him. Archer has saved the three letters from Bartok which she received. She says that it was only after studying with him that she realized what she did not know. She studied violin in a lab course at Juilliard (date?).

Archer began teaching at the McGill Conservatorium.

1947   Archer was awarded the Bradley Keeler Memorial Scholarship for entrance to Yale University and began studies in composition there with Paul Hindemith. She became assistant percussionist with the New Haven

Symphony Orchestra (until 1949). Archer regards Hindemith as one of the great teachers of the twentieth century, and he has had a lifelong influence on her. Composition classes were small – about five students. Hindemith also taught pedagogy of theory, history of theory, and Collegium Musicum – a heavy teaching load – but did not teach in the summer. Archer regarded his pedagogy of theory course as being especially valuable. Collegium was obligatory for all students – all the early music examples were copied out by hand by Hindemith! Not once in two years did he mention his own music. He maintained that in composing music it is not a question of being new and different but of knowing what one is doing. Archer is greatly impressed to this day by Hindemith's integrity and his dedication to teaching. She realizes that his music was in vogue in the 1950s but has since passed out of favour – she feels that it will make a comeback.

In conversation Archer refers to Hindemith's *A Composer's World* (1952), where he says that creativity is like standing at a window just before a storm and there is a flash of lightning – suddenly one sees everything and then it is gone. Later one might not remember everything at once but the brain reconstructs the whole from the various parts and pieces and gradually every piece will be in its place. This was the way in which Beethoven worked. Mental processes are different for each composer – for Mozart the selective process was simply much faster. The nineteenth-century view was that one should not talk about the creative process, and this was the prevalent view when Archer began her studies. Archer views 'teaching as a matter of finding the key to the composer's creative process.'

1948   Completed B MUS degree at Yale. Was awarded Quebec government scholarship and Charles Ditson Fellowship (Yale) for the orchestral work *Passacaglia*. Taught at University of Alberta Summer School.

1949   Completed M MUS degree at Yale. Thesis: *The Bell*. Awarded the Woods-Chandler Prize in composition. Awarded Quebec government scholarship. Taught at University of Alberta Summer School. An award from the Ladies' Morning Musical Club of Montreal allowed her to participate in musical life there. Spent some time in Paris, Geneva, and Italy.

1950-3   Composer-in-residence at North Texas State College (now North Texas State University)

1952   Taught at Cornell University in the summer session (theory, piano, organ, choir) and was chapel organist.

1953   Taught at University of Oklahoma (until 1961). Judge of young composers' competitions – state (1953-61), national (1959-61). Promoter of Canadian music in the United States. Gave series of radio lectures on WNAD, Norman, Okla., 1960-1, on twentieth-century piano teaching materials as well as twentieth-century four-hand piano music.

1956   Awarded a Canada Council Senior Fellowship

1961   Commenced doctoral studies at University of Toronto but was unable to continue because her mother was terminally ill. She spent most of 1961-2 in Montreal.

1962   Began teaching at the University of Alberta as chairman of theory and composition division (until 1978).

1968   Was awarded Yale University citation for distinguished service to music.

1970   Received Alberta Achievement Award.

1971   Was awarded D MUS (honoris causa) from McGill University.

1972   Received City of Edmonton Creative and Performance Award.

1977   Was co-founder (with Richard Johnston) of the Alberta Composers' Association (over sixty members in 1983). Was awarded the Queen's Jubilee Silver Medal for long and distinguished service in the field of music.

1981   Attended an international conference on computer music at North Texas State University.

1983   Was appointed a Member of the Order of Canada (investiture April 1984). Received the 'Composer of the Year' award from the Canadian Music Council on 24 June 1984.

1985   Was appointed a Fellow of the Royal Canadian College of Organists (honoris causa) on 9 July 1985.

F.R.C. CLARKE

Healey Willan's Unfinished *Requiem*

The world première of the first two movements (in a performance version prepared by myself) of the unfinished *Requiem* by Healey Willan (1880-1968) was given on 2 December 1983 by the Queen's University Choral Ensemble. This marked the first time that any of the music of this work had been heard publicly, even though it was composed some seventy years ago.[1] If completed it would have been the composer's largest choral/orchestral composition.

Willan's *Requiem* was conceived for SATB soli, large chorus (occasionally double chorus), and orchestra. There are four movements for which the sketches are fairly complete, at least of the vocal parts: Introitus, Kyrie eleison, Sequentia, and Sanctus (numbered 1, 2, 6, and 7 respectively). There exist also very brief sketches for a Prelude, Offertorium, and Benedictus. Since the Benedictus sketch is called No. 8 and since requiem settings usually have an Agnus Dei and a Lux aeterna following the Benedictus, one can assume that Willan intended to have ten movements in his setting. The four movements that do exist would take nearly forty minutes to perform; had Willan completed his *Requiem* it would have been the longest of all his works except his opera *Deirdre*. On three of the movements appear the dates 1914 and 1918 – one of Willan's most imaginative creative periods (just after he had arrived in Canada), during which he also composed such masterpieces as the *Introduction, Passacaglia and Fugue* for organ and the *Sonata No. 1* for violin and piano. It is not surprising then that there is much beautiful music lying buried within these requiem movements. Unfortunately, as with a number of other projected choral/orchestral works by this composer, the orchestrations were not done and the accompaniments exist in a fragmentary condensed score.

Example 1

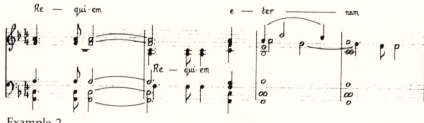

Example 2

The Introitus requires SSAATTBB choir but no soli; the instrumental accompaniment is simple and the movement contains many unaccompanied passages. Like the composer's cantata *Cleopatra* (1907) the Introitus begins with an orchestral passage consisting of a mystical succession of highly chromatic chords bearing little relationship to one another but bound together by a descending chromatic scale in the upper part (Example 1). Given the similarity of the two passages it is possible that Willan began work on this movement while he was still living in England and thus somewhat earlier than the completion (as far as it is complete) date of 31 May 1914 would indicate. The opening bars of the chorus are typical of the serene beauty which pervades the whole piece (Example 2).[2] For the middle section of the movement, the 'Te decet,' the tonality shifts from F major to C major and the tempo increases. This section features some antiphony between the SSAA and the TTBB voices of the choir. The opening text, music, and tonality return at the end of the movement to give an overall ternary structure. There are some places in the Introitus where the harmony might suggest some French influence, particularly that of Fauré (Example 3).

In preparing my performance version of this movement for choir and organ I found that all the notes of the chorus parts existed, although some of the word-underlay had to be supplied. The accompaniment was incomplete and, besides having to rearrange it for organ, I found it necessary to add to and amplify what was left by the composer.

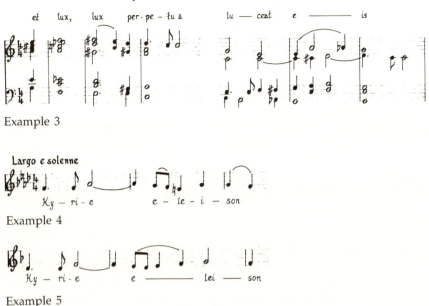

Example 3

Example 4

Example 5

The Kyrie eleison bears the date of March 1918 and seems to be the last of the nearly completed movements to have been composed. Yet an earlier sketch also exists which suggests that the origins of this music predate 1918. This earlier sketch itself appears to stem from at least two separate periods since the original has obviously been added to at a later date with a different ink that is less faded. The manuscript sheets on which the earlier sketch and the 1918 version are written are different, the former being made in Germany. These and other factors lead me to believe that this Kyrie, like the Introitus, was initially conceived before the composer came to Canada in 1913. The Kyrie requires a solo quartet in addition to SATB (divisi) choir. Though cast in a ternary structure like the Introitus, the music for the Kyrie is somewhat more elaborate. The opening section, for choir and orchestra, is based upon a theme (Example 4) which displays a family affinity to the Kyrie of Willan's later *Missa Brevis No. 8* (Example 5). The theme is duly 'answered' by the next voice, indicating that the treatment is going to be fugal. This does not prove to be the case, however, and Willan fools us by proceeding in a very free fashion thereafter. The middle section, Christe eleison, is given over to the soloists and the choir is silent. The solo soprano leads off (Example 6); the solo tenor repeats this theme and the other soloists gradually join in. Although the section is nominally in D flat major, this tonality is evident

Example 6

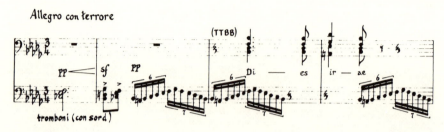

Example 7

only up to the end of the tenor entry; after that it starts to wander. In the third and final section, Kyrie eleison, the home key of F minor returns. Here solo quartet and choir, having previously performed separately, are brought together, sometimes singing antiphonally and sometimes simultaneously. The musical material is similar to that of the opening section but not an exact repetition.[3]

The longest of the nearly completed movements of Willan's *Requiem* is the Sequentia, a setting of the Dies irae. This lengthy text is set in a number of short musical sections. The whole movement, scored for SATB soli, SATB chorus (with divisi), and (intended) orchestra, begins and ends in B flat but employs many other tonalities in between. Some unity is given to this succession of somewhat unrelated sections by the recurrence from time to time of the musical motive used to set the opening words, 'Dies irae.' Terror is depicted in the opening section (Example 7). The 'Tuba mirum' uses the same magnificent funeral march music that is found in Willan's 1912 incidental music for the play *Glastonbury* (Example 8). Which came first? Since the melody seems to fit the words so well I am inclined to think the 'Tuba mirum' version is the original. (This gives further weight of evidence to the speculation that much of the music for the *Requiem* was written before the composer's departure from England.) In his 'Tuba mirum' Willan is not inclined to write for four brass bands à la Berlioz; here his music portrays the aspect of dreadful judgment in the text rather than in the blowing of last trumpets. In the 'Liber scriptus' section a new theme is combined with the 'Dies irae' accompanying motive (Example 9). Of the remaining sections particular mention should be made of the suitably sinister 'Confutatis maledictis' and the poignant 'Lacrimosa.' The Sequentia ends rather abruptly with a somewhat tonally

Example 8

Example 9

Example 10

ambiguous passage which also might indicate Willan's familiarity with Fauré's *Requiem* (Example 10). The manuscript of the Sequentia is not dated and, indeed, appears to be a collection of several different manuscripts and inks. The music is in a less finished state than that of the other movements of the *Requiem*.

The Sanctus is the only other completed movement. Written on the same type of manuscript paper as the Introitus, it appears to be contemporary with it, being dated 26 May 1914. As with the Introitus, no soloists

Healey Willan's sketch for the Benedictus of his *Requiem*
Photograph courtesy of the National Library of Canada

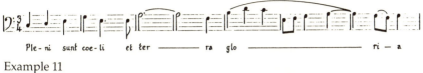
Example 11

are required for the Sanctus. This is the only movement of the four which is set out for SATB/SATB double chorus, an arrangement which permits antiphonal singing between the choirs for the opening repetitions of the word 'sanctus'; however, Willan does not exploit this potential for antiphonal work as much as he might have. The two choirs join together as one in the final section of the movement, a large fugue of over one hundred bars (Example 11). The piece is largely in C major. Although the choral parts are complete, it would appear that large portions of the intended accompaniment were not written in.

Why did Healey Willan start such a large undertaking as this *Requiem*? It is possible he may have begun it on the death of his father, James Burton Willan, in 1912 or 1913. Although I have found no firm evidence to support such speculation, it does seem likely. Mention has been made above of the musical affinity between the Kyrie theme of this work and that found in the later *Missa Brevis No. 8*. Willan wrote the latter in 1938 for his mother, who died about that time. Was this possible association coincidental, conscious, or unconscious?

The *Requiem* was probably left unfinished as a result of the disruption caused by Willan's move to Canada and by his realization, once settled there, that there would be little chance in those days in Toronto of a new work of such dimensions ever receiving a performance. The situation regarding performance opportunities did improve after many years, but by that time Willan was busy with other things. The original source of inspiration and impetus for writing the *Requiem* would have been long gone by then; indeed, the composer may well have forgotten about the project. (Even if he had not forgotten, the problems of stylistic incongruity he had encountered in his later unsuccessful attempts to complete another large work which he had begun much earlier, *The Pageant for Our Lady*,[4] would doubtless have been enough to discourage him.)

It is my intention to complete Willan's *Requiem* by preparing performance versions of the Sequentia and Sanctus, as I have already done for the Introitus and Kyrie, and to add the following movements:

Benedictus Willan's sketch for this is very incomplete and covers only the first part of the text, 'Benedictus qui venit in nomine Domine.' Never-

Example 12

theless, there is enough in the sketch for one to be able to flesh out a short movement. The main tune is rather beautiful (Example 12). The movement appears to be intended for solo quartet. Another interesting feature of Willan's sketch is that it involves within a short space of time three tonalities: E major, A flat major, and C major. Willan leaves no indication for the setting of the remainder of the text, 'Hosanna in excelsis.' Following precedents such as Haydn's *Nelson Mass*, I will adapt part of the final section of Willan's Sanctus ('Pleni sunt coeli . . . Hosanna . . . ') to repeat as a Hosanna for the Benedictus. Conveniently the tonality of C major fits perfectly.

Agnus Dei There being no composer's sketch for this movement, I will use the Agnus Dei from Willan's *Communion Service in E flat and C*, B236, of 1910. This has the advantage of being in the right tonality and of belonging to the same stylistic period. The vocal parts will be slightly altered to accommodate a Latin rather than an English text.

Lux aeterna Following to some extent the example of Süssmayer's completion of Mozart's *Requiem*, I have composed a Lux aeterna (Communion) for Willan's *Requiem* by adapting material found in the Introitus and Kyrie. This adaptation works very well; nearly every note is Willan's, and the return of the opening music gives the *Requiem* a nicely rounded form. Indeed, one wonders why more composers of requiems did not follow the same procedure.

The foregoing plan presents all the essential movements of the Requiem Mass except, perhaps, the Offertorium. Willan's sketch for the Offertorium is much too brief and incomplete to allow completion with any reasonable authenticity.[5]

For the purists who might object to the addition of movements from other sources it would be quite possible to perform the Introitus, Kyrie, Sequentia, and Sanctus as a satisfactory musical entity, much like another 'magnificent torso' (to quote Tovey), the unfinished *Great Mass in C Minor* by Mozart. These four movements contrast well with one another, and the Sanctus, with its big 'Pleni sunt coeli' fugue, would serve as a rousing finale.

ISTVAN ANHALT

Thisness: Marks and Remarks

Stopping by a signpost, a marker meant to stop, a passer-by looks and queries the sign, probes it for meaning as if peering through an opaque window. Others also stop, look, and exchange accounts of what is seen, finding that these are not identical.

A door opens and a visitor enters. Hearing – one of several faculties felt to be active – now comes into play. One listens ... a sound is heard ... and then another. Is this an echo of the 'I,' a reflection of the self, or is it someone else's sign? A voice now ... potentially intelligible. At first the voice says 'this,' then 'this' again, with a slightly different inflection and emphasis. The word 'that' follows, then in a quick succession come 'what,' 'when,' 'where,' and 'why,' all appearing in a compact stretch of time no longer than a slightly drawn-out present. This moment is indissolubly tied together with a place, an environment (not entirely devoid of temporality on its own account) within a compound dual frame. Through memory, experience, and extension, the event couples itself to other events (like and unlike), eventually forming relationships of similarities, adjacencies, collections, categories, scalar and other kinds of orderings, all potential frames themselves and frames framing frames ... forms and structures all containing a multiplicity of substances. A transposition of metaphor shows now a configuration of rapidly expanding concentric circles, the result of the throw of an idea into a receptive, yielding, medium ... interfering circles of transcendences with a suggestion of infinite regress about them. But then due to inertia, the dissipation of energy, fatigue, the figure attenuates to a standstill, or so it seems. But we soon come to realize that motion has not altogether ceased. 'Things' now appear as processes, forever in motion. Neither do ideas stand still; they move with the current of questioning. Names also stand for processes, and their occasional thought-of stability is but an illusion, it seems. At other times the urge is felt to open the 'black box.' As a result words, carrying their past, present, and future within like a secret and precious burden, are unlocked and the energy thus liberated might be found to illuminate for a surprising distance.

A voice from the past interrupts: 'Wait. Just tell me the simple unvarnished truth, please.'

Sorry, this I am unable to do. The time is long past when makers of intricate cabinets were thought of as holding the key to certain secret compartments in the human mind. To be simple is the most difficult act of all, and I haven't mastered it yet. And as to the word 'truth,' I had better just leave it alone.

'Let's try something else then. Where did all this begin for you? Personally, I mean.'

I cannot say for sure, though it seems certain that it started much earlier than the moment when I, so to say, began. The genes ... you know. This can be taken for given.

'What does your own "this," or "thisness," mean then for you?'

They suggest, indicate, and are indicated by, beyond the genes, certain signposts, code-notions: dates, periods, residences, displacements, by the beginnings and the ends of involvements, by days of birth and death of close ones. Most of these data are readily available and map life in its grand contours, but they must be handled with circumspection as they rarely, if at all, match the dynamic landscape of the mind. This topography is formed by feelings, by emerging thought, impressions in constant flux, ongoing relationships, an unceasing stream of actions, reactions, work undertaken, completed, or not, some turning out well enough to cause joy, others proving to be failures (I must soon enough break the silence I have so far kept about some of these); these and many other kinds of marks, marks upon marks, remarks upon marks, and so on, the whole building up into a vast and undecipherable memory-labyrinth, a thought and feeling edifice of inexplicable complexity, an edifice that is unceasingly building itself and appears to be signalling that this very act of continuous building is at the heart of its existence. This would suggest that the ultimate destination is but the journey itself, which at the same time is also the final goal and destiny, should one be inclined to name it so. (Should I ever need a witness for this I could not think of a better man than Helmut Kallmann to say a few words on my behalf. I know him as someone who is aware, with a deep understanding, of what it takes to give the past, his own as well as that of others, its due, with a foresight and care that are essential for this. He brings wisdom and a rare touch to the tending of this garden.)

Thisness: Marks and Remarks

'Slow down for a moment and pause, if you can, please. I want to ask a question.'

Gladly, though this might not be as easy to do as I would like. For example, I still have difficulty in indicating silence or pause . . .

'But Mallarmé . . . '

Of course. He knew how. In any case thanks for bringing up his name at this juncture. It seems it was the right thing to do.

'Let us continue then. What were you doing yesterday? Anything memorable? If not, routine matters would also do.'

Yes, it was a fairly good day, as full as they usually come. Memorable? Difficult to say, but perhaps so on one account: a conversation with a friend during our shared lunch-time. Something that he told me echoed an experience I had before.

'Tell me more about it.'

After our usual opening banter I noticed that he seemed to be preoccupied; a cloud seemed to hang over his head as he spoke, looking ahead as if avoiding eye-contact between the two of us. Then he came to the point: a routine medical check-up showed up a diabetic condition in him. He finds it difficult to come to terms with this new reality and fights it to the point of unfocussed anger. He feels that an earlier state of coherence of self has become irreparably damaged and that he has problems with finding a new equilibrium. Then he stopped and paused.

I replied that this was familiar to me through personal experience, some of it quite recent. This seemed to comfort him a little, and we even laughed afterwards. It was not necessary for me to elaborate on my remark regarding parallel experiences. I could have told him though (he is a good listener) about a few difficult weeks I had in the course of the summer of 1985, during which I felt at times that I had a little too much on my plate. I was in the midst of writing the piano-vocal/choral score of *Winthrop* and also thinking of a promise made a while back to Phyllis Mailing, a friend and a much-admired colleague, to write a few songs for her by the fall. And there were other matters to attend to, besides. By July it became clear that if I was to write a piece for Phyllis I could not delay starting it any longer. Work on *Winthrop* must be interrupted, however reluctantly, and the other matters pushed into the background as much as feasible.

As on other occasions, first I looked into some books, half by design and half serendipitously, in search of ideas for a text that I knew I must write myself and which would deal with one or another facet of existence, a theme to which I had been drawn, in one form or other, for quite a while. (*Foci* is about this, and so are the threefold portrayals in *La Tourangelle* and in *Winthrop*.)[1] By the end of July I managed to write a few dozen lines that constituted what appeared to me as three or four short poems, with some lines still missing. All seemed to belong to – how to put it? – a 'terrain' which, in turn, they defined. But I did not have a name for this 'place,' or idea, or whatever it was. I somehow felt that I would have to find this something, find its name, or give it a name, and then, in turn, this something would give coherence to the whole piece, 'dictate' the still missing texts and act as a motor for the entire work, text and music too.

And one day it happened; not quite by design, but neither entirely by chance. Among the books I was dipping into here and there (I had no patience for a more careful kind of reading at the time) there was a one-volume dictionary of philosophy. It was in this that one morning I stumbled upon the word 'haecceity' (meaning *this* object or person) and I immediately knew that I had found what I was looking for. Besides, the root of the word 'haec,' the feminine form of the demonstrative pronoun in the nominative in Latin, was a familiar companion from my early years in the Dániel Berzsenyi real-gymnasium in Budapest ... I still hear the incantational music of the Latin class drill: 'hic, haec, hoc; hunc, hanc, hoc; huius, huius, huius ... ' which we learned, through innumerable repetitions, day after day, week after week ... And lo: now one of those funny little words that often almost lulled me into a hypnotic daze in the classroom almost six decades ago gives me an electric jolt, energizing whatever it is that gets one to work with an imperative push, providing also at the same time idea after idea in quick succession ... One proceeds almost like a sleep-walker ... no false step is possible. 'Risky' moves can be made, perhaps because they do not appear as such.

Within a few days I had the complete text. It consisted of nine poems and the brief description of a tenth movement, conceived as a short pantomime. They read as follows:

1 QUEST

Go
  bring back the pearl
  from that distant land

Take time to pass
  wonder all along
  until you have the questions right

Listen first
  and then listen some more
  to the voices that come along

Then rest . . .
  and try again

At last
  you will know
  you have heard it right this time
  a voice speaking in silence perhaps

The time
  for return
  is near

You will spot the hour
  whether at night
  or in the day

Depart
  without delay
  on the journey back home

———

2 THISNESS (HAECCEITAS)

On my way I am
  I was before
    and before then
      I shall be and
        shall be again

From there I came
  here I am now
    for a while
      and then a little longer perhaps

Why did I come?
  Why then?
    Why there?
      Where is my home?
        Where shall I be going now?
          For how long?
            And to what end?

How to find?
  How to keep?
    How to lose?
      How to preserve?
        And how to change?

I am here to seek the light
  to while away for a while
    to seek the light again
      and then ... some distraction

It has to be this way
  a truth is hard to bear

Now:
  concealment, diversion, shouting and noise

Do you hear the voice across the din?

---

3 INCANTATION

I want
  hence it is good

I take
  hence it is right

I claim
  hence you yield

My needs
  command your deeds

I like
  hence it is nice
    it is so nice
      I want it twice
        I want it thrice

I crave
  hence you surrender

I must possess
  so you are possessed

You will be mine
  all will be mine
    all is mine

You mime
  all that's mine

You watch
  my every sign

You admire me
  you love me
    you adore me

You despise me
  you fear me
    you hate me

Till the day
  on which I die

Yeah . . .

———

4 DIALOGUE

You, indeed, must.

    Do I really?

You have no other choice but to do;
it has been decided a long time ago.

    Perhaps so, but I still want to wait and see.

You are wasting your time.

    Time is the only thing that I can freely spend.

That's what you think.
The word in the mirrored corridors
of the Labyrinth says differently.

    This wasn't my concern
    until you spoke of it.

Another evasion, perhaps?

    Must I then look into the abyss?

You said it: . . . the cracks . . .

———

Thisness: Marks and Remarks 219

5 VERTIGO

Reeling
    rolling
        into the cracks . . .
  of words . . .   worlds . . .
Failing
    falling
        along an arc . . .

along an arc . . . a long arc . . . arc along . . .
arca long . . . canor arca . . . conar . . . racon . . .
lone agon . . . wrong agon . . . agonarch . . . angor
agon . . . racon . . .

angor agon, agonal, galga agon, agonarch, galga
arc golag, galga lagōr golag, langōr golag, galga
long glagola golag, galga golag, galga galōr glagola
golag, galga galōr glagolag, carna golag,
carna galga golag, glagola galgal golag, glagola
gorgōn golag, gorgōn agon golag, carna gorgōn
agon, carna agon gonal agolag, archōn agolag,
archōn golag, agonal, archōn agon golag galac,
golag glagolag, glogal golag, golan agon, golan
agon, golan agon canān, golan canān agon, galga
canān, agon, angor agon, agon, galga glogal,
can cana agon, cana agon, cana galga agon, angor
agon golag, galga lagōr glagolag, galgal
anarch, archōn anarch . . . orgōn anarch . . . anarch
. . . anarch . . . a narc . . . a narc . . . narc . . .
narc . . . narc . . .

narc . . . narca long . . .
/ɑ/   /ɒ/   /ɔ/   /ʌ/   /o/
/R/   /r/   /x/   /γ/   /X/   /ʁ/   /ʕ/
/l/   /n/
/h̥/

logar . . . arcan logar . . . arca long . . . a
long arc

———

6 REASON

Along this arc
  I can predict

Up to this point
  I understand

There are things
  for which I have a name

I know events
  that are likely to recur

Certain places and faces
  I see day after day

I am able to note
  how things change
  from one hour to the next

I feel the change
  within myself

I know of clocks
  that are set to different times
  clocks that connect
  and those that oft-times divide

I observe myself
  while I am doing this or that
  thinking of days yet to come
  and of those that one ought not to forget

I do devise some rules
  and at times claim
  that I can tell a right
  from a wrong

I am also able to love
  and to attenuate my hate

I have learned how to give
   and have re-learned how to receive

Yes, but I still fail to see
   what all this may add up to be ...
   may come to mean

---

7 UNREASON

Is this the end of your speech, foreigner?
How strangely you speak.

I hate you for it.
I hate you, pharmakos.

They claim: you know all
that I don't understand ...

I fear you, pharmakos,
wizard and poisoner.

You stir up my life,
sacred and accursed soul.

You must be exorcised!

And what's the worst,
you dweller upon the boundary line,
you bring what I've come to need.

I hate you the more for it.

Strain, stress, strife ...
the going gets rougher now.

You, Ishmael, you are at hand to blame.

   'The plague's upon us!
   Bring out the pharmakoi!'

You are handy to strike.

'Blow, pharma, blow, pharma,
pharma, blow!'

More yet to come!

'Attack between the legs!'

'Aim at the head!'

'Blow out their lights!'

'Destroy the forms!'

'Erase their formulas!'

'Kill to clear!'

'Kill to clean!'

'Kill to cure!'

The boil is lanced . . .
the air heavy . . .

Trace and retrace . . .

. . . try to forget . . .

Peace will now return
with the settling dust . . .

And now a warning:

You mustn't ever, ever, bring it up again.
It never even took place.

Then . . . perhaps . . .
the voice, also, will go away . . .
in time . . .

———

8 FILLED PAUSE

[Pantomime with a few
improvised paralinguistic
sounds and instrumental
'noises,' all performed
very sparsely and softly]

―――

9 ABOUT THIS SONG

What makes me sing this song?

Am I the cause or
am I the result?

Could I be both?

Does the song sing itself, or
do I become I as I sing away?

Or did someone script the tune
a long time ago
placing it in the head
to come alive
when the right moment comes along?

How many tunes are thus hiding away?

Does one depart
when the last tune was allowed to sound?

Or when one goes,
goes behind the veil,
do still-born tunes remain
still in the head?

Who composed their potentiality?

―――

10 BEYOND

Beyond . . .
       yet so near . . .
              grasp . . .
                in vain . . .
a spark . . . a shadow . . .
           fleeting . . .
hold on . . .
           slipping away . . .
How long ago?
        One forgets . . .
                a string is trembling . . .

Alone . . .
      just found out
            the others are gone
Silence only
      remains . . .
             wrapped in recall . . .
Still . . .
    but the throbbing within . . .
Wait and listen . . .
         in vain . . .
             as no-one else is here

Wait
   a little longer . . .

Then . . .
      go . . .

Leaving . . .
     nothing at all

Thisness: Marks and Remarks 225

Two of the preliminary sketches for the costume and set designs for Istvan Anhalt's *Thisness* by the Vancouver artist Sylvia Tait, reproduced by permission of the artist

For about two weeks I had to put aside the finished text to attend to other business. But the work kept on churning at the back of my mind during this period, and when I finally got down to the composition of the music it went fast. Knowing that Phyllis Mailing would have much music to learn, I was eager to get the score to her as soon as possible. She must also be informed that *Thisness* had turned out to be a dramatic work, with a simple scenario that could benefit from a staged presentation. With regard to the latter aspect I immediately thought of Sylvia Tait, the Vancouver artist, whose work has been very close to me since the 1960s. I was delighted at her positive and enthusiastic response when I invited her to design the visual side (costumes, props, if any, and lighting) of the presentation. The 'rough' copy of the score now complete, I was eager to tell Phyllis and Sylvia about the work without waiting any longer. I wrote the following letter to them.[2]

10 August 1985

The work is complete, I finished the score yesterday. Of course polishing will go on, especially as I hear you, Phyllis, singing this detail or that. What follows is a first attempt to describe what the piece is about and what it ought to add up to.

It is what I have come to call a 'monodrama[3] cycle' for voice and accompanist. It will take about thirty-five minutes[4] to perform and is a dramatic work, with a not-so-hidden scenario. The ten sections (only some of which are in the nature of a 'song') are interconnected textually as well as musically. They will have to have their visual equivalents as well.

I first encountered the word 'thisness' in its Latin original, 'haecceitas.'

My edition of *Webster's International Dictionary* gives these definitions: '*thisness*: The quality in a thing of being here and now or such as it is; the concrete objective reality of a thing; haecceity; *haecceity, haecceitas*: Thisness; specificity; also the character of being here and now.'

A *Dictionary of Philosophy*[5] gives this information: '*haecceity*: A term originally employed by Duns Scotus (c. 1266-1308) to denote the formal property of an object or person in virtue of which it is uniquely individuated as just this object or person.'

I think the notion also has to do with the concept of 'existence' in some 'existentialist' sense. Heidegger's *Dasein* would be a good example of this. This is how the dictionary of philosophy I've just quoted from defines this: '*Dasein*: (German for: being there) A term employed by Heidegger in the investigation of human existence. Man's particular mode of being-in-the-world is characterized by relatedness to surrounding objects and members of his community, in terms of being concerned with and caring about them . . . ' It also gives these definitions: '*individuation, principle of*: A principle that uniquely identifies one individual . . . the term most commonly occurs now in discussions of personal identity and of the way in which one individual is to be identified in relation to others,' and, finally, '*personal identity*: The concept posing the philosophical problem of explaining what it means to say that this at this time is the same person as that at that time. *See* person; soul; survival and immortality.'

And so it goes; the idea leads one on, and it is difficult to see where the boundaries might be perceived to be . . .

Earlier this summer I also chanced to encounter the old gnostic parable 'The hymn of the pearl' that is reported to be a part of the apocryphal Acts of the Apostle Thomas. It tells of a symbolic journey of *recovery*, as well as *discovery*. The young person who is sent away from the royal house of the 'Father' has the task of retrieving a precious pearl from the clutches of a serpent. Various robes, messages, temptations, and frailties, among other things, play roles here. Finally another word from the 'Father' (in the form of a letter) 'awakens' the one who is on the quest. The set task is now expeditiously accomplished, and a triumphal return home is assured and carried out.

I have taken some features from this tale and made them part of *Thisness*, as you will see from the text and in the comments that follow here. But others (the triumphal return home, for example) I had no use for. But there are more relevant and stronger connections here. The symbolism of the robes and the 'pearl,' particularly, suggested to me that this parable is, in fact, yet another way of speaking about what has come to be referred to a few centuries and paradigmatic changes later by the words that appear as subject-headings in dictionaries and which I have quoted above.

So, we have a theme, a text, and there is now a score that, I am confident, fills this shell with musical substance.

Here follow short descriptions of the ten sections.

1 *Quest* In a completely darkened auditorium one hears a voice (singing), the voice of the one who sends another on a personal quest, punctuated by a few ringings of a bell. These sounds come from backstage. The vocal expression is a mixture of love, concern, strength, authority, and a kind of dignity. (ca 2'30")

2 *Thisness* There is now some visibility (that increases gradually). Entrances (vocalist, accompanist, assistant, if any) are made. The overall character is, along most of the way, song-like and intimate. Towards the end it turns surprisingly raucous – a transition to the next event. (ca 4'30')

3 *Incantation* The mood is showy, aggressive, vulgar, sexy in a rather grossly tempting way. There are in the music tones of several pop idioms (allusions to rather than attempts at faithful imitations of). Towards the end the piece turns into a simulation (in a 'show-biz'-like manner) of introspection, not quite credible. (ca 3')
4 *Dialogue* Two 'parts' of a person are talking to each other. There is a difference in outlook between the two, yet also an underlying empathy and identity. The conclusion prepares the ground for no. 5. (ca 1'30")
5 *Vertigo* From the point of view of sound repertory (vocal and instrumental), this is the most eccentric piece. The vocalist de-composes language and works at certain levels of meaning that are of great expressive power and intimacy. The accompanist complements her in this by producing a 'matching' sound sequence, consisting of hand-stopped strings, uncharacteristic glides, and scraping sounds of various kinds. At one level the movement can be listened to as a kind of nightmare. But I would prefer if it were taken as an attempt at coming to grips with, or confronting, some aspects of existence and/or experience that are often resistant to (or even defy) other approaches. At the end of this the performers emerge with a certain weariness. (ca 5'15")
6 *Reason* It is my hope that this piece (one with a rather consistently carried out contrapuntal construction) will do justice to its title. It is, besides other things, to convey the essence of belief in human reason, cause and effect relationships, scientific procedures, goal-oriented endeavours, value-systems, and perhaps some other fruits of a richly crowned tree with roots in Plato, Hume, etc. right down (or up) to some of the logical positivist thinkers of the Vienna Circle. (This sounds a bit heavy. The piece is, in reality, a delicate two-part canon, song-like, and very intimate in tone.) (ca 4'15")
7 *Unreason* There is a big contrast here. The audience discovers (it might not be a complete surprise for some) that someone has been listening to the preceding three pieces (nos 4-6) with a mounting rage that now erupts. The voice, that of a brutal, rather ignorant, opinionated, and pathologically aggressive person, is hoarse, tense, loud – bespeaking these traits without any attempt to disguise them. Yet this person is also a forceful leader of others, a person of considerable authority, who acts out of a certain logic, based, to be certain, on fatally false premises, hence a doubly or triply dangerous individual. The implications of this piece should be that unspeakable crimes are being perpetrated in the course of its relatively brief duration. The destructive act could not have been undertaken with impunity. A price has to be paid. This

comes in the evidence [now composed] that the perpetrator, who acted out of a high mental-emotive pressure, becomes suddenly stricken. One cannot be certain; it looks as if she has suffered a stroke of some severity. This suddenly inhibits her movements, her speech, which becomes less and less intelligible from that point onwards. The audience may even come to feel a certain amount of compassion mixed with horror for the person in whose fate the roles of tormentor and victim have suddenly come to merge. (ca 4'30")

8 *Filled Pause* After what has just taken place nothing can be said, for a while at least, or so it seems. But the flow of expression cannot and does not stop. Just the contrary. The seeming silence speaks loudly and eloquently, especially given our way of using this potent language of 'negativity.' But of course a perfect silence is difficult to preserve. Small 'parasite' sounds begin to appear: a grunt, a slight moan, a barely audible sigh of relief; one clears one's throat, as if removing an unwanted object (or memory image), etc. The accompanist checks the piano for possible (pseudo) damage incurred in the course of the dangerous experience just enacted. In more practical terms this pantomime movement gives the performers a chance to recover from the effort of having performed no. 7. For the audience it is a breather from a different vantage point, but no less necessary. (ca 1')

9 *About this Song* This section is the closest in tone to a medium-length concert aria. The singer is here herself, a recitalist, also speaking for the composer as composer and, most importantly, for a listener in the audience as a creative person, with a potential for giving voice to his/her personal 'thisness.' Hence the theme is introspection, asking oneself questions once again: about self-expression, communication, and the like. This channels directly to the final stage (no. 10). (ca 4'30")

10 *Beyond* The bell-like tones of the piano call the vocalist to reminisce. The sounds increase in loudness, and at one point a connection between these and the bell tones of the first movement will probably be suggested. These tones now slowly decrease in intensity as the vocalist, who has stopped singing, listens to them. When the last resonance is barely audible she resumes her introspective commentary. After the last sound of the piano has completely died down the accompanist (with assistant, if any) leaves the stage in the dwindling light. The vocalist acknowledges her solitude and prepares for her exit. This will be signalled by the first of two ringings of a distant (off-stage) double bell (a clearly pitched middle-sized bell and a triangle).[6] Almost immediately after she makes her exit complete darkness returns. (ca 4')

Now about the visual side of the piece.

The 'journey" will be expressed by the entrances and exits. Action will be implied by the interpretation of the text and the music, by the vocalist's movements and position on the stage and by her interaction with her accompanist-partner. Different feelings, moods, and thoughts will also be suggested by the costumes. For no. 2, I imagine an ankle-length travelling cloak with a hood for the vocalist and all-black attire for the accompanist and assistant, both of whom should wear a half-mask. Irrespective of gender, the two will be clad in slacks and turtle-neck sweaters. The masks should be removed towards the close of no. 2. In no. 3 the vocalist should wear a Tina Turner-type outfit.

I have problems with envisaging the garment(s) for nos 4-6. I don't even know whether there should be one (with minor 'modifiers'), two, or three. I see the possibility of using an oversized Janus-type double mask in no. 4. (Should one use the mask idea elsewhere? I tend to think not as it would reduce the directness of all the other numbers.) The garb in no. 5 should convey the idea of moving towards the edge of things; an almost reckless tampering with safe boundaries. No. 6, in contrast, should suggest rationality; hope based on this rationality.

From the point of view of the visuals also no. 7 is a climax. While we should avoid depicting an associate concentration-camp commander (I am aiming here at a more general allusion) there should be enough earthy brutality and gore to this scene. (I shall be looking forward to your ideas about a costume, etc. for this, Sylvia.)

In no. 8 the garb of no. 7 will be taken off, revealing the gorgeous evening dress of a concert-singer, who is about to continue her 'normal' recital. (By this time all the previously discarded costumes, modifiers, and the double mask will be seen lying around.)

During the general pause that begins no. 10 the vocalist slowly takes off her gown, revealing a white body-stocking. She stands, symbolically naked, before the audience. As she prepares to leave the stage, at the end, she casually gathers up all (or some) of her discarded garments and, holding these with one limp arm, exits dragging them on the floor behind her, like some kind of appendage which she does not want to, or cannot, get rid of.[7]

I don't see clearly yet the way the costumes could be changed. One way would be an 'onion-peeling' process: the singer would take off one layer showing the one directly under it. (This would work well from no. 2 to no. 3, but I don't quite see it from no. 3 to no. 4, especially if the garment in no. 3 is to be short.) In some changes at least it might be necessary to take the new garb from elsewhere on the stage. (But what would this do to the unity of this aspect? Also, it does not seem to me a simple enough process. Help, please!)

With respect to lighting, a few well-timed changes would be all that would be necessary, in all probability. I sense the need for a rigorously conceived and carried out economy with respect to all movements (especially by the vocalist). I have in mind a mixture of a few stylizations of recognizable models and new invention that is suggested by the music. I would be grateful to have your ideas, suggestions, Phyllis, as to how you would like to proceed in this regard.[8]

A simple setting for the piece ('less is more,' as we have found ourselves saying in unison, Sylvia) might be effective and needed. But what should this consist of? What symbols would grow out of the essence of the piece itself? For one thing: the shed/discarded garments will have to be put/dropped/thrown on/over some surface(s). Your idea of cubes (to be kicked over in a fit of rage at the opening – or close to it – of no. 7) should be considered as a possibly effective solution.

This is all for now about *Thisness*. I am looking forward to working together with you on this – three good friends of old, celebrating our mutual affection in a very special way. Ever since I was commissioned by the Vancouver New Music Society[9] to write a piece for you, I have been thinking a great deal of you, Phyllis, and all through the writing you were an inspiration – your great artistry and much else besides. And it was more than right that you, Sylvia, should be the 'feeling and thinking eye' in this project. I love your visual world and even as I am writing this one of your beautiful canvasses is within my reach.

Phyllis Mailing and Richard Epp gave the première of *Thisness: A Duodrama Cycle* on 19 January 1986 at a concert of the Vancouver New Music Society in the Vancouver East Cultural Centre, with staging and lighting designed by Sylvia Tait.

SUN-FATHER SKY-MOTHER

R. Murray Schafer
for Mignon

NOTE

SUN-FATHER SKY-MOTHER IS INTENDED FOR PERFORMANCE BY A SOLO SINGER IN A MOUNTAIN SETTING, NEAR WATER AND FORESTS. SINCE ECHOS ARE AN IMPORTANT FEATURE OF THE WORK, A VALLEY SURROUNDED BY SEVERAL MOUNTAINS WOULD BE BEST. IN THIS CASE THE SINGER COULD MODULATE THE DURATION AND THE LOCATION OF THE ECHOS BY FACING IN DIFFERENT DIRECTIONS.

I RECALL ISTVÁN ANHALT ONCE SPEAKING OF WISHING TO COMPOSE MUSIC DIRECTLY INTO THE TISSUE OF REVERBERATION. HE WAS SPEAKING OF ELECTRONIC SOUND; BUT WITH THE PRESENT ENVIRONMENT THIS IS EQUALLY POSSIBLE. IN PLACES I'VE TRIED TO SUGGEST HOW THE VOICE COULD WORK OVER THE FOLDINGS OF PREVIOUS ECHOS TO SET UP A KIND OF RHYME WITH ITSELF, SOMETIMES MODULATING THE EFFECT BY THE INSERTION OF NEW NOTES.

WE MIGHT THINK OF SUN-FATHER SKY-MOTHER AS AN EXAMPLE OF ACOUSTIC ECOLOGY. THE SINGER SINGS TO THE ELEMENTS AND ECHOS BRING THE VOICES OF NATURE BACK TO THE SINGER. BUT SINGER AND ECHO ARE THE SAME; THUS THE PERFORMER AND THE ENVIRONMENT HAVE BECOME ONE.

THE WORK WAS FIRST PERFORMED BY ELEANOR JAMES IN AUGUST 1985 AT SPRAY LAKE IN THE ROCKY MOUNTAINS SOUTH OF CANMORE, ALBERTA. THE SINGER MOVED TO DIFFERENT LOCATIONS FOR THE VARIOUS VERSES OF THE WORK.

SUN-FATHER SKY-MOTHER IS INTENDED FOR EVENTUAL INCORPORATION INTO <u>AND WOLF SHALL INHERIT THE MOON</u>.

TEXT

(1) O SUN
FATHER
LIGHT OF THE WORLD
I COME TO YOU
I SING TO YOU
MY SPIRIT SOARS
I AM ONE WITH YOU.

(2) O SKY
MOTHER
CROWN OF THE WORLD
I COME TO YOU
I SING TO YOU
MY SPIRIT SOARS
I AM ONE WITH YOU.

(3) O MOON
LOVER
LIGHT OF MY NIGHT
I COME TO YOU
I SING TO YOU
MY SPIRIT YEARNS
I AM ONE WITH YOU.

(4) O STARS
BROTHERS & SISTERS ABOVE
I COME TO YOU
I SING TO YOU
MY SPIRIT SOARS
I AM ONE WITH YOU.

(5) O MOUNTAINS
PROTECTORS
I COME TO YOU
I SING TO YOU
MY SPIRIT ARCHES
I AM ONE WITH YOU.

(6) O BIRDS
DAUGHTERS
I COME TO YOU
I SING TO YOU
MY SPIRIT FLIES
I AM ONE WITH YOU.

(7) O FISH
ANCESTORS
I COME TO YOU
I SING TO YOU
MY SPIRIT SWIMS
I AM ONE WITH YOU.

(8) O FORESTS
PROVIDERS
I COME TO YOU
I SING TO YOU
MY SPIRIT GROWS
I AM ONE WITH YOU.

(9) O ANIMALS
SONS
I COME TO YOU
I SING TO YOU
MY SPIRIT HOWLS
I AM ONE WITH YOU.

(10) SPIRITS OF THE WORLD
I COME TO YOU
I SING TO YOU
COME... SING...
COME TO THE WILD ONE
I AM ONE WITH YOU
TAKE ME TO THE LAND I LOVE

SIGNS EMPLOYED IN THE MUSIC

⌐⌐ = VERY LONG PAUSE   ⌒ = PAUSE
⌐ = SHORT PAUSE   ⌢ = VERY SHORT PAUSE

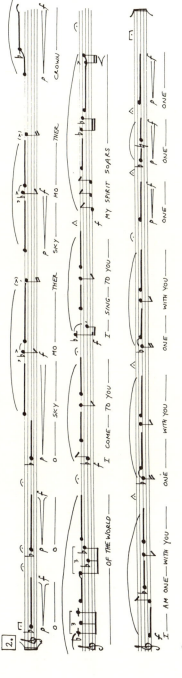

PATRICIA KELLOGG

Sounds in the Wilderness: Fifty Years of CBC Commissions

> I have just received a brochure put out by the Koussevitzky Music Foundations, in which they list all the works they have commissioned. It occurred to me that it would be an interesting idea to have something along similar lines published by the CBC, listing the works and information about them which we have commissioned over the years. I realise that this will take considerable research but think it is a worthwhile project we might get going on with a view to having something ready sometime next fall. Would you let me know if you think this is possible.
> Geoffrey Waddington, Director of Music
> Toronto, March 20th, 1959

This internal memo was addressed to Helmut Kallmann, the person primarily responsible at that time for operating the CBC Music Library in Toronto. Efforts went forward immediately, and the suggested catalogue of CBC-commissioned works became available that fall. On the occasion of the CBC's fiftieth anniversary in 1986, a completely updated catalogue was prepared by the staff of the CBC Toronto Music Library, covering almost all of the serious works commissioned by both the French and English radio networks from the point of the first commission (1939) to the present. Helmut Kallmann's original catalogue from 1959 was a crucial source of information for the compilation of this new one.

Preparations for the celebration of the CBC's golden anniversary included the combing of the corporation's program archives to bring forward examples of the best works from the past so that these achievements could be presented again to the Canadian public in the fall of 1986. Attempts were also made to uncover more information about our broadcasting history so that further research in this area may be facilitated. It is the main purpose of this article, therefore, to document fully for the first time the evolution of the commissioning of Canadian composers by the CBC to create special works for radio broadcast.[1]

The corporation has long been recognized as an important source of classical music and as a major employer of Canadian musical talent. A broad range of activities has meant opportunities for thousands of individuals and groups – from producers to performers, from string quartets to full symphony orchestras, from arrangers to, of course, composers.

For example, over the years, a great many composers have received 'commercial' musical assignments to meet the CBC's production requirements for theme music (program signature tunes) and for incidental music to frame and provide continuity to dramas and documentaries. (In this regard, CBC television has also been a major source of work for Canada's composers.) As Gilles Potvin, a long-time music producer with the CBC, recently pointed out: 'Probably the most played CBC-commissioned Canadian work in existence is the theme music for the farm broadcasts ... it was on daily for years and years.' Hundreds of these 'commercial' commissions advanced the musical development of composers like Howard Cable, Pierre Mercure, Godfrey Ridout, Morris Surdin, Jean Vallerand, and John Weinzweig by providing a degree of financial stability as well as an opportunity to practise their craft, even if it was in a more restricted creative setting than they might have preferred.

The CBC has also encouraged the composition of original music through the less direct means of assuring the broadcast of works by individual composers or of works commissioned by other organizations (the Winnipeg Symphony Orchestra, for example, with funding – possibly in whole or in part from the Canada Council – dedicated to the creation of a specific composition).

As already noted, however, this article focuses exclusively on the direct CBC commissioning of works for radio broadcast. This is only one component – albeit a critically important one – in the overall CBC commitment to classical music. Before a comprehensive picture of the CBC's support of Canadian composers will emerge, much more research will be required in such areas as the corporation's commissioning of incidental music for both radio and television, and the positive influence of the CBC even where works were not directly commissioned.

An outline of the commissioning process under discussion may be needed here. A commission begins as a contract between the composer and the corporation, specifying the type of work desired. This may be any one of a number of musical genres, ranging from chamber music to a work for full orchestra, from concerto to opera, from an unaccompanied choral work to one in experimental electronics. The contract normally arises out of consultations between a producer and a composer. It specifies at least the approximate length of the work, the proposed instrumentation, the date the composition is required to be finished, and the number of broadcasts or performances for which the CBC wishes to contract.

From the earliest days, the CBC paid not only for the creation of the work but also for the copying and reproduction of the orchestration, that is, of all the instrumental and/or vocal parts necessary for the performance (often a considerable cost). The CBC also took responsibility for the determination of venue, the staging and/or recording, where required, and, ultimately, for the broadcast itself. Through all of this, the composer retained copyright of the work and remained eligible for the payment of royalties in the event that the work was used for more than the specified number of performances. After the work had been broadcast, complete control reverted to the composer, who could then authorize any additional performances he or she wished. (Originally, the composer was in a sense further subsidized, because the performing parts for the players became the property of the composer, even though they had been paid for by the corporation. Owing to budget restrictions in recent years, this practice has been discontinued; however, while the CBC now retains the rights to performing materials, these may be leased from the music library for a reasonable fee.)

The term 'wilderness' in the title of this article reflects partly the immense territory over which the CBC must broadcast, sending out original Canadian classical music – among a huge range of other services – to such remote outposts as Tuktoyaktuk in the Arctic and Batteau on the Labrador Coast. But it also refers to the early void in Canada in the support of Canadian composers and in the performance of new Canadian works and the way in which the CBC moved to encourage creative endeavours that would broadcast original Canadian musical sounds into both the geographical and this particular cultural 'wilderness.'

Canada's aspiring composers in the 1930s and early 1940s generally went abroad for most of their studies. As that generation completed its training and became established – usually by teaching at Canadian universities and conservatories (if they returned to Canada at all) – the various Canadian music departments began to acquire the ability to take on increasing responsibility for the training of Canada's subsequent young composers. For all composers at that time, however, whether younger or older, there was little or no 'market' for their skills or opportunity for performances of the works they were creating. Geoffrey Waddington, director of music for the CBC's English network from 1952 to 1964, wrote the following in *Music in Canada* in 1955:

The Canadian composer faces more than the usual number of problems and handicaps in Canada ... It is understandable, but nevertheless regrettable, that for 'box office' reasons works by Canadian composers appear too seldom on the regular programmes of large symphony orchestras. In this field, however, the CBC has been able to fill the gap by giving frequent broadcast performances of Canadian music. Works are commissioned for special occasions and much of the best that is being written today is recorded for distribution abroad by the CBC's International Service.[2]

Geoffrey Waddington and his predecessor, Jean-Marie Beaudet, were in fact the catalysts within the CBC in the development of a unique program to encourage the creation of new Canadian music. Through their efforts the public became increasingly aware of the existence and value of Canadian composers. In addition, following their early lead, various performing groups and arts agencies gradually began to commission works on their own to support creative activities in the field of classical music. As a result, in recent years, the CBC has become only one of several important commissioning agents and is no longer the dominant force on the scene.

Even so, today the CBC remains a significant and still-growing source of commissions. Up to the present, the English and French radio networks have commissioned at least 620 works, representing creative output from about 250 Canadian composers, with 60% of this falling in just the past fifteen years (228 works in the 1970s and 144 more at just over the halfway point of the 1980s).

Apart from the changes in broadcasting conditions and policies that are dealt with in this article, the steady growth of support for original Canadian classical music reflects a number of other developments, including simple population growth, sociological factors within the audiences, and the broader availability of and improvements to musical education. In any event, a review of the evolution of commissioning by the CBC will demonstrate that the Corporation has not only been central to this growth, but was *the* crucial element in creating greater appreciation and support in the first place.

THE EVOLUTION OF COMMISSIONING

The early years

The CBC was created by an act of Parliament in 1936 to replace the Canadian Radio Broadcasting Commission. Modelled largely on the British Broadcasting Corporation, it was given a mandate to create national broadcasting systems to serve both the French- and the English-speaking populations. Its two main objectives, as articulated by Leonard Brockington, first chairman of the CBC board of governors, in a national broadcast on 4 November 1936, were 'to make it possible for every Canadian to hear the CBC's programs, and to provide the best programs from all available sources.' One of the fledgling corporation's first decisions, naturally enough, was to carry out a survey of Canadian talent resources. An assessment of what appropriate programs were available to it from other countries was also undertaken.

As the corporation's executives strove to determine the most effective form of program organization, they sought expert advice on what Canadian talent existed, where it was located, where further training was needed to develop potential, and where regional resources existed that could support decentralized production. The experts engaged by the corporation as music advisers were Sir Ernest MacMillan and Wilfrid Pelletier. Not surprisingly, the first statement of music policy expressed a dedication to Canadian performers and supported the idea of production from all major centres across the country.

In 1938, Jean-Marie Beaudet, who became a noted conductor and champion of modern repertoire, was named national music director. He brought to the position a personal commitment to the live performance of Canadian music. By 1941 he had instituted several showcases for Canadian composers. For example, an orchestral series called 'Tribute to Young Canadians' was presented by Samuel Hersenhoren, the Toronto conductor. It featured already completed works by such young composers – all in their twenties at that time – as Robert Farnon, Barbara Pentland, Godfrey Ridout, and John Weinzweig. (Generally, the young composers whose works were performed on this series were already known to the CBC through their work on 'commercial' assignments to compose incidental music to accompany other programming.)

In a recent interview, Keith MacMillan – a leading proponent of Canadian repertoire – confirmed that 'the idea of commissioning [serious music] in this country was the CBC's in the 1940s and 1950s.' By 1941 Jean-Marie Beaudet had convinced senior management that the CBC should not be content with live performances of existing works, but should become actively involved in the creation of special works for its own purposes.

Up to that point, the CBC had commissioned only one work. Oddly enough, this first-ever commission went to an Englishman – Benjamin Britten. It was issued by John Adaskin, a CBC conductor and producer, for a program called 'Melodic Strings.' *The Young Apollo*, opus 16, a seven-

and-a-half-minute work for piano and string orchestra, was broadcast on 27 August 1939 with the composer at the piano and was dedicated to Alexander Chuhaldin, the CBC conductor of the program.

The first Canadian to be commissioned by the CBC was Healey Willan, and the work involved was an hour-long opera, *Transit Through Fire*, with a libretto by John Coulter. Jean-Marie Beaudet was responsible for the decision to commission this work. Orchestrated by Lucio Agostini, the opera was broadcast in 1942, with the chorus and orchestra conducted by Sir Ernest MacMillan.

Shortly thereafter, a program of suites was developed based on CBC incidental music. This single program, 'Music for Radio,' was broadcast as part of a series called 'Our Canada' on 31 January 1943. The program notes give the following information on these early commissions: 'All the works on the programme were written as musical accompaniment or background music ... In each case, the music heard was a composition written specially for the medium of radio.' The works presented were composed by Howard Cable, Barbara Pentland, Godfrey Ridout, and John Weinzweig and were based on the incidental music they had written for, respectively, 'Comrades in Arms,' 'Payload,' 'For They Are England,' and 'Our Canada.'

During the rest of the 1940s eight more works were commissioned, most notably *Deirdre of the Sorrows* (produced in 1946), the first full-length opera by Healey Willan, again with a libretto by John Coulter and again contracted under Jean-Marie Beaudet's leadership.

The English network

Until well into the 1940s, the commissioning of serious Canadian works as a regular policy was rare. In 1947 Geoffrey Waddington became music consultant to the English network and, continuing the work of Jean-Marie Beaudet (who left the CBC to pursue teaching, mainly at the Conservatoire in Montreal), he was able eventually to make commissioning an established policy.

In 1950 the program 'Opportunity Knocks,' launched in 1947 as a national talent competition, adopted a category for composers, and over the next seven years 101 short pops-concert works were commissioned. When Geoffrey Waddington was named director of music for the English network in 1952 (a position he held until 1964), he became the musician with 'the greatest employment power and programming responsibility in Canada ... Under his direction, the CBC's policy of commissioning Canadian composers became regular practice.'[3] In addition to the large quantity of pops-oriented works for 'Opportunity Knocks,' the CBC commissioned fifty-two other works during the 1950s, including major orchestral compositions for the CBC Symphony Orchestra (founded in 1952) and music for special events – nine works alone for Queen Elizabeth II's coronation in 1953.

The early 1960s brought a period of massive change caused by the advent of television in the previous decade. The CBC's responsibilities for introducing and rapidly expanding the availability of this new medium had placed enormous strains on all CBC budgets, and certainly the shock waves had been felt throughout the radio networks, where, for example, the commissioning of serious music was no longer expanding. Moreover, radio audiences had changed radically: gone was the heavy demand for light entertainment, now supplied by the junior medium, and far greater now was the demand to meet a wide range of more specialized needs – after all, the individual drawn to watching television sitcoms as part of a mass audience is not likely to be found as part of a far smaller audience listening to a fugue by Healey Willan. In retrospect, this need for refocusing and greater specialization proved to be a significant boon to Canadian composers of serious music. In the English network, one of the many results of this refocusing was the rejuvenation of the commissioning process.

In 1965 John Roberts became supervisor of radio music in Toronto. He later went on to serve from 1971 to 1975 as head of radio music and variety for the entire English network. In these management positions he was instrumental in greatly expanding the commissioning of original Canadian music across a broad spectrum. On his arrival in Canada in 1955, Roberts, an Australian, set about trying to familiarize himself with the contemporary work of Canada's composers: 'I knew Canada must have composers ... I asked, where are they?' He found that, with the exception of recordings by the CBC's International Service, very little modern Canadian repertoire was available. Believing that 'creation is the fountainhead of everything and without creation there is no progress,' he was strongly committed to the development of new serious Canadian music – and to creating a permanent record of it.

Thus, his tenure in CBC music management positions was marked by an extensive use of commissions for concert series with featured artists and special programming for such events as the Canadian Centennial celebrations in 1967 and the World Music Week in 1975. He personally took charge of commissioning and offered performance opportunities on an ever-widening range of programs. His conviction that Canadian works, whether new or composed at an earlier time, should be part of a program with other repertoire rather than presented in isolation was reinforced in 1970 when the Canadian Radio-Television Commission established Canadian-content regulations, requiring that a certain minimum proportion of all broadcast music be Canadian in origin. Thanks in part to Roberts's commissioning policies – and to his commitment to CBC recordings – the CBC was the only broadcaster in Canada able to meet Canadian-content requirements from the outset.

In 1976 Robert Sunter became head of radio music for the English network. Fresh from his position as music officer of the Ontario Arts Council, he knew that, beyond the CBC, there were now far more opportunities for composers to receive commissions. This led him to take a somewhat different and more focused approach: 'I never commissioned a work personally – I made sure the proposal came through a producer. Commissions were made for programme purposes; for example, if a programme was doing a contemporary composer's profile and needed an example of his latest work, or if a featured group needed a Canadian work to complete its programme ... or if repertoire was needed for a CBC group such as the Vancouver Chamber Orchestra. The criteria for commissioning were based on what was needed to make the programme successful. On rare occasions, a commission was considered if an eminent composer brought a distinctive idea to a producer.'

Harold Redekopp succeeded Robert Sunter in 1981 and implemented a slightly different commissioning process based on delegating to the producers even more responsibility for program content. As a result, a group of producers, some of whom are themselves composers, share responsibility for artistic decisions (to ensure a national perspective, this group is never chaired by a Toronto-based producer). This Commissions Committee is not a jury; rather, it is mandated to examine the track record of each composer proposed for a commission by another producer. Each proposal is evaluated on the basis of program content needs, forces required (instruments and venue), proposed performers, and rebroadcast possibilities. Harold Redekopp recently commented on this process: 'The object of the exercise is not to play God but, in an orderly fashion, to consider each program idea ... The committee is expected to consider and sample a wide range of writing and style. So far, indications are that inviting the proposing producer to share in the process of decision-making with his colleagues is healthy and productive.'

The French network

As was the case with its English counterpart, the period up to 1940 was a time of evaluation for the French network. As noted earlier, the results of the evaluation work of Sir Ernest MacMillan and Wilfrid Pelletier began to take shape with the appointment in 1938 of Jean-Marie Beaudet as national music director.

From the outset, the performance of contemporary Canadian music was vigorously encouraged by both Jean-Marie Beaudet and Jean-Josaphat Gagnier, the noted conductor and composer, who served from 1936 until his death in 1949 as the director of music for the Quebec Region, centred in Montreal (the genesis of what, through subsequent national expansion, became the French network). During this period the French network commissioned its first serious composition.

In 1948 Roland Leduc founded l'Orchestre des petites symphonies and launched what was to become an extremely popular program called, appropriately enough, 'Les Petites Symphonies.' Over the next seventeen years this program became noted for premières, with many works commissioned expressly for it – beginning in 1948, with Roland Leduc issuing the French network's first-ever commission. It went to a major figure in Canadian music, Claude Champagne, for his *Concerto in D Minor*. This work was broadcast on 'Les Petites Symphonies' in May 1950, with Roland Leduc conducting and Neil Chotem at the piano.

During the 1950s no one was appointed specifically to fill the position of director of music for the French network. Even so, commissioning continued to expand steadily, with producers enjoying considerable latitude in commissioning works for their own particular shows. (At times, unfortunately, this process was not very formal and, as a result, the record of activities for this period remains incomplete, although most commissions appear to have been successfully traced.) The French network tended to feature special musical series – as well as talent contests – providing numerous opportunities for composers, especially in the folk-song area. In addition, as was the case with the English network, there was a considerable need for incidental compositions for program theme music and to accompany dramas and documentaries. This need indeed continues, in both radio and television.

Finally, before moving on to the 1960s, it is important here to consider two other major factors: the interchangeability of music between the networks and the influence of the CBC's International Service (later called Radio-Canada International or RCI).

Both under Jean-Marie Beaudet's national control and subsequently there was no linguistic bias in commissioning. That is, many works by French-Canadian composers were commissioned by the English network and vice versa. Regardless of source (either network or even RCI), commissioned works were broadcast on either network or, more often than not, on both, often simultaneously. This was the case in fact with most classical music programming of live performances. (Indeed, even today, the CBC's contract letter routinely states that the 'CBC shall be entitled ... to broadcast the commissioned work over each station of its English and French AM and FM networks ... ') This meant that, regardless to which 'solitude' the listener belonged, there was full access to the music emanating from the other one. This broader national exposure achieved through complete interchangeability obviously increased both the value and the support of the whole commissioning process.

Because the direction of the French network and RCI were both located in Montreal, cooperation with RCI became a consistent feature of French network music programming. For example, as early as 1947 Alexander Brott was commissioned by RCI to write a descriptive suite about Canada. This work, *From Sea to Sea*, was produced in Montreal and used by RCI in its short-wave broadcasts to other countries (it was also part of a special Canadian tribute to the Unesco General Assembly in Mexico City). Thus, a number of commissioned works have arisen out of co-operation between these two components of the CBC, with RCI recording premières of Canadian compositions to make them available for rebroadcast.

With the growing complexity and breadth of radio music broadcasting, the French network re-established the position of director of music in 1959, and since that time there has been a succession of composers/producers in this post: Roy Royal (appointed in 1959), Hugh Davidson (1962), Jean Vallerand (1964), Jacques Bertrand (1966), and Jacques Boucher (1984). All of these directors of music had been associated with one or more of the CBC's own highly regarded ensembles and had promoted live-performance broadcasting. Under their direction, not surprisingly, many new works were commissioned for these ensembles. In addition, they developed a policy of commissioning major works in connection with high-profile broadcasting opportunities. For example, the French network regularly commissions works to be entered in important international broadcasting competitions.

One such highly esteemed award, the Prix Paul Gilson, is sponsored by the Communauté radiophonique des programmes de langue française. Since the early 1960s the CBC has been entering works in this competition, and in 1969 Otto Joachim won the Grand Prix Paul Gilson for his CBC-commissioned composition *Illumination II*. The Prix Italia is another major international broadcasting competition for which, over the years, the French network has commissioned several entries, and in 1985 Michel-Georges Brégent won honourable mention for his work *Atlantide*. Among the many composers who have been commissioned to provide major works for broadcast and for entry in these competitions are Jacques Hétu, Pierre Mercure, François Morel, Gilles Tremblay, and Claude Vivier.

The impact of other commissioning agents

Before the CBC entered the 'wilderness' and began to issue commissions to Canadian composers of serious music, there were a few existing sources of support – private foundations, personal patronage, performing groups, and, probably of greatest importance, university-associated organizations. Some of this support remains today, but commissions from these sources still represent at best a mere trickle. The CBC's dominant – and perhaps at times lonely – position in the field of commissioning continued right through the 1960s. A number of external factors then began to have a significant impact on both the frequency and particularly the type of CBC commissions.

A gradual rise in cultural awareness – a form of nationalism – on the part of an influential segment of the Canadian public generated efforts to encourage growth in all cultural areas. This in turn motivated governments to take a closer look at what was being done – or not being done – for Canada's artists. In 1974 this led the Canada Council to establish a program for commissioning Canadian composers. Since that time a substantial amount of funding has been made available to performers and groups wanting to commission a Canadian composer to write a specific piece, and these funding decisions are often influenced by the CBC's interest in broadcasting and/or recording the work. (The Canada Council also provides support for individual composers through such means as study grants.)

Decisions on which submissions from performers and groups shall receive funding from the Canada Council are taken, essentially, by a jury of composers. This extensive program, in place now for over twelve years, has become the primary source of commissions for the Canadian composer of serious music. For example, between May 1984 and October 1985 – a period of just seventeen months – five juries met and were involved in issuing 123 commissions (mostly for chamber music, although at least 25 were for compositions for full orchestra). In approximately the same time frame, the CBC issued fewer than forty commissions – still a significant number, but only two were for full orchestra.

Another noteworthy improvement over the years has been the emergence of support from provincial arts agencies or ministries of culture, through programs inaugurated in the 1960s and 1970s. Almost all commissions from these sources, however, are issued by Ontario, through its Arts Council, or by Quebec, through its Ministère des Affaires culturelles.

At this point two other important sources of commissions should be acknowledged: television and films. Although most original Canadian music written for television has been of an incidental nature, CBC-TV has commissioned some works both for programs devoted to the performance of music and for complete, high-profile productions (*Aberfan*, an opera by Raymond Pannell, with a libretto by his wife, Beverly, commissioned by the CBC and telecast in 1977, won the Salzburg TV opera prize). While these works are not great in number, they remain to be clearly identified for inclusion in the CBC catalogue.

Since its inception in 1939, the National Film Board has been an important source of income for Canada's composers. While most of this work has also been of a 'made-to-order' nature – sound tracks to accompany short subjects, documentaries, and feature films, often offering considerable challenge and reward – it may be that some works have been commissioned in their own right for inclusion in films devoted to the performance or explanation of music by Canadians. Again, these commissions would not be numerous.

Although the CBC has been displaced by the Canada Council as the primary source of commissions for concert works, a vigorous and steadily growing program is still in place. It is not, however, growing as rapidly as before, as the reduced frequency of CBC commissions reflects the emergence of other commissioning agents. These combined commissioning activities, in any case, are generating a substantial increase in the amount of original Canadian material available for broadcast.

In addition, responding to changing conditions, some shifting of priorities is gradually occurring. For example, with a lot more major orchestral works now being commissioned by other agents, the CBC is placing more emphasis on works for smaller groups, as well as experimental music, including electronic works, which may be better appreciated through the medium of radio than in live performance. At the same time, the CBC is maintaining or expanding other important facets of its commissioning program – for instance, in the category of opera and large choral works.

Thus, with the CBC having first filled the void and then continued to lead the way for a great many years, the environment for the Canadian composer of serious music is unquestionably more supportive today than ever before.

The influence of the CRTC

Two actions by the CRTC (now called the Canadian Radio-television and Telecommunications Commission) have had a particularly positive impact on commissioning: the introduction of Canadian-content requirements for radio music broadcasting in 1970, and the implementation in

1975 of a policy for FM radio broadcasting that required an 'expansion of imaginative and creative resources and capacity in Canada.'[4] It should be noted here that by 1975 the CBC was operating separate national AM and FM radio networks in both French and English.

From the outset the CBC was able to meet Canadian-content regulations owing to its established policy of encouraging the creation of original Canadian music and, more importantly, the recording of a substantial Canadian repertoire (of a broad range of music – not just serious works). Moreover, the CBC tended to program a lot more classical music than most other outlets, and this was a field which, largely through the CBC's efforts, already offered a relatively high proportion of Canadian work on the basis of both composition and performance. (This is not to say that some significant recording had not occurred previously in the private sector – Glenn Gould, for example, recorded exclusively for Columbia – but there was not enough of it.)

Initially, then, private and institutional broadcasters were obliged to turn, in part, to the CBC's recorded music to meet these Canadian-content regulations. Many of these broadcasters, and the recording industry, moved quickly to produce substantial quantities of Canadian material, although these activities were focused mainly on popular music. In the area of serious music, however, they often had to rely largely on CBC-produced material, thus increasing the exposure and value of this music. This, in turn, tended to strengthen the commissioning program, so that more new material became available.

The policy for FM broadcasting established by the CRTC in 1975 required an 'increase in productive and creative capacity ... to provide programming which is varied and comprehensive, of high standard, using predominantly Canadian creative and other resources.' The CRTC clearly stated that FM radio 'must expand its offering of content with new opportunities for public discovery and appreciation of a greater spectrum of music and the spoken word.'

This meant that FM stations not only had to meet certain minimum Canadian-content requirements but were now obliged, where necessary, to upgrade program content – to improve their foreground broadcasting. Foreground format is virtually the opposite of background music and requires the production of informative and thought-provoking presentations. Music programs, for example, must explain the music or examine a composer's life and/or works through original scripted material or live commentary. Other types of foreground programming would include radio dramas, live concerts (even of rock music), current-affairs documentaries, and newscasts with editorial commentaries.

Obviously, given its mandate to generate distinctive Canadian material to raise and maintain national awareness and identity, the CBC already far exceeded these foreground-format requirements for FM radio. Most other broadcasters, however, suddenly had an even greater need for music produced by and through the CBC. With so many private and institutional FM broadcasters now using the CBC's commercially released recordings as a regular part of their programming, the CBC's commitment to encouraging and commissioning original Canadian music has been further justified and strengthened.

The CRTC's promulgation in the first half of the 1970s of 'nationalistic' regulations coincides rather nicely with the implementation in 1974 of the Canada Council's program in support of Canadian composers. One might be pardoned for suspecting the existence of a comprehensive scheme to promote serious Canadian music in general – and Canadian composers in particular.

A HISTORICAL REVIEW OF COMMISSIONS

Commissions prior to 1950 identified earlier in this article are: Benjamin Britten's *The Young Apollo*; Healey Willan's two operas, *Transit Through Fire* and *Deirdre of the Sorrows*; Alexander Brott's suite *From Sea to Sea*; Claude Champagne's *Concerto in D Minor*; and the four suites based on incidental music (Howard Cable's *Comrades in Arms*, Barbara Pentland's *Payload*, Godfrey Ridout's *For They Are England*, and John Weinzweig's *Our Canada*).

In addition, two other works by Healey Willan were commissioned, both broadcast in 1943: special music to accompany *The Life and Death of Jean de Brébeuf*, the poetic narrative by E.J. Pratt; and a composition for small orchestra and narrator, *Hymn for Those in the Air*, with text by Duncan Campbell Scott. In 1946, 'Music for Radio, No. 2' featured *Edge of the World*, an orchestral work by John Weinzweig. There were two more commissions, bringing the total to fourteen, with the following works performed in 1948: Barbara Pentland's *Variations on a Boccherini Tune*, for full orchestra, and Oskar Morawetz's *Divertimento for Strings*, commissioned by Samuel Hersenhoren for performance by the chamber orchestra, the CBC Strings.

The 1950s

Apart from the 101 short (three-and-a-half minute average) pops-concert works that were commissioned for 'Opportunity Knocks,' fifty-two other works were commissioned in this decade – nearly four times the number of the preceding decade – reflecting Harry Freedman's recently expressed view: 'When Geoffrey Waddington and Terence Gibbs [the noted CBC music producer] came on the scene, things began to improve for all composers.' In the English network, certainly, the influence and opinions of these two men permeated all musical production.

In reviewing the decades, highlights are cited to provide a sense of the progress being made through the years, especially in terms of the types of works being commissioned. No judgments on relative merit are intended; inevitably, many fine compositions have not been mentioned.

There is no better place to begin a review of the 1950s than with 1952's *The Best of All Possible Worlds*. This ninety-minute CBC-commissioned work by Mavor Moore, for actors and singers, with chorus and orchestra, was based on Voltaire's *Candide*. It was a great radio success and was later staged in Toronto in 1956 (as *The Optimist*) and revived under its original title by CBC-TV in 1968.

In 1953 Queen Elizabeth II was crowned, and special works were commissioned for broadcast during Coronation Week. As a result, this was the first year in which commissioning reached double digits (ten), which did not happen again until 1967, the year of Canada's Centennial. Among the compositions commissioned for the coronation were: two choral works, one each by Healey Willan, *Coronation Suite*, and Godfrey Ridout, *Coronation Ode*; two works for full orchestra, one each by Jean Papineau-Couture, *Prélude*, and Alexander Brott, *Royal Tribute*; and a composition for violin and strings by Jean Coulthard, *A Prayer for Elizabeth*.

In 1955 John Weinzweig's *Violin Concerto* was premiered. Another major commission broadcast in that year was Gabriel Charpentier's *Trois Poèmes de Saint Jean de la Croix*, a chamber music work for contralto, violin, and violoncello (with words translated from the Latin into French by Armand Godoy).

François Morel received four commissions during the decade, including one for *Cantate pour la Passion*, an ambitious choral work broadcast in 1957. In that same year Clermont Pépin's CBC-commissioned *Symphony No. 2* was premiered on 'Les Petites Symphonies,' conducted by Roland Leduc.

In the following year Clermont Pépin's *Le Porte-rêve*, a ballet, was telecast by CBC-TV. On radio, Roger Matton's *L'Horoscope*, a 'suite chorégraphique' for orchestra based on an Acadian legend, was premiered by the CBC Symphony Orchestra, conducted by Geoffrey Waddington. That same year brought another major work by John Weinzweig, *Wine of Peace*, for soprano and orchestra, as well as Murray Adaskin's *Algonquin Symphony*.

In the last year of the decade, 'CBC Wednesday Night' (an important showcase program for a number of years) presented a series of intimate chamber operas, including the CBC-commissioned *Night Blooming Cereus* by John Beckwith, with a libretto by James Reaney. Oskar Morawetz's *String Quartet No. 3* was also broadcast in that year, as were two more CBC-commissioned works from Jean Papineau-Couture: *Pièce concertante no. 2 (Éventails)* and *Pièce concertante no. 3 (Variations).*

Before we leave this decade, it is important to comment on the role of 'Opportunity Knocks.' John Adaskin, the originator, producer, and conductor of the program, wanted to give more exposure to the many young composers then emerging across the country. Moreover, since most of his shows were devoted entirely to singers and solo instrumentalists performing with orchestral backup, the introduction of light pops-concert items would provide greater variety for very little money – he paid about $50 per work (a month's rent at that time for modest quarters). As Harry Freedman (then in his early thirties) recently recalled: 'The works were all demonstrations of the "craftsmanship" that they [we] were all learning at the time ... the pieces were for very restricted orchestra and were limited to three to four minutes ... [But at this time, the] CBC was the only group who made known to all Canada that such a thing as a Canadian composer existed. The public thought that all composers were dead.' In the seven years beginning in 1950, 101 works by sixty-seven composers were commissioned by John Adaskin for his series. Among these composers from all regions of Canada whose works were featured on 'Opportunity Knocks' and whose careers were thereby encouraged are John Beckwith, Alexander Brott, Jean Coulthard, Samuel Dolin, Harry Freedman, Hector Gratton, Otto Joachim, Talivaldis Kenins, Horace Lapp, Oskar Morawetz, Jean Papineau-Couture, Godfrey Ridout, Harry Somers, and John Weinzweig. (See Appendix.)

The 1960s

A total of eighty-one CBC-commissioned works from this decade have been identified – a 60% increase over the fifty-two works of the previous decade, and an increase of over 80% on the basis of cumulative durations. In fact, even if the 345 minutes for the 101 short works for 'Opportunity Knocks' are included – and not treated as an anomaly – the increase in total duration is about 30%.

The value of durations should be noted here. A list of the numbers of works, while interesting, becomes much more significant when the timing of works is considered, since cumulative durations yield a more accurate picture of the importance of commissioning activities. After all, works under consideration in this article range all the way from the one-minute *Fanfare* for Canada's Centennial by Sir Ernest MacMillan to the three-hour musical for Radio Variety by Cliff Jones, *For the Love of Howard*, commissioned in the 1980s.

In the early 1960s, as noted previously, radio's refocusing in response to the advent of television led, in part, to the gradual rejuvenation of the commissioning program. In the first five years of the decade, twenty-nine commissions were issued, while in the last five years fifty-two more works were commissioned, bringing the total for the decade to eighty-one.

Another factor that contributed substantially to the increase in commissioning in the latter part of the decade was the creation of special works for the 1967 celebrations in honour of Canada's Centennial. In that single year seventeen CBC-commissioned works were premiered – only the second year in which commissions had reached double figures – and they have never been below double digits since.

In 1961 two of the works for full orchestra commissioned and broadcast by the CBC were Clermont Pépin's *Monologue* and Godfrey Ridout's *Fall Fair*; the latter became the first CBC commission to take a permanent place in the repertoire of Canadian symphony orchestras.

In this decade François Morel again received four commissions, including one for his *String Quartet No. 2*, broadcast in 1963. In that same year, the CBC presented Pierre Mercure's *Psaume pour abri* – a major cantata, involving two choirs, a narrator, a large instrumental ensemble, and electronic tape. Among other commissions premiered in that year were two chamber music works: Oskar Morawetz's *Sonata for Cello and Piano* and Barbara Pentland's *Trio for Violin, Cello and Piano*.

One of John Weinzweig's three commissions in this decade was for his *Concerto for Piano and Orchestra*. This was broadcast in 1966, as was Jean Papineau-Couture's *Concerto* (for piano and orchestra), one of his five commissions in the 1960s. *Kékoba*, an ensemble work by Gilles Tremblay, was also premiered in 1966.

Special works commissioned for presentation during 1967 – Canada's Centennial Year – included three hour-long operas, using subjects reflecting different regions of the country: *The Brideship* (a lyric drama) by Robert Turner, with a libretto by George Woodcock, a story of mail-order brides on the West Coast during the Gold Rush; *Grant, Warden of the Plains* by Murray Adaskin, with a libretto by Mary Elizabeth Bayer; and *Sam Slick* by Kelsey Jones, with a libretto by Rosabelle Jones, based on the Nova Scotian stories written by Thomas Chandler Haliburton. Among other commissioned works that used the human voice were Violet Archer's

Cantata sacra; John Beckwith's *Canada Dash, Canada Dot*, with words by James Reaney; R. Murray Schafer's *Requiems for the Party Girl*; and *Evocations* by Harry Somers, one of his six commissions in the decade. Among works for full orchestra premiered during the Centennial Year were Harry Freedman's *Armana* and Sophie-Carmen Eckhardt-Gramatté's *Symphony-Concerto* (for piano and orchestra).

In 1968 *Amuya*, a work by Serge Garant for small ensemble, was presented on 'CBC Summer Festival,' conducted by the composer. Jacques Hétu's work for full orchestra, *L'Apocalypse (une fresque symphonique d'après saint Jean)*, opus 14, was also premiered in that year.

CBC-commissioned works premiered in the last year of the decade included Jean Papineau-Couture's work for chamber orchestra *Oscillations* and a composition for full orchestra by John Weinzweig, *Dummiyah/Silence*. In addition, as noted earlier, Otto Joachim won the Grand Prix Paul Gilson for his *Illumination II*.

The 1970s

The number of commissions in the 1970s – 228 – was nearly three times that of the previous decade, with cumulative duration showing a gain well in excess of 200%. Here the point is reached where commissioning activities became so extensive and varied that little useful purpose is served by citing specific compositions. An upsurge in the demand for all forms of Canadian music was generated by CRTC regulations regarding, in 1970, Canadian-content requirements for all broadcasters and, in 1975, foreground-format improvements by FM broadcasters. This in turn encouraged even greater activities in both the CBC's commissioning and recording operations.

Gradually, however, some shifting of emphasis also occurred. While almost every category of music showed a significant gain, greater stress began to be laid on music for small ensembles and chamber music. To some extent this reflected a trend that had started in the late 1960s towards the featuring of Canadian artists in recital: for instance, works were specifically commissioned by the CBC for performance by such leading artists as Arthur Ozolins, the Orford String Quartet, the Société de musique contemporaine du Québec Ensemble, and Maureen Forrester. Another factor affecting the types of commissions was the commissioning being undertaken by other CBC departments. For example, Radio Features and Humanities used commissions to enhance programs like 'Celebration.' This often meant that works were commissioned to meet more specific production requirements.

Another major development in the 1970s was the commissioning of

Fifty Years of CBC Commissions 257

rock operas and musicals by Radio Variety. This program concept had been instituted in 1968 with the broadcast of the CBC-commissioned two-hour musical *Lady Emma*, by Doug Randle, with a libretto by Ron Solloway. In the 1970s nine more works were commissioned, varying in length from one to two hours (a total duration of 870 minutes in the decade).

From the many commissions issued in the decade, there emerged a number of truly creative accomplishments – even where a commission did not quite turn out the way the Radio Music department had originally expected. For example, a commission calling for a 'radiophonic' work (something to exploit the advantages of the broadcast medium) expanded into a full-blown pageant based on the concept of involving an entire community – with costumes, banners, actors, singers, chorus, and orchestra (the visual effects obviously going somewhat beyond the nature – and the funding – of radio). This project was *Apocalypsis* by R. Murray Schafer. Finally, through the efforts of the composer and the co-operation of the performing arts faculties of the University of Western Ontario (not to mention some special grants), the production was mounted, and the work was eventually broadcast in 1980.

The 1980s

In this current decade the commissioning program has continued to expand steadily, although emphases are still shifting, mainly according to production needs and funding difficulties. A case in point is that fewer major works for full orchestra are now being commissioned by the CBC – although it would appear that the slack is more than being taken up by commissions from the Canada Council.

At the same time, the demand for new compositions for the CBC's various ensembles continues. Thus, works for chamber orchestra are being commissioned at a rate significantly higher than in the previous decade. In the 1970s nineteen such works were commissioned, whereas to this point in the 1980s sixteen new works for chamber orchestra have already been performed. This is largely due to the particularly strong program being carried out by the CBC Vancouver Chamber Orchestra.

SOME FINAL OBSERVATIONS

In the *Encyclopedia of Music in Canada* Keith MacMillan quotes Geoffrey Waddington – 'The CBC has been the dominant factor in providing some measure of economic security for the Canadian musician' – and then goes on to comment: 'He might have added that the CBC also was the most effective champion of the Canadian composer, through commissions, public performances, payment of royalties, etc. The foregoing no longer would be true by the mid-1970s. Nonetheless, the story of the broadcasting of serious music in Canada virtually begins and ends with the CBC.'[5]

By aiming to provide a comprehensive review of commissioning by the CBC and to stimulate further research into the impact of the CBC in serious music, the present article substantiates this view. It is not within the purview of this article to argue the merits of commissioning per se; rather, the intent was to enumerate some of the benefits that have accrued to Canadian music and musicians because of the existence of the CBC's commissioning program.

By focusing on an area of Canadian culture that was largely being neglected (because of 'box-office' considerations) and establishing a policy to overcome this problem, the CBC – in keeping with its mandate – made a unique effort to raise and maintain national awareness of the Canadian identity in music. As a consequence, the CBC has:

1 identified and encouraged a broad range of composers and presented the results of their creative talents to the Canadian public;
2 raised public awareness of the suitability of Canadian culture and folklore for operatic and symphonic treatment;
3 furnished many works that have become standard repertoire for Canadian symphony orchestras;
4 given international exposure to Canadian composers through broadcasting competitions and RCI broadcasts and recordings;
5 provided distinctive repertoire for Canada's leading performing artists, who have presented many of these works to audiences around the world;
6 made a contribution of about thirty pieces to the available international repertoire for chamber orchestras by producing Canadian repertoire for its own specialized ensembles and other artists.

The corporation's most significant accomplishment in this area, however, is that it created a climate that nurtured development in all phases of Canadian music. Thus, talented Canadian students now largely acquire and improve their skills at universities and conservatories in their own country – and more composers are able at least to earn a decent living in Canada.

The list of 242 composers who have been commissioned by the CBC yields some interesting facts:

1 Only four commissions have been issued to foreign nationals not residing in Canada.

2 Over 70% of the composers were born and/or raised in Canada and largely educated here – and this percentage has become even higher in recent years.
3 About 7% of the composers came from the United States, 6% from the United Kingdom, and 15% from various European countries.
4 Of the composers born or raised in Canada about 38% came from Ontario, 34% from Quebec, 23% from the western provinces, and 5% from the Maritimes.

It is evident, then, that the results relate to the concept of 'national distribution' and to the original policy of producing music in major centres of all regions. An assessment of those results may be made in both qualitative and quantitative terms. The name of almost every renowned Canadian composer of the past fifty years appears on the list, often with one or more commissions in early career. These creative artists went on to fame – if not necessarily fortune – in a broader context beyond the CBC, thereby demonstrating the validity of the CBC's commitment to identifying and encouraging promising composers. Even so, over half of all commissions have gone to composers who could not be described as famous. This reflects the efforts of the CBC to extend support as well on the bases of geography and quantity. After all, where is the Solon who can decree that all worthy Canadian composers shall be from Montreal or Toronto, and who can likewise perceive and guarantee future prominence?

Beyond hard facts and cold history, it is essential that we remind ourselves that the composition of serious music is a high and difficult human endeavour, as well as a very personal form of expression. The CBC's files bear witness to the concern for the individual composer that informed the decisions of those in the corporation most closely associated with commissioning serious music.

APPENDIX

Number of works commissioned and total minutes by decade

Type of work	1939–49		1950–59		1960–69		1970–79		1980–86		Totals	
Chamber music			4	86	20	305	80	1320	44	728	148	2439
Chamber orchestra and	5	44	4	49	7	107	19	356	16	266	51	822
'Opportunity Knocks'			101	345							101	345
Opera and large choral	3	233	11	318	9	345	14	320	11	381	48	1597
and radio variety					1	120	9	870	2	300	12	1290
Chorus a cappella					4	62	6	67	7	65	17	194
Full orchestra	4	72	19	253	14	178	36	636	5	80	78	1219
Concerto	1	14	4	77	4	75	16	357	12	275	37	798
Small ensemble			4	40	17	287	38	760	15	323	74	1410
Solo voice and orchestra			1	17	4	51	8	168	4	79	17	315
Unidentified instrumentation	1	(ND)	4	(ND)	1	(ND)	1	20	3	104	10	124
Unfinished/in progress			1	(ND)			1	(ND)	25	(ND)	27	(ND)
TOTALS	14	363	153	1185	81	1530	228	4874	144	2601	620	10553

Notes on durations

ND = no duration available (timing of the work is not on record or, in the case of works that are unfinished or in progress, not yet available). In most cases where no duration was on record, a duration was assigned based on the averaging of all similar works. Since duration was missing for some major works, cumulative duration figures may be taken as somewhat less than actual.

Definitions of types of work (genres)

Chamber music All standard chamber groups such as string quartets, woodwind quintets, etc.; all solo voice and instrumental works, and all ensembles of standard instruments from two to five players.

Chamber orchestra All string orchestra works and works for reduced orchestras such as the Vancouver Chamber Orchestra.

Opera and large choral Operas, oratorios, cantatas, musicals and pieces for soloist(s), chorus and orchestra.

Chorus a cappella All unaccompanied vocal ensembles.

Full orchestra Overtures, symphonic works, concertos for orchestra and concerti grossi.

Concerto Solo instrument(s) and full orchestra or string orchestra.

Small ensemble Groups of instruments and/or voices for six to twenty players/singers, including electronic or non-standard instruments, and tapes.

Solo voice and orchestra A solo voice or voices with full or string orchestral accompaniment.

Unidentified instrumentation All works for which adequate information could not be found at time of printing.

RONALD NAPIER

The Canadian Music Council: A Brief History

The Canadian Music Council began immediately following the presentation to Parliament in 1944 of briefs from various national organizations representing all areas of Canadian arts and culture. All areas, that is, except music, for alone among the arts there existed no national or even provincial organization which could speak for music, or for any substantial section of the Canadian musical community.

When it was realized that no musical group was willing or able to send a representative with a prepared brief to Ottawa, Sir Ernest MacMillan was urged by several interested persons to give music a voice among all the other arts. This he did, at his own expense, and the brief that he presented still stands today as a well-reasoned portrayal of music in Canada at that time.[1]

Following his Ottawa visit MacMillan did what he could, personally, to enlist the continued support of musicians throughout Canada. However, few musicians of standing in their community had either the time, the ability, or the inclination for the arduous work of organization that was needed. There was no money for a secretary or for postage, let alone for widespread publicity about a new organization.

MacMillan soon asked Charles Peaker to take over as chairman of the 'Music Committee,' which was the name its supporters had given to it so that it could be listed as a member of the newly formed Canadian Arts Council. Since Dr Peaker was at that time director of the Toronto Conservatory of Music, he was able to arrange for some essential office help for the infant organization.

The present honorary secretary, John Cozens, was asked by Charles Peaker to help him in organizing the various interested friends of Canadian music into a body which would represent as far as possible all parts of the country, and to this end letters were sent to a great many Canadian musicians. Twenty of these accepted the dubious honour of membership and were promptly assessed a fee of $1 per year 'to cover postage.' Thus, on a budget of slightly over $20 annually (there were a few small donations), Canada had its first 'national' music organization.

Shortly afterward the Canadian Federation of Music Teachers' Associations had a meeting in Toronto, and since most of the twenty members were delegates the Music Committee could count on a good attendance for its first round-table meeting, which took place on 2 July 1946. The initial work done by the three original and more or less self-appointed officers was enthusiastically endorsed, and the name 'Canadian Music Council' decided upon.

Peaker found it necessary to resign in 1947, and MacMillan was re-elected as chairman.

In 1948 the first test and opportunity for the council arose when news was received from London, England, of the forthcoming 'Olympic Arts Competition.' The Canadian Olympic Committee had not considered the arts to be of sufficient interest to this country and so had not advised anyone of this recently revived event. There were fewer than a hundred copies of the rules and application forms available from England, and very little time left to advertise the competition. In co-operation with the Arts Council the Canadian Music Council managed to get a Canadian version of the rules and regulations printed in French and English and distributed throughout Canada. As there were then no comprehensive listings of Canadian composers, all kinds of "free advertising" facilities were sought and used to let Canadians know about this opportunity. From the large number of entries received the council had to choose nine scores to send to England for the final judging.

Most Canadians became aware that the first prize in skating in the 1948 Olympics went to Barbara Ann Scott, but few realized that the next highest prize won by any Canadian was the second prize in chamber music which went to the Toronto composer John Weinzweig, or that the fourth prize won by Jean Coulthard of Vancouver was one of the few remaining prizes to come to Canada at that Olympiad. These successes by a country not previously known for the quality of its music drew considerable international attention.

In 1949 the Canadian Music Council was incorporated by Dominion Charter. Sir Ernest MacMillan became the first president, and the other directors were Lyell Gustin, a prominent Saskatoon piano teacher and lecturer at the University of Regina; Jean-Marie Beaudet, a Quebec conductor and pianist; Dr Arnold Walter, a music educator, administrator, and composer who was then director of the Senior School of the Royal

Conservatory of Music of Toronto; and W. St Clair Low, a Toronto accountant who was general manager of the performing rights society the Composers, Authors and Publishers Association of Canada (CAPAC), of which MacMillan was the president. John Cozens was the secretary.

During these years, when the council was continually seeking ways of increasing the representation of Canadian musical life in its membership, some fifty Canadian musicians from various parts of the country were invited to join. Most accepted, despite a frank statement from the president enumerating the many problems that the council faced. Now that it had its charter, fund-raising could begin, and Kenneth Ingram, who had been associated with the British Council, was engaged to run a full-time secretariat. Almost immediately, however, the federal government appointed the Massey Commission (officially the Royal Commission on National Development in the Arts, Letters and Sciences), which was expected to recommend the creation of a national organization similar to the Arts Council of Great Britain (the Massey Commission's report was issued in 1951, and did indeed recommend the establishment of a 'Canada Council'). This severely handicapped the Canadian Music Council in its drive for funds, and the secretariat had to be closed down after only a few months.

Although membership fees and occasional donations were still the only source of revenue, it is surprising how much was accomplished in those early years. By 1953 membership had grown to forty individual members and three national organizations – CAPAC, the Canadian College of Organists, and the Canadian Federation of Music Teachers' Associations. The council undertook to select the Canadian entries for the 1954 Olympic Arts Festival, at which Canadians again received acclaim; a library of published Canadian music was assembled with the aid of the Canadian Music Publishers' Association, and in 1955 the Department of External Affairs collaborated with the council in the selection and reproduction of five orchestral works which were included in the libraries of our embassies throughout the world. Also that year the Council produced *Music in Canada* (University of Toronto Press, 1955) a collection of contributions from nineteen writers, each dealing with a different aspect of the subject. MacMillan was its editor. This was the most ambitious work of its kind up to that time. Included were articles on folk song (Marius Barbeau), composition (Jean-Marie Beaudet), orchestras (Wilfrid Pelletier), recordings (John Beckwith), film music (Louis Applebaum), and broadcasting (Geoffrey Waddington), to mention just a few. The opening chapter, 'Historical background,' was by Helmut Kallmann and constitutes the first substantial writing about music in Canada by the then CBC music librarian, apart from his *Catalogue of Canadian Composers*, published by the CBC in 1952.

The next major project of the CMC was the launching of the *Canadian Music Journal* in 1956. The *Encyclopedia of Music in Canada* has called the *CMJ* 'the most consistently scholarly music periodical to appear in Canada until that time.'[2] A significant two-part article by Helmut Kallmann appeared in the first two issues. It was entitled 'A Century of Musical Periodicals in Canada.' At the end of the article is a checklist of no fewer than seventy-two Canadian musical periodicals.

The *Canadian Music Journal*, vol. 1, no. 1, opens with an introduction by Sir Ernest MacMillan describing the origins, present functions, and hopes for the future of the CMC (at that time it was still hoped that the formation of the projected Canada Council would alleviate the Music Council's financial deficiencies): 'The long delay of the Government in implementing this section of the report leaves the Council still struggling with wellnigh insuperable difficulties but with hopes that relief is not too far distant.' A further quotation gives a vivid picture of the CMC as it was in 1956:

The Council ... endeavours to keep in touch with various regional and provincial organizations interested in promoting the cause of music in Canada. In 1953 the Council was constituted a national committee of the International Music Council of UNESCO, with headquarters in Paris. Especially since the end of World War II, bewildering numbers of musical organizations have been established throughout the world with aims and objects similar to our own; with these too the Council endeavours to maintain contacts and to publicize their activities. What does the Council actually do? In the first place it deals with a mass of correspondence from people both in Canada and other countries who wish information on Canadian musical life. A music club, let us say, somewhere in Iowa, wishes to give a concert of Canadian music. Its resources are so-and-so. Will we suggest a programme? Can we recommend a good pianist or violinist to represent Canada in an international artists series in such-and-such a city (this calls for much judgment and diplomacy!). What information can we give a student who wishes to study in Canada? What provision can be made for exchanges of music students? Countless letters are received from musicians – often of high standing in their own countries – who wish to settle in Canada and who want information as to conditions here. Only too often have replies to be negative and discouraging, and nearly always framing such replies calls for much cogitation and expenditure of time.

The long-awaited Canada Council that the Massey Commission had recommended in its 1951 report finally came into existence in 1957.

Although MacMillan was appointed to the Canada Council and continued as a member of it until 1963, the Canadian Music Council was not asked to act for it in musical matters as had been anticipated. Instead the CC formed its own music section. With little hope of establishing a permanent secretariat, the CMC remained a wholly volunteer organization. However, there was at least now an agency to which it could turn for the funding of special projects, and for such needs as travel grants to attend meetings.

A cherished dream for many years of both the Canadian League of Composers and the Canadian Music Council had been establishing a music centre that could house the council's by now considerable library of published and unpublished compositions and would act as an information centre and library for the promotion and distribution of the works of Canadian composers. Already in the spring 1957 issue of the *Canadian Music Journal*, a special issue entitled 'Music and the Canada Council,' comprehensive plans were outlined in a report prepared for the Music Council by John Weinzweig and John Beckwith of the Canadian League of Composers. These plans became a reality when the Canadian Music Centre opened its doors on 1 January 1959, with initial grants from the Canada Council and CAPAC. Later additional grants were made by the Ontario Arts Council, BMI Canada, and others. The Canadian Music Council maintained a controlling interest in the centre for several years, but the latter is now a wholly independent agency.

The *Canadian Music Journal* was respected for the high standard of its articles and reviews, but by 1962, although foreign readership was increasing, domestic circulation was declining, and with it advertising revenue. When the two performing rights societies, CAPAC and BMI Canada, withdrew their support, publication had to be discontinued after the Summer 1962 issue. By this time almost all national music organizations were members of the Music Council, which had, however, continued to maintain a rather low profile. This situation began to change with the institution of a series of conferences which were held in conjunction with the annual meetings. Beginning in Toronto in 1965, when the topic 'The pros and cons of the competitive festival' generated a remarkable degree of interest – and controversy – the location was changed to Ottawa in 1966 ('Music in Canada, its resources and needs'). 'Music and media' (Toronto, 1967) brought speakers and delegates from as far away as Japan and Australia. During the following decade conferences were held on a wide variety of topics in most of Canada's principal cities.

MacMillan retired as president in 1966 and was succeeded by Arnold Walter, another founding member, who had been vice-president. Dr

Walter was followed in 1967 by the composer Jean Papineau-Couture, and from 1968 the council informally adopted the policy of a two-year presidential term. The first president under this new procedure was John Peter Lee Roberts, 1968-71.

In 1969 the council's second full-length book appeared, *Aspects of Music in Canada*, edited by Arnold Walter (University of Toronto Press, 1969). Though more comprehensive than *Music in Canada*, it was similarly a collection of essays on various activities and organizations, again with a chapter on the historical background, substantially revised and expanded from his earlier essay, by Helmut Kallmann, then just appointed chief of the Music Division of the National Library. The book also appeared in French in 1970, edited by Gilles Potvin and Maryvonne Kendergi, as *Aspects de la musique au Canada*.[3]

Another 1969 innovation was the establishment of honorary memberships, and this was followed in 1970 by the decision to admit performing groups as members (until that time the only two categories of membership had been those of individual members and national organizations).

The Canada Music Book/Les Cahiers canadiens de musique first appeared in an issue dated Spring-Summer 1970. The second issue, almost one year later, was dated Spring-Summer 1971, after which it appeared semi-annually. An editorial announcement by Gilles Potvin in the first book stated that the new publication 'without being a replica of the defunct *Canadian Music Journal*, has retained some features of the former, if only the collaboration of several of the same contributors.' One of these was Helmut Kallmann, and the first issue contained a major article, 'James Paton Clarke – Canada's first Mus. Bac.' from his pen.

In 1970 the council also became the Canadian section of the International Society for Contemporary Music, in which capacity it organizes and co-ordinates (with the co-operation of the Canadian League of Composers and the Canadian Music Centre) Canada's role in the selection of music for 'World Music Days,' the annual festival of the ISCM.

Although honorary memberships had been established in 1969, the council's directors felt that some additional, more tangible means should be found to recognize 'outstanding service to music in Canada,' so the distinguished Quebec sculptor Charles Daudelin was commissioned to design a medal to be presented annually. It was awarded for the first time at the 1971 conference in Quebec City, the first recipients being Jean-Marie Beaudet (posthumously), Leo Barkin, and Serge Garant.

By this time preparations were well under way for Canada's role as host country to the sixteenth General Assembly of the International Music

Council and the first 'World Music Week,' which was also held under the IMC's auspices. In 1969 Canada had proposed to act as host for 1973, but since Switzerland had prior claim Canada's invitation was changed to 1975 (the meetings are held biennially) and was formally adopted at the IMC's General Assembly in Moscow in 1971. This gave the Canadian Music Council more time for planning, and also the opportunity to mount a substantial exhibition at the Lausanne meetings in 1973 calling attention to Canada's musical life. This may have helped to persuade some delegates and observers from Europe and Asia to make the effort to come and investigate Canada in 1975.

The council's directors soon realized that the two-week program that gradually took shape during the innumerable planning sessions and discussions constituted not only the CMC's most ambitious undertaking to date, but perhaps also the most significant and important artistic endeavour of its kind that Canada had yet undertaken. John P.L. Roberts, the council's past president and chairman of the planning committee, who was also an individual member of the International Music Council, is the best authority on what had been planned, and how some of the activities had evolved. Writing in the introduction to the bilingual, hundred-page program, which covered everything from the IMC executive meeting in Calgary on 23 September to the individual pieces to be performed by the Montreal Symphony in Montreal on 5 October, he stated:

What we have tried to do is to evolve a series of major music events which would give to our overseas visitors and even to some of us at home a remarkable picture of the wide contrasts and elements of great quality which make up Canadian musical life.

... The National Film Board of Canada was approached and, thanks to the cooperation of the performing unions, the American Federation of Musicians and ACTRA, the initial discussions developed into a major project sending crews all over the country capturing on film different aspects of Canadian musical life. Plans were devised and frequently revised to bring together a wide variety of outstanding musicians, ensembles and groups, and we kept wishing we had six months or longer for a festival which would do justice to all of Canada's performing talent.

Because the International Music Council's General Assembly in Toronto will consist of the working meetings of that organization and is primarily intended for its members, something needed to be scheduled opposite it. The result was the International Exhibition of Music for Broadcasting which will be presented by the English and French Radio and Television Services of the CBC, Radio Canada

The Canadian Music Council 269

International and the International Music Centre (IMZ), Vienna. From the beginning, as a project of the CBC's music co-ordinating committee, this developed into two separate international events, one concerned with television and films, and the other with radio and recordings. At a later date, a project by the American-Canadian Music Critics' Association was also included at the request of William Littler of *The Toronto Star*. It is an Institute for the study of Canadian music by Canadian and American critics.

Opening in Ottawa on September 30th and continuing in Montreal will be the World Music Week conference, Music as a Dimension of Life. This will have 14 different sessions, some of which occur simultaneously in different locations. Altogether these sessions group themselves into seven sections and a variety of topics. We had to plan a conference which would also serve other musics besides those in the West. The topics to be dealt with include The Role of the Media in a Changing World, The Music of Young People, organized in association with the International Institute of Music, Dance and Theatre, Vienne, The World Soundscape, Music and Tomorrow's Public, The Roles of the Composer and Performer, and The Preservation and Presentation of Traditional Music and Dance. Montreal events are creating a great deal of interest but a 'first' for most people will be the performance of the Musicians and Dancers of the Burmese State Theatre at the Salle Claude Champagne. *Solstices* by Gilles Tremblay to be presented at the Place des Arts is arousing considerable interest.

... Several sessions of the World Music Week conference are tied to on-going projects of the International Music Council such as the Preservation and Presentation of Traditional Music and Dance, and Music and Tomorrow's Public. Works from the International Rostrum of Composers are on the New Music Concerts programme in Toronto and that of the Montreal Symphony Orchestra. Peter Toperczer, the soloist with the National Arts Centre Orchestra, is a winner from the International Rostrum of Young Interpreters. Looming large in the events will be the President, Yehudi Menuhin, who apart from appearing on several panels in the conference will give a recital in the National Arts Centre on International Music Day. A new venture of the International Music Council is International Music Day which will be widely celebrated all over the world and have a very particular focus in Ottawa through conference sessions and several contrasting music events.

The two activity-filled weeks proved more successful than even the planning committee had dared to hope. In addition to some 350 Canadian participants and observers there were slightly over 200 musicians and delegates from forty-five countries and all continents. Some highlights not already mentioned included Harry Somers's *Louis Riel* by the Canadian Opera Company; R. Murray Schafer's *Lustro* by the Toronto Symphony conducted by Marius Constant; and the People of 'Ksan from British Columbia, who performed in Ottawa, where the first International Music Day celebrations got under way with the recital by Yehudi Menuhin. On that program was Somers's *Music for Solo Violin*, commissioned by Menuhin, who later that afternoon received an honorary doctorate from the University of Ottawa together with Somers, the Montreal composer Jean Vallerand, and the Vietnamese musicologist Trân van Khê. That evening the first IMC awards were presented to Ravi Shankar, Yehudi Menuhin, and (posthumously) Dmitri Shostakovich. The prime minister, the Rt Hon. Pierre Trudeau, made the presentation.

Enough has been said to indicate the wide scope of these events. They resulted in a greatly increased awareness of Canada's music, both at home and abroad, and a perception by the Canadian musical public, and especially by government and non-government funding bodies, of the extent of the council's activity and influence.

In 1976 funds were made available by the Canada Council to engage a secretary general, with one assistant and modest office space in downtown Ottawa. Guy Huot was appointed, and John Cozens, who had served the organization since its very beginnings as volunteer (that is, unpaid) secretary, was officially named honorary secretary. That same year he was awarded the council's medal.

In November 1976 appeared the first issue of what has become the CMC's longest-running periodical, *Musicanada*, a bilingual quarterly edited by Guy Huot. *Musicanada* was originally the house organ of the Canadian Music Centre and had been edited by the centre's executive secretary, Keith MacMillan, until publication was discontinued in 1970. The revived *Musicanada* – the first issue was published as no. 30 – is a magazine-style periodical containing regional reports and general news, book and record reviews, and some short articles.

Several new awards were instituted in 1977, most of which are now awarded annually. They include Artist of the Year, Composer of the Year, and a special award made to 'bodies or individuals who have provided help and encouragement to music in Canada.' In addition, media awards are made in the fields of radio, television, and recordings. These last are 'alternately biennial' and are made for radio production one year, followed the next year by recordings and television. The growth in activity since the secretariat was formed has been rapid and substantial. Since 1978 the CMC has administered both the Jules Léger Prize for new chamber music and the Robert Fleming Award for young composers.

By the early 1980s council membership had grown to almost 250 individuals and close to 100 organizations. In 1984 another major international festival was held in Canada for the first time; this was World Music Days, the annual festival of the International Society for Contemporary Music. This festival, co-ordinated by Guy Huot for the CMC as Canadian section of the ISCM, was almost two years in preparation. World Music Days comprised over forty events in Toronto and Montreal, from 23 September to 3 October, and was preceded (21-22 September) by a two-day symposium in Toronto on 'Contemporary Music Theatre,' featuring participants from Europe and America. Delegates to the festival came from twenty-nine of the thirty-one member countries of the ISCM. The new works from Canada and abroad (approximately 150 in all) were performed by Canadian soloists and ensembles as well as musicians from the United States, Italy, Britain, and Argentina.

In the secretary-general's report to the 1985 annual meeting of the Canadian Music Council, Huot identified four main areas of the council's activity as follows:

1 Information and promotion. The Council receives numerous requests from Canada and abroad ... Partly to answer these requests, several lists are published
   (summer camps, festivals, international competitions, music schools, contemporary music societies etc.) ... *Musicanada* is an important vehicle for promoting our music and musicians ...
2 Lobbying.
3 International representation (ISCM, IMC, CIDEM (Inter-American Music Council)). For the IMC the Council promotes International Music Day throughout the world ... Every year it organizes Canada's participation in the ISCM World Music Days ... For two years we have been taking part in the Cannes MIDEM Classique ... The Council is also taking an active part in planning the International Year of Canadian Music in 1986.
4 Special projects. We organize conferences, symposia and studies ...

It is now more than forty years since a group of interested and committed musicians organized themselves with a determination to see Canada's musical accomplishments recognized both at home and abroad. Progress was slow, and was often hampered by indifference as well as chronic underfunding and the fact that until 1976 all of the council's activities were conducted by individuals working on a part-time voluntary basis. The above summary of the secretary-general's outline of activities demonstrates how far the organization has come in those forty years. Let us hope that the next forty will be as rewarding.

PRESIDENTS OF THE CANADIAN MUSIC COUNCIL

1949-66	Sir Ernest MacMillan	1975-7	John Peter Lee Roberts
1966-7	Arnold Walter	1977-80	Maryvonne Kendergi
1967-8	Jean Papineau-Couture	1980-2	George Laverock
1968-71	John Peter Lee Roberts	1982-3	Micheline Tessier
1971-3	François Bernier	1983-6	Patricia Tompkins
1973-5	Ronald Napier		

RECIPIENTS OF THE CANADIAN MUSIC COUNCIL MEDAL

1971 Jean-Marie Beaudet (posthumously), Leo Barkin, Serge Garant
1972 John Beckwith, Lionel Daunais, Lois Marshall, R. Murray Schafer
1973 Sir Ernest MacMillan (posthumously), Eric McLean, Lyell Gustin, Soeur Marie-Stéphane, Jean Papineau-Couture, Gilles Tremblay
1974 François Brassard, Helen Creighton, Luc Lacourcière
1975 Elmer Iseler, Yehudi Menuhin, Wilfrid Pelletier
1976 Alexander Brott, John Cozens, Nicholas Goldschmidt
1977 Phyllis Mailing, Helmut Kallmann, André Prévost
1978 Keith Bissell, Mario Duschenes, Keith MacMillan, Olivier Messiaen, John Weinzweig
1979 Richard W. Cooke, Yvonne Hubert, John Newmark
1980 John Avison, Norma Dickson, Nicholas Koudravtzeff (posthumously)
1981 Mario Bernardi, Glenn Gould, Nicholas Kilburn
1982 Robert Aitken, Maryvonne Kendergi, Gilles Lefebvre
1983 Rolland Brunelle, Maureen Forrester, Ruby Mercer
1984 George Little, Frances James Adaskin, Henry Mutsaers, Ronald Napier
1985 Louise André, Louis Quilico, Peggie Sampson
1986 Franz Kraemer, Paul Loyonnet
1987 Walter Homburger, Gilles Potvin, Simon Streatfeild

CONFERENCE TOPICS

1965 'The Pros and Cons of the Competitive Festival'
1966 'Music in Canada, its Resources and Needs'
1967 'Music and Media'
1968 'Music Education in Canada'
1969 'Contemporary Music and Audiences'
1970 'The Musician in 2001'

1971 'Music and Youth in Canada'
1972 'The Development of a Music Policy for Canada'
1973 'Music Criticism in Canada'
1974 'Folk Music in Canada'
1975 'Music in Canada: Survey and Perspective'
'Music as a Dimension of Life' in collaboration with the International Music Council (Paris) and the International Institute for Music, Dance and Theatre (Vienna)
1976 'Music in a Restrained Economy: From Proliferation to Consolidation'
1977 'Music in the Community'
'International Symposium on Singing'
1978 'Music and Television'
1979 'For all Children, their Daily Music'
1981 'The Serious Music Recording Industry in Canada'
1982 'The Plight of the Canadian Performer'
1984 'World Music Days'
'Symposium on Contemporary Music Theatre'
(No conferences were held in 1980, 1983, 1985, or 1986.)

WALTER H. KEMP

Three Masses by Maritime Composers

Composers, filled with the Christian spirit, should feel that their vocation is to cultivate sacred music and increase its store of treasures.

Let them produce compositions which have the qualities proper to genuine sacred music ... for the active participation of the entire assembly of the faithful.[1]

The Ordinary of the Mass is not a principal source of interest for the majority of contemporary Canadian composers. In the concert hall, Harry Somers's *Kyrie* (1972) and Clifford Ford's *Mass* (1976) are masterly pieces, but lonely. One work which Canada has produced in tune with the *Missa Luba, African Sanctus*, et al is Pierick Houdy's *La Messe québécoise*, for small choir, organ, fiddle, bass, and spoons: a delightful synthesis of art music and the indigenous, fulfilling to a high standard Article 119 of the Vatican II *Constitution on the Sacred Liturgy*, which urges non-Europeanization of national traditions, 'adapting worship to their native genius.'[2]

In the first half of the 1980s, three composers employed at institutions of higher learning in the Maritime Provinces – Michael Parker (Sir Wilfred Grenfell College, Corner Brook), Dennis Farrell (Dalhousie University, Halifax), and myself (University of King's College and Dalhousie) – have each written a Mass. These settings illustrate possibilities open to composers of church music working within a North American society where there is high tension between the cultural and the doctrinal goals towards which their craft is applied.

Also, if we accept Georgiades' statement that 'the language of the Mass is the conveyor of an idea, of an event,'[3] each of these compositions demonstrates a role which a late-twentieth-century Mass may fulfil. Pursuing and elaborating upon Georgiades' concept,[4] we can consider that the early Christian Mass was an event taking place in an enclosed space –

celebrants and singers, liturgy and action, were as one. By the Gothic era, when art triumphed as a vessel of worship, the liturgical action was still unified in one space, but the event was divided between clerics and choristers. The Reformation took the choristers from their proximity to sacramental activity, providing a new space for sung leadership and/or accompaniment some distance removed, usually in a gallery. As participants and listeners the congregation had to divide their attention between the two sound sources of the worship. The potential for congregational passivity within the bi-polar spatial situation of post-Reformation liturgical worship was realized by the Romantic concert Mass, during which a large impersonal space was shared by two separate micro-communities engaged in a one-way communication chain. A static, liturgically inactive choir delivered the 'radiant energy' of the text to passive consumers, neither group encountering the actual event of the Mass except through individual image processes or associative memories raised by the musical performance. My *Mass in Honour of St Thomas Aquinas* was designed for a small chapel setting perpetuating the Medieval idea of sacramental action shared by priests and choir. Michael Parker's *Missa silvatica* interprets the Ordinary in terms of contemporary tensions, a small community of intelligent actors in vocal sound delivering an 'effect' to a passive community of listeners and thereby hoping to excite in them a sympathetic perception, psychological awareness, and response that are equally contemporary. Dennis Farrell's *Civic Mass* attempts to fill the spatial vacuum of the concert Mass by inviting the listener to become a singer, the meaning of the original event breaking through into an ecumenical, pluralistic secular society to create a revived communality active within a symbolic space whose boundaries are the modern metropolis.

The *Mass in Honour of St Thomas Aquinas* (1983) was written for the Chapel Choir of the University of King's College, Halifax, and dedicated to the chapel's music leaders, Helen and David Buley. Completed on the feast of the dedication of the chapel, 6 October 1983, this Mass was in regular eucharistic use for the second half of the 1983-4 academic year and has been adopted for services at St John the Evangelist, Montreal. The first concert performance was given by the St Paul's Singers of Halifax under the direction of the composer on 4 March 1986. The *Aquinas Mass* was intended for joyful and transcendent eucharistic celebration. Its brevity was dictated by the dimensions of the King's Chapel in which the action of the Mass is enacted and by the relatively small number of communicants. There was also a didactic element involved in the composing of this piece, to provide university students who were not music majors with a simple introduction to certain aspects of contemporary sound through direct participation in an event the musical expression of which is not the goal but the vehicle (Example 1).

The unaccompanied SATB choral texture is occasionally broken by solo soprano and baritone, in the Christe and in the responsorial Agnus Dei (Example 2). The irregular metres of the Gloria and the swinging Sanctus (with its Trinitarian symbolism of line, harmony, rhythm, and metre) ensure that the earthly dimension of the sacrifice is present. While considering the economy of duration, material, and difficulty required by a 'brief Mass' composed for a university chapel choir, the expansion of the soul's prayer and praise is not forgotten. The 'Hosannas' refer back to the acclamations of an earlier Christian era, and the lyrical 'Domine fili unigenite' recalls nostalgically the sentiment of an ultramontane Catholicism officially put away several decades ago (Example 3). The 'Dona nobis pacem', in which material from the opening Kyrie is rescored, reminds the worshipper that 'Ite missa est' implies a welcome to return.

Aquinas, patron saint of education, wrote that beauty requires integrity, proportion, and brilliance (*claritas*), so that a thing which gives pleasure when it is perceived may be called beautiful.[5] The beauty of the event: that is what the *Mass in Honour of St Thomas Aquinas* is about.

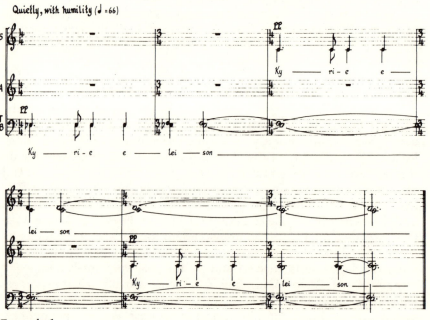

Example 1

Example 2

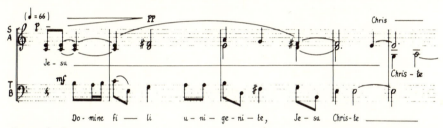

Example 3

Michael Parker's *Missa silvatica* (Missa Brevis No. 1), opus 26, won first prize in the 1981 Competition for Choral Composers sponsored jointly by the Newfoundland and Labrador Arts Council and the Department of Music of Memorial University. Written for SATB a cappella choir, it has significant passages for soprano solo in the 'Et in terra pax' and Agnus Dei and for a quartet of soloists in the opening of the Sanctus. Like the *Aquinas Mass*, the *Missa silvatica* was composed with ears attuned to the sound and expertise of a specific choral ensemble: the Memorial University of Newfoundland Chamber Choir, directed by Donald Cook, who gave the première performance on 25 January 1982 and subsequently recorded it.[6] The musical complexity, therefore, is appropriately greater than that of the eucharistic Mass tailored for the King's Chapel Choir and, because the *Missa silvatica* is intended for the concert hall, the durations of its individual sections are not determined by requirements of liturgical action.[7] The music 'breathes' well, and Parker's feeling for the shape and quality of the Latin is very much in evidence, as might be expected from a composer holding an MA in classics from the University of Toronto who teaches a combination of college classes in arts and music.

In the prefatory remarks to the published edition of the *Missa silvatica*,[8] it is stated that each section 'is characterized by a separate series of notes derived from key words in the individual texts.' Listeners may not apprehend that logic as much as they may appreciate the composer's employment of the sound-values of certain intervals, through which he achieves accumulation and variation of mood, developing a musical Mass that has undeniable affective purposes.

Each section of the *Missa silvatica* furnishes illustrations of these calculated sound-values. In the Kyrie are exposed successively groupings of intervals which will be used in the rest of the work:

Kyrie   narrow steps; leaps in tertial consonance; the tritone introduced gradually within each entry of the voices participating in the gestural imitation, the tritone modified through concordant harmonization with the other voices.

Christe   unison/octave statements of melodic cells with small range and chromatic content; the starker sound of fifths and fourths, the parallelism of which (one of the fingerprints of this Mass) is foreshadowed in bar six (compare Sanctus, bars 32-40).

Kyrie   a combination of these sound-values, until the texture unwinds, ending in a soprano solo which refashions the initial pitch series in retrograde order.

Already the planned intensification of interval sound-values is felt in the first ten bars of the Kyrie (Example 4). The splendid glow of the Gloria is imparted by the rich sonancy of the third, in variform piling up for petition and for acclamation (bars 54-63). The alteration in mood-affect from the splendour of the Gloria to the mystery of the Sanctus is wrought by removing the third as the dominating interval sound-value and making the fourth, in both its perfect and augmented forms, constitute the line and harmony (Example 5). The contrapuntal motif of the 'Pleni' articulates the ambit of the fourth, its chromatic content progressively filled in. The engagingly rhythmic 'Osanna' extends this practice to the ambit of a sixth (Example 6). In a similar manner the concluding soprano solo of the Agnus Dei stretches to the complete octave but uses only ten of the twelve available notes; the two notes omitted, E flat and C, would have been identified with the framing A flat as triadic consonance, a quality which would detract from the tensions of this solo, described in the prefatory note as a 'last agonizing petition.' (Example 7). The Agnus Dei is a summation of the work's interval sound-values, introducing each in turn (Example 8).

Example 4

Parker's *Missa silvatica* is not 'sylvan,' not idyllic.[9] It is tough, even in its praising. It is tough in its immediacy, in the toughness of Bonhoeffer's image of 'Christ in the world today.' Erik Routley has described the secularized modern composer as being no longer inside the church; the church must deal with the composer: 'The church has had to get used to being in a position where it could not escape conversation with "the world": to travel, as it were, second class ... What we are witnessing is the first few sentences of a conversation whose end will surely be more

Example 5

Example 6

Example 7

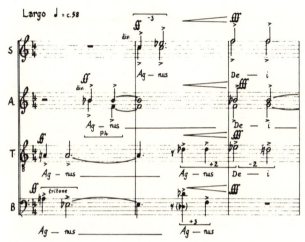

Example 8

creative than the former state of things was ... no longer monologue but rather conversation: and the theological result is, precisely, the "Religionless Christianity" cult.'[10] The voices that cry out from the *Missa silvatica* give a sharp edge to the authenticity residing in the text. Contemporaneity is a special value of Parker's Mass.

The *Civic Mass* by Dennis Farrell involves more performers than the two works previously discussed, the title 'Civic' lending itself to an occasion of large urban forces brought together in celebration rather than a more parochially specific people's 'dialogue' Mass. A frequently subdivided SATB chorus is accompanied by an organ. The festive tone given by a brass choir and timpani may be replaced with a more reflective spirit by omitting these orchestral instruments, thereby allowing the work to function as a four-voice parish high Mass. There is a part for the congregation, which the composer's program note confesses to be 'frankly melodic, attempting the attractiveness of brand-new chorale tunes as a practical solution to the problem of (active) populist participation in a piece of sophisticated church music.' By calling this congregational music a 'populo part,' Farrell declares himself as a mover in the revival of the 'populo' Masses fostered by the *Missa choralis* of Licinio Refice and similar Masses by Perosi and Carnavali. During the course of an interview, the composer asserted: 'My liturgical guidelines are still the *Motu proprio* of St Pius, the *Sacrae musicae disciplinae* of Pius XII. Church music imprinted me strongly, strongly enough to want to compose, and even more strongly to write better than I heard. Liturgical formation and artistic development are life-long apprenticeships for the church composer.'

Haligonians have experienced the *Civic Mass* in two quite different sets of performance circumstances. The première of the work at St Mary's Roman Catholic Basilica on 4 May 1980 featured the main choral part sung by the Halifax Chamber Choir, directed by Paul Murray, to whom the Mass is dedicated; the six hundred members of the congregation were rehearsed and led in performance by a second conductor, Alexander Tilley, whose St Andrew's Presbyterian Church Choir was placed at the front of this assembly. The orchestral instruments and ample gallery pipe organ contributed to the complex of sound resonating within the broad acoustic of the basilica. To one adding his voice among the populace the impact of the event was driven both by an energy in the art music that was Tridentine, Mannerist, and an enthusiasm in the 'populo' that was summoned from both the hymnodic response innate in the Protestant and the discovery of the same among the modern Catholic laity. On 20 November 1983, in the Rebecca Cohn Auditorium of the Dalhousie Arts Centre, I conducted all performing forces in the second presentation of the *Civic Mass*, rebroadcast on regional CBC Radio. The ecumenical power could be apprehended again, but this time with more clarity in the score's musical detail because of the drier acoustic of the concert hall setting. With the exception of the brass choir, which had a membership almost identical to the original ensemble, the performing circumstances differed significantly from those of the première. Instead of a chamber choir, the one hundred voices of the Dalhousie Chorale sang the choral material; unfortunately, a rather tired electronic organ of early vintage placed on the stage had to stand in for a pipe organ; the paying congregation of roughly the same number as that of the première mastered the 'populo part' quite quickly, there being a fair number who had participated at the basilica. The work was able to accommodate itself to the spatial, aesthetic, practical, and liturgical differences, and in both settings put across its message, in this way realizing the composer's remarks to me: 'Church music should not be solely an aesthetic experience. We must, however, remove the "anaesthetic" element. We must aesthetize liturgical feeling and thinking ... [The Liturgical Movement's] calculation of real, liturgical time fails to build in such notions as contrast, delight, sublimity, and profound sense of occasion.'

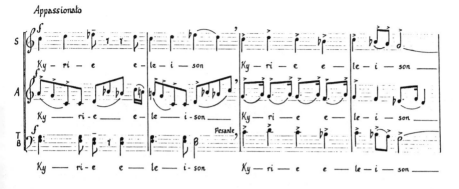

Example 9

Example 10

The musical style of the *Civic Mass* is eclectic, the composer drawing from the techniques and spirits of various past eras to inform his personal neo-Romanticism (Example 9). The 'populo part' seems to appeal to its singers, who find the lines musically challenging and spiritually refreshing (Example 10).

Example 11

The ecumenicity of the *Civic Mass* is present in both text and music. Other than the Kyrie, the sections of the Ordinary appear in English with slight texted variants, offering to the various denominations represented at the performances what Farrell calls 'options in the translation that would incorporate a familiarity.' There is a *cantus firmus* quotation from Merbecke in the Gloria (Example 11). The melody for the final 'Amens' of the Gloria is derived from the plainsong *Missa de angelis*. The Mass concludes with a quodlibet, combining the 'Grand Amen' and the tune 'Old St George' to the favourite Presbyterian psalm 'Ye gates lift up your heads on high.' As a prelude to the Mass, there is a 'solemn setting' of the Royal Anthem.

Such selectivity exercised upon denominational repertoires, each of whose mix is peculiar to its own urban Christian population, is a type of ecumenism which a church musician may practise within the modern Canadian cultural mosaic. The pluralism forming the metropolitan-specific pattern of church music traditions can be mined, producing an artistic-liturgical representation of a shared, common life of worship through music. The North American Catholic composer is caught up with the question of how 'unity-in-diversity' may permit 'the adaptation of Catholicism to a pluralistic sociocultural system,' for

> if we accept the notion that the sociocultural system is integrated by the highest values held by the people, and that these highest values are contained in religion, then we have a distinctly American problem of religious pluralism ... A free society like ours resists authoritarian coercion to a basic, integrating, and overarching value system such as the Catholic Church claims to possess ... the continued Americanization of Catholicism will depend upon the way in which the solution is attempted.[11]

It would seem that one solution a modern Catholic composer could attempt is a creative selectivity, the model for which would be Farrell's *Civic Mass*.

When it is stated in the *Constitution on the Sacred Liturgy of the Second Vatican Council* that 'every Mass has of itself a public and social nature,'[12] the addresses of Popes Pius X, XI, and XII encouraging 'participatio conscia et actuosa' are being reaffirmed.[13] In Article 30 of the *Constitution* Vatican II seeks to stress that, in addition to 'the expression of inner sentiments by external deportment . . . practising the politeness proper to God's sanctuary,'[14] active participation should be promoted by the people taking part 'by means of acclamation, responses, psalmody, antiphons and songs.'[15] The door is open: many musics 'are by no means excluded from liturgical celebration, so long as they accord with the spirit of liturgical action as laid down in Art. 30.'[16] Thus the contemporary liturgical movement, by using translations, new melodies, and new performance practices 'seeks to extract from the early Christian liturgy only a mode of operation, namely the active participation of the community in the liturgical event.'[17] Although proceeding from liturgical considerations, the liturgical movement in being also 'sociologically oriented . . . seeks the authentic not in its *origins* but in its *effect*.'[18]

Seeking the authentic in an equilibrium sustained between *modus operandi* and 'effect' is at the heart of the three Masses under discussion, dissimilar as they are in original function, style, and practice. Each was composed to serve an identified community – chapel, collegiate, civic. Each was to develop that community's life of worship conceptually and actively. Each is intended to be an awakening through musical idioms that are 'new,' singing of joy, suffering, and communal festivity. 'Our liturgical gatherings have only begun to awaken to the meaning of communal liturgy after centuries of passivity. But though a thaw has set in, we have yet to experience the warmth and enthusiasm that should characterize our liturgical celebrations in community.'[19] Each of the three Masses raises that 'warmth,' pouring into the old authentic chalice of the Ordinary their new wine.

KENNETH WINTERS

Towards the 'One Justifiable End': Six Discs

In music the middle 1980s may be looked back upon as the time when we extricated ourselves with painful slowness but absolute determination from a thrall under which, for rather a long time, only a few of Canada's hundreds of composers, and those few in only some of their works, had managed to sting their audiences to more than dutiful curiosity or involve them in more than temporary inconvenience. Those same middle 1980s may also be recalled as the years of a slightly quickened perception that music is made by no one alone, not even the composer, but by every hand, ear, heart, and mind that touches it, however briefly, on its way from its composer's first awareness to its hearer's expanding awareness.

Ralph Vaughan Williams put this another way when he said that a composer's score bears about the same relation to the experience of a work of music that a railway schedule bears to a journey. Ruskin said it when he pointed out that 'the power which causes the several portions of a plant to help each other we call life; the ceasing of this help is what we call corruption.'[1] In one of the many ideas he contributed personally to the work he co-edited – the *Encyclopedia of Music in Canada* – Helmut Kallmann restated the principle from a particular standpoint. The *Encyclopedia*, he said, 'is the beginning of a process of understanding that has only one justifiable end: a deeper participation in music itself, as listener, interpreter, or creator.'[2]

Music comes into being along a symbiotic chain in which we all are links. No one concerned is exempt, either from a hands-on, ears-on role or from the linking function of that role. We may of course determine which roles are ours, but we may not shirk them and their interconnection and still maintain the life, the music.

In *Le Monde musical* in May 1919 Nadia Boulanger wrote: 'Nothing is better than music; when it takes us out of time, it has done more for us than we have the right to hope for: it has broadened the limits of our sorrowful lives, it has lit up the sweetness of our hours of happiness by effacing the pettinesses that diminish us.'[3] That sounds a bit high-falutin, doubtless, yet think of it. Music itself – a Bach fugue, say – is surely better than it can be played, or the millions of hours of lonely ecstatic striving to achieve its clarity would cease. It must be better than it can be heard, or why would we return to it so hungrily again and again, to listen and seek? It must even be better than it can be composed, or the obsessive search of creation would surely have stopped with Bach, Haydn, Mozart, Schubert, Stravinsky.

Small wonder, then, that music is better than it can be afforded or programmed or 'encyclopediated' or discussed or criticized or broadcast or recorded. Yet all these functions contribute to its abiding life, and their individual strengths or weaknesses quicken or diminish that life.

Not to follow sententiously every avenue for discussion opened by this preamble, let us stroll down just one by way of example.

'Music is better than it can be recorded.' Yes, I believe that, even now when monophonics have given way long since to stereo- and quadraphonics, 78 rpms have been supplanted by 33⅓ rpms, and these needle-played systems in turn are being put out of fashion by laser-read compact discs recorded digitally. Each new discovery is a kind of plucky, wistful, striving proof that some profound and essential aspect of the musical experience evades – probably always will evade – capture by technology. Nevertheless, from the time of its discovery to the present, recording has undertaken, as its most graceful function, the reproduction of superior musical performances, and its importance in that connection has grown until, today, it is probably music's most efficient and valuable disseminator – valuable not only because it can take music anywhere (after all, radio can do that too, and more cheaply) but also because it gives the listener a performance of some music of his choice in a form in which he can carry it in his hand into the inner sanctum of his musical life, his life of the mind, and in his own time revisit it and reconsider it again and again. The value of this volition and peace and privacy, to the listener and to the living composer whose deepest thoughts and furthest flights he may want to know, can hardly be overestimated. The normal long chain of communication between the mind of the composer and the mind of the listener can be abbreviated thus into a single manageable package.

The road to the package is not so simple, alas. Canada by the mid-1980s still had no appreciable serious-music record industry. There are numerous reasons given for this: cost, population base (available profits), the bias of governments (they get into oil and sell Canadarms and Candu reactors and hydro-electric power, but their advocacy on behalf of Canadian music is nominal), the taste of corporation magnates (which runs to the buying and selling of paintings, horses, and ballplayers), and the commercial gumption and merchandising adroitness (or lack thereof) of Canada's cautious, poverty-fixated little serious-music record industry itself. 'Leave it largely or at least partly to the CBC' seems to have been its sad refrain; and indeed we must all thank Heaven that the Canadian Broadcasting Corporation has had a certain conscience and shown a degree of initiative in the cause of recordings of Canadian music, and of making those recordings generally available – at first awkwardly, by mail order, more recently more gracefully, over the counters in leading record stores.

What is remarkable in the circumstances is that over some twenty years, from the mid-1960s to the mid-1980s, some authentic Canadian masterworks recorded by the best possible performers have become available and have illuminated for us aspects of the musical minds of some of our best composers. Perhaps I can give an idea of my own encounters with six such recordings.

The earliest of the six – a 1968 CBC recording which reached at least the Canadian public via a special distribution arrangement with the Canadian arm of the US company RCA – gave us a brilliant performance, by pianist Anton Kuerti and a very good no-name (well, 'CBC Festival . . . ') orchestra conducted by Alexander Brott, of Sophie-Carmen Eckhardt-Gramatté's *Symphony-Concerto*. This large work, and with it something of the essence of its composer, came home to me for the first time through the good offices of this recording. I heard here the natural vigour and technical assurance which sustained Eckhardt-Gramatté's best music even when the notation was erratic, the expression impulsive, aggressive, or temperamental. A naturalized Canadian (she arrived in Canada in 1953 with her Austrian husband, Ferdinand Eckhardt, who had been appointed director of the Winnipeg Art Gallery), Eckhardt-Gramatté brought onto the Canadian scene a rigorous European training and a personality of large dimension, startling force, and a swift, tactless, scintillating charm that some sobersides found daunting. Her wrath – and she did feel strongly about things – was best avoided. She had vocation, dedication, and ambition, and declared them in a rather challenging way, coming as she did from a crowded culture where even the best talents had to fight for ground. With the Kuerti-Brott recording of her *Symphony-Concerto* I came to realize that, unlike some of our more tentative geniuses, she was all there in her music: the compact figure, the dark gleaming eye, the splendid, hoarsely-expressive voice, the large hands which in their quickness and sinew described her early career as an authentic virtuoso of piano and violin, the devastating bluntness, the genuine and imaginative sweetness, the fascination with everything alive. Through this recording of this work I came to realize that it was not Eckhardt-Gramatté, flags flying and signals flashing, who was daunting, either personally or in her art, but rather the flat-eyed establishment figures, the theatrical opportunists, the cynical gimmick artists, the methodologists; these, with their calculated ease, were infinitely more menacing than this volatile European-Canadian woman from the prairies.

The next of the six – a 1970 Radio Canada International recording also released through the Canadian branch of RCA – gave us one of Harry Somers's most beautiful early works (1956; he was 31) marvellously sung by Maureen Forrester, with the National Arts Centre Orchestra in its shining young elegance under Mario Bernardi. The music – *Five Songs for Dark Voice* – is in reality a cantata, in which Michael Fram's linked, cyclic verses are sensitively encompassed by Somers's neo-Stravinskyan score. (The echo from Jocasta's aria is probably no accident and certainly no drawback.) The haunting music of the first song pervades the rest, without nagging, and the variety within the tragic unity is exquisitely elaborated. The fine, simple canon at the end of the fourth song, on the wonderful words 'At four o'clock, before the dawn / In the echoing street, there is yourself,' is expanded luminously in the first part of the last song. This, in turn, is tenderly broken in upon by the flute solo which leads to the grieving reprise of the first music, subtly altered, fulfilling the cycle of feeling. Somers has often been more ostensibly dramatic than here, but seldom more unaffectedly communicative. The recording, sad to say, is aging, and the sleeve design is discouragingly drab. Oh that this wonderful performance of this small (twelve-minute) masterpiece could be remastered, perhaps even rerecorded, but somehow recaptured and repackaged for today's public.

The third of my six – another 1970 CBC recording freed for sale to the public, this time by an arrangement with Decca – brings us Harry Freedman's remarkable work for choir and woodwind quintet, *The Tokaido*. Freedman had long been fascinated by things oriental, especially visual and literary things, and *The Tokaido*, a set of verses and colour prints by the nineteenth-century Japanese artist Ichiryusai Hiroshige, captured his imagination both ways. From the verses Freedman selected nineteen, arranging sixteen in four groups and saving one for a prologue, two for an epilogue.

Tokaido means 'the way facing the Eastern Ocean' (that is, the road between Kyoto and Tokyo), and Hiroshige's work is a record of the fifty-three stopping places along the road. Freedman's journey, with its impatient western tendency to abridge, contents itself with the high spots.

Nevertheless it is a curiously, almost soothingly, satisfactory work. The severe serial techniques Freedman used in its composition and the distinctive but limited colours of the woodwind quintet sit particularly well with the delicate objectivity and fatalistic humour of Hiroshige's verse. Without once resorting to Japanese musical sources or attempting to achieve any kind of obviously Japanese effect, Freedman has avoided the worst trap of western orientalism: the chintzy limbo of chinoiserie, the complacent offensiveness of the handily spurious.

What he has achieved is a quiet, rather static, but strangely evocative and haunting monochrome, far more Japanese than it would have been if it had striven to be, and yet not necessarily Japanese at all, but, rather, a firm, gentle grasp of some exportable, transplantable essence in oriental thought. My only criticism would be that in making nineteen Japanese epigrams last twenty minutes it has expanded the unexpandable.

Never mind. It is nearly the best thing Freedman has done (I'm similarly partial to *Encounter*, for violin and piano), and the performance – by Elmer Iseler's now gone Festival Singers of Canada (for whom it was written) and the Toronto Woodwind Quintet – achieves a cool and subtle perfection that does it justice. Again, the sleeve design is a serious drawback; who, searching through a record bin, would give it the second look that might lead to a purchase? What a relief it was, later in the 1970s, to see our precious few good recordings of Canadian music appearing in jackets which allowed, at last, that we might have eyes as well as ears. The remaining three of my six are quite handsomely clothed; another link in the symbiotic chain decently forged at last.

Before discussing those three recordings I'd like to digress briefly on the subject of that other all-important link, the performer. It is the performer, after all, who carries the terrible burden of choice. It is the performer who must decide which of the hundreds of works available will suit the instrument, fit the program, satisfy the audience; which will be chosen or rejected, which performed once or sometimes or often or never. To the listener such decisions are more significant than he is in any position to know; to the composer such decisions are life or limbo. Not only does it matter deeply whether or not his works be chosen. It matters how many of them, and by whom. Certainly, when it comes to a publicly available recording it matters very much whether the performers are a pianist like Kuerti, a singer like Forrester, a choir like the Festival Singers, or some nonentity. Surely it matters also whether that performer chooses one work by each of a dozen composers, as a token of democratic duty done, or a dozen works by one composer, as a declaration of championship. Beecham was of more use to music through his passionate advocacy of Sibelius and Delius, whom he understood, than he ever could have been through reluctant presentations of Schoenberg and Webern, whom he did not. Repertoire may be enlarged by numbers, but music itself is enlarged only by understanding. Naturally, if the performer's understanding can encompass a dozen composers instead of one, we are all enriched; but if his choice exceeds his grasp nothing is gained. Discrimination, fashionable or not, remains a virtue.

A performer – or, rather, a performing group – well worth considering in this light is Canada's prodigious Orford String Quartet: Andrew Dawes and Kenneth Perkins, violins; Terence Helmer, viola; Marcel St-Cyr and, later (1980), Denis Brott, cello. This quartet came into existence in 1965, and during the 1970s it emerged as not merely the finest Canadian string quartet since the noted Hart House Quartet of the second quarter of the century (1923-45), but as one of the finest in the world, able to represent Canada and the string quartet literature with distinction before sophisticated audiences in any country in the world. The Orford Quartet has played throughout Continental Europe and the USSR, in the United Kingdom, and all over North America to admiring audiences and critics. It has mounted all the pinnacles of the repertoire – the main works of Haydn, Mozart, and Bartok; Schubert, Schumann, and Dvorak; all of Beethoven, Mendelssohn, and Brahms; the Debussy, the Ravel, pieces of Berg and Webern, and a wide selection of other twentieth-century quartets, by Prokofiev, Shostakovich, Ives, Britten, Tippett, Carter, Lutoslawski, Penderecki, and Crumb.

Significant for Canada is the substantial number of twentieth-century Canadian works the Orford Quartet has performed, always scrupulously, and with conscience enough to perpetuate some and subsequently deliberately neglect others. By 1980 its Canadian repertoire included some twenty-five quartets, by Murray Adaskin, Brian Cherney, William Douglas, Robert Fleming, Alan Heard, Jacques Hétu, Luigi von Kunits, Oskar Morawetz, Jean Papineau-Couture, Clermont Pépin, Harry Somers, John Weinzweig, and Charles Wilson, and other pieces for quartet by Samuel Dolin, Harry Freedman, Srul Irving Glick, Stephen Pedersen, and Gerhard Wuensch. Many people probably do not realize there are in existence as many Canadian string quartets as can be found in the Orford Quartet's repertoire. If, said quickly, a repertoire containing twenty-five Canadian works does not seem phenomenal for a group then fifteen years old, compare it with the repertoire of its famous predecessor, the Hart House Quartet which, in the twenty-two years of its existence, played just two Canadian quartets, one of them (by a composer whose name is forgotten) only once, and the other (by Sir Ernest MacMillan) not much oftener. The Hart House Quartet preferred to hold its audience in softer bonds. A typical program would offer perhaps one standard classic, then a string of arrangements of familiar melodies; 'Old Black Joe' was a favourite. This is not to sneer; the Hart House Quartet did what it could in the context of its time. But what it did helps us to appreciate, by contrast, the Orford's achievement, in particular that portion of the Orford repertoire which is unique and for which no norms of performance had been established – that is to say, the Canadian portion.

Which leads to my fourth recording: the Orford's 1977 Melbourne release of John Beckwith's only *Quartet* (composed that year) and R. Murray Schafer's *String Quartet No. 2*, subtitled 'Waves,' composed in 1976.

The Schafer is a singular work and, in a particular and perhaps restricted way, an unimpeachably elegant one. The restriction – if such it be – lies in its deliberate representation of the unfolding, the unfurling, the exfoliation, of a single concept, based in nature, in the infinitely recurrent, subtly variegated simplicity of nature, and in the intellectual perception of that simplicity. During the World Soundscape Project (an elaborate investigation into the relationships of sound to the human environment) Schafer discovered that the endlessly recurrent waves of the ocean were not equidistant in time from one another but tended to be almost so, within a narrow variation of between six and eleven seconds. This principle – of recurrence and infinite variation within a narrow frame – lodged in his consciousness like a seed, then grew into a work of one indivisible movement which lasts just over eighteen minutes and achieves remarkable freedom of expression within something close to absolute unity of structure, played out in terms of a rhythm that is at once contained, flexible, coherent, and varied within the confines suggested by its inspiration, the waves. Schafer has worked with a refined proliferation of small means: prolonged miniature ostinati, tremolos, trills and near-trills, melismas, short scalic sequences, little running figures one note shorter or longer on the fifth or seventh or tenth repetition, myriad tiny asymmetries. The result is not so much a tour-de-force as a tour-de-délicatesse, orientally abstract. Within the fragile, busy fabric, the cold mind of the romantic or dramatic artist is selecting, shaping, constructing small shocks and graduated peaks, but astutely never violating continuity or imperilling unity. The result is not a piece that would survive imitation or a concept that Schafer could risk reusing. It is even a piece that on the wrong occasion might seem not so much hypnotic as humdrum. Nevertheless, it is original, virtuosic, and very, very remarkable.

John Beckwith's *Quartet* is near Schafer's in length – perhaps a minute longer – but it occupies a much wider and more sectional musical canvas. Schafer's piece, though founded in a fascinating fact underlying the habit of ocean waves, is a transmutation into sound of implications of that fact, not at all a musical picture of waves. Beckwith's piece, while organized rigorously on a twelve-note series and worked out intellectually in terms of contrasts, textures, and balances, is fundamentally expressionistic and connotative, full of this era's deposits in humanity's memory bank. If a member of some late evolution of our race were to open a time capsule and find the Beckwith *Quartet* and listen once, twice, three times, I feel certain that even without a printed program (or even the ability to read one) he would feel a stirring of race-memory.

The composer has talked candidly about the connotative elements of the music, saying that it

> incorporates images of kinds of string music which one might regard as indigenous to Canada – banjo, guitar, ukelele, mandolin and, above all, old-time fiddling traditions are in a state of vigorous good health in some parts of the country ... Although the *Quartet* contains no actual quotations, it invokes ... these instrumental colours and the literature associated with them ... I do not regard music as a pure or abstract phenomenon, even in such a traditionally rarefied Western-Art medium as the string quartet. Connections with tradition, with a social environment, and with human-life attitudes are bound to be apparent.[4]

As for the constructional elements in Beckwith's work, though they reach away from string quartet tradition they have their feet planted in it. The five sections almost flow into one another to make one continuous movement. Yet we realize on a second hearing that the first section is an introduction, the fourth a minute-long interlude. Thus we are left with a near-relative of the old three-movement form, with two spirited fast movements separated by a pensive slow one. A subtler departure from tradition lies in the composer's strophic approach to the construction of the three main movements. He describes the successive periods of serial permutation within each movement as 'verses,' and so, within the practical old abstract three-movement form, we have the humanizing spirit of the narrative song.

'Listen!' says the startling fortissimo pizzicato of the uneven entrance of the four instruments. 'We have something to tell you,' say the ensuing busy whispers. 'Let us step into the chambers of memory,' say the clock-like, dream-like harmonics. These initial elements of the introduction take less than a minute. The second section – the equivalent of the first main Allegro – is quick to introduce the banjos and mandolins. The movement ends, after a massive, crowing, fiddle-tuning effect on open-string intervals, with an obstinate cadence that sounds like a bulletin of imperious nostalgia from the *Rite of Spring*.

The central section – the equivalent of the traditional slow movement – is at once a surprise and a simple necessity: the shadow between the twanging walls of the outer sections. Banjos and mandolins are banished here. The thoughtful, seriously lyrical string discourse is like a descendant of the austere female-voice duet in Bach's *Christ lag in Todesbanden* or the confiding romantic dialogue of the 'Duetto' from Mendelssohn's *Songs without Words*, but of course it's not a duet but a quartet, and what it suggests most of all is the fugue of human voices rising and falling against each other in Glenn Gould's radio composition 'The Idea of North.' It is always dangerous to pin labels onto music or to impose environments for it, but speaking subjectively I heard this as Canadian winter music, the loneliness of four imaginations over sublimina of hymn tunes, wood stoves, the warm but fragile haven of the Canadian house or church or school. In this surely Canadian mood a quiet, worried yearning rises to a frugal but open eloquence, plain yet intense, austere but not cold, troubled but dignified.

After this section – for me the most thought-provoking part of the work – we move across the minute-long fourth section (interlude) to the exuberant fiddle fest of the finale with, in its penultimate bars, the return of the memory-chamber device of the introduction.

In the excellent recording, produced for Melbourne records by the CBC's Anton Kwiatkowski and handsomely jacketed, the Orford Quartet conveys the filigreed textures of the Schafer and the medallion-like sonorities of the Beckwith with equal but aptly different poetry.

My fifth disc – a 1985 release by Centrediscs (the recording arm of the Canadian Music Centre), digitally recorded by the CBC sound engineer James Reid at the University of British Columbia – presents four piano works by Barbara Pentland finely and subtly played by Robert G. Rogers who, at the time of this writing, has been a champion of this composer's work for over thirty years. The results of this long advocacy are apparent in the commitment, lucidity, and quiet eloquence of these performances, and make this disc one to which I expect to return again and again.

Responses to Pentland's music are often socially polarizing. I think of the reaction of a friend – highly intelligent if not particularly sophisticated musically – to this recording.

'But it's not music,' she said, in a hurt voice.

'But it is,' I replied, 'and very good music, too.'

'Well, if it's music, and good music, will you tell me what it is you like about it?' she asked. And all I could think of was an adaptation of Gertrude Stein's Picasso answer:

'I like to listen to it.'[5]

On reflection, however, though the main reason is still that I like to listen to it, I would add that, for me, Pentland's music is a very particular but very real music, its roots in Bach and Webern, its cool, intellectual, delicately manipulated geometrics a natural outcome of musical thought, but an outcome still sufficiently individual – sufficiently new – to continue polarizing responses to it, praise be. Of the four works on the record – the five-movement *Suite borealis* (1966), the small single piece *Vita brevis* (1973), the five-piece collection *Ephemera* (completed in 1978), and the large single piece *Vincula* (1983) – I've returned most often to *Ephemera*, but *Vincula* (Bonds), mysterious, tragic, impassioned, is increasingly enthralling.

My sixth recording – another Centredisc, recorded in 1985 in the singer's kitchen in rural Ontario by the CBC sound engineer Ed Marshall and released in 1986 – offers songs by seven Canadian composers sung by the great tenor Jon Vickers with the pianist Richard Woitach.

There are twenty-six songs in all: Sir Ernest MacMillan's disarming arrangements of *Three Indian Songs of the West Coast*; Harry Somers's *Three Songs to Words by Walt Whitman* – musical confessions, really, sensitively curved and subtly frank; the *Six Medieval Love Songs* of Jean Coulthard, with their graceful, unblushing debt to the piano intermezzi of Brahms; Godfrey Ridout's pleasant arrangements of two *Folksongs of Eastern Canada*; John Beckwith's early *Five Lyrics of the T'ang Dynasty*; the late Bernard Naylor's suite *Speaking from the Snow* (1947), based on four Cecil Day Lewis poems – music curiously frail, austerely obsessive, probably profound; and three 1949 settings of William Blake by Oskar Morawetz, their Czech rhythms in arresting counterpoint to Blake's English ones.

The focus here is not, perhaps, so directly the music, but rather the fact that one of the world's most illustrious singers has chosen to devote an entire, publicly available recording to these twenty-six songs by Canadians. The performer's 'terrible burden of choice' has not been shirked here, and the choice is more than justified by superb performances, fine recording, and attractive, articulate packaging. It is safe to assume that because of all the presentational virtues represented here these songs will travel far and wide, ultimately lodge themselves in the imaginations of many, many listeners, and help in a decisive way to shorten the distance between the ideas of composers and the responses of those listeners. The essential links of the chain of communication are all contained in this single package.

In discussing these six Canadian recordings of Canadian music I do not wish to imply that they are – or even that I believe they are – all of their calibre that we have achieved. On the contrary; though these are six in which I have taken particular pleasure, and though for me they are certainly in the nature of artistic milestones, there have of course been others, especially, in the 1980s, through the Canadian Music Centre's briskly improved (though still heavily subsidized) recording operation, Centrediscs. There still are not many, however, and they still, I submit, are far too little bought, talked of, written about, *played*, even though, given purchase, discussion, criticism, and *hearings*, the best of them are probably the most effective advocates of the vitality of Canadian music imaginable.

Which leads, I suppose, to the final and burning question: 'Now that ways have been found – albeit in only a few instances and with a great deal of political and economic finagling – to provide listeners with the ideal means of acquainting themselves with some of the best Canadian music, how do we persuade them to avail themselves of those means? Now that technology has so miraculously shortened the road between Canadian listeners and Canadian music, how do we further entice them to travel that road and to fulfil their crucial role as the end links in the symbiotic chain?'

The answer, like so many answers, is elusive. We know that listeners understand the principle of the recorded-music revolution very well. In their hundreds of thousands they pay their money and rush off to closet themselves happily with the wonderful performances of Bach, Mozart, Chopin, Verdi so expensively but readily available in the record shops of the world. They are less ready, it seems, in such numbers to sample the delights of Canadian music. In their natural caution, or their conviction of inferiority ('If it's made in Canada, how can it be any good?'), or their still unstimulated appetites, they pass it over. Non-Canadians go blank on the subject; Canadians regard their music as still unproven, still unendorsed by universal approval. They look at the latest musical creation by one or another of our numerous accomplished university professors, mutter wryly to themselves 'I bet that's a real toe-tapper!' and move on to the Beethoven bin or the Tchaikovsky display.

How shall they be won over, induced to submit their time, made adventurous, fearless, independently discriminating, curious to know, willing to discover, open to possibility? Which are still the missing links? Must composers resort to the extravagant theatrics and japes of recent R. Murray Schafer to draw attention to their art? Must merchandisers find new, more insidiously intrusive hard sells to bamboozle and trap the obstinately unaware? Must critics supress their candid thoughts about the paralysing tedium of the bulk of new music in order to keep the atmosphere hospitable for the tiny delectable quintessence of it? Between the musical object and the listener's submission to it still falls the shadow. I have tried to describe six instances of light which might dispel that shadow, and I only wish description could turn the trick; of course, it cannot, or anyway not much, not enough.

The turning inevitably will be slower and more painful than any of us would wish or even dream. Doubtless on the way to the towering Canadian musical genius who will seize the world by the beard and compel it to listen, many more modest geniuses, in every field of Canadian musical endeavour – along every link of the symbiotic chain – will be sacrificed to slowness and pain. How shall it be otherwise?

GEOFFREY PAYZANT

The Glenn Gould Outtakes

My book on Glenn Gould came out in the spring of 1978, the first (and in 1986 still the only) monograph on its subject.[1] A year later it had sold almost 5000 copies, the magic number in Canada to qualify as a 'best seller'; I believe it was the first Canadian title on a musical topic to achieve this status. Subsequently it was published in Japanese by Tappan in Tokyo and in French by Fayard in Paris, so there are now more than 20,000 copies in print in three languages. I do not know the exact number because ownership of the copyright changed hands four times in the first five years as one publisher after another went out of business; this is surely another record. That twenty-five or more publishers declined my offer to show them the manuscript, or accepted the offer but rejected the book, may be yet another. As Glenn Gould wrote at the beginning of his own review of it, 'Geoffrey Payzant has written a book like no other about a performing musician.'[2] He echoed the first sentence of the book's preface: 'This book is not like other books about pianists.' These statements were true in many ways, some of which neither of us could have predicted at the time we wrote them. One way or another, and whatever its merits, *Glenn Gould, Music and Mind* made history.

Eventually came two offers to publish the manuscript, one from an American university press and one from the Toronto subsidiary of an American trade house. I accepted the latter, mainly because proximity had obvious advantages, but also because I met the editor, Garry Lovatt, and liked him. But it meant that I had to rework some of the manuscript to make it less philosophical and psychological than it might have been if it had gone to a university press.

I was happy with the result, and remain so. There is nothing in the book that I would do differently if I were to start all over again, barring a few minor details. However, some of my favourite bits ended up on the cutting-room floor, not because I was dissatisfied with them, but because Garry persuaded me that they would not do in a trade book. In part they read like the earnest efforts of an aging academic philosopher to gain a belated promotion, which in fact they were. But they also contain some useful material.

The following are the opening paragraphs of my original introduction to Glenn Gould, Music and Mind. *For reasons which may be obvious to the reader, I did not show this version to any trade publisher. But this is the clearest of the many statements I wrote of the purpose of the book.*

THE ORIGINAL INTRODUCTION

This book is not a biography of Glenn Gould. It is a study of his musical aesthetics. He and I live in the same city, and we are acquaintances of more than twenty years' standing, but I have made a point of not seeking inside information for this book from him or from anyone close to him. My sources are public and open to anyone, although some of them take a little digging.

The primary sources for this study are Gould's own recordings and his writings. My use of the word 'writings' needs explanation. Gould is the author of more than twenty-five articles about music, and of perhaps as many liner notes to his own recordings. These have been published in the ordinary way and are known to readers world-wide. But together they are only a relatively small part of his writings. His many radio broadcasts and television and film appearances must be considered writings because most of them are carefully worked up from scripts, even the seemingly most spontaneous and informal ones. They are little known outside Canada.

This book examines Gould's musical thought as put forward in his writings and exemplified in his recordings. It is only incidentally concerned with his life and times. Unavoidably the first chapter is a brief account of the emergence and early development of his musical abilities and interests. But there are no such cloying vignettes as are to be found in some accounts of the early lives of 'Sepperl' Haydn and 'Wolferl' Mozart and other famous musicians in their childhood. The reader will have to look elsewhere for stories about clever little Glenn in short pants.

In his writings Gould has developed a philosophical position on matters relating to the nature of music; the role of performer, composer, and listener; art and morality; and most particularly the interaction of music and technology. Some of his discussions of these matters are in the form of philosophical arguments; most are not arguments but confessions of his personal likes and dislikes as a working artist. I attempt to separate arguments from confessions, to evaluate the arguments and to suggest causes for the preferences.

Several months after I had prepared this selection of 'outtakes' I received notification from the present copyright owners that they had sold rights to yet another publisher, the book's fifth, to reissue Glenn Gould, Music and Mind *in, of all things, a biography series! This reissue contains an additional preface written by me explaining that, while the book is not a biography in the accepted sense, Glenn Gould's life was a life of the mind, and this is what I examine in the book.*[3]

IDEALISM, MATERIALISM, EMPIRICISM

According to Artur Schnabel, music exists mentally not physically, ideally not materially. 'The music itself' consists of auditory mental images; Schnabel calls them 'tonal ideas.' These tonal ideas precede and determine their materialization in visible notation and audible sounds. Schnabel regards this materialization as a secondary function. We can think in tones, just as we can think in words without uttering them or writing them down.[4]

To think in music is to combine and arrange musical ideas into coherent structures, or to recollect such structures, in the imagination. It can be done without singing or humming, and without touching a musical instrument. Examples of these structures are: melodies or parts of melodies; intervals; scales or parts of scales; chordal progressions or chords or parts of chords; rhythmic configurations; combinations of any or all of these. A musician could 'think' a melody either by inventing it or by recollecting it. Having thought it, he could then play it, sing it, or notate it, and it would be the same melody in each case, 'the melody itself,' no matter in which way it was materialized. All this is implicit in the way both Gould and Schnabel talk theoretically about musical thinking. Theirs is an *idealistic* theory of music.

By 'idealistic' I mean 'of ideas,' or 'of the mind,' as opposed to the material or the physical. The idealistic theory of music denies that music consists primarily of audible sounds and that music depends for its existence upon audible sounds. To make music, and to hear it *as* music and not as mere noise, depends upon a certain prior mental activity: the activity of thinking music, or, as Schnabel says, thinking *in* music; it does not depend upon any kind of performance, whether sung or played. In musical thinking, auditory mental images are combined systematically, deliberately, and according to musical principles.

In philosophy the word 'idealism' has two opposites. One of these opposites derives from metaphysics and the other from epistemology. In metaphysics the opposite of idealism is *materialism*, and the metaphysical question is whether ultimate reality is constituted of minds and thoughts, or of matter and its various determinations. In epistemology the opposite of idealism is *empiricism*, and the epistemological question is: Do our minds come into being equipped with ideas or with direct access to knowledge of the real world, or do our minds come into being empty but ready to be filled with ideas and knowledge obtained through the senses? Idealism stands opposite to materialism from one point of view and to empiricism from another, but it is the same idealism in both.

The word 'materialism' is not used here in the everyday sense of preferring material goods to spiritual goods; nor is it used in the metaphysical sense of affirming that the universe is constructed entirely of material particles: atoms, for example.

In our present sense of the word, 'material' is that out of which a work of art is made; it is that upon which the artist works to produce, by means of his skills and tools, the completed work of art. It is the Aristotelian 'material cause.' And 'materialism' is the name of a theoretical position which is opposed to 'idealism' in musical philosophy. This opposition presents itself when we consider the relation between the artist and his materials.

According to the idealist position, the artist forms 'in his mind' an image of what he proposes to do with the material; to make the work of art is to impose that image upon the material, or to reproduce the form of the image in the material. Thus a painter might have in his mind an image of a leaping animal, or of an abstract pattern. To make his painting he will manipulate his pigments in such fashion that the completed work can be seen as having the one form or the other. The material, coloured pigments forming a surface, is passive and receptive, and in an important sense the work of art may be said to exist ideally, as mental image, prior to the artist's taking up his material.

According to the materialist position, the artist takes up his material with no finally or fully formed mental image and solicits from his material its collaboration, allowing it to suggest the direction his work will take, to impose its own characteristic form upon the work. Thus a sculptor in wood will allow the grain and its changes of direction to lead him; thus Michelangelo did not hack his shapes out of the stone but 'found' them in it. The artist enjoys and respects his material, accepts its suggestions, gives it an active role in the creative process. The work does not exist until this active collaboration between the artist and his material has ceased.

Martin Heidegger says that thinking is a kind of 'craft,' indeed a kind of handicraft:

The hand is a peculiar thing. In the common view, the hand is part of our bodily organism. But the hand's essence can never be determined, or explained, by its being an organ which can grasp. Apes, too, have organs that can grasp, but they do not have hands. The hand is infinitely different from all grasping organs – paws, claws, or fangs – different by an abyss of essence. Only a being who can speak, that is, think, can have hands and can be handy in achieving works of handicraft.

But the craft of the hand is richer than we commonly imagine. The hand does not only grasp and catch, or push and pull. The hand reaches and extends, receives and welcomes – and not just things: the hand extends itself, and receives its own welcome in the hands of others. The hand holds. The hand carries. The hand designs and signs, presumably because man is a sign. Two hands fold into one, a gesture meant to carry man into the great oneness. The hand is in all this, and this is the true handicraft. Everything is rooted here that is commonly known as handicraft, and commonly we go no further. But the hand's gestures run everywhere through language, in their most perfect purity precisely when man speaks by being silent. And only when man speaks, does he think – not the other way around, as metaphysics still believes. Every motion of the hand in every one of its works carries itself through the element of thinking, every bearing of the hand bears itself in that element. All the work of the hand is rooted in thinking. Therefore, thinking itself is man's simplest, and for that reason hardest, handiwork.[5]

Etienne Gilson is either more cautious or less figurative (I am not sure which) than Heidegger in some of his remarks about the relation between the artist's thinking and his hand:

Man does not think *with* his hands, but the intellect of a painter certainly thinks *in* his hands, so much so that, in moments of manual inspiration, an artist can sometimes let his hand do its job without bothering too much about what it does ... it cannot be doubted that the art of a painter resides in his hands, in his fingers, and probably still more in his wrist, at the same time as it resides in his intellect. The art of the painter is the art of the whole man ...

If ... creative work is at stake, many other factors than intellectual knowledge become involved in the process. The hand is one of them, and the hand of a painter is for him full of surprises. But even when his hand does exactly what he wanted it to do, the knowledge that an artist has of his own art is not an abstract notion of lines, surfaces, and colors to be seen on a piece of canvas; it is the concrete cognition of the very acts and motions whereby a certain pattern of lines, surfaces, and colors can actually be produced. In painting, it is impossible to distinguish between art itself and execution, as if art were wholly in the mind, and execution wholly in the hand.[6]

Victor Zuckerkandl discusses both Heidegger and Gilson in a chapter entitled 'The Musician's Hand.' But Zuckerkandl claims that musical thinking is unlike the thinking of which Heidegger speaks, and that the creative work of the musician is unlike the creative work of the painter as described by Gilson. Unlike them he makes a distinction between 'outer hand' and 'inner hand.' It is of the 'outer hand' that Gilson speaks in the above quotations; Zuckerkandl agrees with what Gilson says about the painter's hand and thinking. But he says: 'The painter or sculptor needs two organs, a perceiving one and a working one, the eye and the hand: the eye sees what the hand does. The musician can, as it were, dispense with the eye. His work is done inside, not outside himself. In his case, external perception, actual hearing, at best serves to confirm the correctness of what he has done inwardly or to verify it for the purpose of subsequent adjustments.'[7]

Zuckerkandl says that the 'thinking hand' alone, unaided by the 'physical hand,' creates music, and that the 'thinking hand' is not a mental image of the 'physical hand.'[8] He goes so far as to say that a musician does not need a physical hand: 'The handless painter is a musician.'[9] He goes still further to say that the thinking hand is guided, not by remembered and imagined contact with musical instruments, but by musical tones themselves, which for him have a purely mental form of existence: 'We have come to recognize the musician's hand as a purely intellectual organ, and its formative activity as purely intellectual in character.'[10] Thus Zuckerkandl denies that there is any analogy or similarity between painting and music, at least so far as hand and thinking are concerned. Music for him is a wholly abstract art – abstract in the sense that it owes nothing to auditory or tactile experience.

Some people seem to be capable of regularly making responses in one sensory mode to stimuli in another sensory mode: they 'see' certain audible tones, or 'feel' certain odours. This is called 'synaesthesia.' There is disagreement among psychologists as to whether this is a genuine kind of perception or merely a strong imaginative association. Glenn Gould's friend the psychiatrist Peter F. Ostwald (who studied harmony with Arnold Schoenberg) has encountered synaesthesia as a form of psychological disturbance.

Cases of crossed reactions to sensory stimuli, seeing colors that correspond to particular sounds, for example, are reported from time to time, and some authorities think the experience is not uncommon. Dr. Peter F. Ostwald of the University of California Department of Psychiatry in San Francisco estimates that as many as 14 percent of men and 31 percent of women experience some kind of double sensation, usually color hearing, and he notes that medical papers describing the phenomenon date back at least 200 years.

Usually there is a pitch relationship: low sounds are associated with dark colors. Vowels and pure tones come through as more defined in hue than consonants or noise ...

Whether such associations represent true crossties that are present in the brain at birth, or occur as a result of accidental or mental illness, is hard to say. They may simply represent early conditioning experiences.[11]

'Early conditioning experiences' might include the acquisition of the highly specialized skills and perceptions required to be a musician, either composer or performer. Learning to play a musical instrument, or to write music, is not a matter merely of learning to translate between notation (visual), fingering (tactile), and sound (auditory). It is a matter of abolishing the ordinary distinctions among all three. The musician does not translate; he hears with his eyes, sees with his ears, touches with his eyes and ears. The mind has its eye, its ear, its hand; but the eye has a mind, and so do the ear and the hand, and in advanced levels of musical skill these several faculties of mind and sense merge into one.

Synaesthesia, or something very like it, is what Gould has in mind in the anecdote of the Vacuum Cleaner where he says 'in the softer passages, I couldn't hear any sound that I was making at all. I could feel, of course – I could sense the tactile relations with the keyboard which is replete with its own kind of acoustical associations.'[12] He could *hear* his fingers when he could not hear the piano.

He talks about recordings made by pianists who were dead or in retirement before he was born, but whose 'supplementary choreography of movement and gesture' was apparently audible to him. He could 'see' their gestures by listening to their recordings.[13]

In his experiment to discover whether or not people could accurately locate splices in recordings, Gould noticed that 'tactile associations' produced a noticeable effect upon the judgments of those of his subjects who were instrumentalists; he would like to explore this further in subsequent experiments.[14]

Arnold Schultz describes the role of bodily movements in our thinking, and particularly in the way in which certain bodily movements cause certain mental images to 'erupt,' or (as we might say) to emerge into awareness:

> If by good chance the reader is a pianist, even of slight attainment, he can observe these finer movements to especially good advantage. If he is asked to think the appearance of a C-chord, the finger adjustments necessary to play the chord are practically certain to precede the image (he may use eye-movements alone, but this is much more difficult). If he is asked to tell the number of keys, black and white, between C and the B-flat above, he will probably play or touch all the intervening keys imaginatively, having each erupt as an image as he goes along, and counting them one by one. If he is skillful enough to think piano music away from the instrument, he will find that he 'thinks with his fingers,' that the images of the keys which produce the music appear only after he has made appropriate imaginative movements towards them. If he is skillful enough to think in terms of printed note-imagery, he will find *that he is putting his fingers on the printed characters* (a procedure not easily explained to the non-pianist) and that the appropriate notes erupt only after the appropriate movements have been stimulated in the imagination.[15]

One is tempted to dismiss all this by saying that in the imagination we are free to associate anything with anything: sights with sounds, touch with abstract concept, and so forth. An external stimulus to the eye can produce only a visual response; an external stimulus to the ear can produce only an auditory response. But this would be too simple and mechanical an account of perception, whether or not one accepts the notion that a stimulus in one sensory mode can produce a genuine response in another.

Actual visual perception and (by derivation) imagined visual perception do not spring solely from the activation of optical receptors and their associated neural circuitry. Visual perception relies partly on this, but also, as Michael Polanyi reminds us, on 'the intricate pattern of internal stimuli arising from the adjustment of the lenses in our eyeballs, from the muscles controlling the convergence of the eyeballs, from the inner ear, etc.'[16] What it *means* to be aware of something visually, whether actually or in the imagination, includes all of that, and much more, not just the contribution of the light-sensitive retinal cells and the parts of the brain with which they communicate by way of the optic nerves. The same is true also of perception in the auditory and the other sensory modes: they are inextricably bound up with actions and bodily dispositions of which we may not be explicitly aware, but without which we could not be aware of anything whatever, either in direct sensory experience or in the imagination. Etienne Gilson said that the art of the painter is the art of the whole man. But we can go further and say that the whole man is involved in *every* perceptual act. Ernst Bacon says much the same thing in these wise and moderate words:

Music seems the most nearly abstract of the arts, by very nature; but perhaps that is because we habitually think of only our five senses, forgetting a kind of sixth sense of interior feeling, the sense of tension and release, muscular movement, the visceral feeling (all connected in a way with the sense of touch, but never quite the same). So we may say that music springs as much from the *sixth sense*, as from that of hearing, but in part too from the sense of touch and sight, for we are affected not only by musical sounds, but by their analogies of experience. Who has not at some time translated the forms of trees, of clouds, of hills, inadvertently into melodies? But, being the least palpable, music begins, if not belongs, closest to abstraction.[17]

In Bacon's 'sixth sense,' if we understood it correctly, we might hope to discover how to reconcile music as *abstract* ('the music itself') and music as *appearance* (including its 'tactilia'), and hence also how to reconcile Gould the idealist and Gould the empiricist.

R.G. Collingwood's The Principles of Art *was published in 1938 and is a major classic in philosophical aesthetics. The opposition between Gould and Collingwood in the matters here under discussion is almost total, but by juxtaposing them I clarified for myself Gould's utterances regarding the relation between performers and audiences.*

PERFORMER AND AUDIENCE

Does the performer need an audience?

The sense of 'audience' used here is that of the physical presence of a number of people who have come for the purpose of listening to a performance.

Glenn Gould prefers not to have an audience at his performances, and can point out that this preference has not, in the long run, damaged his career as a performer. He believes that audiences do not go to concerts for reasons having to do with the music, so according to him there is no musically significant way in which audiences can participate. R.G. Collingwood took the opposite view: 'The position of the audience is very far from being that of a licensed eavesdropper, overhearing something that would be complete without him. Performers know it already. They know that their audience is not passively receptive of what they give it, but is determining by its reception of them how their performance is to be carried on.'[18]

Four ways in which the audience can 'determine' how the performance is carried on are mentioned by Collingwood:

1 The artist may take his audience's limitations into account when composing his work; in which case they will appear to him not as limitations on the extent to which his work will prove comprehensible, but as conditions determining the subject-matter or meaning of the work itself.[19]
2 The artist, like anyone else who comes before an audience, must put a bold face on it; he must do the best he can, and pretend that he knows it is good. But probably no artist has been so conceited as to be wholly taken in by his own pretence. Unless he sees his own proclamation, 'This is good,' echoed on the faces of his audience – 'Yes, that is good' – he wonders whether he was speaking the truth or not.[20]
3 The aesthetic activity is the activity of speaking. Speech is speech only so far as it is both spoken and heard.[21]
4 What happens at the dress rehearsal ... can be described by saying that every line, every gesture, falls dead in the empty house. The company is not acting a play at all; it is performing certain actions which will become a play when there is an audience present to act as a sounding-board.[22]

We shall look at these items in sequence.

Item 1 seems at first reading to suggest that the artist must 'play down' to his audience. But this is not what Collingwood means or, for that matter, what Gould does. Collingwood continues the quotation: 'In so far as the artist feels himself at one with his audience, this will involve no condescension on his part; it will mean that he takes it as his business to express not his own private emotions, irrespectively of whether any one else feels them or not, but the emotions he shares with his audience.'[23] Gould works from a different set of principles. For him the task of the artist is to create structures, or to reveal structures, which are intelligible in and for themselves. His is not an expression theory of art. But Gould would agree with Collingwood's view that the role of the artist is to share his specialized understanding with an audience, and that he must be capable of being understood. In items 2 and 3 Collingwood says that the artist needs to be able to see evidence that he is being understood while actually performing; Gould denies this. And far from patronizing or playing down to his solitary, thoughtful listener, Gould pays the listener a high compliment by expecting a high degree of understanding from him.

But since the listener does his listening at some other time and place than those in which Gould does his performing, there is no possibility that the listener's degree of understanding can be reflected directly. (It can be reflected indirectly in royalty payments, of course.)

Item 2 reminds us that artists, like the rest of us, suffer anxiety and uncertainty. Gould has never found relief from these afflictions in the faces of his audiences at concerts, although he is aware that some musicians do find relief there. On external evidence alone we form the impression that Glenn Gould possesses a healthy ego, that he sets a supremely high artistic standard for himself and knows when he has approached that standard and when he has not. He claims to be indifferent to criticism,[24] but such claims are always open to question. Many of his published remarks appear to be justifications of certain of his wilder flights of recording to which critics have objected.[25]

Item 3 is the one with which Gould would disagree most particularly: 'The aesthetic activity is the activity of speaking.' Although Gould frequently speaks of musical 'statements,' he does not mean the word in its linguistic sense. Somewhere he talks about J.S. Bach's 'incredibly complicated statements.' He speaks of a studio take as a particular 'statement' of the piece. This is the sense of the locution 'an architectural statement' and not the sense in which we ordinarily define a statement as a verbal affirmation or denial. Collingwood's expression theory of art maintains that all art is language, but for Gould art is primarily structure, and if art says anything it is not the sort of thing that is said in verbal languages, whether literally or figuratively. Structures are intelligible as structures, and not as communications. This, at any rate, is what I take to be Gould's position in aesthetic theory.

Item 4 compares a dress rehearsal of a stage play with a performance of the same play before an audience. In the absence of an audience as 'sounding-board,' the dress rehearsal is a dead affair. Collingwood intends that this example should cover all similar instances, including the instance of a soloist or a group of musicians rehearsing in an empty auditorium compared with those same musicians performing the same music before an audience. Gould would admit that there is a kind of excitement in the performance before an audience that is lacking in the rehearsal in an empty hall. His objection to that excitement is that it is unpredictable and uncontrollable. Since recording makes it possible to avoid much that is unpredictable and uncontrollable, he thinks recording is to be preferred. We might ask: can anything replace the excitement that is lost in recordings but is (sometimes) present in live performance? I suggest for Gould an answer which he might not want to put forward himself: yes, something can and in his case does replace that excitement, and this is Gould's own astonishing mental concentration on the music and his ecstatic disposition as a music-maker. But we will not go into his notion of 'ecstasy' here.

Collingwood refers to the recording industry as 'a recent one which has the outspokenness of an *enfant terrible.*'[26] And he says that art and technology are incompatible. Gould would say that the technological apparatus provides a link between the artist and his audience, a link effective across gaps in space and time. Collingwood says that the technological apparatus constitutes a barrier between the artist and his audience, and speaks of this barrier as an 'evil':

It is intensified by every new mechanization of art. The reason why gramophone music is so unsatisfactory to one accustomed to real music is not because the mechanical reproduction of the sounds is bad – that could be easily compensated by the hearer's imagination – but because the performers and the audience are out of touch. The audience is not collaborating, it is only overhearing. The same thing happens in the cinema, where collaboration between author and producer is intense, but as between this unit and the audience nonexistent.[27]

Does the audience need the artist?

This question is seriously intended. Gould's theory in its mildest version asserts that the distinction between artists and audiences is in process of dissolution; in its wildest version it asserts that everyone is, or must become, an artist. The performer as member of a separate and exalted caste has been made superfluous by modern technology.

We are asking the question in the familiar sense of an artist performing for an audience, both being in the same place at the same time. Gould notwithstanding, this remains a familiar way of using the words 'artist' and 'audience.' We could ask it in another way: Do we sacrifice anything of aesthetic significance when we listen to a recording, which would not be lacking if we had listened to the same performance as 'audience' in the above sense?

Setting aside the social and ritual aspects of attending a live performance (these aspects have never been shown to be of no aesthetic significance), and applying ourselves to the purely perceptual aspects of the situation, we reformulate the question once more: Does the audience need to see the artist?

Two assumptions. The first is that when we compare a live performance with a recorded performance of the same piece, each is good, or at any rate unobjectionable, in its own way. The second is that we are speaking of people who have normal or corrected vision.

Glenn Gould, of course, would say that the audience does not need to see the artist because the real musical experience is purely auditory. Let us hear from a representative of the opposite view, Ernst Bacon.

An artist should be seen as well as heard. A record may reinforce our impressions of him, but it will never establish him as a personality. A record does less for the musician than did the silent pictures for an actor. Not to be seen is an even greater handicap than not to be heard. If the actor must overact or remake his gesture to compensate for the absence of speech, so must the musician remake his performance to compensate for not being seen.

But the musical remake reduces, rather than expands his declamatory powers. Accuracy becomes his main concern. He must level off his extremes and if he does not, they will be levelled off for him by the 'dial maestro' anyway, all at the cost of a spontaneity impossible (or else rehearsed – a self-defeating thing) before that grim little gustograph, the microphone, that remorseless stenographer, who records sounds without the smile or frown of the occasion.[28]

He continues: 'The way a man puts his hand on the piano affects a musician as a brushstroke would affect a painter. The first gesture, like the first sound, reveals the player's sensibility. One knows the artist the moment he begins.'[29] Bacon is here saying that the visible gesture is an aesthetically significant aspect of a musical performance, and that it is entirely sacrificed in a recording. Without it we cannot 'know' the artist as we can when we see his gestures: of hand, of face (the smile or frown), and, we may add, of the whole body.

A middle position is possible, one which asserts that in a certain sense the visual component is present in a musical recording. Gould unconsciously hints at it where he speaks about the 'visual connection . . . the supplemental choreography of movement and gesture' of the older generation of recording musicians, who unavoidably brought concert hall mannerisms into the recording studio.

In my chapter 'Burnished Singing Tone' I reviewed the evidence concerning the relation of touch to tone quality in piano-playing, and then formulated this question: Can a pianist, by altering his manner of pressing down a key, produce two or more notes of equal loudness but different tone quality? Among scientific investigators of this problem the question is unanimously answered in the negative, and that is the answer I gave. Glenn Gould vigorously rejected it. 'Of course, that's all nonsense!' he told me on the telephone, and in his own review of my book he wrote that this was the sort of thing that could only be said by an organist (which

I was). My wife, Mary Lou, rejected it with equal vigour, saying 'Now I know why you get such lousy tone out of the piano.' Though still unrepentant a decade later, I sometimes wish I had insisted upon leaving the next passage in my text; it might have averted some of their wrath.

TOUCH AND TONE

I am far from saying that Gould plays the piano without control of tone-colour; indeed I believe that he and every other master pianist must ignore almost all that has been scientifically established concerning the problem of relation of touch to tone. It is not a centipedal problem but an apiarian one: it has been proved scientifically that bees cannot fly, given their power-to-weight ratio, their wing-loading, and the physical properties of air. But bees don't know this, so they fly anyway.

Despite the scientists, pianists know that they control tone quality by the exercise of skills at the keyboard; they are not concerned that physical measurements of the sounds will refute the notion that touch controls tone quality. There are at least two reasons.

The first is that small differences in tone quality are much more readily noticed by humans than are small differences in loudness, hence an imperceptible difference in weight or velocity of touch might have a clearly audible difference in tone as its correlative.

The second leads to a fundamental problem in aesthetic perception. It can be illustrated by an example from visual art. When we talk about warm and cold colours in a painting, we are not talking about qualities which can be measured on a thermometer; but neither are we talking nonsense or talking figuratively. These are qualities which exist *aesthetically*, as appearances only. How these appearances are related to their physical correlates is not well understood, and it is the subject of ongoing study by aestheticians. When we talk about a pianist's tonal palette we are really talking about aesthetic properties like warmth and coldness in colour, and not about patterns on an oscilloscope.

Joseph Hofmann 'maintained that the piano was a "monochromatic" instrument capable only of light and dark shading.'[30] Sometimes Gould displays a similar view of the piano, or rather, he seeks pianos and piano actions which seem to make monochromatic sounds: 'Once, to the despair of the audio engineers at Columbia, who applied the latest high-fidelity techniques to the recording of the sonatas, Gould said that he wished his rich-toned record had, instead, the constricted sound quality he hears in the low-fidelity Schnabel records made nearly thirty years ago. To this the recording director retorted, "All you have to do is listen to the record on a long-distance telephone." '31

The old acoustical recording process excluded the extreme upper and lower ranges of sound-frequencies which give characteristic tone-colour to musical sounds; in a modern recording these ranges give the illusion of the actual presence of the instrument or instruments in the room in which we hear the recording. But just as in a concert hall the personality or identity of the virtuoso intrudes upon our awareness of the music and steals from its glory, so a particularly opulent sound calls attention to its own glory; or a technological device by which the full frequency range of musical sound is transmitted to us calls attention to its noteworthiness as a technological achievement. Gould seems to think that this gets in the way of 'the music itself.' Pre-electric discs by Artur Schnabel are mentioned in the above quotation. What Gould learned from them was not how to produce tone-colour, but how to let the music 'give,' and how to 'take' from it, as Schnabel would say.

Erwin Stein wrote: 'Beauty of tone is a fine thing, but it is not the only quality to which the attribute of musical beauty applies. Musical sound is shaped, and beauty lies as much in the proportions of the shapes as in the physical phenomena of sounds.'[32]

Gould might ask about a piece of music as we might ask about a house: Of what, and how well, is it constructed? While he probably would not claim that tone-colour is merely ornamental, he is more interested in structure than in paint. Yet there is another side to this. When we talk about colour in musical sounds, or about the piano being monochromatic, we borrow from visual art. And as Clive Bell says of painting, colour is not entirely distinct from form: 'The distinction between form and colour is an unreal one; you cannot conceive a colourless line or a colourless space; neither can you conceive a formless relation of colours. In a black and white drawing the spaces are all white and all are bounded by black lines; in most oil paintings the spaces are multi-coloured and so are the boundaries; you cannot imagine a boundary line without any content, or a content without a boundary line.'[33] This does not deny that in one painting there might be a greater emphasis upon colour than upon form, and in another the reverse. (We are here using 'form' and 'structure' synonymously.) And one person looking at a painting might attend more to the colour than to the form, while another person looking at the same painting might attend more to the form than to the colour; or the same person might attend more to the one on one occasion and more to the other on another. A musician might be more aware that two flutes are playing than that they are playing a canon, or the reverse.

Gould's expression 'instrumental indifference' implies an interest more in form or structure than in colour. 'Colour' in our present sense of the word is mainly a matter of what we might call by contrast 'instrumental interest,' since colour is determined by the specific physical characteristics of musical instruments and their varieties and modifications.

But no musical instrument is truly one-coloured. Every instrument has different colours at different registers of its compass, hence any two notes of different pitch will also have a different colour. And even if it were possible to produce musical sounds monochromatically, the ear itself adds and subtracts colours in everything we hear. Furthermore it is impossible to write an absolutely unspecified or instrumentally indifferent score; we cannot legislate that a score must be read colourlessly. Horn-fifths will sound like horns no matter what instruments play them. Certain arpeggiated figures on the tonic triad in D major will sound like ceremonial trumpets whether played on piano or violin or any other instrument. Indeed to an orchestrator the horn-fifths on the page of score 'look' like horns, and the D-major arpeggios 'look' like baroque trumpets.

Those are some of the philosophical outtakes from my manuscript. The psychological ones are more extensive and varied, because I had been working towards a long chapter with the title 'Music of the Hemispheres' in which I speculate upon the details of Glenn Gould's musical aptitudes. Perhaps they can be salvaged for another such occasion.

Writings by Helmut Kallmann

The following bibliography lists chronologically Helmut Kallmann's writings from 1949 to 1987 and includes books, major articles, prefaces, short dictionary articles, bibliographical compilations, editorial contributions, reviews, concert program notes, and miscellaneous published· and unpublished material.

'Canada on the Musical Map.' *Music and Art* (Los Angeles) 3 (October 1949) 3

'Canadian Music as a Field for Research.' *Royal Conservatory of Music of Toronto, Monthly Bulletin* (March 1950) 2

'Music in Early Canada [part 1].' *The Muse* (Toronto) 1 (April 1950) 2-3. Reprinted in *Music and Art* 4 (Fall 1950) 5

'Music in Early Canada [part 2].' *The Muse* 1 (May 1950) 3-4

'Canadian Music in the Nineteen Forties.' *Music and Art* 4 (Summer 1950) 2

Catalogue of Canadian Composers. Edited. Revised and enlarged edition. Toronto: Canadian Broadcasting Corporation, [1952]. Preface by Charles Jennings. Republished, Scholarly Press, Inc., 1972

'First Opera Arrived by Stagecoach.' *Globe and Mail*, 8 July 1953 15

'Foreword.' Canadian League of Composers concert program, Eaton Auditorium, Toronto, 28 November 1953. (Brief history of all-Canadian concerts.)

'The New Grove's: Disappointment to Canada.' *Saturday Night*, 12 March 1955 25

'Music Festivals in Canada.' The annual Stratford Shakespearian Festival of Drama and Music 1955. (Souvenir program.)

'Historical Background.' *Music in Canada*. Edited by Sir Ernest MacMillan. Toronto: University of Toronto Press, 1955

'Music in Canada and the Canadian Music Council' (No. 1 of 'Two Canadian Musical Organizations'). *Canadian Library Association Bulletin* 12 (April 1956) 178-80

'A Century of Musical Periodicals in Canada.' *The Canadian Music Journal* 1 (Autumn 1956 and Winter 1957) 37-43, 25-30

'A Check-list of Canadian Periodicals in the Field of Music.' *The Canadian Music Journal* 1 (Winter 1957) 30-36

Review of *Canadian Portraits: Famous Musicians* by Louise G. McCready and *Musiciennes de chez nous* by Claude Gingras. *The Canadian Music Journal* 1 (Summer 1957) 76-8

'Der deutsche Beitrag zum Musikleben.' *Mitteilungen, Institut für Auslandsbeziehungen* (Stuttgart) 7 (July-September 1957) 200-04. (Canada issue; written 1955.)

'Audio-visual Aids to Music Education in Canada.' In *Technical Media in Music Education*. International Society for Music Education, 1957. (Mimeographed.)

Catalogue of Orchestral Music. Toronto: Canadian League of Composers, 1957. (Unsigned. Compiled by HK.)

'The Percy Scholes Collection: Nucleus for a National Music Library.' *The Canadian Music Journal* 2 (Spring 1958) 43-5

'From the Archives.' *The Canadian Music Journal* 2 (Summer 1958) 45-52. (Documents related to music in early British Columbia; 'selection and comments' by HK.)

Review of *Past and Present: A Canadian Musician's Reminiscences* by Louise McDowell. *The Canadian Music Journal* 2 (Summer 1958) 81, 83

'Kanada.' In *Die Musik in Geschichte und Gegenwart*. Vol. 7. Kassel and Basel: Bärenreiter Verlag, 1958

'Heintzman, Theodore August.' In *Encyclopedia Canadiana*. Vol. 5. Ottawa: Canadiana Co., 1958

'Music Composition.' In *Encyclopedia Canadiana*. Vol. 7. Ottawa: Canadiana Co., 1958. Rev. ed Toronto: Grolier, 1966 and 1975

'Musical Instruments, Making of.' In *Encyclopedia Canadiana*. Vol. 7. Ottawa: Canadiana Co., 1958. Rev. ed. Toronto: Grolier, 1966. (Co-author with John Beckwith.)

'From the Archives: Organs and Organ Players in Canada.' *The Canadian Music Journal* 3 (Spring 1959) 41-7

Review of Johann Sebastian Bach's *Concerto in F Minor* and Ludwig van Beethoven's *Concerto in C Major*, opus 15, by Glenn Gould. *The Canadian Music Journal* 3 (Summer 1959) 51-3

A History of Music in Canada 1534-1914. Toronto: University of Toronto Press, 1960. Foreword by Sir Ernest MacMillan. (Reprinted 1969 with minor corrections and new cover design in hard cover and paperback editions. Reprinted 1978 in Scholarly Reprint Series.)

Review of Dmitri Shostakovich's *Symphonies Nos. 6 and 11* and works by various other Soviet composers. *The Canadian Music Journal* 6 (Autumn 1961) 40-5.

A Bio-Bibliographical Finding List of Canadian Musicians and Those Who Have Contributed to Music in Canada. Ottawa: Canadian Music Library Association (1961).

Compiled by Melva J. Dwyer (chairman), Lucien Brochu, and Helmut Kallmann ('who was responsible for beginning this project,' Preface). Second edition edited by Kathleen M. Toomey and Stephen C. Willis as *Musicians in Canada: a Bio-Bibliographical Finding List/Musiciens au Canada: Index bio-bibliographique*. Ottawa: Canadian Association of Music Libraries, 1981. (Based on extensive corrections and additions by HK.)

'From the Archives: The Montreal Gazette on Music from 1786 to 1797.' *The Canadian Music Journal* 6 (Spring 1962) 3-11

'RISM Report about Canada.' *Fontes Artis Musicae* 9 (January-June 1962) 21-2

'The Siege of Quebec' (Kotzwara-de Krifft). Program note, Ten Centuries Concerts, 8 December 1962. (Mimeographed.)

'Papineau-Couture, Jean.' 'Pentland, Barbara.' In *Die Musik in Geschichte und Gegenwart*. Vol. 10. Kassel and Basel: Bärenreiter Verlag, 1962

'Music.' In *1962 Britannica Book of the Year/The Year in Canada*. Chicago, Toronto, London, Geneva: Encyclopaedia Britannica, Inc., 1962

'Music.' In *1963 Britannica Book of the Year/The Year in Canada*. Chicago, Toronto, London, Geneva, Sydney: Encyclopaedia Britannica, Inc., 1963

'Joseph Quesnel's Colas et Colinette.' Program note, Ten Centuries Concerts, 6 October 1963. (Mimeographed.)

Directory of Degree Graduates. Toronto: University of Toronto Music Alumni Association, 2 March 1964. Preface by Arnold Walter

'History of Opera in Canada.' *Opera Canada* 5 (September 1964) 10-12, 78

'Music in Canada.' *CBC Times* 17 (15-21 May 1965) 11-12

'Joseph Quesnel, Pioneer Canadian Composer/Joseph Quesnel: ancêtre des compositeurs canadiens.' *The Canadian Composer* 3 (October 1965) 22-3, 36, 44

'Heinz Unger†.' *Zeitschrift für Kulturaustausch* (Stuttgart) 15 (1965) 291

Canadian-built 19th Century Musical Instruments, a Check List. 1965. (Mimeographed.)

– second edition, revised. Edmonton: Canadian Music Library Association, 1966

'First Fifteen Years of Canadian League of Composers/La Ligue canadienne des compositeurs, quinze ans d'activité.' *The Canadian Composer* 7 (March 1966) 18-19, 36-7, 45

'The Acceptance of "O Canada"/L'adoption d' "O Canada."' *The Canadian Composer* 8 (April 1966) 18-19, 38-9, 40-1

'Music Library Association Digs up Our Musical Past/L'Association des bibliothèques musicales explore notre passé.' *The Canadian Composer* 11 (October 1966) 18-19, 28, 46

'Vogt, Augustus Stephen.' In *Die Musik in Geschichte und Gegenwart*. Vol. 13. Kassel and Basel: Bärenreiter Verlag, 1966

'Dangé, François.' 'Merlac, André-Louis de.' In *Dictionary of Canadian Biography*. Vol. 1. Toronto: University of Toronto Press, 1966

'Toronto's Music – Before 1867.' Ten Centuries Concerts, 8 January 1967. (Mimeographed.)

'Composition in Canada: 1867-1967.' *The Telegram*, Toronto, 28 January 1967. (Special advertising section, Women's Committee, Toronto Symphony Orchestra Association.)

'Music in Canada, 1867, A Long Glance Backward/Musique au Canada, 1867, un long regard vers le passé.' *Musicanada* 3 (July 1967/juillet-août 1967) 5-6

Musical Canadiana: A Subject Index. Preliminary edition compiled by a committee of the Canadian Music Library Association. Introduction signed by Helmut Kallmann, Laura Murray, and Grace Pincoe. Ottawa, 1967

Calixa Lavallée, *The Widow.* CBC International Service – RCA Victor Centennial Series Record 231, 1967. (Record jacket notes.) Reissued 1986, Radio Canada International 231

Light Canadian Orchestral Classics/Les Classiques de la Musique d'Orchestre au Canada. CBC Winnipeg Orchestra. CBC International Service – Capitol Records (Canada) ST 6261, 1967. (Record jacket notes.)

Joseph Quesnel, *Colas et Colinette.* CBC International Service 234 – Select Records 24.160, 1968. (Record jacket notes.) Reissued 1986, Radio Canada International 234.

'Weinzweig, John.' 'Willan, Healey.' In *Die Musik in Geschichte und Gegenwart.* Vol. 14. Kassel and Basel: Bärenreiter Verlag, 1968

'Notes From the Canadian Music Library Association.' [US] Music Library Association *Notes* 25 (December 1968)

'The CBC Toronto Music Library.' *CMLA Newsletter* (December 1968).

'Canada.' In *Harvard Dictionary of Music.* Rev. ed. Cambridge: Harvard University Press, 1969

'Martin, Charles Amador.' In *Dictionary of Canadian Biography.* Vol. 2. Toronto: University of Toronto Press, 1969

'Composers in a New Land; Musical Composition in Canada from 1867/Compositeurs d'un monde nouveau; la création musicale au Canada, depuis 1867.' *Musicanada* 20 (June 1969) 5-9, 14-16

Review of *Historical Sets, Collected Editions, and Monuments of Music* compiled by Anna Harriet Heyer. *Canadian Library Journal* 26 (November-December 1969) 486

'Music.' *Canadian Annual Review 1968.* Toronto: University of Toronto Press, 1969

'Historical background.' In *Aspects of Music in Canada.* Edited by Arnold Walter. Toronto: University of Toronto Press, 1969. (Revision of chapter written for *Music in Canada*, 1955.)

'Aperçu historique.' 'Bibliographie.' In *Aspects de la musique au Canada.* Edited by Maryvonne Kendergi and Gilles Potvin. Montreal: Centre de Psychologie et de Pédagogie, 1970. (French version of 'Historical background,' 1969.)

'James Paton Clarke – Canada's First Mus. Bac.' *The Canada Music Book* 1 (Spring-Summer 1970) 41-53

'Music.' *Canadian Annual Review 1969*. Toronto: University of Toronto Press, 1970

'Music, An Introduction.' *Rare and Unusual Canadiana*. Montreal: Lawrence Lande Foundation, no. 6, 1971

'Music Division/Division de la musique.' *National Library News* 3 (January-March 1971) 3-7. (Unsigned.)

'Canadian Music Council. 7th Annual Conference.' *CMLA Newsletter* (May 1971)

'Canada's Musical Heritage a Concern of the National Library/La Bibliothèque nationale du Canada et l'héritage musical canadien.' *The Music Scene/La Scène musicale* (May-June 1971) 4, 21

'Canadian League of Composers, 20 Years, 1951-1971, Chronology/La Ligue Canadienne de Compositeurs, 20 Ans, 1951-1971, Chronologie.' *The Canada Music Book* 2 (Spring-Summer 1971) 81-90

'Beethoven and Canada, A Miscellany.' *The Canada Music Book* 2 (Spring-Summer 1971) 107-17

'Music.' *Canadian Annual Review 1970*. Toronto: University of Toronto Press, 1971

'Preface/Préface.' *Healey Willan Catalogue*. Edited by Giles Bryant. Ottawa: National Library of Canada, 1972

'Toward a Bibliography of Canadian Folk Music.' *Ethnomusicology* 16 (September 1972) 499-503

'Barbeau, Marius.' 'Beckwith, John.' 'Bernardi, Mario.' 'Kallmann, Helmut.' 'von Kunits, Luigi.' In *Riemann Musik Lexikon*. Ergänzungsband, Personenteil. Vol. 1. Mainz: B. Schott's Söhne, 1972. (All entries unsigned.)

'Brauneis, Jean-Chrysostome (junior).' 'Clarke, James Paton.' 'Dessane, Marie-Hippolyte-Antoine.' 'Humphreys, James Dodsley.' In *Dictionary of Canadian Biography*. Vol. 10. Toronto: University of Toronto Press, 1972

'Who, What and Where in Canadian Music/Du nouveau sur la musique canadienne.' *National Library News* 5 (March-June 1973) 4-7

'Music and Criticism in Canada, A Preface/Musique et critique au Canada, une préface.' *The Canada Music Book* 7 (Autumn-Winter 1973) 69-73

'Albani, Emma.' 'Brott, Alexander.' 'Champagne, Claude.' In *Die Musik in Geschichte und Gegenwart*. Vol. 15. Kassel and Basel: Bärenreiter Verlag, 1973

'Weinzweig, John.' In *Dictionary of Contemporary Music*. Edited by John Vinton. New York: E.P. Dutton, 1974

'Coron, Charles-François.' In *Dictionary of Canadian Biography*. Vol. 3. Toronto: University of Toronto Press, 1974

'Colas et Colinette. Introduction.' *Colas et Colinette*, by Joseph Quesnel. Reconstitution by Godfrey Ridout. Vocal score. Toronto: Gordon V. Thompson, 1974. (English and French.)

'Canada.' In *Guide for Dating Early Published Music*. Chapter 17. Compiled by D.W. Krummel. International Association of Music Libraries. Kassel and Basel: Bärenreiter, 1974

'Heinz Unger Scores Donated to the National Library/Don des partitions de Heinz Unger à la Bibliothèque nationale.' *National Library News* 7 (January-February 1975) 10-12. (Unsigned.)

'The Music Division of the National Library: The First Five Years.' *The Canada Music Book* 10 (Spring-Summer 1975) 95-100. Reprinted in *Musikbibliothek Aktuell* no. 2-3 (1976) 67-73

'Dimitri Shostakovich.' *The Canada Music Book* 11/12 (Autumn-Winter 1975) 81

'The German Contribution to Music in Canada.' *German-Canadian Yearbook* 2 (1975) 152-66. Revision and translation by the author of 'Der deutsche Beitrag zum Musikleben,' 1957

'Lavallée, Calixa.' 'Mercure, Pierre.' 'Molt, Theodore.' 'Parlow, Kathleen.' 'Quesnel, Joseph.' 'Somers, Harry.' 'Willan, Healey' (supplement to article). In *Riemann Musik Lexikon*, Ergänzungsband, Personenteil. Vol. 2. Mainz: B. Schott's Söhne, 1975. (All entries unsigned.)

'Canadian Music Publishing.' *Papers of the Bibliographical Society of Canada* 13 (1975) 40-8

'Coates, Richard.' 'Nordheimer, Abraham.' 'Perrault, Joseph-Julien.' 'Wugk, Charles-Désiré-Joseph (Charles Sabatier).' In *Dictionary of Canadian Biography*. Vol. 9. Toronto: University of Toronto Press, 1976

'A National Music Collection/Une collection musicale très accessible.' *Musicanada* 30 (November 1976) 7, 12

'Music.' *Ontario Library Review* 60 (December 1976) 231-2. (Part of reading list entitled 'Canadian Materials on the Arts.')

'Foreword/Avant-propos.' *Canadian Music: A Selected Checklist 1950-73/La musique canadienne: une liste sélective 1950-73*. Edited by Lynne Jarman. Toronto: University of Toronto Press, 1976

'Subject Bibliography – Music.' *National Conference on the State of Canadian Bibliography. Proceedings.* Ottawa: National Library of Canada, 1977

'The National Library; New Acquisitions/Bibliothèque nationale; acquisitions récentes.' *Musicanada* 37 (November 1978) 11

'Beethoven and Canada: A Miscellany.' *German-Canadian Yearbook* 4 (1978) 286-94. Reprinted with slight changes from *The Canada Music Book* 2. (See above, 1971.)

'Eckhardt-Gramatté, Sophie-Carmen.' 'Fricker, Herbert Austin.' 'Hambourg, Michael, Mark, Jan, Boris, Clement, Klemi.' 'Harriss, Charles Albert Edwin.' 'Kallmann, Helmut.' 'MacMillan, (Sir) Ernest Alexander Campbell.' 'Morawetz, Oskar.' 'Pelletier, Wilfrid.' 'Somers, Harry.' 'Walter, Arnold.' In *Die Musik in Geschichte und Gegenwart*. Vol. 16. Kassel and Basel: Bärenreiter Verlag, 1979

'Le Fonds Claude Champagne à la bibliothèque nationale du Canada.' *Com-*

positeurs au Québec, 11, Claude Champagne. Montréal: Centre de Musique Canadienne, Montréal, 1979

'The Mysteries of "O Canada"/Les mystères d' "O Canada."' *Musicanada* 43 (Summer 1980). Reprinted in abridged version as 'Mystery surrounds first edition of "O Canada."' *The Recorder* 23 (Fall 1980) 34-5

'Clarke, James Paton.' 'Codman, Stephen.' 'Fricker, Herbert Austin.' 'Harriss, Charles Albert Edwin.' 'Jehin-Prume, Frantz.' 'Lavallée, Calixa.' 'Molt, Theodore Frederic.' 'Quesnel, Joseph.' 'Vogt, Augustus Stephen.' In *The New Grove Dictionary of Music and Musicians.* London: Macmillan, 1980

'Historical Setting.' *Music Resources in Canadian Collections.* Vol. 7, chapter 2. *Research Collections in Canadian Libraries.* Ottawa: National Library of Canada, 1980. (Unsigned.)

'The Music Division/Division de la musique.' *National Library News* 13 (March 1981) 4-5 (Unsigned.)

Review of *Canadian Music of the Twentieth Century* by George A. Proctor. *Canadian Association of Music Libraries Newsletter* 10 (April 1981) 8-13

Encyclopedia of Music in Canada. Edited by Helmut Kallmann, Gilles Potvin, and Kenneth Winters. Toronto: University of Toronto Press, 1981. (See also *Encyclopédie de la musique au Canada.*)

[The following is a list of Helmut Kallmann's extensive contributions to the *Encyclopedia of Music in Canada.* Some unsigned articles and those in which Kallmann supplied supplementary contributions are not included. EDS.]

'Introduction' (with Potvin and Winters). 'The Anglo-Canadian Music Company.' 'Archives.' 'Art, Visual' (supplemented by Potvin and Patricia Wardrop). 'Art Song' (supplemented by Potvin). 'Edwin Ashdown Ltd.' 'Bands' (with Jack Kopstein and Wardrop). 'Barkin, Leo.' 'Barrel Organs.' 'Battle Music.' 'Bayley, John.' 'Bibliography.' 'W.H. Billing.' 'Blain de St-Aubin, Emmanuel' (with Denise Ménard). 'The Blue and White.' 'Bohrer, family.' 'Brass' (historical section). 'Brauneis [Family].' 'William Briggs.' 'Canada in European and US Music' (with Potvin). '*Le Canada musical.*' '*The Canada Music Book/Les Cahiers canadiens de musique.*' 'Canadian Academy of Music' (with Wardrop). 'Canadian Association of Music Libraries/Association canadienne des bibliothèques musicales' (unsigned). 'Canadian Folk Music Society/Société canadienne de musique folklorique.' 'The Canadian League of Composers/La Ligue canadienne de compositeurs.' 'Canadian Music Council/Conseil canadien de la musique.' '*The Canadian Music Journal*' (unsigned). 'Canadian Music Library Association/Association canadienne des bibliothèques musicales' (unsigned). '*Canadian Music Trades Journal.*' 'Canadian Society of Musicians.' 'CBC' (unsigned). 'The Children of Peace.' 'Choral Singing.' 'Clarke, James P. and Hugh A.' 'Claxton, Thomas.' 'Coates, Richard.' 'College Songs' (with Nancy McGregor). 'Concert Halls and Opera Houses' (supplemented by Potvin and Wardrop). 'Concerts' (with Thomas C. Brown and David Sale). 'Conductors and Conducting' (with Potvin and Winters). 'Confederation and Music.' 'Copyright' (section 5, Historical Notes; unsigned). 'Coron, Charles-François.' 'Coronations.' 'Crozier, St George B.' 'Dancing, Pre-Confederation.' 'C.C. De Zouche.' 'Dinner Horn.' 'Discography' (supplemented by Mark Miller). 'Doyle, Joseph Nevin' (unsigned). 'W.R. Draper Co Ltd' (supplemented by Miller and Wardrop). 'Dulongpré, Louis.' 'Du Mesnil, Pierre' (unsigned). 'Ecuyer, Charles.' 'Education, Professional' (section 1, 1600-1950). 'Eglauch, Leonard.' 'Emigration.' 'England' (with Winters). 'Ethnomusicology' (draft for article by Beverley A. Cavanagh). 'Fields, Harry.' 'First Symposium of Canadian Contemporary Music.' 'Fisher, Arthur Elwell.' 'Fontaine, L.J. Oscar.' 'Fox, George.' 'France' (supplementing article by Potvin). 'Gilkison, Margaret.' 'Girard, Jean' (unsigned). 'Glackemeyer [Family]' (with Cécile Huot). 'Gledhill, Edwin.' 'Godfrey, Henry Herbert.' 'Graham, George F.' 'Griebel, Ferdinand.' 'Hayward, Richard.' 'Hecht, Julius or Jules.' 'Heintzman & Co Ltd' (with Wardrop). 'Hesselberg, Edouard.' 'Hirvy, Michel.' 'History of Canada in Music' (supplemented by Potvin). 'W.H. Hodgins & Co.' 'Hughes, Arthur Wellesley.' 'Humphreys, James Dodsley.' 'Hutton, Charles' (unsigned). 'Imrie & Graham.' 'Indians' (draft of introduction, unsigned). 'Instrument Collections' (supplemented by Wardrop, McGregor). 'Irving's Canadian Series of Five Cent Music.' '"The Island Hymn."' 'Jenkins, Annie.' 'Jingles' (with Thomas C. Brown). 'Johnstone, John Francis' (with Wardrop). 'Jolliet, Louis' (with Potvin). 'Jordan, Henri K.' 'Jourdain dit Labrosse, Paul' (supplemented by Potvin). 'Kalejs, Felicita.' Kalejs, Janis.' 'Kallmann, Helmut' (unsigned). 'Keillor, Elaine.' 'Key, Harold Eustace.' 'Koldofsky, Adolph.' 'Koldofsky, Gwendolyn.' 'Lagacé, Pierre.' 'Lauder, W. Waugh.' 'Lemon, Laura.' 'Leupold, Ulrich.' 'Libraries.' 'Macdonald, Jean' (unsigned). 'Maffré, Joseph.' 'Manuscript Books' (supplementing Stephen Willis's article). 'Maple Leaf.' '"The Maple Leaf For Ever."' 'March "de Normandie."' 'Marcus, Erwin.' 'Mother Marie de St-Joseph.' 'Martens, Theodor(e).' 'Martin, Charles-Amador.' 'Massey Commission.' 'Mead, George, James, and John.' 'Mechtler, Guillaume.' 'Medley, John.' 'Ménard, René.' 'Metropolitan Opera' (with Potvin and Winters). 'Mills, Frederick.' 'Missionaries in the 17th Century.' 'Molt, Theodore Frederic.' 'Moogk, Edward B.' (with Clifford Ford). 'Moussart, François du.' 'Musgrave.' *Musical Canada.* 'Musicology.' *The Music Scene/La Scène Musicale* (with Florence Hayes). '"My Ain Folk"' (unsigned). 'Niagara Falls in Music.' 'Nordheimer Family.' 'A&S Nordheimer Co.' *Opera Canada.* 'Opera Performance' (with James B. McPherson, supplemented by Potvin). 'Organ Playing and Teaching' (section 1). 'J.L. Orme & Sons' (supplemented by Florence Hayes). 'Parkhurst, Edwin.' 'Patriotic Songs.' 'Periodicals.' 'Publishing.' 'Quesnel, Joseph.' 'Read, Angelo.' 'Recorded Sound' (with Edward B. Moogk).' 'Reed, William.' 'Robb, Morse.' 'Sabatier, Charles Wugk.' 'Sakos,

Kenneth.' 'Schallehn, Henry.' 'Schott, Adam.' 'Schubert Choir.' 'Sefton, Henry Francis.' 'Semple, Arthur.' 'Sewell, Jonathan' (with Margaret Holden). 'Singing Schools.' 'Sippi, George B.' 'Smith, Gustave.' '"Sol canadien, terre chérie."' 'H.H. Sparks Music Co.' 'Strange Co.' 'I. Suckling & Sons.' 'Theory Textbooks' (with Ménard, supplemented by Potvin and Wardrop). 'Thompson, Gordon V.' 'Gordon V. Thompson Ltd' (with Marlene Wehrle). 'Toronto String Quartette' (with Wardrop). 'Transportation' (with Hayes). 'Unger, Heinz.' 'Wars, Rebellions, and Uprisings' (sections 1-4, 6-7, and, with Edward B. Moogk, 9). 'Western Music Company, Ltd.' 'Whaley, Royce & Co Ltd.' 'Whyte, John M.' 'Willan, Gladys.' 'Women's Musical Clubs.' 'Woodwinds, Playing and Teaching' (section 1). 'Zealley, Alfred E.'

'Panneton, Charles-Marie.' In *Dictionary of Canadian Biography*. Vol. 11. Toronto: University of Toronto Press, 1982

'Preface/Préface.' *Alexis Contant Catalogue*. Edited by Stephen C. Willis. Ottawa: National Library of Canada, 1982

Encyclopédie de la musique au Canada. Edited by Helmut Kallmann, Gilles Potvin, and Kenneth Winters. Montreal: Fides, 1983

'Periodicals Selected For Priority Indexing. II, North America; Canada.' *Periodica Musica* 1 (Spring 1983) 4

'The German Contribution to Music in Canada – A Bibliography.' *German-Canadian Yearbook* 7 (1983) 228-33

Directory of Music Research Libraries, Volume 1: Canada and the United States. Second rev. ed. General editor, Rita Benton. Directory for Canada compiled by Marian Kahn and Helmut Kallmann. Kassel and Basel: Bärenreiter, 1983. (Includes 'Introduction – Canada,' signed by HK.)

'Major Music Acquisition by the National Library/Acquisition d'une importante collection musicale par la bibliothèque nationale.' *National Library News* 16 (June 1984) 1-2. (Sir Ernest MacMillan papers; unsigned.)

'Music Division Acquires Quentin Maclean Library and Papers/Acquisition des documents et de la bibliothèque de Quentin Maclean par la division de la musique.' *National Library News* 16 (September-October 1984) 7. (Unsigned.)

'The Canadian League of Composers in the 1950s: The Heroic Years.' *Célébrations*. Toronto: Canadian Music Centre, 1984. (Also in *Studies in Music from the University of Western Ontario* 9 (1984) 37-54.)

'Music Materials Fund Yields First Acquisition/Première acquisition fait grâce au fonds pour documents musicaux.' *National Library News* 17 (February 1985) 6, 8. (On Edward B. Moogk Memorial Fund and Moogk bequest; unsigned.)

'Music in Upper Canada.' *The Shaping of Ontario*. Belleville: Mika Publishing Company, 1985

'Canadian League of Composers.' 'Music History.' 'Robb, Morse.' In *The Canadian Encyclopedia*. Edmonton: Hurtig Publishers, 1985

'Griebel, Ferdinand.' In *Dictionary of Canadian Biography*. Vol. 8. Toronto: University of Toronto Press, 1985

'Istvan Anhalt Papers/Documents d'Istvan Anhalt.' *National Library News* 18 (February 1986) 7. (Unsigned.)

Review of *Student's Dictionary of Music* by Wayne Gilpin. *Canadian Association of Music Libraries Newsletter* 15 (March 1986) 10-12

'Canada and the Music of the Grand Siècle/Le Canada et la musique du Grand Siècle.' *Musicanada* 58 (December 1986) 3-4

'Lavallée, Calixa.' In *The New Grove Dictionary of American Music*. Vol. 3. New York: Grove's Dictionaries of Music, Inc., 1986

'Music Librarianship.' *Careers in Music*. Oakville: Frederick Harris Music Co., 1986

'Le Répertoire international de la presse musicale (RIPM): II Les sources canadiennes et le RIPM.' *Les Cahiers de l'ARMuQ* 8 (May 1987) 20-21

'Frédéric Glackemeyer: des données nouvelles sur sa vie et son style musical.' *Les Cahiers de l'ARMuQ* 8 (May 1987) 86-92

'Brauneis, John Chrisostomus.' 'Mechtler, Guillaume.' In *Dictionary of Canadian Biography*. Vol. 6. Toronto: University of Toronto Press, 1987

'Remembering the Conservatory.' *Performing Arts in Canada* 24:1 (June 1987) 9-11

Notes

CAVANAGH The Transmission of Algonkian Indian Hymns

Field work for this project was supported through the Research Grants Programme of the Social Sciences and Humanities Research Council of Canada.
1 Walter J. Ong, *Orality and Literacy, the Technologizing of the Word* (London and New York: Methuen, 1982) 11
2 Ibid. 73
3 This assumption is implicit in: Gertrude Kurath, 'Catholic Hymns of Michigan Indians,' *Anthropological Quarterly* 30 (1957) 31-44; Willard Rhodes, 'The Christian Hymnology of the North American Indians,' in Anthony F.C. Wallace, ed., *Men and Cultures* (Philadelphia: University of Pennsylvania Press, 1960) 324-31; Vincent J. Higginson, *Hymnody in the American Indian Missions*, Papers of the Hymn Society, 18 (New York: Hymn Society of America, 1954).
4 John W. Grant, *Moon of Wintertime* (Toronto: University of Toronto Press, 1985)
5 See Lynn Whidden, 'Les hymnes, une anomalie parmi les chants traditionnels des Cris du Nord,' *Recherches amérindiennes au Québec* 15(4) (1985) 29-36; Richard Preston, 'Transformations musicales et culturelles chez les Cris de l'Est,' *Recherches amérindiennes au Québec* 15(4) (1985) 19-28.
6 For repertoire selection and performance practice, see David E. Draper, 'Abba Isht Tuluwa: The Christian Hymns of the Mississippi Choctaws,' *American Indian Culture and Research Journal* 6(1) (1982) 43-61; for performance practices studied by von Rosen, Cronk, and Cavanagh in Eastern Canada, see Beverley A. Cavanagh, 'The Performance of Hymns in Eastern Woodlands Indian Communities,' in *Sing Out the Glad News* (Toronto: Institute for Canadian Music, 1987).
7 The Algonkian language family embraces the Naskapi-Montagnais, Cree, Ojibway, and several other languages on one hand, and a second group with

Micmacs, Abenaki, Penobscot, and so on on the other. Although certain vocabulary ('nikamun' or 'nakamun', the word for song, for example) is pan-Algonkian, the dialect differences, even between two Montagnais communities, can sometimes be substantial.

8 *Mingan, qui es-tu?* (Mingan: Conseil de bande, 1983) 30
9 See Frank Galway, *A Pilgrimage of Faith* (St John's: Harry Cuff, 1983) for anecdotes of a priest who disguised himself as a fisherman to avoid capture.
10 W.G. Gosling, *Labrador: Its Discovery, Exploration, and Development* (London: Alston Rivers, 1910) 297
11 Nigel Markham, 'Monsignor Edward O'Brien, Missionary to the Innu,' *Them Days* 10 (1985) 4-28
12 'In the country' is the phrase used in Labrador to refer to the forest and lake areas away from the villages.
13 Adrian Tanner, *Bringing Home Animals: Religious Ideology and Mode of Production of the Mistassini Cree Hunters* (St John's: Memorial University of Newfoundland, Institute of Social and Economic Research, 1979) 130
14 In Mingan the lead singer is male, although most of the other people who are recognized as good hymn singers are female.
15 The Algonkian language family includes some dialects in which 'l' is phonemic and others in which 'n' is the phonemic equivalent. Hence 'miluetam' in the former is pronounced 'minuetam' in the latter.
16 Author's collection, Lab 3
17 The word for hymn, 'aiamieu nikuman' is a modification of the word for dream song, 'nikamun.' Other genres of song do not have connotations of power; lullabies or 'bebe ataushu,' for example, are never referred to as 'nikumana.'
18 Clifford Geertz, *The Interpretation of Cultures* (New York: Basic Books, 1973) 93-5
19 [Father Joseph Brachte, OMI] *Saulteux Hymnal: Anicinapemowining* Anamie-Nakamonan (Saint-Boniface, Manitoba: Oblate Fathers, 1942)
20 [Jules Leguerrier, OMI] *Cree Hymnal* (Moosonee: Diocese of Moosonee, 1971)
21 2nd ed. (Le Pas, 1983, mimeographed). I am indebted to Elaine Keillor for acquiring and giving me a copy of this book.
22 Hymns are organized initially according to the liturgical year, but later sections are arranged according to themes such as God, salvation, the sacraments, hymns to Mary and the saints, subjects relating to morality, and finally 'class' songs.
23 Claude Rozier, *Histoire de dix cantiques* (Paris: Editions Fleurus, 1966). See the chapter on 'Reviens pécheur' 17-53.
24 Amédée Gastoué, *La Cantique populaire en France* (Lyon: Janin, 1924)
25 See Laverlochère (1854).
26 This is illustrated in Cavanagh, 'The Performance of Hymns.'

BEAUDRY Catalogue des imprimés musicaux

1 Helmut Kallmann, *A History of Music in Canada 1534-1914* (Toronto: University of Toronto Press, 1960) 61
2 *Répertoire international des sources musicales*, série A/I: *Einzeldrucke vor 1800* (Kassel: Bärenreiter, 1971-81), 9 vol. Aussi: *Répertoire international des sources musicales*, série B6: *Ecrits imprimés concernant la musique* (Munich: Henle, 1971) 2 vol.
3 Lucien Brochu, 'Catalogue des imprimés et manuscrits de musique d'avant 1800 conservés à la bibliothèque de l'Université Laval' (Québec: Université Laval, 1955), 19p., inédit
4 Anthony van Hoboken, *Joseph Haydn: Thematischbibliographisches Werkverzeichnis* (Mainz: Schott, 1957), vol. 1
5 Rita Benton, *Ignace Pleyel: A Thematic Catalogue of His Compositions* (New York: Pendragon, 1977)

SCHWANDT *Musique spirituelle*

I am grateful to Sr Claire Gagnon, AMJ, archivist of the Hôtel-Dieu de Québec, for permission to publish material from the archives. This study was supported by a grant from the Social Sciences and Humanities Research Council of Canada.

1 *Les Annales de l'Hôtel-Dieu de Québec: 1639-1716*, composées par les Révérendes Mères Jeanne-Françoise Juchereau de Saint-Ignace et Marie-Andrée Duplessis de Sainte-Hélène, anciennes Religieuses de ce Monastère, ed. Dom Albert Jamet (Québec, 1939).
2 For a thematic catalogue of all the extant music in manuscript at the Hôtel-Dieu and at the Convent of the Ursulines, see Erich Schwandt, 'The motet in New France: some 17th- and 18th-century manuscripts in Québec,' *Fontes Artis Musicae* 28(3) (1981) 194-219. I have edited a representative selection of motets in *The Motet in New France* (Victoria: Éditions Jeu, 1981).
3 For an annotated and illustrated catalogue of items connected with the history of music in New France, see Elisabeth Gallat-Morin and Antoine Bouchard, eds, *Témoins de la vie musicale en Nouvelle-France* (Québec: Archives Nationales du Québec, 1981).
4 For an extended biographical notice of Mère de Sainte-Hélène, see *Les Annales* xxxiii-xxxvii.
5 The little manuscript, written on paper and bound in paste-board covers, has the call number Bn-1 MS 1. Its pages measure 16 × 10 cm, and the decorated covers 16.6 × 11 cm. The watermarks of the paper are too fragmentary to be of any use. The complete text is presented at the end of this article. The orthogra-

phy is that of the original, but some punctuation has been added for clarity.
6 Charles Hamm, *Music in the New World* (New York: Norton, 1983) 46
7 For the complete text of Tufts's introduction, see Irving Lowens, *Music and Musicians in Early America* (New York: Norton, 1964) appendix A.
8 Ibid., chapter 3

POIRIER Deux oeuvres de Jean-Jacques Rousseau

1 La thèse de doctorat de Marcel Trudel, 'L'influence de Voltaire sur les écrivains français du Canada, de 1760 à 1900' (Québec: Université Laval, 1945), demeure l'ouvrage fondamental en la matière.
2 Voir Jacques Mounier, *La Fortune des écrits de Jean-Jacques Rousseau dans les pays de langue allemande de 1782 à 1813* (Paris: Presses universitaires de France, 1980).
3 Baudouin Burger, *L'Activité théâtrale au Québec (1765-1825)* (Montréal: Les Editions Parti pris, 1974) 89
4 Daniel Heartz, 'Rousseau' dans Stanley Sadie, édit., *The New Grove Dictionary of Music and Musicians* (Londres: MacMillan, 1980) vol. 16, 271
5 Les nombreuses représentations en sol américain, entre 1790 et 1800, revêtent un intérêt particulier dans le cadre de cet article. Voir Paul Merrill Spurlin, *Rousseau in America, 1760-1809* (Alabama: University of Alabama Press, 1969) 83-4, 135.
6 Helmut Kallmann, dans l'introduction à l'enregistrement: disque Select CC 15 001 et Service international de Radio-Canada 234, Montréal, 1968. Parmi les auteurs à avoir repris l'idée mentionnons Willy Amtmann, *La Musique au Québec, 1600-1875* (Montréal: Les Editions de l'homme, 1976) 324, 331; Denise Ménard et Annick Poussart, 'Colas et Colinette ou le Bailli dupé,' dans Helmut Kallmann et al. (dir), l'*Encyclopédie de la Musique au Canada* (EMC) (Montréal: Fides, 1983).
7 EMC 201
8 Livret de *Colas et Colinette* (Québec: Chez John Neilson, 1808) 8. Comme pour la citation suivante provenant de *La Gazette de Québec*, le souligné est de nous.
9 Rousseau ne fait lui-même que reprendre à son compte une expression qui remonte aux troubadours dans la littérature française, comme le prouve la délicieuse pastourelle de Marcabru (première moitié du XIIe siècle), 'L'autrier jost' una sebissa.'
10 *La Gazette de Québec*, no 2077, 31 janvier 1805, 4. Ecrite vers 1789, la pièce de Quesnel fut représentée d'abord à Montréal, le 17 janvier 1790 (voir EMC 201). Cette dernière date marque le début de la période sur laquelle porte notre étude.
11 Heartz, 'Rousseau.' Kallmann écrit dans le même sens: 'Des pages comme la

deuxième ariette du Bailli et celle de Colas ont une agréable saveur folklorique ... ' Voir l'introduction à l'enregistrement.

12 Voir le livre 8 des *Confessions* et le 2e Dialogue de *Rousseau juge de Jean-Jacques*, note 131.

13 Pour une édition moderne de 'Allons danser' de Rousseau, avec les parties instrumentales, voir Archibald T. Davison et Willi Apel, dir, *Historical Anthology of Music: Baroque, Rococo, and Pre-Classical Music* (Cambridge, Mass.: Harvard University Press, 1950) no 291, 235; et le no 14 de la partition publiée dans la collection Kalmus Vocal Scores (New York: Edwin F. Kalmus, s.d.).

14 L'hypothèse que Daulé soit redevable à Quesnel de l'arrangement de la musique de 'Allons danser' demeure séduisante pour deux raisons. Dans l'avertissement placé en tête du *Nouveau Recueil de cantiques*, Daulé reconnaît sa dette à l'égard 'des personnes de goût et d'expérience qui ont bien voulu [l'] aider ... dans la Musique' (p. i). Or, ces titres conviennent à Quesnel, que Daulé eut probablement l'occasion de rencontrer (et de consulter?) lors de la première (1805) ou de la seconde (1807) représentation à Québec de *Colas et Colinette*. Sur la présence de Quesnel à Québec lors des représentations, voir EMC 201.

15 *Le Canadien* 8(32), 20 juillet 1838, 1

16 La représentation du 4 juin est annoncée dans le *Quebec Mercury* du 30 mai 1846, 3c. Comme le texte du *Quebec Mercury* indique 'last performance' à la date du 4 juin, on peut supposer qu'il y eut d'autres présentations de l'oeuvre avant cette date. De fait, Nazaire LeVasseur donne la date du 16 mai 1846, dans 'Musique et musiciens à Québec,' *La Musique*, 1(9) (septembre 1919), 98. Notons toutefois qu'Alfred Loewenberg, dans *Annals of Opera 1597-1940* (2e édition, New York: Rowman and Littlefield, 1970), 218, inscrit celle du 26, et Pierre-Georges Roy celle du 25, dans 'Le Théâtre Saint-Louis, à Québec,' *Le Bulletin des recherches historiques* (Lévis) 42(3) (mars 1936) 187.

17 Voir, à titre d'exemple, *La Gazette de Montréal* du 20 janvier 1817, 3. Une réponse aux attaques de Rousseau sur le théâtre remplit de nombreuses colonnes du *Canadien* de 1824. Voir les livraisons des 12 et 19 mai, en première page.

18 LeVasseur, 'Musique et musiciens à Québec'

19 Tome 3 des *Oeuvres complètes* (Paris: Chez Furne, 1835) 248

20 Jean-Jacques Rousseau, *Dictionnaire de musique* (Paris: Chez la Veuve Duchesne, 1768) préface, iii et iv

21 Ibid. iv et vi

22 Pierre-Georges Roy, *Les Juges de la Province de Québec* (Québec: Rédemptori Paradis, 1933) 39; et fiche d'étudiant conservée aux Archives du Séminaire de Québec

23 Les informations puisées à ce cahier s'ajoutent à celles contenues dans Marc Lebel, Pierre Savard et Raymond Vézina, *Aspects de l'enseignement au Petit*

Séminaire de Québec (1765-1945), vol. 20 des Cahiers d'histoire (Québec: La Société historique de Québec, 1968).

24 Le Séminaire de Québec possède un manuscrit de huit pages intitulé *Principes de musique par Monsieur Dupon par lequel toutes personnes pourront apprendre d'eux mêmes à Connoitre toute la musique*, datable de la fin du XVIIIe siècle. Communication de Mme Vivianne Emond, que je remercie.

25 Rousseau ('Accompagnement,' *Dictionnaire* 9) répond à ceux qui voudraient faire passer l'étude de la composition avant celle de l'accompagnement: 'Combien de gens, au contraire, veulent qu'on commence par l'*Accompagnement* à apprendre la Composition? & cet ordre est assurément plus raisonnable & plus naturel.'

26 Anton Bemetzrieder, *Reflexions sur les leçons de musique* (Amsterdam: Chez l'auteur, 1778) 6-7; Diderot est identifié au moyen de l'initiale P mise pour Philosophe.

27 Rousseau, 'Expression,' *Dictionnaire* 214. Au moins un autre auteur québécois de manuels de théorie musicale, Théodore-Frédéric Molt, aurait emprunté à Rousseau, comme l'indique Claire Grégoire-Reid, dans une thèse de maîtrise en musique récente (Université Laval) intitulée 'Les manuels de théorie musicale imprimés au Québec entre 1811 et 1911,' pp. 120-4.

28 D'une manière qui n'est pas sans rappeler les propos récents de Daniel Heartz sur la musique de Rousseau dans *The New Grove*, Napoléon Aubin écrit, à propos de la musique des trois marches composées par Sauvageau et exécutées en 1840, que le compositeur 'a heureusement conservé le style gai pastoral et naïf qui distingue la musique canadienne' (Napoléon Aubin, 'Célébration de la St. Jean-Baptiste. A Quebec,' *Le Canadien* 13(26), 5 juillet 1843, 3).

29 La planche N du *Dictionnaire* reproduit 'Chanson des sauvages du Canada' et 'Danse canadienne,' deux pièces insérées plus tôt dans l'*Encyclopédie*. L'attribution à Mersenne est faite par Rousseau à l'article 'Musique' (*Dictionnaire* 317). De fait, le livre III (p. 148) de l'*Harmonie universelle* de Mersenne est la source. Mais Rousseau a modifié les titres donnés par Mersenne: 'Chanson des sauvages du Canada' remplace 'Trois Chansons des Amériquains,' et 'Danse canadienne' est substitué à 'Chanson canadoise.' De plus, comme l'a déjà fait remarquer Julien Tiersot, Rousseau a 'reproduit les notations du P. Mersenne, en ajoutant par endroits à l'intonation et au rythme des altérations, tout arbitraires, qui ne contribuent guère à rapprocher les mélodies de leurs formes authentiques et primitives' (Julien Tiersot, *Notes d'ethnographie musicale: La Musique chez les peuples indigènes de l'Amérique du Nord (Etats-Unis et Canada)* [Paris: Fischbacher, 1910] 141). Rousseau est allé plus loin, en coulant dans une même mélodie les 'Trois Chansons des Amériquains' de Mersenne!

30 Rousseau, 'Musique,' *Dictionnaire* 317

VOGAN Music Instruction in Nova Scotia

This paper was presented in an earlier form as an illustrated lecture for the Royal Nova Scotia Historical Society with assistance from members of the High Schools' Chorus of Dartmouth directed by James Farmer.

1 Phyllis Blakeley, 'Music in Nova Scotia, 1605-1867,' *Dalhousie Review* 31 (1981) 94
2 Timothy J. McGee, 'Music in Halifax, 1749-1799,' *Dalhousie Review* 49 (1969) 377-81
3 Helmut Kallmann, *A History of Music in Canada 1534-1914* (Toronto: University of Toronto Press, 1960) 53
4 Ibid.
5 William S. Bartlett, ed., *The Frontier Missionary: A Memoir of the Life of Rev. Jacob Bailey, A.M., Missionary at Pownalborough, Maine, Cornwallis and Annapolis, N.S.* (Boston: Ide and Dutton, 1853) 221-2
6 The title page of the third edition of this publication reads: *The Harmonicon: A Collection of Sacred Music, consisting of Psalm and Hymn Tunes, Anthems, &c. Selected from the Best Composers and Adapted to the use of the Churches in British North America*, 3rd ed. (Pictou: James Dawson & Son, 1855).
7 Interview with Anderson Murray, Scotsburn, NS, 27 December 1985. Some of the wallpaper scrolls used by Mackay are housed in the Public Archives of Nova Scotia in Halifax and in the First Presbyterian Church in Pictou.
8 Blakeley, 'Music in Nova Scotia' 224-5
9 Rules and Regulations of the Halifax Harmonic Society, 1843, 2-5
10 Blakeley, 'Music in Nova Scotia' 100
11 Interview with Nancy Hood, Yarmouth, NS, 22 March 1986
12 Frederick A. Hall, 'Musical Life in Eighteenth-Century Halifax,' *Canadian University Music Review* 4 (1983) 284
13 Blakeley, 'Music in Nova Scotia' 225
14 Hugo Talbot, ed., *Musical Halifax* (Halifax: McAlpine Pub. Co. Ltd. 1903-4) 7
15 Superintendent of Education, *Annual Report of the Common, Superior, Academic, and Normal and Model Schools in Nova Scotia for the School Year 1865* (Halifax, 1866) 96
16 *Acadian Recorder*, 27 February 1867, 2
17 Halifax *Citizen*, 21 July 1868, 3
18 W.O. Perkins and J.B. Norton, eds, *The Dominion Songster for School, Classes and for the Family Circle* (Halifax: Connelly & E. Kelly, 1870) preface
19 Superintendent of Education, *Annual Report of the Common, Superior, Academic, and Normal and Model Schools in Nova Scotia for the School Year 1871* (Halifax, 1872) 93
20 Ada F. Ryan, *School Day Melodies* (Halifax: T.C. Allen & Co., 1898)

21 'Tonic Sol-fa in Nova Scotia,' *The Educational Review*, January 1891, 131
22 *Journal of Education*, April 1893, 22
23 *Journal of Education*, October 1905, 198
24 Ibid.
25 *Proceedings of the Dominion Educational Association*, 1898, xxxvi
26 Talbot, *Musical Halifax* 3

BRYCE John Lovell

1 *Canadiana 1867-1900: Monographs/Monographies* (Ottawa: National Library of Canada/Bibliothèque nationale du Canada, 1985)
2 André Beaulieu and Jean Hamelin, *La Presse québécoise, des origines à nos jours*, vol. 1: 1764-1859, vol. 2: 1860-79, vol. 3: 1880-95 (Québec: Presses de l'Université Laval, 1973-7)
3 *Mackay's Montreal Directory for 1866-67* (Montreal: John Lovell, 1866) 63
4 George L. Parker, *The Beginnings of the Book Trade in Canada* (Toronto: University of Toronto Press, 1985) 175
5 For more details on music typography, see William Gamble, *Music Engraving and Printing* (London: Pitman, 1923) 168-201.
6 I am grateful to Dr Parker for bringing this delightful account to my attention, and to the Douglas Library at Queen's University for lending it to me.
7 Susanna Moodie, *Letters of a Lifetime*, ed. Carl Ballstadt, Elizabeth Hopkins, and Michael Peterman (Toronto: University of Toronto Press, 1985) 96-8
8 Edited by W.W. Pasko (New York: Howard Lockwood, 1894; reprinted by Gale Research, Detroit, 1967). Lovell's entry (p. 352) is a faithful condensation of his own submission.
9 The purpose of this pamphlet, headed 'Confidential – To be published in my Reminiscences of an Eventful Life,' was to expose his unchivalrous, indeed insulting, treatment at the hands of his bank manager over a small money matter. It includes correspondence to and from bank officials, an article showing the trust and esteem in which he is held by others, correspondence about the dictionary and his entry, a letter to his wife and children, and a description of his memoirs, which he promises to publish 'within a year from March, 1892.'
10 Biggar Papers, Public Archives of Canada, MG29, D23
11 By Lovell's account it remained closed for six months, reopening in December 1838. But first-hand reports of his role in the November 1837 skirmishes, and the fact that *The Literary Garland* must have required some preparation and work before it made its first appearance in December 1838, would be cause to doubt Lovell's memory of events which had taken place fifty-five years earlier.
12 Biggar Papers and 'Reminiscences of the Rebellion of 1837,' two notebooks by an unknown writer, 'read to the Women's Club of Montreal, December 4,

1900.' Public Archives of Canada, MG55/29, no. 49

13 Lovell's obituaries in the *Montreal Daily Star* and *The Gazette* (3 July 1893) claimed the reverse: that Lovell responded to Wetherall's plea for a volunteer and that Bellingham offered to accompany him.
14 Biggar Papers. Sydney Bellingham was also listed as a provisional director of the Lovell firm in a stock offer dated 9 March 1874 for an expansion of the business at Montreal and Rouse's Point, New York (Public Archives of Canada, MG24, D16, vol. 112, file I-M).
15 Parker, *Beginnings of the Book Trade* 167-75
16 Further details can be found in Maria Calderisi, *Music Publishing in the Canadas/ L'Edition musicale au Canada 1800-1867* (Ottawa: National Library of Canada/ Bibliothèque national du Canada, 1981).
17 A branch of the firm was established in Toronto in 1850 to publish government papers. Gibson's wife (John Lovell's sister) and sons continued the business after his death until 1868. See Parker, *Beginnings of the Book Trade* 83 and Elizabeth Hulse, *A Dictionary of Toronto Printers, Publishers, Booksellers and the Allied Trades, 1798-1900* (Toronto: Anson-Cartwright, 1982) 150-3. Since John Lovell was not directly connected with Lovell & Gibson, Toronto, discussion and description of its music publications are not included in this article.
18 In her dedication to him of *Geoffrey Moncton, or, The Faithless Guardian* (New York: DeWitt & Davenport, 1855)
19 *The Literary Garland*, 1(1) (December 1838) 48
20 *The Snow-Drop; or Juvenile Magazine*, July 1850, 32
21 Montreal: Printed by Lovell and Gibson, 1846; reprinted by the Bibliographical Society of Canada, 1975
22 It is in this category of Lovell's output that I feel most uneasy about setting out a list of titles. The retrospective national bibliography is just beginning to document systematically the 1800-67 segment; not all contributing libraries have been consistent about indicating the presence of musical notation in a book or pamphlet, and not all books and pamphlets from this period are in fully catalogued collections.
23 'Home Industry: To the Editor of the Montreal Gazette,' *Canadian Manufactures* (1858); *A Letter to Sir John Rose, Bart., K.C.M.G., on the Canadian Copyright Question by two members of the Native Book Trade* (1872); *Statement of the Tenders for the Printing and Stationery required by the Corporation of the City of Montreal, for Six Years: John Lovell's Exposé of the Unfairness and Trickery of Two Members of the City Hall Committee* ... (1881); and *John Lovell and the Bank of Montreal* (1892).
24 At the end of his biographical sketch, dated 25 February 1892, in *John Lovell and the Bank of Montreal* 6
25 These include the Montreal imprints of Lovell & Gibson (1843-50), Lovell Printing and Publishing Company (1877-86), and John Lovell & Son (1888).

26 *Symbols of Canadian Libraries/Sigles des bibliothèques canadiennes*, 11th edition (Ottawa: National Library of Canada/Bibliothèque national du Canada, 1985)
27 From their appearance and other clues, these pieces were printed in the late 1850s or early 1860s.
28 James Constantine Pilling, *Bibliography of the Iroquoian Languages* (Washington: Government Printing Office, 1888) 21
29 'Note historique' in the seventh edition (Montreal: H. et M. White; Springfield, Mass.: L.E. Rivard, 1891) iii-v; the note also states that the first edition (1862) had been stereotyped in Boston and printed by Lovell.
30 Pilling, *Bibliography* 50
31 Ibid. 50
32 Ibid. 101
33 James J. Fuld, *The Book of World-Famous Music* (New York: Crown Publishers, 1971) 95

MOREY Orchestras and Orchestral Repertoire

1 *Mail*, Tuesday, 23 February 1892
2 *Globe*, Saturday, 11 October 1856
3 *Globe*, Thursday, 3 June 1869
4 *Globe*, Friday, 13 December 1907
5 *Globe*, Wednesday, 8 December 1909
6 For information about the group and its tours see H. Earle Johnson, 'The Germania Musical Society,' *Musical Quarterly* 39(1) (January 1953) 75-93.
7 *Examiner*, Wednesday, 25 June 1850
8 *Globe*, Tuesday, 2 July 1850
9 *Mail*, Saturday, 4 October 1873
10 *Daily Mail and Empire*, Saturday, 23 March 1895. The receipts of the earlier concert were recalled as being $70.
11 *Globe*, Saturday, 5 March 1881
12 *Globe*, Monday, 4 December 1882
13 *Globe*, Tuesday, 8 May 1883. The concerts were on 15 and 16 May.
14 *Mail and Empire*, Saturday, 23 March 1895
15 See C. Morey, 'The Beginnings of Modernism in Toronto,' in G. Ridout and T. Kenins, eds, *Célébration* (Toronto: Canadian Music Centre, 1984) 80-6.
16 *Correspondent and Advocate*, Thursday, 31 December 1835
17 Minute Book in Baldwin Room, Metropolitan Toronto Public Library. The book includes copies of programs from 1845 to 1847. The last entry to use the name 'Toronto Choral Society' is 2 May 1845. See also Helmut Kallmann, *A History of Music in Canada 1534-1914* (Toronto: University of Toronto Press, 1960; reprinted 1969) 98.

18 For details on Clarke's activities, see Helmut Kallmann, 'James Paton Clarke – Canada's First Mus. Bac.,' in *The Canada Music Book* 1 (Spring-Summer 1970) 41-53; also Kallmann's article on Clarke in Helmut Kallmann et al., eds, *Encyclopedia of Music in Canada* (Toronto: University of Toronto Press, 1981).
19 *Globe*, Saturday, 1 February 1851. The concert was on 6 February.
20 *Globe*, Thursday, 30 September 1858
21 *Globe*, Thursday, 5 December 1867
22 *Globe*, Monday, 28 February 1881
23 *Empire*, Saturday, 18 November 1893
24 *Globe*, Wednesday, 25 April 1900
25 *Globe*, Friday, 6 December 1901
26 *Mail*, Wednesday, 9 January 1889
27 Mary E. Joliffe, comp., *The Welsman Memoranda* (Toronto: Northern Miner Press, 1971) 6
28 *Globe*, Saturday, 16 February 1907
29 *Globe*, Thursday, 26 November 1908

KEILLOR Musical Activity in Canada's New Capital City

1 Charles Roger, *Ottawa Past and Present* (Ottawa: Time Print and Publishing Co., 1871) 52-3
2 Ibid. 88
3 I am indebted to several students of my undergraduate course in Canadian music at Carleton University, Loretta Beninger, Sandra McLauchlan, Glen Carruthers, and Henri Steenaart, and particularly to a former graduate student, Elizabeth Chrysler, for compiling the information from the *Ottawa Citizen* (OC). The *Ottawa Free Press* (OFP) began publishing in the spring of 1870 and continued until the end of February 1880. For the latter half of 1870 and the first half of 1873 no issues are available from either paper. Neither paper uses pagination at this time. In the programs cited from these sources the original style and layout have been retained.
4 William P. Lett, *Recollections of Bytown and its Old Inhabitants* (Ottawa: 'Citizen' Printing and Publishing, 1874) 72-3
5 Albert A. Gard, *The Hub and the Spoke; or the Capital and its Environs* (Ottawa/ New York: The Emerson Press, 1904) 103
6 David A. Morris, *The Canadian Militia from 1855: An Historical Summary* (Erin, Ont.: The Boston Mills Press, 1983) 14
7 John Hart (Bookseller, Stationer, &c., Perth, Ontario) (author?), *Ten-Cent Canadian Ball-Room Companion and Guide to Dancing* (Toronto: Wm. Warwick, 1871) 7
8 R.H. Hubbard, *Rideau Hall: An Illustrated History of Government House, Ottawa, From Victorian Times to the Present Day* (Montreal/London: McGill-Queen's University Press, 1977) 25

9 Lady Dufferin, *My Canadian Journal 1872-1878*, ed. Gladys Chantler Walker (Don Mills: Longmans Canada Limited, 1969) 175
10 Irwin and Co., comp., *City of Ottawa Directory*, August 1873 to August 1874 (Montreal: John Lovell, 1873) 5
11 Dufferin, *Canadian Journal* 166
12 David James Trotman, 'Ottawa in 1878: Land-Use Pattern in a Canadian City,' MA Thesis (Ottawa: Carleton University, 1977) 26
13 Other minstrel troupes appearing in Ottawa were: New Orleans Minstrels, 11 and 13 May 1872; Hamall's Serenaders and Brass Band, 10-11 September 1873; Benedict and Clarke's New Orleans Minstrels and Brass Band, 11-12 May 1874; LaRue's Minstrels and Hamall's Serenaders, 7-8 October 1874; Wares' and Bryant's Combination, 6-7 November 1874; Hibernian Minstrel Troupe, 9-11 September 1875; McGill and Strong's Emerald Minstrels, 16-18 December 1875; Wilson and Mack's Serenaders, 8 April 1876; Happy Cal Wagner's Minstrel Troupe, 2-4 December 1876; Walhalla's Minstrels, 19 February 1877; Madame Rentz's Female Minstrels and Mabel Stanley's London Burlesque Troupe, 25-6 May 1877; The Original Georgia Minstrels, 4-5 February 1878; Haverly's Minstrels, 18-19 February 1878; and Duprez and Benedict's Famous Minstrels and Royal Brass Band, 27 October 1879.
14 These performances may have been complete versions because reviews do not mention any extra skits added as fillers.
15 Rosa d'Erina's performances included 15-16 February and 8-9 October 1872; 12 and 28 January, 9 February, 17 March, and 8 July 1874; and 6, and 12 August 1875.
16 *City of Ottawa Directory* (1877) 4
17 Frederick W. Mills and Frederick A. Dixon, *The Maire of St Brieux*: an operetta in one act. [Ottawa?: s.n. 1875?] (Ottawa: J. Bureau). ISBN 0-665-10114-7 (Positive copy). – C182-607183-X. (CIHM/ICMH Microfiche series = CIHM/ICMH collection de microfiches: no. 10114)
18 Dufferin, *Canadian Journal* 166
19 Arthur A. Clappé and Frederick A. Dixon, *Masque entitled 'Canadas* [sic] *welcome'*: as shown before His Excellency the Marquis of Lorne, and Her Royal Highness, the Princess Louise on February 24, 1879 at the Opera House, Ottawa. – Ottawa: J.L. Orme, 1879. – ISBN 0-665-08594-X (Positive copy). – C 184-624528-0. – (CIHM/ICMH Microfiche series = CIHM/ICMH collection de microfiches: no. 08594)

MCINTOSH Ships of the Fleet

1 'Diary of Robert Melrose,' entry for 18 October 1853, MS, Provincial Archives of British Columbia; see also W.K. Lamb, ed., 'The diary of Robert Melrose,

1852-57,' *British Columbia Historical Quarterly* 7 (1943) 132. The frigate HMS *Trincomalee* was on Pacific Station in 1853 and again between 1885 and 1888.
2 'Diary of Robert Melrose,' entries for 26 September and 25 October 1855
3 'Diary of Martha Cheney Ella,' MS, Provincial Archives of British Columbia, entry for 18 October 1853; see also 'The diary of Martha Cheney Ella, 1853-1856,' ed. J.K. Nesbitt, *British Columbia Historical Quarterly* 13 (1949) 91-112, 257-70.
4 Most likely the band of HMS *Monarch*, on the Pacific Station 1855-6. The rear-admiral was William Henry Bruce.
5 'Diary of Martha Cheney Ella,' entry for 16 September 1856
6 The corvette HMS *Satellite* was on the Pacific Station 1856-60.
7 'Journal of Arthur Thomas Bushby,' MS, Provincial Archives of British Columbia, entry for 22 January 1859; see also D.B. Smith, ed., 'Journal of Arthur Thomas Bushby,' *British Columbia Historical Quarterly* 12 (1957-8) 130.
8 *British Colonist*, 24 April 1860, 2. The screw-frigate *Topaze* was on the Pacific Station 1860-3.
9 *Daily British Colonist*, 27 December 1862, 3
10 Ibid., 5 February 1863, 3
11 From a printed program in the Provincial Archives of British Columbia
12 *Daily British Colonist*, 19 June 1863, 3
13 The *Tribune* was on the Pacific Station 1859-60 and again 1864-5, the *Ganges* 1858-60, and the *Sutlej* 1863-7. They were all screw-frigates.
14 *Daily British Colonist*, 6 September 1865, 3
15 *Daily British Colonist and Victoria Chronicle*, 24 September 1866, 2
16 Ibid., 26 September 1866, 2
17 A manuscript of this work is located in the Provincial Archives of British Columbia (item S/M/H78). It appears to have been copied by George H. Elliot (1st Lieutenant Marine) and is dated 2 October 1860.
18 D.B. Smith, ed., *Lady Franklin Visits the Pacific Northwest: Being Extracts from the Letters of Miss Sophia Cracroft, Sir John Franklin's Niece, February to April 1861 and April to July 1870*, Provincial Archives of British Columbia Memoir No. 11 (Victoria, 1974), 33
19 *Daily British Colonist*, 24 March 1864, 3
20 Ibid., 3 February 1866, 3
21 *Daily British Colonist and Victoria Chronicle*, 5 August 1867, 2
22 *Victoria Standard*, 7 July 1870, 3
23 *Daily British Colonist and Victoria Chronicle*, 7 September 1868, 3
24 Ibid., 14 July 1869, 3
25 Ibid., 17 July 1869, 3
26 Ibid., 12 May 1880, 2
27 The *Swiftsure* was on the Pacific Station until 1885 and did another tour of duty

there 1888-9. The Swiftsure Yacht Race is held annually on the last weekend in May.
28 *Daily British Colonist and Victoria Chronicle*, 22 August 1883, 3; see also 'Diary of Susan Crease,' MS, Provincial Archives of British Columbia, entry for 21 August 1883.
29 *Daily Colonist*, 25 August 1889, 1
30 Ibid., 25 September 1889, 4
31 John T. Walbran, *British Columbia Coast Names: 1592-1906* (Ottawa: Government Printing Service, 1909; reprint ed., Vancouver: J.J. Douglas, 1971) 273

POTVIN Maurice Ravel au Canada

L'auteur désire remercier la compositrice Jean Coulthard de Vancouver qui lui a fait part de ses souvenirs personnels sur le concert de Ravel à Vancouver et l'a autorisé à les publier. Il remercie aussi pour leur collaboration John Cull de la Vancouver Public Library, Juanita Renaud de la Bibliothèque nationale du Canada et Patricia Wardrop de l'*Encyclopédie de la musique au Canada* ainsi que Susan Spier.
1 Voir Madeleine Goss, *Bolero: The Life of Maurice Ravel* (New York: H. Holt, 1940); Vivian Perlis, *Two Men for Modern Music* (New York: Institute for Studies in American Music, 1978); et Joseph Roddy, 'Ravel in America,' *High Fidelity*, March 1975
2 Harry Adaskin, *A Fiddler's World* (Vancouver: November House, 1977, 1982)
3 René Chalupt, *Ravel au miroir de ses lettres* (Paris: Laffont, 1956)
4 Carl Morey, 'The Beginnings of Modernism in Toronto,' dans G. Ridout et T. Kenins, dir, *Célébration* (Toronto: Canadian Music Centre, 1984); lettre de Carl Morey à l'auteur, 4 décembre 1985.
5 Robert Kimball et Alfred Simon, *The Gershwins* (New York: Atheneum, 1973)
Ouvrages et journaux consultés:
Jankélévitch, Vladimir. *Maurice Ravel*. Paris: Rieder, 1939
Vancouver Daily Province, 12 and 15 February 1928
Vancouver Sun, 11 and 15 February 1928
The Toronto Daily Star, 19 March 1928
The Evening Telegram, Toronto, 17, 19, 22, 23 March 1928
The Globe, Toronto, 17, 20, 22 and 23 March 1928
La Presse, Montréal, 14, 19 et 20 avril 1928
Le Devoir, Montréal, 20 avril 1928
Le Canada, Montréal, 20 et 28 avril 1928
La Patrie, Montréal, 20 et 21 avril 1928
The Gazette, Montreal, 20 April 1928
Montreal Daily Star, 21 April 1928

MACMILLAN Ernest MacMillan: The Ruhleben Years

1 Diary, kept by ECM from 5 September to 31 October 1915. This quotation is taken from the entry of 26 September 1915.
2 J. Davidson Ketchum, *Ruhleben: A Prison Camp Society* (Toronto: University of Toronto Press, 1965)
3 Memoirs. Unless otherwise indicated, subsequent quotations are taken from this source.
4 Ketchum, *Ruhleben* 3
5 Ibid. 92-3
6 ECM exchanged letters with his family and his fiancée, Laura Elsie Keith (LEK), in Toronto throughout the war years; the prisoners were allowed two letters per month, so ECM wrote once a month to his family and the other monthly letter went to LEK. Most of the correspondence with LEK has survived, as has much to and from the MacMillan family and others. See ECM to LEK, 17 May 1915 for the second of these quotations.
7 ECM to LEK, 21 April 1915
8 For example, see John Beckwith, 'Sir Ernest MacMillan,' in Helmut Kallmann et al., eds, *Encyclopedia of Music in Canada* (Toronto: University of Toronto Press, 1981).
9 ECM to LEK, 15 July 1915
10 ECM to LEK, 12 August 1917
11 Ketchum, *Ruhleben* 167
12 ECM's diary
13 ECM to his family, 15 December 1916
14 ECM to LEK, 2 December 1917
15 ECM to LEK, 20 July 1918
16 ECM to LEK, 12 July 1918
17 Alfred Hollins, *A Blind Musician Looks Back* (Edinburgh: Blackwell, 1936)

PROCTOR Notes on Violet Archer

1 Evidently this refers to 'Directory of American and Foreign Contemporary Operas ... 1975-1980,' *Central Opera Service Bulletin* 22(2) (1980) 35.

CLARKE Healey Willan's Unfinished *Requiem*

Music examples are included with permission of the estate of James Healey Willan.
1 Space limitations in my book *Healey Willan: Life and Works* (Toronto: University of Toronto Press, 1983) precluded detailed discussion of Willan's unfinished works.

2 An early sketch for this section reveals that the composer originally conceived the music in G flat major.
3 In preparing my performance version of the Kyrie I encountered similar problems to those of the Introitus except that in this case a larger proportion of the accompaniment had to be created.
4 See *Healey Willan* 163-4
5 A full orchestral score and a vocal/organ version are available from the Canadian Music Centre.

ANHALT *Thisness*

1 [Istvan Anhalt: *Foci*, for soprano, instrumental ensemble, and prerecorded tape, 1969; *La Tourangelle*, musical tableau for five singers, instrumental ensemble, and prerecorded tape, 1975; *Winthrop*, musical pageant for soloists, chorus, and orchestra, 1985. In both *La Tourangelle* and *Winthrop* the central character is portrayed by three different vocalists.]
2 The letter is edited here.
3 I later changed it to 'duo-drama.'
4 It has proved to be about forty minutes long.
5 A. Flewe and J. Speake, eds. (London: Pan Books 1979)
6 In the final version two crotales and a bell are used.
7 This feature was not used at the première.
8 The understated acting of Phyllis Mailing at the première was very effective.
9 Made possible through a grant by the Canada Council

KELLOGG Sounds in the Wilderness

Of necessity, a study of this nature depends every bit as much on the oral history provided by individuals as it does on bibliographical and archival research. Many of those who provided invaluable assistance through interviews are identified in the text: Jacques Boucher, Harry Freedman, Helmut Kallmann, Keith MacMillan, Gilles Potvin, Harold Redekopp, John Roberts, and Robert Sunter. In addition, the following gave freely of their time and information in interviews: Norma Dickson, CBC secretary to John Adaskin and other music producers in Toronto (retired); Franz Kraemer, head, music section, Canada Council (until June 1986); George Laverock, radio producer, CBC Vancouver; Fraser Macdonald, radio producer, CBC Toronto (retired); Laurent Major, assistant to the manager, musical programs, French Networks-Radio, CBC Montreal; Jean Piché, music officer, Canada Council.

Expert assistance was also unfailingly provided by library staffs across the country in CBC music libraries and Canadian Music Centres, especially Mark

Hand, national librarian, CMC Toronto; Claire Métras, librarian, CMC Montréal; Jan Cornish, librarian, CBC Toronto Music Library; and Lynn McIntyre, CBC Toronto Music Library.

1 In almost every case works have been dated according to the point of first broadcast by the CBC rather than the date on which the commission was issued or the composition was completed. Likewise, where the title of a work in the CBC's music library differed from that in Helmut Kallmann et al., eds, *Encyclopedia of Music in Canada* (Toronto: University of Toronto Press, 1981), the latter source was used.
2 Geoffrey Waddington, 'Music and Radio,' in Ernest MacMillan, ed., *Music in Canada* (Toronto: University of Toronto Press, 1955) 131-2
3 Helmut Kallmann, 'Waddington, Geoffrey,' *Encyclopedia of Music in Canada* 982
4 *FM Radio in Canada* (Ottawa: CRTC, 1975)
5 Keith MacMillan, 'Broadcasting,' *Encyclopedia of Music in Canada* 117

NAPIER The Canadian Music Council

1 A copy of this paper is in the MacMillan Collection at the National Library of Canada, Ottawa.
2 'The Canadian Music Journal,' in Helmut Kallmann et al., eds, *Encyclopedia of Music in Canada* (Toronto: University of Toronto Press, 1981)
3 The French edition was substantially corrected and updated, and provided with a discography by Gilles Potvin, and a bibliography by Helmut Kallmann.

KEMP Three Masses by Maritime Composers

1 *The Constitution on the Sacred Liturgy of the Second Vatican Council* . . . (Glen Rock, NJ: Paulist Press, 1964) Art. 121, 70
2 *Constitution* 69. One of the notable features in the constitution's chapter on sacred music is that 'even new creations need no longer be confined to hymns in the traditional sense' (Josef Andreas Jungmann, 'Constitution on the Sacred Liturgy,' in *Commentary on the Documents of Vatican II* [New York: Herder and Herder, 1967], vol. 1, 80).
3 Thrasybulos Georgiades, *Music and Language: The Rise of Western Music as Exemplified in Settings of the Mass*, trans. Marie Louise Göllner (Cambridge and New York: Cambridge University Press, 1982) 3
4 Ibid. 9-10, 118-19
5 *Summa theologiae* I, 5, 4; I, 39, 8; see translation by Vernon J. Bourke, ed., *The Pocket Aquinas* (New York: Washington Square Press, 1960) 262-4.
6 Waterloo Record 8027
7 The composer does report that by special ecclesiastical permission this Latin

concert Mass was sung during morning Holy Communion at Exeter Cathedral when the Memorial University Chamber Choir was on its 1983 English tour; in his opinion it proved to be quite effective within the context of the Church of England service.

8 The Waterloo Sacred Choral Series, Waterloo Music Co. Ltd., Waterloo, Ont.
9 In a telephone conversation, the composer did agree that the forest scene around Corner Brook might support Don Cook's translation, 'Woodland Mass,' suggested in the publication; however, he points out that the Mass is dedicated to Marcia and Paul *Woodford*.
10 Erik Routley, *Twentieth Century Church Music* (London: Herbert Jenkins, 1964) 210-11
11 Joseph H. Fichter, SJ, 'The Americanization of Catholicism,' in Thomas T. McAvoy, ed., *Roman Catholicism and the American Way of Life* (Notre Dame: University of Notre Dame Press, 1960) 127
12 *Constitution on the Sacred Liturgy* Art. 27, 40
13 *Sacred Music and Liturgy: Instruction of the Sacred Congregation of Rites*, 3 September 1958, trans. J.B. O'Connell (Westminster, Maryland: The Newman Press, 1959) 37
14 Ibid. 37
15 *Constitution* Art. 30, 41
16 *Constitution* Art. 116, 68
17 Georgiades, *Music and Language* 125
18 Ibid. 126
19 Leon Joseph Cardinal Suenens, *A New Pentecost?* (London: Collins Fountain Books, 1977) 103

WINTERS Six Discs

1 Quoted in Kenneth Clark, *Ruskin Today* (London: John Murray, 1964) 89
2 Helmut Kallmann et al., eds, *Encyclopedia of Music in Canada* (Toronto: University of Toronto Press, 1981) xiv
3 Quoted in Alan Kendall, *The Tender Tyrant* (London: Macdonald and Jane's, 1976) 110
4 John Beckwith, notes to the recording, Melbourne SMLP 4038
5 When someone asked Gertrude Stein what she liked about Picasso's paintings, she replied: 'I like to look at them.'

PAYZANT The Glenn Gould Outtakes

1 Geoffrey Payzant, *Glenn Gould: Music and Mind* (Toronto: Van Nostrand Reinhold, 1978; rev. ed. Toronto: Key Porter Books, 1984)

Notes to pages 298-309 343

2 Glenn Gould, 'Gould by Payzant/Payzant by Gould,' *Globe and Mail*, 27 May 1978, 41
3 The reissue is published by Formac Publishing Company Ltd in their Goodread Biography Series.
4 Artur Schnabel, *Music and the Line of Most Resistance* (New York: Da Capo Press, 1969) passim
5 Martin Heidegger, *What Is Called Thinking*? trans. J. Glenn Gray, (New York: Harper & Row, 1968) 16-17
6 Etienne Gilson, *Painting and Reality* (New York: Meridian Books, 1959) 52-3
7 Victor Zukerkandl, *Man the Musician* trans. Norbert Guterman, (Princeton: Princeton University Press, 1973) 283
8 Ibid. 282
9 Ibid. 285
10 Ibid. 285
11 Joan Steen Wilentz, *The Senses of Man* (New York: Thomas Y. Crowell Company, 1968) 316
12 Glenn Gould, 'Address to a Graduation,' *Bulletin of the Royal Conservatory of Music of Toronto* (Christmas 1964)
13 Glenn Gould, 'An Argument for Music in the Electronic Age,' *The Varsity Graduate* (University of Toronto) 11(3) (1964) 118-20
14 Glenn Gould, 'An Experiment in Listening: The Grass Is Always Greener in the Outtakes,' *High Fidelity Magazine* 25(8) (August 1975) 59
15 Arnold Schultz, *A Theory of Consciousness* (New York: Philosophical Library, 1973) 23
16 Michael Polanyi, *Knowing and Being* (London: Routledge & Kegan Paul, 1969) 115
17 Ernst Bacon, *Notes on the Piano* (Seattle and London: University of Washington Press, 1968) 124
18 R.G. Collingwood, *The Principles of Art* (Oxford: Clarendon Press, 1938) 322
19 Ibid. 311-12
20 Ibid. 314
21 Ibid. 317
22 Ibid. 322
23 Ibid. 312
24 'Some of my best friends are critics, although I'm not sure I'd want my piano to be played by one.' Glenn Gould, 'Glenn Gould Interviews Glenn Gould about Glenn Gould,' *High Fidelity Magazine* 24(2) (February 1974) 75
25 For an example, see Gould's account of the recording session for his *Art of the Fugue* disc in Payzant, *Glenn Gould*, 46
26 Collingwood, *Principles of Art* 11
27 Ibid. 323

28 Bacon, *Notes on the Piano* 145
29 Ibid. 151
30 Rafael Kammerer, insert notes to disc 'Josef Hofmann: The Legendary Casimir Hall Recital of April 7, 1938,' VM 101, International Piano Library
31 Joseph Roddy, 'Apollonian,' *The New Yorker* 36(13) (14 May 1960) 89
32 Erwin Stein, *Form and Performance* (London: Faber & Faber, 1957) 13
33 Clive Bell, *Art* (London: Chatto & Windus, 1914) 19-20

Notes on Contributors

ISTVAN ANHALT is a composer and former head of the Department of Music, Queen's University. He has written a number of important compositions, including the opera *Winthrop* (1986); his interest in the use of voice and text has resulted in several articles and the book *Alternative Voices* (1983).

CLAUDE BEAUDRY est bibliothécaire en musique à l'Université Laval et organiste à St. Charles de Limoilou de Québec. Il travaille depuis quelques années à un projet d'inventaire des fonds anciens de musique conservés dans la ville de Québec. Beaudry est auteur de *Guide de rédaction de travaux de recherche en musique* (1985).

MARIA CALDERISI BRYCE is head of the Printed Collection, Music Division, National Library of Canada and the author of *Music Publishing in the Canadas, 1800-1867/L'Édition musicale au Canada, 1800-1867* (1981). She is also president of the International Association of Music Libraries, Archives and Documentation Centres (1986-9).

BEVERLEY CAVANAGH, associate professor in the Department of Music, Queen's University, is an ethnomusicologist specializing in the music of the Inuit. Her publications include *Music of the Netsilik Eskimos: A Study of Stability and Change*, 2 vols (1982).

F.R.C. CLARKE, professor and head of the Department of Music, Queen's University, is a composer and church musician. He chaired the music subcommittee for *The Hymn Book* of the Anglican and United Churches (1971) and is the author of *Healey Willan: Life and Music* (1983).

CLIFFORD FORD is a composer and executive secretary of the Canadian Musical Heritage Society. Among his commissioned works are *Mass* (1976) and *Day of Wrath* (1979). He edited volume 2 (*Sacred Choral Music I*, 1984) in the *Canadian Musical Heritage* series.

Notes on Contributors

RICHARD JOHNSTON is a composer and former dean of fine arts and professor of music at the University of Calgary. In addition to his active composing career he has arranged and edited several collections of Canadian folk-songs.

ELAINE KEILLOR is an associate professor at Carleton University, a pianist, and an ethnomusicologist. She is the editor of volumes 1 and 6 (*Piano Music I*, 1983, and *Piano Music II*, 1986) in the *Canadian Musical Heritage* series and is preparing a study on the life and works of John Weinzweig.

PATRICIA KELLOGG came to Canada in 1970 after teaching music history at the University of Miami (Fla.). She became music librarian for CJRT-FM in Toronto and in 1977 joined the CBC as supervisor of Music Library Services and Radio Program Archives; she is now supervisor of Radio Network Program Services.

WALTER KEMP is professor and chairman of the Department of Music, Dalhousie University. He is active as a musicologist, organist, choir director, and composer. He is the author of *The Evolution of Musical Composition from the Middle Ages to Bach and Handel* (1979).

ROBERT DALE McINTOSH is associate professor and chairman of the Department of Art and Music Education, Faculty of Education, University of Victoria. He specializes in the musical history of British Columbia and has published *A Documentary History of Music in Victoria, British Columbia* (1981).

KEITH MacMILLAN is former executive secretary of the Canadian Music Centre (1964-77) and former chairman of the Department of Music, University of Ottawa (1977-85). He is the author of many articles on Canadian music and co-editor of *Contemporary Canadian Composers* (1975).

CARL MOREY, professor and dean of the Faculty of Music, University of Toronto, has written articles on Canadian music for many publications, including *The New Grove Dictionary* (1986), the *Encyclopedia of Music in Canada* (1981), and *Célébrations* (1984). His main areas of research are opera and the musical history of Toronto.

RONALD NAPIER is a music administrator and amateur musician who is a former chairman of the Canadian Music Publishers Association and past president of the National Youth Orchestra of Canada. He was also president of the Canadian Music Council from 1973 to 1975.

GEOFFREY PAYZANT, professor of philosophy at the University of Toronto, edited the *Canadian Music Journal* from 1956 to 1962. Among his publications are *Glenn Gould: Music and Mind* (1978) and *On the Musically Beautiful* (1986), his translation of Eduard Hanslick's *Vom Musikalisch-Schönen*.

Notes on Contributors

LUCIEN POIRIER est auteur, interprète, professeur agrégé (Université Laval), éditeur (Société pour le patrimoine musical canadien, Editions Jacques Ostiguy), et spécialiste de l'histoire de la musique au Québec. Il poursuit actuellement des recherches sur la presse québécoise (1764-1918) et la musique.

GILLES POTVIN est depuis 1966 conseiller spécial aux émissions musicales de Radio Canada International. Il a été codirecteur d'*Encyclopedia of Music in Canada* (1981) et de l'*Encyclopédie de la musique au Canada* (1983). Il a été critique musical aux quotidiens montréalais *Le Devoir* et *La Presse*.

GEORGE PROCTOR (1931-85) was a professor at the University of Western Ontario and former head of the Department of Music, Mount Allison University (1967-74). Among his publications are *Sources in Canadian Music: A Bibliography of Bibliographies* (1979) and *Canadian Music of the Twentieth Century* (1980).

R. MURRAY SCHAFER is a composer, writer, and educator. In addition to his extensive compositional activities, Schafer founded the World Soundscape Project at Simon Fraser University and has published several books, including *E.T.A. Hoffmann and Music* (1975), *Creative Music Education* (1976), and *The Tuning of the World* (1977).

ERICH SCHWANDT, an authority on sacred music in New France, has edited motets and Masses performed in Québec in the seventeenth and eighteenth centuries. He is a professor in the School of Music, University of Victoria.

NANCY F. VOGAN is associate professor of Music and Education, an associate of the Centre for Canadian Studies, and co-ordinator of the Integrated Music Education Program at Mount Allison University in Sackville, New Brunswick.

JOHN WEINZWEIG has taught several generations of composition students at the Faculty of Music, University of Toronto, where he is now professor emeritus. He was founding president of the Canadian League of Composers and is the only composer among the distinguished Canadian artists who have been awarded the Molson Prize.

KENNETH WINTERS is a former critic for the *Winnipeg Free Press* (1956-66) and the Toronto *Telegram* (1966-71) and former executive director of the Ontario Federation of Symphony Orchestras (1971-5). He is a writer and commentator for numerous CBC Radio productions and was one of the editors of the *Encyclopedia of Music in Canada* (1981) and *L'Encyclopédie de la musique au Canada* (1983).

Index

Page numbers in **bold type** indicate that the person or subject of an index entry is the subject of an essay in this volume. Page numbers in *italics* refer to illustrations and illustrative material within the text – charts, musical examples, tables – or to information contained in the captions for such materials. French-language essays have been assigned French index terms, modifiers, and, in some cases, *see* references; English terms have been assigned to essays in English. Subheadings have been arranged alphabetically. The method of alphabetical arrangement is word by word.

Abenaki, 12
Aberfan Pannell, 250
Abrégé de l'antiphonaire romain ..., 32
acoustic ecology, 232
ACTRA, 268
Adams, L.T., 122
Adaskin, Harry: quoted, 151–2
Adaskin, John, 243, 254
Adaskin, Murray, 253, 255, 291
Adler, Charles, 166
The Adopted Child Clappé, 132
Agius, Antonio, 146
Agostini, Lucio, 244
Ah! say, lovely Emma ... Stevenson, 49
Ahearn, John, 122
Aiamieu kie nikamu, 9, 12, 13
Albert, Eugène d': works performed in Victoria, 144

Alberta Composers' Association, 202
Alembert, Jean le Rond d', 32, 64
Algonkian language groups. *See* Abenaki; Cree; Micmac; Montagnais; Naskapi; Saulteux
Algonquin Symphony M. Adaskin, 253
Allen, John, 146
Amadeus Quartet, 177
Amateurs canadiens de Québec, 64
American Dictionary of Printing and Bookmaking, 80
American Federation of Musicians, 268
L'Ami du peuple de l'ordre et des lois, 81
Amuya Garant, 256
And Wolf Shall Inherit the Moon Schafer, 232
Anderson, Rev. James, 76–7
Andrews, F.H., 92

Index

Anger, Humphrey, 111
Anhalt, Istvan, **211–31**, 232; works, 340 n. 1
Les Annales de l'Hôtel-Dieu de Québec, 50–1
Antiphonarium various, 32–3, 93, 94
L'Apocalypse (une fresque symphonique d'après saint Jean) Hétu, 256
Apocalypsis Schafer, 257
Applebaum, Louis, 264
Archer, Violet: Proctor notes on, **188–202**; awards, honours, 201, 202; biographical checklist, 197–202; commissions, 193, 255; early life, 188–91; musical influences, 191–2; opera, 192; performer, 194, 200; professional activities, 191; studies with Bartok, 199–200, with Hindemith, 200–1; teaching, 194–7, 201–2; texts, 193; works, 192, 193, 201, 255
Armana Freedman, 256
Arne, Michael, 33
Aspects of Music in Canada/Aspects de la musique au Canada, 267
The Assembly Waltzes Schallehn, 88
Association of Canadian Television and Radio Artists, 268
Astor, W.H., 33
Athanasii Kircheri ... musurgia universalis ... Kircher, 40
Atlantide Brégent, 248
Auber, Daniel: works performed in Ottawa, 126; in Toronto, 108
Aubin, Napoléon, 70; et première du *Devin du village* au Canada, 65
Augustines de l'Hôtel-Dieu, 50, 51
Augustinians of the Mercy of Jesus. *See* Augustines de l'Hôtel-Dieu
Aux-Cousteaux, Artus, 30

Bacchus and Mars Arne, 33
Bach, J.S.: works performed in Ottawa, 128, 130, 131, 132; in Toronto, 182
Bacon, Ernest: quoted, 306, 310
Bailey, Rev. Jacob: quoted, 72
Le Bailli dupé. Voir Colas et Colinette ou le Bailli dupé
Bainton, Edgar, 170
Balestreri, Violet. *See* Archer, Violet
Balfe, M.W.: works performed in Ottawa, 124, 126, 127
Ballard, Father, 123
Band of the 81st Regiment, 108
Band of the Queen's Own Rifles, 109
Band of the 60th Regiment, 120; repertoire, 118
bands: in British Columbia, 143–8; in Nova Scotia, 73; in Ottawa, 118–23; resident and touring in Toronto, 100–2; in Victoria, 146. *See also* Quadrille bands
Banff Centre, 192
Banks, Joyce, 14
Barbeau, Marius, 264
Barkin, Leo, 267
Barrett, James, 122
Barry, Philips, 23
Bartok, Bela, 199–200
Bayer, Mary Elizabeth, 255
Bayley, John, 101, 109
Beaudet, Jean-Marie, 242, 243–4, 247, 263, 264, 267
Beckwith, John, 264, 266; quoted, 293; works, 254, 256, 292, 293–4, 295
Bédard, Pierre, 67–9; cahier manuscrit, *68*; table de sujets, *69*
Beethoven, Ludwig van: works performed in Ottawa, 128, 129, 130;

in Toronto by visiting orchestras, 102–7; by resident groups, 108, 109, 110, 113
Bell, Clive: quoted, 312
Bell, H.P.: cité, 161–2
The Bell Archer, 201
La Belle Canadienne polka Vilbon, 91
Bellingham, Sidney R., 81, 82
Bellini, Vincenzo: works performed in Ottawa, 127
Bemetzrieder, Anton, 33, 69
Berlioz, Hector: works performed in Toronto, 103, 104, 106
Bernardi, Mario, 289
Bernier, Nicolas, 33
Bertrand, Jacques, 248
The Best of All Possible Worlds Moore, 253
Béthizy, Jean Laurent de, 33
Biggar, E.B., 80
Bizet, Georges: works performed in Toronto, 101
Blachford, Frank, 112
Blackstone, Milton, 156
Blake, William, 295
Blanchin, [?], 15
Bloom, Joseph, 144
BMI Canada Ltd., 266
Bogue, Lucy, 151
Bohrer, William, 95
Bohrer's Automatic Piano Hand-Guide, 95
Le Bon Vieux Temps Defoy, 90
Bonner, John C., 120, 121, 132
Boucher, Jacques, 248
Boucke, P.S., 131
Bouhier, Louis, 15, 17
Boulanger, Nadia: quoted, 287
Bourdon, Louis-H., 159, 160
Bousquet, [?]: works performed in Victoria, 145

Brahms, Johannes: works performed in Toronto, 104, 105, 106, 113
Braidi, Edgar, 160
Braman, Amasa, 71
Brault, Victor, 150
Brauneis, Jean-Chrysostome, II, 89
Brégent, Michel-Georges, 248
Brewer, James, 122
The Brideship Turner, 255
Bridle, Augustus: cité, 156
British Columbia: music activities on Pacific Station, **143–8**
See also Victoria
Britten, Benjamin: CBC commission, 243, 252
Brochu, Lucien, 29, 31
Brockington, Leonard, 243
Brott, Alexander, 254, 288; works, 248, 252, 253
Brott, Denis, 291
Bruch, Max: works performed in Toronto, 113
Brunettes ou petits airs tendres . . ., 33
Buck, Edgar, 132
Buley, David and Helen, 275
Bushby, A.T., 143
Business Guide to the City of Montreal. With a Collection of Popular Songs, 93
Butler, E.J., 129, 130

Cable, Howard, 240, 244, 252
Les Cahiers canadiens de musique, 267
Campra, André, 34
Canada, Department of External Affairs, 264
Canada Council, 240, 265, 266, 270, 340 n.9; and commissioning, 249, 257

Canada Dash, Canada Dot Beckwith, 256
The Canada Music Book, 267
Canada Music Week, 191
Canada's Welcome Clappé, 132–3
Canadian Academy of Music, 182
Canadian Arts Council (1945–58), 262
Canadian Association of University Schools of Music, 195
Canadian Broadcasting Corporation. *See* CBC
Canadian College of Organists, 264
Canadian Conference of the Arts. *See* Canadian Arts Council
Canadian Federation of Music Teachers' Associations, 191, 263, 264
Canadian Forces School of Music, 148
The Canadian League of Composers, 266, 267
Canadian Music Centre, 266, 267, 270, 294, 296, 340 n.5. *See also* Centrediscs
Canadian Music Council, **262–73**; activities, 271; awards, 270; Canadian Music Centre, 266; conferences, 266, 272–3; International Music Council Assembly, 267–70; international representation, 271; library, 264; medal, annual recipients, 267, 272; origins, 262–3; presidents, 272; publications, 264–5, 266, 267, 270; secretariat, 170
The Canadian Music Journal, 265, 266
Canadian Music Publishers' Association, 264
Canadian Opera Company, 269
Canadian Radio Broadcasting Commission. *See* CBC
Canadian Radio-Television and Telecommunications Commission. *See* CRTC

Canadian Radio-Television Commission. *See* CRTC
Canadian University Music Society, 195
Cantata sacra Archer, 192, 256
Cantate pour la Passion Morel, 253
Cantiques à St. Joseph, 93
Cantiques populaires du Canada français Gagnon, 26
Cantus diversi ex graduali romano ..., 34
Cantus ex graduali et antiphonario romano ..., 94
CAPAC, 264, 266
The careful wife ... Hook, 38
Carleton Wix Associated, 157
Carré, Rémy, 34
Carter, James, 121
Carter, John, 101
Casseres, Louis G., 74
Catalogue of English and French Books in the Quebec Library, 60
Catéchisme, recueil de prières et de cantiques Laverlochère and Garin, 25
The Cathcart Polkas Schallehn, 84, 88
CBC: and Canadian Music Council, 268–9; CBC Festival Orchestra, 288; CBC Strings, 252; CBC Symphony Orchestra, 245, 253; CBC Vancouver Chamber Orchestra, 257; music library, 239; recordings, 251–2, 288, 289. *See also* CBC and commissioning; RCI
CBC and commissioning, **239–61**; benefits of, 258–9; for CBC-TV, 250, Centennial commissions, 245, 255–6; durations, 254, 256, 257, 260; English network, 244–6; evolution, first commissions, 242–4, 247; external influences, 249–50; French network, 246–8;

incidental music, 240, 243, 244, 247; process, 240–1, 246, 248; review of commissions, 252–7, 260, 261. See also 'Opportunity Knocks'; 'Les Petites Symphonies'
CBC International Service. See RCI
Cellarius Waltz Schallehn, 88
Centrediscs, 294, 295, 296
Cérémonial des soeurs des SS. Noms de Jésus et de Marie, 96
CFCA: radio, 158
Champagne, Claude, 198, 247, 252
Chants évangéliques pour le culte public ... Rivard, 93
Chants religieux et civiques pour les fêtes décadaires J.-B. Rousseau, 47–8
Charpentier, Gabriel, 253
Cheltenham, J.: cité, 155
Cheney, Harriet, 84
Cherney, Brian, 291
Cherry, William, 122
Cherubini, Luigi, 34
Chipewyan, 12, 14, 21
Chisholm, Professor, 77
Chopin, Frédéric: works performed in Ottawa, 130; in Toronto, 105, 112
Chotem, Neil, 247
Chubb, Frederick, 154
Chuhaldin, Alexander, 244
Church Hymnal 2 edns, 96
Civic Mass Farrell, 275, 281–4, *283*, *284*
CKAC: radio, 158
Clappé, Arthur A., 121, 132
Clarke, Douglas, 192, 198
Clarke, Herbert L., 101
Clarke, James Paton, *97*, 108, 267
Clarke, John, 35
Claxton, Thomas, 111
Claypole, A.G., 177
Clementi, Muzio, 35
Cleopatra Willan, 204

Colas et Colinette ou le Bailli dupé Quesnel: rapport entre *Le Devin du village* et, 61–2
Collection complete des oeuvres de J.J. Rousseau, 62
A Collection of Original Sacred Music Andrews, 92
Collingwood, R.G.: quoted, 306–7, 309
Communauté radiophonique des programmes de langue français, 248
Communion Service in E flat and C Willan, 210
Composers, Authors and Publishers Association of Canada. See CAPAC
Comrades in Arms Cable, 244, 252
Concerto, piano and orchestra, Papineau-Couture, 255
Concerto for Piano and Orchestra Weinzweig, 255
Concerto in D Minor Champagne, 247, 252
Conn, John Peebles, 170
Consolations des misères de ma vie J.-J. Rousseau, 63–4
Constant, Marius, 270
Cook, Donald, 277
Cornell University, 202
Coronation Ode Ridout, 253
Coronation Suite Willan, 253
Costellow, Thomas, 35
Les Couleurs du Canada Peltier, 90
Coulter, John, 244
Coulthard, Jean, 253, 254, 263; cité, 154; recording, 295
Coulthard, Mrs Walter, 150, 154
Couture, Guillaume, 129
Cowan, William, 121
Coward, Henry: and première of *England*, 182
Cozens, John, 262, 264, 270

Cree, 7, 20
Cree Hymnal, 14, 15, 17, 20, 25, 27
Crozier, St George, 101, 108
CRTC: effect of policies on CBC, 246, 251–2, 256
Cunnabel, Jacob, 72
Cuoq, Jean-André, 12, 15, 94, 95
Cusheon's Naval and Military Theatre, 144
Cushing, Mrs E.L., 84
The cypress wreath Gresham, 37

The Daffodils Archer, 193
d'Albert, Eugène. *See* Albert, Eugène d'
Dale, Benjamin, 170, 171, 177
d'Alembert, Jean le Rond. *See* Alembert, Jean le Rond d'
Dalhousie Chorale, 282
Dalhousie University, 75, 274
Damrosch, Leopold, 104
Damrosch, Walter, 105, 106
Daudelin, Charles, 267
Daulé, l'abbé Jean-Denis: et Quesnel, 63, 329 n.14; et Rousseau, 63–4
D'Auria, Francesco, 111
Davidson, Hugh, 248
Davies, Merlin, 190, 197
Davis Inlet, Labrador. *See* Hymnody, Algonkian
Dawes, Andrew, 291
Dawson, James, 72
De cantu et musica sacra a prima Ecclesiae ... Gerbert, 36
de Kresz, Geza, 152, 156
De Sève, Alfred, 129
Death alive ... Dibdin, 36
Decair, Louis, 194
Decca Records Inc., 289
Defoy, Joseph A., 90
Deirdre Willan, 203; — *of the Sorrows*, CBC commission, 244, 252

Del Caro's hornpipe, with variations ... Latour, 40
del Vecchio, Rosita, 129
Démonstration du principe de l'harmonie ... Rameau, 46
d'Erina, Rosa, 129, 336 n.15
Derveau, Rev. Père Adrien, 14, 17, 20
Desbarats, la famille: recueils, 30–1
d'Eschambault, Guillaume Fleury. *See* Eschambault, Guillaume Fleury d'
Dibdin, Charles, 36
Dickinson, James, 111
Dictionnaire de musique J.-J. Rousseau, 60, 61; influence au Canada, 66–70
Dictionnaire de musique, par J.-J. Rousseau éditions divers, 48
Le Devin du village J.-J. Rousseau, 61–6, *Airs principaux*, 62; extrait, *63*; rapport entre *Colas et Colinette* et, 61–2; représentations au Canada, 64–6, 329 n.16
Diderot, Denis: cité, 69
Dinelli, Giuseppe, 111
Divertimento (1949) Archer, 192
Divertimento (1957) Archer, 193
Divertimento for Strings Morawetz, 252
Dixon, F.A., 132
Doane, Arnold, 73
Dolin, Samuel, 254, 291
The Dominion Songster for Schools, Classes and the Family Circle, 76
Dominion State Ball Raineri, 118
Donizetti, Gaetano: works performed in Ottawa, 126, 127; in Toronto, 101; in Victoria, 145
Don't Laugh MacMillan, 166
Douglas, William, 291
Down in the valley the sun setting clearly ... Hook, 39
Drechsler-Adamson, Bertha, 111, 112
Dubois, Jean-Baptiste, 160
A duet for two performers on the

piano forte ... Ross, 47
Duff, Alex, 132
Dufferin, Lady, 120; quoted, 124, 132
Dufferin, Lord, 120
Dukas, Paul: works performed in Toronto, 107
Dummiyah/Silence Weinzweig, 256
Dvorak, Antonin: works performed in Toronto, 105

T. Eaton Co., 158
Les Echos du sanctuaire Gagnon, 89
Eckhardt-Gramatté, S.C., 256, 288–9
Edge of the World Weinzweig, 252
education. *See* Instruction in music; Instruction manuals; Singing schools; Tonic sol-fa
E'er Laura met my ravish'd view ... Percivall, 42
Elemens de musique théorique et pratique ... Alembert, 32
Elgar, Edward: works performed in Toronto, 107; visit to Montreal, Toronto, 113
Elgar Choir of Hamilton, 113
Ella, Martha Beeton Cheney, 143
Elliott, James, 122
Elnointoasimgeoel Alasotemagan, 23
Encounter Freedman, 290
Ephemera Pentland, 295
Epitome antiphonarii ... various, 36
Epitome gradualis romani ... various, 36
Epp, Richard, 231
Eschambault, Guillaume Fleury d', 91
Evocations Somers, 256
Excerpta è cantibus liturgicis ..., 95
Exposition de la théorie et de la pratique de la musique ... Béthizy, 33

Fall Fair Ridout, 255
Fanfare and Passacaglia Archer, 193

Fanfare for a Centennial MacMillan, 255
Farnon, Robert, 243
Farrell, Dennis, 274; works, 281–4, *283*, *284*
Favreau, Paul, 118
Fecht, Louis, 132
Festival Singers of Canada, 290
Field, Harry, 171, 174
Fisher, Edward, 131
Five Lyrics of the T'ang Dynasty Beckwith, 295
Five Songs for Dark Voice Somers, 289
Fléché, Father Jessé, 71
Fleming, Robert, 270, 291
Flotow, Friedrich von: works performed in Ottawa, 126; in Toronto, 102; in Victoria, 145
Foci Anhalt, 213
Folksongs of Eastern Canada Ridout, 295
For the Love of Howard Jones, 255
For They Are England Ridout, 244, 252
Ford, Clifford, **97–9**; 274
Form Riflemen Form! Prince, 89
Forrester, Maureen, 256, 289
Foster's Pier, Esquimalt, 144, 145, 146
Fram, Michael, 289
Franck, César: works performed in Toronto, 106
Freedman, Harry: quoted, 253, 254; recording, 289–90; works, 256, 291
French Canadian Institute. *See* Institut canadien français
Fricker, H.A., 182
Fripp, Herbert G.R., 131
From Sea to Sea Brott, 248, 252
La Frontière Eschambault, 91
Fuller, F.H., 128

Gade, Niels: works performed in Toronto, 103
Gagnier, Jean-Josaphat, 247

Gagnon, Sr Claire, 327 n.
Gagnon, Ernest, 26, *85*, *86*, 87, 89, 90, 91
Garant, Serge, 256, 267
Gastoué, Amédée, 23
Gauthier, Eva, 150, 159
Geertz, Clifford, 11
Gelinek, Joseph, 36
Georgiades, Thrasybulos: quoted, 274
Gerbert, Martin, 36
Germania Musical Society, 102
Gibbs, Terence, 253
Gibson, John, 83, 333 n.17
Gilbert and Sullivan: works performed in Nanaimo, 147; in Ottawa, 127–8; in Victoria, 147
Gilmore, Patrick, 101
Gilson, Etienne: quoted, 302
Glaholm, Aggie, 147
Glastonbury incidental music, Willan, 206, *207*
Glenn Gould, Music and Mind Payzant: additional material, **298–313**
Glick, Srul Irving, 291
Godoy, Armand, 253
Goetz, Hermann: works performed in Toronto, 112
Goldmark, Karl: works performed in Toronto, 106
Gorazzi, Signor, 131
Gosling, W.G., 6
Gould, Glenn, 294, **298–313**; art as structure, 308; idealism and empiricism, 300–6; and performer–audience relationship, 306–10; scope of writings of, 299; and synaesthesia, 304; touch-tone relationship, 310–13
Governor-General's Foot Guards Band, 120–1
Gowan family, 120, 123, 131, 132; Gowan's Hall, 123, 124, 130; Opera House, 124, 126, 127, 132
Gowan's Band/Orchestra, 118–20, 122, 126, 127
Graduale romanum ... various, 36–7, 94
Grand concerto for the harp ... Steibelt, 48
A grand concerto for the piano forte ... Steibelt, 48
Grand Pré Seminary, 74
Grande Marche Canadienne Sabatier, 90
Grant, Warden of the Plains M. Adaskin, 255
Gratton, Hector, 254
Gray, Alexander, 190
Gregoire, Charlotte, *20*
Gresham, William, 37
Grétry, André-Ernest-Modeste, 37
Grounds and Rules of Musick Explained Walter, 54
Guerrero, Alberto, 150
Guida di musica ... Hook, 39
Le Guide-mains automatique Bohrer, 95
Gunther, Henry, 146
Gustin, Lyell, 263

Hague, John, 110
Haliburton, Thomas Chandler, 255
Halifax: church music, 71; conservatories, schools, 75; music clubs, 77–8; music instruction, 72–4; school music instruction, 75–7; singing societies, 73. *See also Civic Mass; Mass in Honour of St Thomas Aquinas*
Halifax Chamber Choir, 282
Halifax Harmonic Society, 73, 74
Hambourg, Boris, 156
Hambourg Concert Society, 158
Hamm, Charles, 53
Handel, George Frideric: works

performed in Halifax, 73; in Ottawa, 128, 129, 130
The Harmonicon Dawson, 72
Harner, F.W., 131
Harrison, A., 131
Harrison, J.W., 132
Hart House String Quartet, 172, 177, 291, 292. *See also* Quatuor Hart House
Harze, Mr, 132
Haydn, Joseph, 37–8; works performed in Halifax, 73; in Ottawa, 129, 130, 131; in Toronto, 109
Haynes, William, 146
Heard, Alan, 291
Heartz, Daniel: cité, 61, 62
The heaving of the lead ... Shield, 48
Heidegger, Martin: quoted, 302
Helmer, Terence, 291
A Help to Country Congregations ... 2 edns, 94, 95
Herbert, Victor, 101, 105, 106
Hérold, Ferdinand: works performed in Toronto, 102, 108; in Victoria, 144
Hersenhoren, Samuel, 243, 252
Hétu, Jacques, 248, 256, 291
Hindemith, Paul, 192, 200–1
Hiroshige, Ichiryusai, 289
Hither, Mary, hither come ... Hook, 39
HMS *Parliament* Fuller, 128
Hofmann, Joseph: quoted, 311
Hollins, Alfred, 168, 181
Holman, Harriet, 127
Holman English Opera Company (Opera Troupe), 126, 127
Holt [bandmaster], 101
Hook, James, 38
Horne, William K., 145
L'Horoscope Matton, 253
Hôtel-Dieu, 50–1

Hotham, Rear-Admiral Charles Frederick, 147
Houdy, Pierick, 274
Hounsell, John, 131
Hull, Percy, 171
Humbert, Stephen, 72
Humperdinck, Engelbert: works performed in Toronto, 179
Humphreys, J.D., 101
Huot, Guy, 270, 271
Hyler, G., 39
Hymn for Those in the Air Willan, 252
hymn-books, 4; contents and arrangements of for Indians, 15–27; French Catholic and Methodist for Indians, 12–15; use by Indians, 6, 8–9; use in Algonkian hymnody, 11, 27. *See also* Hymnody; Hymns
hymn singing. *See* Hymnody
hymnals. *See* Hymn-books
Hymnes et proses de l'Eglise ..., 39
hymnody: Algonkian, **3–28**; in missionization, 4–5. *See also* Hymn-books; Hymns
hymns: as dream songs, 10, 326 n.17; interpretation by native and non-native, 9–11. *See also* Hymn-books; Hymnody

Ienenrinekenstha kanesatakeha, ou Processional iroquois ... Cuoq, 94
Iesus, Maria ..., 39
Illumination II Joachim, 248, 256
imprimés musicaux d'avant 1800: catalogue des, **32–49**
Improvisations Archer, 192
In festo vitae interioris Domini nostri Iesu-Christi, 39
L'incantation de la jongleuse Gagnon, 85, 87, 91

Indian Good Book Vetromile, 12
Indians. *See* Abenaki; Chipewyan; Cree; Micmac; Montagnais; Naskapi; Saulteux
Ingram, Kenneth, 264
Institut canadien français, 116–17, 124
instruction in music: in Nova Scotia, **71–8**; in Ottawa, 130–1; by Roman Catholic Orders, 71, 74, 130. *See also* Singing schools; Tonic sol-fa
instruction manuals, **50–9**, 72
International Music Council, 265; International Music Day, 191, 269; 16th General Assembly, World Music Week, 245, 268–70. *See also* Canadian Music Council
International Music Day, 191, 269
International Society for Contemporary Music, 267; World Music Days, 267, 271
International Year of Canadian Music, 271
Introduction, Passacaglia and Fugue Willan, 203
Iseler, Elmer, 290

James, Eleanor, 232
Jamieson, Rhynd: cité, 154, 155, 156
Jansen, L[ouis?], 39
Jarrett, F., 144
Jeans, E., 74
Jehin-Prume, Frantz, 129
Joachim, Otto, 248, 254, 256
John Lovell and the Bank of Montreal, 80, 332 n.9
Johnson, Mrs Della, 154
Johnston, Richard, **134–42**, 202
Jones, Cliff, 255
Jones, Kelsey, 255
Jones, Peter, 12
Jones, Rosabelle, 255

Jules Léger Prize, 270

Kaiatonserase ..., 93
Kallmann, Helmut, 29, 61, 212, 239, 264–5, 267; quoted, 286; writings, **315–24**
Keats, John: quoted, 6
Keel, Frederick, 170
Keith, Laura Elsie. *See* MacMillan, Lady
Kékoba Tremblay, 255
Kelly, Michael, 39
Kemp, Walter H., 274, 275-6, 276, 277, 282
Kendergi, Maryvonne, 267
Kenins, Talivaldis, 254
Kerrison, J. Davenport, 109
Ketchum, J. Davidson, 165, 171
Kircher, Athanasius, 40
Klingenfeld, Heinrich, 111
Kotzwara, Franz, 40
Kotzwara's Battle of Prague ..., 40
Kreith's celebrated twenty-four airs and waltzes ... Jansen, 39
Kreutzer, Conradin: works performed in Victoria, 145
Kuerti, Anton, 288
Kunits, Luigi von, 291
Kwiatkowski, Anton, 294
Kyrie Somers, 274

La Feillée, François de, 40
Labelle, Jean-Baptiste, 92
LaBerge, Bernard R., 151
Laberge, Dominique: cité, 162, 163
Lady Emma Randle, 257
Laffey, Mr, 147
Lalo, Édouard: works performed in Toronto, 113
Landscapes Archer, 193
Lapierre, Eugène, 157
Lapp, Horace, 254

Latour, Conrad, 15, 17
Latour, T., 40
Lauder, Waugh, 104, 110
Laval University. *See* Université Laval
Lavallée, Calixa, 129
Laverlochère and Garin, *15, 25*
Laverock, Lily J., 152
Le Vasseur, Nazaire: cité, 65
Lecocq, Alexandre: works performed in Ottawa, 126, 127
Leduc, Roland, 247, 253
Lehmann, J.F., 84, 88
Lewis, Cecil Day, 295
Lewis, Matthew Gregory, 40
Liberati, Alessandro, 121, 131
The Life and Death of Jean de Brébeuf Willan, 252
Lindsay, William, 170
Lisgar, Sir John Young and Lady Lisgar, 120
Liszt, Franz: works performed in Ottawa, 130; in Toronto, 103, 104, 105, 106, 112
The Literary Garland, 82, 83–4
Littler, William, 269
Littmann, Mr, 126
liturgical music. *See* Antiphonarium; Cantus; Epitomes; Graduale romanum; Mass; Messe; Processional; Psalterium; Québec (ville)
Loredan, Signor P., 130–1
Lorne, Marquis of, 132
Loseby, H.E., 147
Louis Riel Somers, 269
Louise, Princess, 132
Lovatt, Garry, 298
Lovell, John, **79–87**; activities as music printer, 83–7; life and career, 81–2, 87, 332 n.9; music imprints, 87–96, 333 n.22, 334 n.25; role in 1837 Rebellion, 81–2, 332 n.11. *See also John Lovell and the Bank of Montreal*
Lovell, Robert, 81
Lovell, Sarah, 80
Lovell & Gibson, 79, 84, 334 n.25
Lovell Litho & Publications Inc., 79
Low, W. St Clair, 264
Ludlow, Godfrey, 170
Lustro Schafer, 269
Lyon, Rev. James, 72

MacDowell, Edward: works performed in Toronto, 113
McFarlen, Reuben, 71
McGill Conservatorium, 190, 194, 200
Mackay, Andrew, 72
Mackay, Robert W.S., 79
Maclean, Quentin, 170, 171
MacMillan, Alexander, 167
MacMillan, Sir Ernest Campbell: Canadian Music Council, 262–6; CBC and, 243, 244; works, 255, 292, 295
– at Ruhleben, **164–82**: as an actor, 172–4, *173*; in Bayreuth and Nuremberg, 168–9; *Cinderella*, 175; conducting, 167, 174–5; doctoral studies, 176, 179; *Don't Laugh*, 197; England, 176, 179, 182; lectures, 171–2, 182; *Mikado*, reconstruction, 177–8, *178*; *String Quartet*, 169, 177. *See also* Ruhleben
MacMillan, Keith, 243, 270; quoted, 258
MacMillan, Lady, 168, 182
Maffré, Joseph, 83
Maguire, Edmond, 146
Maience walse ... Gelinek, 36
Mailing, Phyllis, 213, 226, 231
The Maire of St Brieux Mills, 132
Le maistre des novices dans l'art de chanter ... Carré, 34

Marchand, J.U., 91
Marchand, Louis, 40
Marche de la St. Jean Baptiste Brauneis, 89
Marie-Andrée Duplessis de Sainte-Hélène, Mère, 51–4
Marier, A., 132
Marier, E., 132
Marier, J., 132
Marier, K., 132
Mariott, [?]: works performed in Victoria, 144
Marley, E., 131
Marshall, Ed, 295
Marshall, Robert, 109
Martin Platts' periodical collection of popular dances, walzes, etc ... Platts, 42
Martini (Schwartzendorf), Jean-Paul-Egide, 41
Martini's grand overture to Henry the Fourth ... Martini, 41
Mascagni, Pietro: works performed in Toronto, 101
Mason, Lawrence: cité, 158
mass: liturgical music performed in Quebec city, 50; Naskapi celebration of, 7–8. *See also* Civic Mass; Mass in Honour of St Thomas Aquinas; La Messe québécoise; Missa Brevis No. 8; Missa silvatica; Requiem
Mass Ford, 274
Mass in Honour of St Thomas Aquinas Kemp, 275–6, 276, 277
Massey Commission, 264
Massey Hall, 105, 110, 111, 168
Mastrocola, Joseph, 160
Matton, Roger, 253
Maul, Adam, 101
The May Queen Workman, 132

The Meal Archer, 192
Meiachkauat, Charles: quoted, 5
Melbourne, 292, 294
Melrose, Robert, 143
Mémoire sur la musique des Anciens ... Roussier, 48
Mémoires ou essais sur la musique par le citoyen Grétry Grétry, 37
Memorial University of Newfoundland Chamber Choir, 277, 342 n.7
Mendelssohn, Felix: works performed in Ottawa, 129, 130; in Toronto, 101, 102, 113
Menuhin, Yehudi, 269, 270
Mercer, John, 131
Mercure, Pierre, 240, 248, 255
The Merry Bells of England Lehmann, 84, 88
Mersenne, Père Marin, 70, 330 n.29
Messe pour choeurs, solistes et orchestre ... Martini, 41
La Messe québécoise Houdy, 274
Messe royale et messe du second ton, 94
Méthode nouvelle pour apprendre parfaitement les règles du plain-chant et de la psalmodie ... various, La Feillée, 40
Meyerbeer, Giacomo: works performed in Toronto, 103; in Victoria, 144
Michaels, H., 131
Micmac, 5, 21, 71
Millea, Mildred, 23
Mills, F.W., 131, 132
Milton, H., 122
La Minerve, 80, 81
Ministère des Affaires culturelles, 249
minstrel companies, touring

entertainers: in Ottawa, 124–6, 336 n.13
Missa Brevis No. 8 Willan, 205, *205*, 208
Missa silvatica (Missa Brevis No. 1) Parker, 275, 277–81, *279*, *280*, *281*
missionaries: Jesuits, 5, 6; Moravians, 6
Molt, Théodore-Fréderic, 330 n.27
Monologue Pépin, 255
Montagnais, 5, 6, 9, 12, 21, 23, 25, 27
Montéclair, Michel Pignolet de, 41
Montfort, Grignon de, 23
Montreal: publishing and printing in, 79–96; Ravel à, 159–62; World Music Days in, 271; World Music Week in, 269
The Montreal Bazaar Polka Brauneis, 89
Montreal Gazette, 81
Montreal Symphony Orchestra, 198, 269
Montreal Women's Symphony Orchestra, 194, 199
La Montréalaise, chant d'union Sabatier, 90
Moodie, Francis, 83
Moodie, J.S. Dunbar, 83
Moodie, Susanna, 80, 83
Moore, Mavor, 253
Morawetz, Oskar, 252, 254, 255, 291, 295
More, Mrs [?], 131
Moreau, Hegespipes, 64
Morel, François, 248, 253, 255
Morey, Carl, 157, 158
Morin, Jean-Baptiste, 41
Morin, Léo-Pol, 150, 161; cité, 163
Motets various, Campra, 34
Mottets à une, deux et trois voix ... Bernier, 33

Mount Allison Ladies' College, 74
Mozart, Leopold: works performed in Toronto, 108
Mozart, Wolfgang: works, 41; performed in Ottawa, 129, 130, 132; in Toronto, 102, 103, 104, 106, 108, 109, 110, 113
Murray, Paul, 282
Music Critics' Association, 269
Music for Solo Violin Somers, 270
Music in Canada, 264
Musical Halifax, 78
The Musical Miscellany, 95
Musical Society of Antigonish, 73
Musicanada, 270
Musique spirituelle où l'on peut s'exercer sans voix, bibliographic description of, 327 n.5; text of, **54–9**
Myrand, Ernest, 23

Naden Band, 147
Nanaimo Operatic Company, 147
Naskapi, 5–7, 9, 10, *15*, 20, 21, 25, 27
National Arts Centre Orchestra, 269, 298
National Film Board of Canada, 250, 268
National Library of Canada, 87, 177
Naylor, Bernard, 295
New Music Concerts, 269
Newfoundland and Labrador Arts Council, 277
Nicks, G., 41
Niecks, Friedrich, 168
Night Blooming Cereus Beckwith, 254
Nikamo masinaigan Prévost, 12, *13*, 14
Nikisch, Arthur, 107
Nivers, Guillaume-Gabriel, 41
Noëls anciens de la Nouvelle France Myrand, 23

A&S Nordheimer, 132
North Texas State College, 201
Norton, Jacob B., 75
Nos jours de gloire Eschambault, 91
Notions élémentaires de musique, tirées des meilleurs auteurs et mises en ordre par Chs. Sauvageau, 70
Nouveau Recueil de cantiques à l'usage du diocèse de Québec Daulé, 63
Nouveau système de musique théorique ... Rameau, 46
Nouvel essai sur l'harmonie ... Bemetzrieder, 33
Nova Scotia: bandmasters and bands, 73; music instruction in, **71–8**; singing schools, 71–2; school music instruction, 74, 75–7. *See also* Halifax
Novello, 182
Nui, Mani Shan, 20, 25

O strew the sweet flower ... Ross, 47
Oblate Fathers, 14
O'Brien, Father Edward, 6
Ocki aii masinaiganikikinohamagan, ou Nouveau syllabaire algonquin Cuoq, 95
Octo cantica Divae Mariae Virginis Aux-Cousteaux, 30
Offenbach, Jacques: works performed in Ottawa, 117, 120, 126, 127
The Office of Tenebrae, 96
Olympic Arts Competition/Festival, 263, 264
Ong, Walter J.: quoted, 3–4
Ontario Arts Council, 249, 266
opera performances: in Ottawa 126–8; in Toronto, 179
'Opportunity Knocks': commissions for, 244, 252, 254
The Optimist. See The Best of All Possible Worlds

orchestras and orchestral music in Toronto, **100–14**; resident orchestras and repertoire, 108–14; touring orchestras and repertoire, 102–7
Orchestre des petites symphonies, 247
Orchestre symphonique de Montréal. *See* Montreal Symphony Orchestra
Ordo ad visitandas parochias ..., 96
Orford String Quartet, 256, 294; repertoire, 291–2
J.L. Orme and Son, 124, 132
Oscillations Papineau-Couture, 256
Ostwald, Peter F., 303–4
Ottawa: bands, 118–23; chamber music, 129, 131; music instruction, 116, 130–1; music in the 1870s, **115–33**; opera, 126–8; organizations, 131–2; patriotic societies, 116; street musicians, 116; touring minstrel, stage companies, 124–6, 336 n.13; World Music Week in, 269, 270. *See also* Quadrille bands
Our Canada Weinzweig, 244, 252
Ozolins, Arthur, 256

Pacific Station. *See* Royal Navy: and music in British Columbia
Pageant for Our Lady Willan, 208
Palmer, Harold F., 92
Pannell, Raymond and Beverly, 250
Papineau-Couture, Jean, 267; works, 253, 254, 255, 256, 291
Pardon, H., 131
Parker, Michael, 274, 275, 277–81, *279, 280, 281*
Parlow, Kathleen, 113
Passacaglia Archer, 201
La Patrie avant tout Marchand, 91
Pauer, John, 170

Pauer, W., 177
Paur, Emil, 105, 106
Payload Pentland, 244, 252
Peaker, Charles, 262, 263
Pedersen, Stephen, 291
Peiler, Carl, 101
Pelletier, Frédéric: cité, 161
Pelletier, Wilfrid, 243, 264
Peltier, Octave, 90
Pentland, Barbara, 243, 244, 252, 255, 294, 295
People of 'Ksan, 270
Pépin, Clermont, 253, 255, 291
Percivall, G.A.F., 42
Perkins, Kenneth, 291
'Les Petites Symphonies,' 247, 253
Pièce concertante No. 2 (Éventails), Pièce concertante No. 3 (Variations) Papineau-Couture, 254
Pièces choisies pour l'orgue ... Marchand, 40
Piwas, Agathe, 23
Platts, Martin, 42
Pleyel, Ignace: works, 42-5
A Pocket Song Book for Use of the Students and Graduates of McGill College, 96
Polanyi, Michael: quoted, 305
Pontificale romanum Clementis VIII Primum ..., 45
Porter, Charles, 75
Le Porte-rêve Pépin, 253
The post captain ... Shield, 48
Pot-pourri for the violin obligato ... Rosquellas, 47
Potvin, Gilles, 267; quoted, 240
Pratt, E.J., 252
A Prayer for Elizabeth Coulthard, 253
Prélude Papineau-Couture, 253
Premier livre de motets de monsieur Morin ... Morin, 41
Prévost, Mederic, 12, 13, 14

La Prière des anges Sabatier, 89
Prince, Henry, 89
Prince Arthur Galop Gowan, 119
Principes de musique ... Montéclair, 41
Prix Italia, 248
Prix Paul Gilson, 248
Processionale ... various, 45
Proctor, George, 188
Pro-Musica Society, 150, 151
Psalterium romanum ... various, 45-6
Psaume pour abri Mercure, 255
Public Archives of Canada, 80
publishing and printing, **79-96**
Purcell, Henry: works performed in Ottawa, 132; in Toronto, 179

quadrille bands, 120, 122
Quatuor Dubois, 150, 160
Quatuor Hart House, 151-2, 156, 158. *Voir aussi* Hart House String Quartet
Québec (ville): imprimés musicaux d'avant 1800 à l'Université Laval, **29-49**; performance of liturgical music in, 50-1; Quebec Public Library, 60. *See also* Rousseau, Jean-Jacques; Séminaire de Québec
Queen's University Choral Ensemble, 203
Querelle des bouffons, 64-5, 329 n.17
Quesnel, Joseph: et Daulé, 63; rapprochement entre Rousseau et, 61-2

Rachmaninoff, Sergei: works performed in Toronto, 101, 102; visit, 113
Radio Canada International. *See* RCI
Raff, Joachim: works performed in Toronto, 106

Raineri, G., 118
Rameau, Jean-Philippe, 46
Randle, Douglas, 257
Ravel, Maurice: au Canada, **149–163**; à Montréal, 159–62; à Toronto, 156–9; à Vancouver, 152–5; aux chutes Niagara, 157; programmes des concerts, *153*, 154, 157–8, 160–1; sa musique executée au Canada, 107, 150
RCA, 288, 289
RCI, 242, 247–8, 269, 289
Reaney, James, 254, 256
recordings, Canadian, **286–97**
Recueil anglais St Basil, 17
Recueil de cantiques Latour, 15
Recueil de cantiques montagnais Derveau, 14, 16
Recueil de cantiques d'Ottawa Blanchin, 15
Recueil de prières et cantiques Saurin, 17
Recueil du Scolasticat St-Joseph, 17
Redekopp, Harold, 246
Reflexions sur les leçons de musique Bemetzrieder, 69
Reid, James, 294
Reminiscences of Seventy Years S. Lovell, 80
Répertoire de l'organiste ... Labelle, 92
Répertoire international des sources musicales. See RISM
Requiem Willan, 209; realized by F.R.C. Clarke, **203–10**; première, 203
Requiems for the Party Girl Schafer, 256
La Revue canadienne, 80
Rich, Chief Joseph, 6
Ridout, Godfrey, 240, 243, 244, 252, 253, 254, 255, 295
RISM, 29–30, 31–2
Rivard, L.E.: compiler, 93
Robert Fleming Award, 270

Roberts, John Peter Lee, 245, 267; quoted, 268
Robinson, Jean Blake. *See* Coulthard, Mrs Walter
Roger, Charles: quoted, 115
Rogers, Robert G., 294
Roma, Lisa: au Canada, 152, 155, 156, 159
Romberg, Andreas: works performed in Toronto, 108
Romberg, Bernard Heinrich, 46
Rosen, Franziska von, 5
Rosquellas, P., 47
Rosquellas' Spanish guitar tutor, 47
Ross, John, 47
Rossini, Giacomo: works performed in Ottawa, 120, 126, 127, 129; in Toronto, 101, 102, 103, 104, 108, 109; in Victoria, 144, 145
Rousseau, Jean-Baptiste, 47–8
Rousseau, Jean-Jacques, 48; cité, 66; influence au Canada, **60–70**, 330 n.27
Roussier, Pierre-Joseph, 48
Routley, Erik: quoted, 279, 281
Roy, Nare, 123
Royal, Roy, 248
Royal Canadian Band of HMCS Naden, 147
Royal Commission on National Development in the Arts, Letters and Sciences, 264
Royal Lyceum, 102
Royal Navy: and music in British Columbia, **143–8**
Royal Nova Scotia Historical Society, 331 n
Royal Tribute Brott, 253
Rozier, Claude, 21
Rubinstein, Anton: works performed in Toronto, 113
Ruhleben, 164–7, 171, 180; musicians

and music activities in, 170–2, 174–5, 177–8; theatrical activities, 172–4
Ruskin, John: quoted, 286
Ryan, Ada, 77

Sabatier, Charles Wugk, 89, 90, 91
Saffrey, E.C., 74
St Andrew's Presbyterian Church Choir, 282
St. Clair, Charles Emery, 92
St-Cyr, Marcel, 291
St Helen of the Cross, Sister, 74
St Mary's Roman Catholic Basilica, 282
St Paul's Singers, 275
Saint Saëns, Camille: works performed in Toronto, 106, 107, 113
Sam Slick K. Jones, 255
Sancta Maria, Succurre Miseris! Sabatier, 91
Sandrie, George, 144
Sarnia Independent Band, 121
Saulteux, 20, 21, 23, 25
Saulteux Hymnal, 14, *15*, 15–17, 20, *20*, 23, 25, 27, 326 n.19
Saurin, [?], 17
Sauvageau, Charles, 70, 83
Say not that minutes swiftly move ... Lewis, 40
Schafer, R. Murray, 197, **232–8**, 256, 257, 269, 292, 296
Schaffer, Charles, 146
Schallehn, Henry, 84, 88, 108
Schmitz, Elie Robert, 150
School for the Blind, 75
Schnabel, Artur, 300, 312
Schubert, Franz: works performed in Toronto, 101, 112, 113
Schultz, Arnold: quoted, 305
Schumann, Robert: works performed in Ottawa, 130; in Toronto, 104, 106

Scott, Duncan Campbell, 252
Scriptores ecclesiastici de musica sacra potissimum ... Gerbert, 36
Second concerto for the violin ... Rosquellas, 47
Seidl, Anton, 105, 106
Seitz, Ernest, 113
A Selection from the Psalms of David for Morning and Evening Service Warren, 92
Séminaire de Québec, 30, 60; les Archives du, 67; éducation en musique au, 69, 330 n.24
Sénécal, Eusèbe, 80
Sganarelle Archer, 192
Shaftesbury Hall, 102
Shankar, Ravi, 270
sheet music: first known printed in Canada, 84; Lovell imprints, 88–92
Sheppard, la famille: recueils, 30–1
Sheshus nashatau Oblate Fathers, 9, 14
Shield, William, 48
Shostakovich, Dmitri, 270
Sicotte, Lucien, 160
sight-singing manuals: basis of allegorical treatise, 52
singing schools: in Nova Scotia, 71–2; in Ottawa, 116
Six Medieval Love Songs Coulthard, 295
Small Book Containing 20 Psalm Tunes with Directions How to Sing Them Tufts, 54
Smetana, Bedrich: works performed in Toronto, 105
Smith, Eliza, 116
Smith, Gustave, 123, 132
The Snow-Drop; or, Juvenile Magazine, 84
Snow Show Galop St. Clair, 92
The Snow Shoe Tramp Palmer, 92
Social Sciences and Humanities

Research Council of Canada, 325 n., 327 n.
Société de musique contemporaine du Québec: ensemble, 256
Société Radio-Canada. *See* CBC; RCI
Solloway, Ron, 257
Solstices, Tremblay, 269
Somers, Harry, 254, 256, 269, 270, 274, 291; recordings, 289, 295
Sonata for Piano and Cello Morawetz, 255
Sonata No. 1 Archer, 192
Sonata No. 1 Willan, 203
Sonatas various, Clementi, 35
Sound-Producing Instruments in Native Communities Research Group (SPINC), 27
Sousa, John Philip, 101
Souvenir de Venise Gagnon, *86*, 87, 90
A Spanish air Astor, 33
Sparahawk, Edward Vernon, 81
Speaking from the Snow Naylor, 295
Specimen of Printing Types and Ornaments, in Use at the Printing Office of Lovell & Gibson, 84
The sportsman's rhapsody ..., 48
Stadaconé Gagnon, 89
Stark, Ethel, 194, 199
Steibelt, Daniel, 48
Stein, Erwin: quoted, 312
Stevenson, Sir John Andrew, 49
Stock, Frederick, 105, 106
Stoeckel, [?] bandmaster, 101
Strathy, George, 109
Strauss, Johann: works performed in Toronto, 101, 103
Strauss, Richard: works performed in Toronto, 101, 106–7
Strephon and Lucy ... Percivall, 42
String Quartet No. 3, Morawetz, 254
String Quartet No. 2 Morel, 255

String Quartet No. 2 'Waves' Schafer, 292
Suite borealis Pentland, 295
Sullivan, A. *See* Gilbert and Sullivan
'Summer and Winter' Clarke, 97
Sunter, Robert: quoted, 246
Surdin, Morris, 240
Sutherland, George, 118, 131
Sweet Marianne ... Hyler, 39
Symmes, Thomas, 53
[Symphonies: arr.] Haydn, 37–8
[Symphonies concertantes: arr.] Pleyel, 44
Symphony-Concerto Eckhardt-Gramatté, 256, 288–9
Symphony No. 2 Pépin, 253

Tait, Sylvia, 225, 226, 231
Talbot, Hugo: quoted, 78
Tanner, Adrian: quoted, 7
Tartini, Giuseppe: works performed in Ottawa, 128
Tasse, H., 132
Tchaikovsky, Pyotr: works performed in Toronto, 105, 106, 107, 113
Tell! Ah! tell me is it love ... Nicks, 41
Ten-Cent Canadian Ball-Room Companion and Guide to Dancing, 120
Tendresses bacchiques ..., 49
Thalberg, Sigismond: works performed in Ottawa, 128, 130
Theodore Thomas Orchestra, 102, 103, 104, 105, 106
theory texts. *See* Instruction manuals
Therefore with Angels & Archangels, &c., 90
Thisness: A Duo-Drama Cycle Anhalt, **211–31**; composer's notes, 227–9; costumes, lighting, set design, 225, 230–1; première, 231; text, 215–24; themes in, 226–7

Thomas, Ambroise: works performed in Toronto, 104
Thou dear native land Clarke, 35
Three duets, for two violoncellos ... Romberg, 46–7
Three easy divertimentos for the piano forte ... Costellow, 35
Three favorite airs ... Weidner, 49
Three Indian Songs of the West Coast MacMillan, 295
Three Sketches for Orchestra Archer, 193
Three sonatas for the piano forte, composed by D. Steibelt, 49
Three Songs to Words by Walt Whitman Somers, 295
Tiepke, H.G., 116, 132
Tilley, Alexander, 282
Timothy Eaton Memorial Church, 182
The Tokaido Freedman, 289–90
tonic sol-fa: in Nova Scotia, 76–7, 332 n.21
Toronto: bands, local and touring in, 100–2; local orchestras and repertoire, 108–14; music organizations and repertoire, 107–9; opera performances, 179; Ravel visit to, 156–9; visiting performing artists, 104, 105, 106, 112, 113; visiting orchestras and repertoire, 102–7; World Music Days in, 271; World Music Week in, 269
Toronto Conservatory of Music, 111, 157, 182
Toronto Conservatory Opera Company, 179
Toronto Conservatory Symphony Orchestra, 111
Toronto Mendelssohn Choir, 106, 182
Toronto Philharmonic Society, 101, 104, 108

Toronto Symphony Orchestra (1890, 1897, 1901), 111; (1908), 106, 107, 111–14; (1922), 269
Toronto Woodwind Quintet, 290
Torpadie, Greta: au Canada, 160
Torrington, F.H., 104, 109, 110
La Tourangelle Anhalt, 213
Traité de composition de musique ... Nivers, 41
Traité de l'harmonie réduite à ses principes naturels ... Rameau, 46
Transit Through Fire Willan, 244, 252
Tremblay, Gilles, 248, 255, 269
Trio for Violin, Cello and Piano Pentland, 255
Trio No. 2 Archer, 192
[Trios] Pleyel, 44–5
Tripp, J.D.A., 112
300 Cantiques anciens et nouveaux Bouhier, 15, 17
Trois poèmes de Saint Jean de la Croix Charpentier, 253
Tsiatak nihonon8entsiake ... Cuoq, 12, 94
Tufts, John, 54
tune-books. *See* Instruction manuals
Turner, Robert, 255

Un Soir à bord Gagnon, 90
Union Harmony Humbert, 72
Université Laval, la bibliothèque de, 29–30, 60; collection des imprimés musicaux d'avant 1800, **29–49**; imprimés 'unica,' 32; recueils des familles Desbarats et Sheppard, 30–1
University of Alberta, Department of Music, 191, 192, 196, 201, 202
University of King's College, Chapel Choir, 275
University of Oklahoma, 202

University of Ottawa, 270
University of Toronto, 168, 202
University of Western Ontario, 257
Urania or a Choice Collection of Psalm Tunes, Anthems, and Hymns Lyon, 72
L'ut dreze Smith, 132

Vallerand, Jean, 240, 248, 270
van Khê, Trân, 270
Vancouver: Ravel visit, 152–5; *Thisness* première, 231
Vancouver New Music Society, 231
The Vancouver Waltz Horne, 145
Vandusen, James W., 122, 131
Variations on a Boccherini Tune Pentland, 252
vaudeville. *See* Minstrel companies
Vaughan Williams, Ralph: works performed in Toronto, 179
Verdi, Giuseppe: works performed in Toronto, 101, 104, 113; in Victoria, 144, 145
Vetromile, E., 12, 14
Vickers, Jon, 295
Victoria: bands, local, 146–7; bands, naval, 145–7; concert repertoire, 144, 145; orchestras, 146, 147
Victoria! Loseby, 147
Victoria Galop Sandrie, 144
Victoria Musical Society, 146
Victoria Symphony Orchestra, 148
Vieuxtemps, Henri: works performed in Toronto, 103
Vilbon, Charles, 91
Vincula Pentland, 295
Violin Concerto Weinzweig, 253
Vita brevis Pentland, 295
Vivier, Claude, 248
Vogt, Augustus: quoted, 100

Waddington, Geoffrey, 239, 242, 244, 253, 264; quoted, 239, 257
Wagner, Richard: works performed in Ottawa, 129, 132; in Toronto, 101, 103, 104, 105, 106
Wallace, William: works performed in Ottawa, 127
Walter, Arnold, 263, 266–7
Walter, Thomas, 54
Walters, Elena, 129
Warren, W., 132
Warren, W.H., 83, 92
Warren and Sons, 131
Weber, Carl Maria von: works performed in Ottawa, 130; in Toronto, 101, 102, 103, 104, 108, 110
Weber, Charles, 170, 177
Weidner, T.C., 49
Weinzweig, John, **183–7**, 263, 266, 291; and the CBC, 240, 243, 244, 252, 253, 254, 255, 256
Welsman, Frank, 106, 111
When pensive I thought of my love ... Kelly, 39
Who Killed Cock Robin? Tiepke, 132
Willan, Healey, **203–10**, *209*, 244, 252, 253
Willan, James Burton, 208
Wilson, Charles, 291
Winderstein, Hans, 107
Wine of Peace Weinzweig, 253
Winnipeg Symphony Orchestra, 240
Winthrop Anhalt, 213, 214
Wodson, Edward W.: cité, 158
Woitach, Richard, 295
Wolf, Hugo: works performed in Toronto, 107
Woodcock, George, 255
Workman, W.G., 116, 130, 132
World Music Days, 267, 271

World Music Week, 245, 268–70
World Soundscape Project, 292
Wuensch, Gerhard, 291

Yale University, 200

Yarmouth Citizens' Concert Band, 73
The Young Apollo Britten, 243–4, 252

Zerrahn, Carl, 104
Zuckerkandl, Victor: quoted, 303